A History of Greatham

by Peter Gripton

A History of Greatham

an illustrated history of Greatham, a parish and village in Hampshire.

This book is dedicated to all residents, past and present, of the Parish of Greatham.

Peter Gripton, 2003.

"For life to be large and full, it must contain the care of the past and of the future in every passing moment of the present"

Joseph Conrad, 'Nostromo'

Third Edition 2007 by Las Atalayas Publishing
First Published 2003

Author and Editor Peter Gripton
Copyright © Peter Gripton 2003-7

ISBN 978-0-9556753-1-7

Design and Typesetting by kenandglen.com

Contents

Introduction		1
Chapter 1	Conservation Area	11
Chapter 2	The holding of the manor	14
Chapter 3	Le Court	16
Chapter 4	Manor House	20
Chapter 5	The new Church	33
Chapter 6	The Old Rectory	38
Chapter 7	Gold's House	40
Chapter 8	Gold's Barn	44
Chapter 9	Greatham Mill	45
Chapter 10	Greatham School	47
Chapter 11	Greatham Village Hall	49
Chapter 12	Nursery School	51
Chapter 13	Welldigger's Cottage	52
Chapter 14	Other dwellings	55
Chapter 15	Village Inns	61
Chapter 16	Village Businesses	63
Chapter 17	Village Organisations	64
Chapter 18	Woolmer Forest	65
Chapter 19	Albert Baker	75
Chapter 20	Leonard Cheshire	77
Chapter 21	The Corytons	79
Chapter 22	Michael Digby	81
Chapter 23	Heath Harrison	83
Chapter 24	The Shotter Family	85
Chapter 25	Henry Press Wright	92
Chapter 26	Elsie Collins	93
Chapter 27	Brenda and Jack Dunn	94
Chapter 28	Kath & Charlie Hanson	96
Chapter 29	The Haywards	98
Chapter 30	May and George Lockley	105
Chapter 31	Jackie & Bill Marie	107
Chapter 32	Audrey and Bill Moseley	109
Chapter 33	The Redmans	111
Chapter 34	George Wakeford	117
Chapter 35	Joe Leggett's memoirs	119
Chapter 36	Alan Siney's story	133
Epilogue		166
Appendix 1	Parish Registers	167
Appendix 2	Trade Directories	170
Index		184

About the author

Perhaps the term 'author' is too strong a word here, as I have been mainly a collator of information and fact-gatherer. Indeed, I have been both amazed and delighted to have had the privilege of putting together this 'History of *Greatham*', a task I have found most enjoyable and stimulating. I have produced a list of contributors elsewhere and sincerely hope that I haven't missed anyone out. The biggest problem encountered during my project was 'when and where to stop' and I am sure that there will be many anecdotes and memories that do not appear here. If so, I apologise and hope that some future historian will take up the challenge of re-writing this work to a satisfactory conclusion. Meanwhile here it is – 'warts and all' – and I hope that its readers will have as much pleasure as its scribe.

On a personal note, here's the low-down on me! I was born in Liverpool in 1940, educated first at Arnot Street School in Walton and then at the Liverpool Institute High School for Boys in the city centre. This famous school lay between the city's twin Cathedrals, Anglican and Roman Catholic, on the appropriately named Hope Street. The 'Inny', as it will always affectionately be known to former pupils, has a number of famous celebrities among its list of ex-boys – Arthur Askey the comedian, Sir Paul McCartney & George Harrison of 'The Beatles' and Peter Sissons the newscaster, to name but a few. The school is now world-renowned as the Liverpool Institute of Performing Arts.

I joined the Army directly from school in 1956, serving as an electronics technician, and was at nearby Bordon in 1967 when the time came for me to leave. Having decided to stay on as a civilian instructor, my wife Joyce and I settled in *Greatham* that same year and have been here ever since. Both my daughters, Lorraine and Michelle, were pupils at the Primary School, back in the days when Gwen Brooker was headmistress. For a number of years, Joyce assisted with the Brownies, designated as 'Tawny Owl', with Rita Gerard as 'Brown Owl'.

Joyce also participated in local sports, being a keen member of 'The Jays' netball team for a number of years. The team played in the Petersfield League and Joyce's team-mates included Helen Gould, Jackie Marie and Shirley Redpath, all from *Greatham*. Upon my arrival in the village, I worked as a part-time barman at the 'Silver Birch' for about two years. This was at a time when Longmoor Camp was still being well used and evenings 'at the pub' were very popular with the soldiers! Monday evenings in particular were most enjoyable, as local folk singers would provide some entertainment. The back bar would reverberate to the sounds of 'Liverpool Lou', 'The leavin' of Liverpool' & 'The streets of London',

I finally retired from the Civil Service in August 2000, having spent the last 18 years as a computer manager, still at Bordon, and I hope to continue living in *Greatham* for many years to come.

'Greatham Corner' as it was known and situated on the junction of the roads to Liss and to Selborne. Children used to catch the school bus to Alton from here.

Foreword

At a public meeting held in March 1998, the villagers of **Greatham** decided that it would be to their advantage to carry out a *'Village Appraisal'*. At a subsequent meeting, I was appointed Chairman of the Steering Group, set up to follow the project through. At regular meetings over a period of about 9 months, the Group discussed and determined the method by which the Appraisal was to be conducted. Finally, starting in February 1999, questionnaires were distributed to all villagers.

As they were returned an analysis of the data began, I read that there was a need to provide some background information, in order to put the Appraisal into the context of how **Greatham** village life had both changed and developed through the ages. As the guidelines so aptly declared, an Appraisal provided the chance to *'discover the past, document the present and debate the future'*. In trying to carry out the first two of these three worthy endeavours, it came as no surprise that there was no single document that said it all. However, I was delighted at the response from so many local people to the idea of producing this short history and amazed at the amount of relevant information that has subsequently come to light.

I feel it is necessary to state, from the beginning, that I could not produce a chronological history from say the Stone Age to the present-day, thinking that it would be virtually impossible. Instead, I tended to gather information relating to certain areas of interest, i.e. people, buildings, localities, events, etc., and to present these in as logical an order as possible. I am grateful to the many people of the village who have assisted in this work, and to the many sources of information which, although originally not intended to impinge on **Greatham**, have indeed done just that. Reference to, and acknowledgement of, all source information will be found at the end of this work.

Pete Gripton, 2000

'Study the past, if you would divine the future'

Confucius (551 – 479 BC)

Introduction

The present-day Parish of **Greatham** lies in the county of Hampshire, on either side of the old Farnham (Surrey) to Petersfield Turnpike, later the A325 road, the modern version of which was laid down in 1822 and constructed by 1826. At the southern end of the village, the B3006 road branches off towards Selborne and on to Alton. Recent road improvements have led to **Greatham** being by-passed and the road through the village no longer carries the full weight of through traffic, having been downgraded to a 'C' class road. It is the hope and wish of local people that traffic-calming measures recently implemented can lead to the rehabilitation of **Greatham** in the future.

The Parish is presently home to some 850 residents, living in just over 300 dwellings, based upon the 1991 census and predictions by Hampshire County Council. The area of the Parish measures 1,273 acres, there are 16 public rights of way and a *'Conservation Area'* containing 16 listed buildings.

The 'Domesday Book' of 1086 recorded **Greatham** as being 'Terra Regis', a Latin term meaning 'Land of the King', indicating that this was once a Royal manor (or estate) belonging to William the Conqueror himself. In later years, the manor passed through many families by marriage and by purchase, including the Devenish,

Marshall, Norton, Freeland, Love, Chawner and Coryton families.

Some recent researchers and historians throw doubt on Domesday as being a *de facto* record of the actual location of some of the place names written down. They say that Domesday was designed essentially to aid the collection of taxes. However, this does not change the fact that Greatham – or Greteham - was recorded, so this history presumes that the present location is where the village has always been sited.

The name of the village has changed many times, however slightly, over the years. **Greteham** (1086), **Grietham** (1167), **Gretham** (1179), **Grutham** (1235), **Gratham** (1262) - all derived from two separate words, the 'Old-English' (Anglo-Saxon) *'ham'*, meaning *'village, estate, manor or homestead'* and an old Scandinavian word *'griot'* or *'gryt'*, meaning *'stones or stony ground'*. Thus the name **'Greotham'** came into being, literally a *'stony estate'* or *'farm on gravel'*.

Formation

About 100 million years ago, fresh water covered this area, depositing layers of sand brought down by the wearing of siliceous

Tollgate House, demolished in the 1950's, as viewed from the approach to the village from West Liss.

rocks elsewhere. This sand exists in huge tracts to the north and east of the Parish. Eventually seawater flooded in up to those sandy wastes and, over millions of years, built up a thick deposit of chalk from animal remains. This sea receded and the earth shrank, pushing up the chalk hills that are now evident at Hawkley and Empshott, bordering the western side of the Parish. **Greatham**, lying between the higher chalk and the sand, became a swampy fresh-water lake, which extended southwards through to Petersfield, turned eastwards through the Rother Valley and into the whole Wealden area stretching as far as Kent.

The sandy sediment brought down into this lake settled down to form a layer of clay sub-soil, which is a dominant feature in much of **Greatham's** ecology to the present day. As the water finally receded, some of the lower areas built up a varying overlay of sand, sediment and loam, from the decayed vegetable material washed down onto the flood plain. For tens of millions of years **Greatham** was to be ruled by the dinosaurs, with evidence of that pre-historic past all around. For every flint-stone that works itself up through the clay is, in all probability, a piece of fossilised sea-sponge.

Pre-history

It is probable that man lived and hunted in the area now known as **Greatham** as long as 9,000 years ago. A Mesolithic (Stone Age) site was excavated at Longmoor as recently as 1979 and contained around 15,000 pieces of worked flint, which included some 200 arrow barbs and tips, plus many skin-scrapers. That site, measuring some 8 metres in diameter, was probably used by the hunter-gatherer tribes for flint-blade manufacture and was dated to around 7,000 years BC.

Recent research by the Natural Environment Research Council seems to indicate a lifestyle change, around 6,000 years ago, every bit as intense as the technological one in modern times. The Ancient Britons appear to have switched from being hunter-gatherers to farmers in a time-span of as little as a century.

Natives began making artefacts like pottery, putting Britain on the path to civilisation. They abandoned hunting for fish, shellfish and berries, replacing this with a diet of wheat and barley, with meat coming from domesticated cattle, sheep and goats. Their previous wandering lifestyle was left behind, as the creation of villages and towns began to take shape.

The original small, dark-skinned Iberic inhabitants of this area were probably nomadic in their habits, wandering over the downlands with their herds of grazers and ruminants. They were driven out by the tall, fair and savage Celts, a typical branch of the diverse Aryan race, who tilled the land and were consequently of a more stationary culture. With their bronze, and later iron, weapons and tools, as opposed to the stone ones of the previous inhabitants, they were able to clear the primeval forests for their settlements, at a time when agriculture and animal husbandry were being introduced.

There is plenty of visible evidence of Neolithic (Bronze Age) habitation, in the form of round 'barrows', which are shown on present-day maps as 'tumuli'. These were probably the burial mounds of the leaders of local settlements and are in such abundance as to suggest an area of some sacred significance, in an age some 1,200 to 1,400 years before the Christian era.

There is little remaining evidence of any local Iron Age habitation but samples of iron clinker, possibly from iron-kilns of those days, can still occasionally be found. Also, early Romano-British pottery shards, found at nearby Alice Holt, seem to have belonged to an established pre-Roman industry, which had then attempted to adapt its style to suit the demands of the Roman Empire. Some 82 separate kiln sites have been identified in the area. In the 4th-century, it is recorded that the thriving ceramic industry of Hampshire, mainly based in the later royal Alice Holt forest area, 'captured the London market and flourished greatly'.

Prior to the Roman invasion, the area now called 'Hampshire' was in the hands of two main tribes. The 'Regni' were original ancient Britons, while the 'Belgae' were settlers from the Low Countries across the Channel. The Britons' name for the area was 'Gwent' or 'Y Went', while the Anglo-Saxon termed it 'Hamptuncure', based upon Hamptun (now Southampton). Hampshire is believed to have been the first county to fully accede to Roman rule, and the capital city, now Winchester, was first named 'Venta Belgarum', literally 'market-place of the Belgae'.

The chief evidence of a Roman presence in the area are the remains of the main 1st-century road, which joined together the two settlements at Chichester and Silchester, only discovered in 1949, in the course of routine examination of aerial photographs at the Archeological Division of the Ordnance Survey. The road enters Ministry of Defence land at the south-western end of Weaver's Down, and passes right through Longmoor Camp along Roberts Road and Methuen Road. It then skirts the south-western edge of Woolmer Road, before heading off in roughly the direction of Behham's Lane, to neatly bisect the West site of what is now RAF Oakhanger.

As was typical of Roman roads, it had three layers – large grit, small grit and flat stones, with a camber to prevent rain from collecting on its surface. The original road must have been a busy one, connecting these two cantonal capitals as it did. Chichester (*Noviomagus Regnensium*) was a port of some importance, while Silchester (*Calleva Atrebatum*) was a major centre of communication, and the road was used for carrying troops and supplies, right up to the 5th-century. Many English towns and cities bear the term *'chester'*, derived from the Roman word *'castra'*, meaning a fortified town, and these fortifications or walls are still much in evidence today.

Hoards of Roman money and medals were found at or near to Woolmer Pond, when it dried out in the 1700s. Gilbert White of Selborne wrote *'In the dry summer of 1741, Woolmer Pond dried up, and they found great heaps of coins, the one lying on the other as if shot out of a bag'*. Another hoard of nearly 30,000 coins was found, in two broken pots, in 1873. Thought to have been left by a fleeing Roman army centuries before, the coins did not hold much value at the time they were found. Some were catalogued by the British Museum, while others are now tucked away in private collections. The coins show emperor's heads, the inscription *'Pax' (peace)*, and illustrations of panthers and women. Such regal names as Tetricus, Gallienus, Victorinous and Claudius can be seen on both the coins and medals. Local residents have continued to find the odd coin in fields and on the Army ranges, and although of little monetary value, they are collector's items.

Domesday (1086)

The *'Domesday Book'*, officially called 'The Great Description of England', was the record of a survey conducted on behalf of William the Conqueror in 1085 – the term Domesday indicates *'day of judgement'*, though here it is used in a strictly economic context. Notable features were the amount of detail included, and the speed of its accomplishment.

Completed in 1086, the survey ascertained and recorded the King's fiscal rights, in line with William's policy of maintaining a strong central government and taxation system. The survey also gave accurate information about the exact holdings of the King's feudal lords and their ability to raise armies of fighting men, should the need arise. Domesday not only provided William with a record of England prior to 1066, but also attempted to legalise the many changes that had occurred since his Conquest.

No other country in the world possesses such a historical record from so far back in the mists of time. Domesday must indeed have seemed like the dawn of civilisation to the generations that followed. However, some of the basic tenets of English culture, such as marriage, property and inheritance, were already deeply rooted in the social order. The first shoots of

the manorial system had already been planted during the late Roman period. The Norman system was not so much imposed upon, as grafted upon, a well-regulated English society.

The survey itself was carried out by royal officers, visiting the assemblies known as the county courts, attended by township representatives and local lords. A local jury of six Englishmen, along with six Normans, supplied the answers to the officers' questions, and swore to their validity. The survey contained a roll of land-holders in each county, the size of the land, number of farm workers, any mills, fish-ponds or other features, and their value at that time. As late as the reign of Henry II (1541-59), the Domesday Book was recognised as a record above appeal and is still cited in lawsuits.

Map showing the Roman Road

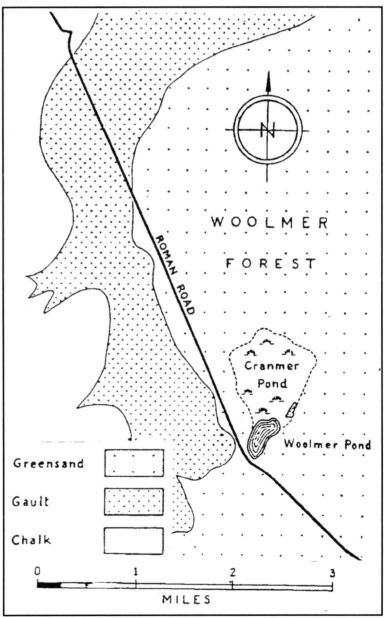

Greatham's entry:

The Latin text reads:

'Ipse Rex tenet Greteham. Eddid Regina tenuit. Tunc, se defendebat pro una hida. Modo non geldat. Terra est 3 carucutae. Ibi 7 villani habeny 3 carucutas. Ibi silva de 30 porcis. Tempore Regis Edwardi et post, et modo, valet 60 solidos.'

This can be interpreted as:

*'The King holds **Greteham**. Queen Edith held it. It was then assessed at 1 hide, but is not now assessed. Here are 3 plough-lands, held by 7 villeins, and woods for 30 hogs. Its value in the time of King Edward and afterwards was, as now, 60 shillings.'*

(The term 'hide' is thought to equal the modern 120 acres and was nominally the area needed to support a free peasant cultivator and his family. A 'villein' (or sometimes 'villain') derives from the Latin 'villa' — a farm. Thus a 'farmer' or 'farm-worker' is indicated. Ed.)

William the Conqueror enclosed large tracts of local land, thought to be mainly for the pleasure of hunting. The whole area that now encompasses **Greatham** and Longmoor was part of the *'Andredsweald'*, the great Saxon forest that enclosed Wolfmar Forest, now called Woolmer Forest.

Local government

Greteham, as it was named at the time, was one of the *'manors'* belonging to Neatham Hundred, the foundations of Neatham having been laid down by the Romans, below the Iron Age enclosure at Holybourne Down, not far from Alton. Neatham must have been a major Roman settlement; it certainly appears on maps used to illustrate the Roman road between Chichester and Silchester. The element 'ham', when used in a place-name, seems to indicate an early manorial centre, often near a Roman road.

The term *'hundred'* is generally agreed by historians to be of Anglo-Saxon origin, and was normally a distinct division of a County, containing 100 families. The most likely constitution of such a hundred would have been a combination of a small number of manorial families, with the remainder consisting of *'yeomen'* and/or tenant working families. The hundred also served its purpose in the realm of defence, with musters of able-bodied men being led by their *'gentry'*. Local men probably served in 1545, either voluntarily or by coercion, when the French landed on the Isle of Wight, and again against the Spanish Armada of 1588.

A manor was a land-based unit, or area, of authority, controlling both the individuals who dwelt and those events that occurred within its bounds. At the heart of each early district was a Royal manor house or 'tun', run by a local official but visited by the King and his retinue at frequent intervals. 'Tun' is still recognisable in the names of such areas as 'Kingston', literally meaning King's Tun or manor house. The origin of the manor as a private unit of jurisdiction and revenue is obscure, but some historians place it near the very beginnings of English society, probably emerging in Saxon times, and reflecting the insecurity of those times. For his own protection, a small freeholder might *'commend'* himself to a powerful lord, usually a nobleman or clergyman, and be seen to be holding his land from that lord.

(The term 'manor' can sometimes be misunderstood, referring at one time to the authority over an area and at another time to the house within which that authority is held. Ed.)

The lord, either on his own account as an owner, or for Crown or Church as a 'vassal', was then in a position to appoint his own officials. These could be such as a 'reeve' (a sort of foreman) and a 'hayward' (who would ensure that people kept their hedges and fences in good repair, to prevent livestock from straying). The medieval division of estates into 'demesne' or domains (exploited directly by the lord) and peasant land is recorded by the late 7th-century, and much of the manpower on demesne was provided by slaves, usually managed by the lord's 'bailiff'.

(A 'yeoman' is a man-servant or steward; a 'vassal' is one who holds and/or administers land on behalf of a superior authority; a 'bailiff' is also a land-agent, managing the practical working of a farm for a land-owner. Ed.)

The size of a hundred or manor varied greatly in medieval times, possibly a mere 30 hides, and up to an estate of some 120 hides. As previously mentioned, the hide was a Saxon measurement, which continued in use for a long period after the Norman Conquest of 1066. Tax avoidance specialists in the Middle Ages often resorted to variations in the size of a hide, and this could be anywhere between 60 and 120 acres. As land was taxed by the number of hides owned, it was an advantage if the size of a hide was enlarged, so that less tax was eventually paid.

The *ecclesiastical 'parish'* has been the measure of the English landscape since Anglo-Saxon times. Boundaries dating back more than a thousand years are still traceable in some areas. In Tudor times, the parish replaced the manor as the vehicle of government. The vestry appointed constables, overseers and even highway surveyors. Churchwardens supervised both the fabric of the church and people's religious behaviour. The village priest became responsible for

> Greatham March 25.ᵗʰ 1788.
>
> My Lord,
>
> It is not in my power to tell you with any exactness what compass of ground there is in this parish. I suppose the widest extent of it may be about one mile from North to South and rather more than one mile from West to East. But I have not been able to get any accurate information concerning the Eastern boundary of the Parish, which on that side making part of Wolmer Forest.
>
> II The inhabitants amount to one hundred and forty six.
>
> III At a medium there are two Marriages, five Births and four Burials per Annum.
>
> IV. The patroness of the living is Mrs Beckford.
>
> V. There is no chapel.
>
> VI. There is no lecturer. I officiate for the Rector, and am not licensed to this curacy.
>
> VII. There are no papists, nor any meetings held of protestant dissenters in this parish.
>
> VIII. There is no school in this parish.
>
> IX. There is not any hospital, nor any endowed charitable in=stitution, nor any fixed annual Donation for the benefit of the poor in this parish. The return to the late Parliamentary enquiry on this subject was made by my predecessor

A letter to the Bishop, dated 1788, giving sparse details about the Parish.

the recording of births, marriages and deaths. The *civil parish* did not emerge until the 1890s, as the smallest theatre of democracy.

Agriculture and Economy

The north-eastern Weald, spread across east Hampshire, north-west Sussex and south-west Surrey, is characterised by the poverty of its soils. In the north of this area the soils are heavy clays, associated with the forest of Alice Holt; in the south, the soils are light and sandy, giving rise to the extensive heath-lands within the triangle formed by Petersfield, Frensham and Haslemere. Judging by the number of tumuli, these sandy lands must have been agriculturally very important in the Bronze Age, but in historical times they have been thinly populated.

The heaths provided commons for grazing, wood, turf and peat for fuel, sand for glass-works, furze for fodder and bracken for cattle litter, but were never able to support the same density of population as maintained on richer soils. This poverty has been revealed in a number of ways, some still evident. Thus, whereas the villages at the foot of the Downs, such as Selborne, Buriton and East Meon, have splendid large churches, with much surviving Norman work, the original heath-land churches are small, and date only from the 13ᵗʰ-century, as at West Liss, Bramshott and **Greatham.** This suggests that a more prosperous and dense population resided at the foot of the Downs in the

11th and 12th-centuries, with only a slow growth on the sandy soils, as the population as a whole grew during the 13th and early 14th-centuries.

This interpretation is supported by the statistics of the Domesday Book. Mapledurham (in Buriton) had 24 ploughlands and a population of 34 villeins, 15 bordars and 8 serfs. There was also a large demesne with another 4 ploughlands. East Meon had 64 ploughlands, 8 in demesne, the remainder owned by 72 villeins and 32 bordars. In contrast, **Greatham,** which held no demesne, had only 3 ploughlands held by 7 villeins.

In 1290, with Edward I on the throne, the income of William Mote, the Rector, made up of glebe and tithes, was £6.7s.6d. In 1334, during the reign of Edward III, the valuation of the tithes of wheat, lambs and wool was only 20s.4d, compared with £19.6s.9d for Mapledurham.

(A 'bordar' is 'a tenant who holds his cottage and small parcel of land from his lord, in return for menial services'. The term 'glebe' indicates land held by the Church, while 'tithe' is a tax equal to one tenth (Ed.)

The poverty of the heath-lands is also illustrated by the lack of any major town development. The towns of the Weald, established in medieval times to meet the marketing needs of the local population are, in general, spaced at a distance conveniently covered in half a day by a man and his livestock. No such town developed on the heath-lands, and thus the pattern was broken. Had the soil been more fruitful, a town would probably have developed in medieval times in the vicinity of Whitehill, or even at **Greatham** itself.

Enclosure

The medieval system of open strip-fields, with certain common rights, was still the custom in Hampshire in 1700, with William II now King. A large part of its arable land still lay in great open fields. This began to change in Tudor times, when some landowners decided to enclose their fields for the purpose of sheep and cattle grazing. The Enclosure Acts of 1752, during the reign of George II, eventually legalised these procedures.

The term *'enclosure'* implied just that, the surrounding of a piece of land by hedge, fence or wall. But in the more restricted legal sense, it was the process by which *'common'* rights were abolished, and the land divided amongst those with claims upon it. Thus the heath, scrub and woodland, which had dominated so much of this area, was to mainly disappear.

This continued gradually and reached its peak during the period 1760–1820, by which time *most* agricultural land had become enclosed. Enclosure certainly led to more efficient agriculture, but although some land was maintained as *'common ground'*, it caused great hardship to the majority of cottagers. They found that they had lost their ancient rights to a plot of land, either to graze sheep or cattle, and/or to gather fuel for heating and cooking.

This presented a severe grievance, helping lead to the agricultural riots raging throughout the region during the 1830s. This grabbing of common land continued right up until 1875, until halted by an Act of Parliament in Queen Victoria's time. As a result, that land which remained was generally of the poorest quality. Those large areas of common land within **Greatham** Parish, still intact on an 1842 tithe map, were to disappear within 20 years of that date, with the exception of a piece of unkempt wetland at the end of Church Lane.

Grievances and disturbances

In the autumn of 1830, starting in Kent, disturbances that became known as the 'Swing Riots' swept across southern England, reaching Hampshire in the second week of November. Actions taken by the rioters differed from place to place, depending upon local grievances, but were mainly centred on discontent at falling wages and rising prices. Locally, Selborne and Headley were almost unique, in that workhouses for the poor were also attacked. It is known that farms in Kingsley, Empshott and **Greatham** were ransacked, as the mobs moved across the countryside.

Men from ten local parishes were involved. Amongst the 22 local men, known to have eventually been tried at Winchester, was one John Kingshott, aged 35 and married with five children, a farm labourer from **Greatham**. He was arrested for stealing loaves of bread, cheese and beer from Mary King of Kingsley. Mr Charles Alcock, vicar of Empshott, observed on Sunday 28th of November that *"almost all **Greatham** labourers are in custody"*, while Kingshott in particular *"made great resistance and attempted the life of young Debenham"*.

He was sentenced to death on account of the robbery, although his offence was recorded as *'machine breaking'*, and indeed much of the rioting was aimed at threshing machines. First introduced in the 1780s, they were now seen as a threat to the winter livelihood of farm workers. Kingshott's sentence was commuted to 'life transportation', so he was sent down to Portsmouth and confined on one of the prison-ships moored in the dockyard. On Thursday 14th of February 1831 he sailed on board the 'Proteus', which landed in Tasmania on August 14th of the same year.

It is recorded that John Kingshott worked for John Kingstall in 1833 and a Mrs Bridger in 1835, before being granted a conditional pardon on April 5ᵗʰ 1838. He never returned to England and nothing is recorded about the fate of the wife and family he left behind. The romantics amongst us may consider that the row of houses in **Greatham**, called 'Kingshott Cottages', was named after this unfortunate man, but there is no evidence that this was the case.

Tithes

Since it was deemed that all crops were harvested by the *'grace of God'*, it seemed fitting that *'one tenth'* of all produce should be given back to the Church, to help towards its upkeep and pastoral care. Around the year 930, tithe payments became obligatory under English law. Eventually, **Greatham** Parish provided a building for this very purpose. This *'tithe barn'*, which would probably date back to the 1500s, may well have been used for other purposes prior to this usage, or indeed may have been purpose-built, but this is not known. By an Act of Parliament in 1836, at the time of William IV, this often impractical method of collecting tithe dues was replaced by a rental charge, paid annually according to a Commissioner's assessment of the property.

The meetings of the Tithes Commissioners for the County of Southampton, with **Greatham** landowners on the one hand, and the Reverend Thomas Agar Holland, Rector of **Greatham** as tithe owner on the other, had taken place in 1840. The nominal tithe assessment was agreed at £247.6s.8d per annum, to be apportioned fairly throughout the Parish. A countrywide survey took place, whereby every enclosure and piece of managed land was measured to the nearest 160th part of an acre, and mapped. The *'tithe map'* of **Greatham** was completed in 1842. The Parish assessment was apportioned on 223 pieces of land, totalling 979 acres, or 396 hectares.

All of the local landowners and occupiers were listed, with an itemised description of their land on which tithes were due. This was assessed on arable land, pasture, meadow (e.g. coppicing), hops (which carried an extraordinary charge of 13 shillings & fourpence per acre), glebe land (rented from the church) and certain areas of common land.

('Coppicing' is one of the oldest forms of woodland management, dating back at least 5,000 years. It fell out of fashion over the last century, falling from 100,000 acres to only 5,000 acres in Hampshire alone, but is currently enjoying something of a revival. It involves cutting a broad-leaved tree back to a stump, allowing it to send up new shoots from just above ground level. These 'poles' can then be cropped and will re-shoot to provide further crops. As the experts say – "A wood that pays is a wood that stays". The term 'coppice', or 'copse', comes from the French 'couper', meaning 'to cut'. Ed.)

No charge was levied on this common land, normally used by commoners, which included roads and rights of way, homesteads (but excluding paddocks and farmyards, which were liable) and large areas of Woolmer Forest within the Parish boundary. The apportionment could vary according to the current grain prices, amounts of land and the crops grown thereon. The initial assessment of £247.6s.8d was actually £262.7s.6d after appraisal. The Government eventually

A typical old barn in Greatham, which has since been renovated and converted into a habitable residence.

A local dewpond

network of 'green lanes' evolved, to link with the firmer main roads and highways. It was essential to the system that the herds could feed and rest up overnight within the confines of these lanes, so in much of the trackway no hard-core was laid down, and the herbage remained undisturbed.

Dewponds were dug out at regular intervals, in order to provide drinking water for the herds. **Greatham** had one outside Deal Farm, and another in Church Lane, alongside Cam Green Cottage, which has in fact been reinstated in recent years. The green lane from Church Lane to the Selborne Road, directly opposite the dewpond, is almost as original, being now classified as a *'bridleway'*, while another wide stretch can be seen, leading up from Deal Farm and bordering the northern edge of the sports-field (Dubbersfield). A further example runs as a continuation of Snailing Lane across to the Liss/Hawkley Road.

(A 'dewpond' is an artificial ancient pond, always containing water, probably fed by dew from the surrounding area draining into it, or by over-night mists. Ed.)

took on the role of tax collector on behalf of the Church until 1936, when tithe payers were finally freed of these obligations.

Tithe Map (1842)

The map previously mentioned was based upon the first Ordnance Survey 1" (one-inch) scale map of Great Britain. The primary triangulation for this began in 1792, about halfway through King George III's reign. It was carried out by Royal Military Surveyors, Captain (later Colonel) William Mudge, Captain Thomas Colby and Isaac Dalby. They were no doubt assisted in their project by local surveyors, hired for some particular task, probably on a daily or weekly basis. The whole project took many years to bring to a conclusion.

They fixed the positions of key trigonometrical stations on the highest points, such as hills and ridges. From there, they were able to fan out and take fixings on precisely located points. These would be major landmarks, church spires and steeples, and even well established tall trees. The survey measurements all had to be made on foot, using compasses to fix the angles.

As far as **Greatham's** map was concerned, the original drawings were cut with the north-south line passing through the centre of the village. The western half of the parish appeared on the Hampshire map, while the eastern half formed part of the West Sussex map. The subsequent edging and copperplate engraving left a geographical gap, centred on Swain's Cottages and the old 13th-century church.

Green lanes or Drover's roads

Apart from local movements of cattle and sheep, all meat had to be delivered to major towns and cities *'on the hoof'*. Thus a nation-wide

Registers and the Census

Registers of births, marriages and deaths have been the responsibility of the Parish priest (or incumbent) since the order issued by Thomas Cromwell, during the reign of Henry VIII around 1538, and it is to these ancient records that we usually go, when trying to trace a family history. Thirty years into the reign of Elizabeth I, in 1588, Jacob Williams, the Rector of **Greatham,** following a parliamentary injunction of that year, was made responsible for copying all previous records onto parchment. Unfortunately, he appears to have muddled things up somewhat, and those early records in the register may be considered as suspect.

The first nation-wide 'census' took place in 1801. Derived from the Latin term for *'rating of property'*, this ten-yearly event was designed to record data about the whole population. As well as numbers of citizens, it would also provide information concerning sex, age and occupation. Four years after Queen Victoria's ascension to the throne, the one that took place in 1841 was the first in which the names of individuals, along with their birth-dates, were recorded. However, it must be said that, with the inability of many people to read and write properly, much of the recorded data should be looked upon with not a little suspicion. Occasionally too, local inhabitants would be listed against the house in which they lived, so the ability to trace heredity and ownership was enhanced by these regular surveys.

(As an example, see the story of the Redman family history elsewhere in this account. Ed.)

Twentieth century

Early in the 20th-century, 'A history of Hampshire' described **Greatham** in the following manner:

" ... *an agricultural parish, containing 2,030 acres, situated on the western side of Woolmer Forest, part of which forest is in the parish, near the Sussex border. The soil is extremely varied and hops are cultivated in some parts. The river Rother forms the boundary on the west, the parish of Selborne on the north, and the parish of Liss on the south and east. To the north the land is high and wooded. A considerable part of the parish is occupied by* **Greatham Moor** *or Long Moor, across which runs Little Dean Bottom. There is a rifle range on the moor.*
The road from Petersfield to Farnham runs through the parish, and near the church throws off a branch to the north, in the direction of Alton. The War Office has recently established a military camp in the parish. **Greatham** *bridge is situated in the south-west corner, and carries the Petersfield/Farnham road over the river Rother.* **Greatham Mill** *stands on this river.*"

The modern landscape

As we enter the third Millennium, it is gratifying to find that those much-maligned people, the planners, seem to have woken up to the fact that rural dwellers do not want urbanisation thrust upon them, and that any development of country areas must be within the bounds already set. Unfortunately, there is no ability to legally enforce the retrospective correction of any planning errors already made, but a recent 'Countryside Design Summary' has at least set some bounds upon future development.

Here in **Greatham**, we are indeed fortunate to find that we are located at the meeting place of three varieties of landscape, as defined in the Design Summary. Lying, as it does, in the flat or very gently undulating 'Rother Valley' area, to the west is the area described as 'Heathland', with its acidic sandy soil and distinctive vegetation, while to the east we have 'The Hangers'. The first two are adequately described by their names, but just to quote the Design Summary, the Hangers is described thus:

"A diverse landscape of steep wooded slopes, narrow valleys, hills, enclosed fields and woodland pasture; unmaintained understorey vegetation and trees along the sunken lanes are

a particular and dramatic feature".

(The term 'Hanger' is derived from the old Saxon word 'hangra', meaning a steeply wooded incline. Ed.)

The sunken lanes mentioned above are there for anyone to see in the surrounding areas of Blackmoor, Empshott, Hawkley, etc. They would have been cut through by the continuous movement of horse-drawn carts over many centuries, while the adjacent trees literally cling to their sides, their exposed roots presenting wonderful intricate displays for the passing rambler. An earlier description of the Hangers was given by William Cobbett of Farnham, in his book 'Rural Rides', written in the 1820s, and still vividly correct today –

"These hangers are woods on the sides of very steep hills. The trees and underwood hang, in some sort, to the ground, instead of standing on it. Hence these places are called Hangers. From the summit of that which I now had to descend, I looked down upon the villages of Hawkley, **Greatham**, *Selborne and some others."*

It is hoped that any future development can be structured to fit in with the natural beauty of our surrounding landscape, so that future inhabitants continue to enjoy the benefits of what many of us today take for granted.

The modern village

It can be presumed that for many centuries, there was little visible change in the appearance of the village up until the coming of the motor vehicle. Time itself must have passed by slowly for those inhabitants of earlier ages. There is no escaping the fact that the 20th-century, like no other one before it, brought change at a somewhat alarming pace. Read Joe Leggett's description of riding with his father on a pony and cart, his thrill at seeing his first motor-car, and compare that with the speed and volume of traffic on today's roads, accompanied by all its noise and pollution.

The character of the village has also changed, and not always for the best. Even as a fairly recent arrival (1967!), I remember two 'village shops' in Longmoor Road alone and, during the course of researching this short history, older members of **Greatham** recalled to me that at one time the village was full of shops, even if some of them only operated from the front room of a house. Villagers themselves tend nowadays to be of a different breed. Once tied to the village boundaries by

Well I suppose the traffic is calmer. Pity we can't say the same of the drivers ....

lack of transport, they were self-sufficient in all manner of ways, with everyone willing to both live and work within the village confines. Today's villager is more likely to be a commuter, able to work many miles away, shop in the large supermarkets of neighbouring towns, only returning to **Greatham** for over-night rest and recuperation.

But we must also see cause for hope. Le Court may no longer reign over the ancient manor of **Greatham**, but just think of the way its influence has extended throughout the world, as it has become the focal point of the Cheshire Homes Foundation, with the ability to aid suffering and disability. The Manor House is no longer quite so grand, without its previous social functions and hunt meetings, but the L'Abri Fellowship also plays its part on the world's education. One does not need to be a religious zealot to understand the basic good work that is now achieved under those towering chimneys.

Along with the rest of mankind, the inhabitants of **Greatham** stand at the threshold of a new Millennium. It is still a small village by most standards, with no real heart, except perhaps the Church on one hand and possibly the Village Hall on the other. Perhaps this is due to the fact that the A325 main Farnham to Petersfield road literally cut the village in half, with its ever-increasing and faster traffic. However, with the opening of the Woolmer Road link, the village is now effectively by-passed to most of the heavy traffic.

At the time of this being written, traffic-calming measures have also been introduced, slowing down the speed of vehicles that still need to pass through. The result of a 'Village Appraisal' has led to the formation of a group of volunteers, whose aim is to improve the leisure and playground facilities in the area adjoining the Village Hall. Perhaps this will point the way ahead to a future where people can gather together more often and with less difficulty. It is to be hoped that this will be the case, but, as always, this is down to the people themselves. To paraphrase the words of the late President of the United States, John Fitzgerald Kennedy, at his inaugural address on January 20th 1961:

> *"Ask not what your village can do for you, ask what you can do for your village"*

Another quotation which springs to mind, particularly appropriate to the Village Appraisal, is:

> *"For life to be large and full, it must contain the care of the past and of the future in every passing moment of the present"*
> **Joseph Conrad, Nostromo**

The ruins of Greatham's old church are now the responsibility of a village trust of volunteers, who offer maintenance and loving care.

Chapter One
Conservation Area

Greatham lies just beyond the northern fringe of the East Hampshire Area of Outstanding Natural Beauty (AONB), as designated by the Countryside Commission in September of 1962. The AONB is one of 40 such nationally important areas that, together with the National Parks, provide some of the country's finest scenery. We are indeed lucky here in **Greatham** to have this most beautiful landscape, all the way down to the South Downs, *'upon our doorstep'*. For a more detailed description of the AONB, and the reasons for its existence, it is recommended that one makes a trip to the Visitor Centre, based in the Queen Elizabeth Country Park, on the southern side of Petersfield.

Although not strictly within this AONB prescribed area, a total of 16 buildings within the village have been 'listed' within a Conservation Area, under the definition of the AONB, since 1994. These include both the 'new' Church of St. John the Baptist and ruins of the old one; Case's House; Swain's Cottage; Rook's Farm; The Rectory (now a private residence); Gold's Cottage and Gold's (or Gould's) House, together with Gold's Barn, which may well have been the original 'tithe barn' of medieval times. Descriptions regarding these buildings are given elsewhere, under individual headings.

The character of the Conservation Area is essentially determined by the following four factors:

- The tightly grouped enclave of historic buildings, dating from the 17th and 19th-centuries, which surround the surviving remains of the old 13th-century Church of St John.
- Opposite the old church, and framed by trees to the north, lies the new 19th-century Church of St John, with its prominent tall spire. The church is set in a distinct flat pasture of open glebeland, which provides views into and out of the village.
- The skyline of Greatham's Manor House, its various steeply pitched roofs and tall chimneys set amongst trees, and all enclosed by a long ironstone wall.
- The visually unifying effect of the use of local ironstone for both buildings and boundary walls.

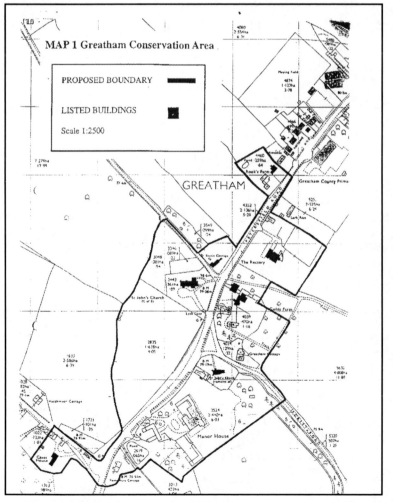

Greatham Conservation Area since 1994

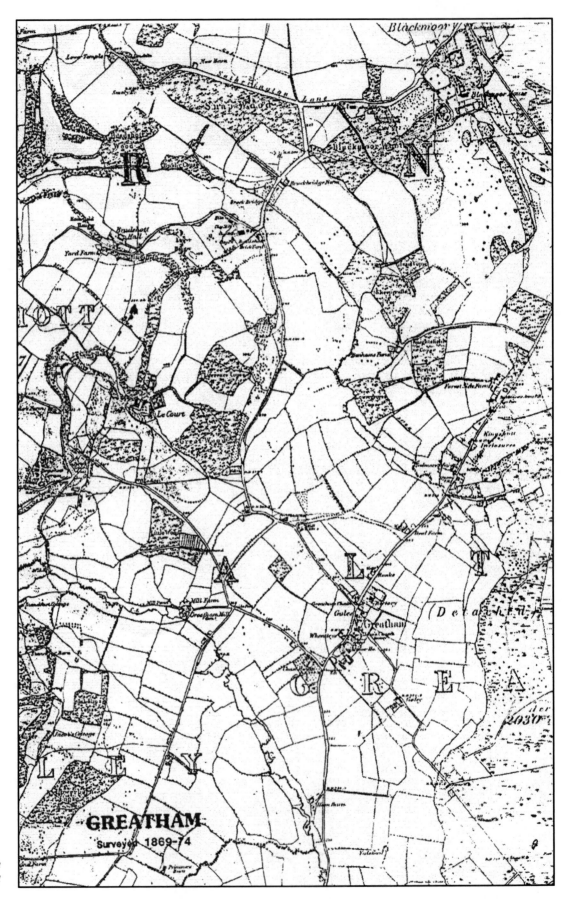

Map of Greatham
1869-1874

Chapter Two
Thele - an ancient holding

Thele was an ancient holding in **Greatham**, first being mentioned as the property of the de Winsors as early as 1390, with Miles Winsor (or Windsor) dying *'seized of it'* in 1452. It was described at the time as a *'messuage and 40 acres of land'*. By a fine levied in 1714, a Spencer Cowper acquired the manor of Thele from R Kynnesman and his wife.

The site is no longer easily identifiable, but a map of Hampshire dated 1801 shows Thele Bridge as the bridge which stands across the Rother, at what is now the bottom of Longmoor Road. An auction notice dated June 1899 mentions *'an enclosure of meadowland, known as Thele or Bridgeford Meadow, in extent 10 acres, 2 rods and 24 perches'*, but no exact location can be gleaned.

It is almost certain that the name lives on today in the property named 'Deal Farm', because it was formerly known as Theale Farm. The terrace of four cottages on the opposite side of the Petersfield Road, to the south of Longmoor Road, originally carried the name Deal Cottages. They were probably built towards the end of the 18th-century, as the type of brickwork at the gable ends was only popular for a few short years at that time.

In the mid-19th-century, they belonged to William Goodeve of Deal Farm. He must have been a man of some considerable influence in the Parish, as testified by the inscription on a marble wall tablet within the old church. It reads:

The area once known as Thele, looking down the hill from the site of the present school, where Henry Trigg's barn can be seen along-side Deal Farm.

It is sad to realise from this monument that both William and his wife outlived all of their five children, a circumstance thankfully less familiar in present times.

Towards the end of that century, Deal Cottage's original roof was blown off during a storm and replaced with slate, which was then becoming more popular and more easily available, thanks to the expanding national railway system. Now converted to two semi-detached houses, the northern-most one has been named Thele Knapp Cottage, with the second carrying the earlier name of Deal Cottage.

> In affectionate remembrance of
> WILLIAM GOODEVE
> Born June 2nd 1785, Died Nov 28th 1867
> Also of MARTHA his wife
> Born Feb 19th 1788, Died June 23rd 1838
> and of the following children of the above
> JAMES, born Nov 7th 1831, died Feb 25th 1832
> ELLEN, born Sept 15th 1822, died Jan 31st 1837
> HENRY GOSDEN, born April 27th 1826, died Sept 8th 1852
> MARY ANN, born Oct 12th 1817, died Oct 21st 1852
> and Thomas, born Jan 31st 1816, died Oct 27th 1866

('Thele' is believed to be an old term for 'boggy, or marshy, meadow', while 'knap' can mean to 'break with a sharp blow, especially a flint or stone'. A modern residence, Thele Knapp House, now stands alongside the cottages. Signs of a bed of flint within the garden area may well indicate evidence of the original holding. Ed.)

Chapter Three
The holding of the manor

As recorded in the Domesday Book, Queen Edith held the manor of **Greatham** before the Norman Conquest. She was the daughter of Godwin, Earl of Wessex, who by the 1030s had become one of the wealthiest and most powerful noblemen in the land. Edith was married to King Edward, also known as 'the Confessor'. Edward ruled England from 1042 – 1066, destined to become venerated as the principal English royal saint.

Greatham was probably part of an extensive estate that included the hunting ground of Woolmer Forest. After the Conquest, it remained a Royal possession until sometime during the 12th-century and is recorded as being *'held by Roger'* in 1167, at the time of Henry II. In 1223, with Henry III now on the throne, the manor was possessed by William Aquilon (or Aguillun in some archives). By 1286, during the reign of Edward I, a Robert de Aquilon died *'seized of it'*. This would indicate that Robert was probably the son and heir of William.

(The term 'seized of' is another way of saying 'in possession of'. Ed.)

Robert de Aquilon left a daughter and heir, Isabel, wife of Hugh Bardolf. Robert's widow Margaret died six years later (1292), having held the manor *'in dower'*, so the manor then passed on to the aforesaid Hugh and Isabel. Hugh Bardolf died in 1304, leaving a son Thomas as his heir. Although Thomas was only 22 years old at the time, he appears to have been out-lived by his mother, who also held the manor in dower, until her death in 1324, by which time Edward II had ascended to the throne. She was succeeded by another son, William, who in turn left the manor to his son, again named Thomas.

(The term 'dower' indicates property held by a widow, upon the death of her husband. Ed.)

This later Thomas died in 1329, at the start of Edward III's long 50-year reign, passing on title of the manor to his son and heir, John Bardolf. Although John survived until 1371, it would appear that by then he had parted with a considerable part of his property, because it is recorded that Nicholas de Devenish of Winchester died *'seized of'* the manor of **Greatham** in 1351. Some 40 years later, at least part of the estate appears to have passed into the possession of a family named de Winsor, together with a farm and demesne of 40 acres known as *Thele*.

Nicholas and his wife Edith, who was apparently more commonly known as Maud, left a son Thomas, only 17 years old at the time and, when he himself died in 1374, he was succeeded by his son and heir, John, an even younger boy of only 10 years of age. Thomas's widow Elizabeth held the manor in dower, until she re-married, to one William Marsh, sometime between 1376 and 1386, probably with Richard II on the throne. At this later date, the manor was dealt with by a fine, to which John Englefield and his wife Nichole were parties. Nichole was the daughter and heir of the previously mentioned Thomas Devenish.

By 1403, Henry IV was ruling England and John Englefield had died, leaving Nichole in possession of the manor as *'tenant for life'*. Before 1417, she had re-married to become the wife of John Golafre and the manor was then settled upon Philip Englefield, together with his wife Ismania and their issue. This would indicate that Philip was the eldest son of John and Nichole, because only a portion of the estate was given to Philip's brother Robert, with the ultimate remainder passing to *'the right heirs of Nichole'*.

The manor eventually descended to John Skylling and Elizabeth, the wife of Richard Norton. Around 1508, with the Tudor Henry VII on the throne, it then appears to have been conveyed to a William Faukener. Some 70 years later, a William Faukener still held title, though it is unlikely that this is the same person, rather another descendant. In 1578, the manor was conveyed to Richard Cooke and Nicholas Freeland for the sum of £200.

Richard Freeland, brother of Nicholas, then took possession and, when he died in 1609, having settled the estate upon his wife Elizabeth for life, a portion passed to their son John, then aged 30. Some time prior to 1610, probably during the kingship of James I, it is recorded that the site farm (i.e. Le Court) and its demesne was separated from the manor lands and conveyed by Sir John Webb to James Percy.

John Freeland died in 1610, leaving a daughter and heir, Margery. She married Sir Richard Caryll of Harting, whose family also held extensive estates in Sussex. When Dame Margery died in 1632, at the time of Charles I, a monument to her memory was erected by her kinsman, John Love, who was the Rector of

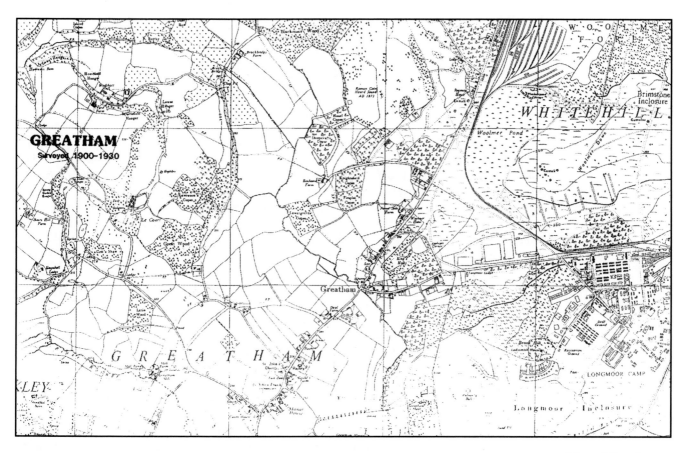

GREATHAM
Surveyed 1900-1930

*Map of Greatham
1900 to 1930*

Greatham at that time.   Her remains now lie in the chancel of the old church and her death is recorded in the register as follows:

"1632, Margery the Lady Carrel widow dyed at London May 11, betwene 2 and 3 o'clock and was buried on the 15th day of May in the morning".

John Love conveyed the manor to Thomas Cowper in 1633, the conveyance at that time including a 'free fishery'. This was probably for the purposes of a trust, as members of the Love family are recorded as *'presenting to the living'* from 1661, right through until 1754, when Susannah Love also *'presented'*, during the reign of George II. The final hereditary trace is in 1785, when the manor was presented by Susannah Beckford, widow, with George III now King of England.
(The custom of 'presenting to the living' is to nominate, especially to a Bishop, the person for institution to an incumbency or benefice – probably best described today as 'sponsorship'. Ed.)

Thus, lords or owners of the manor can be traced down to 1785, but details of subsequent holders of the title have become obscure. However, assuming that by now the title had become inherent with the manor house, the following details seem to fit in quite well. Captain E H Chawner is recorded as having bought Manor House in 1821, from local farmer Richard Hearsey, just after the start of George IV's reign. Both of these gentlemen were listed in the 1855 edition of Kelly's Directory, Hearsey as a farmer and Chawner as *'lord of the manor'*, by which time Queen Victoria had ascended the throne.

The 1880 Kelly's Directory still showed Captain Chawner as titleholder, and it was his son, Edward, who then sold Manor House to the Coryton family in 1883. By 1885, the Kelly's Directory for **Greatham** was then listing G E Coryton as lord of the manor, although still residing at West Liss. It is known that around 1900, the Coryton family moved to Manor House, just south of the Liss Forest Road junction, from Lyss Place at West Liss, on the Hawkley road. Frederick Coryton, son of G E, inherited the title, before passing it on to his own son, Augustus Frederick Coryton, or Captain 'Gussy', destined to become *the 'last squire of* **Greatham'**. A F Coryton died in 1976, bringing the *'holding of the manor'* of **Greatham** to a sad but inevitable close.

Chapter Four
Le Court

The entrance to Le Court, now world-renowned as a home for disabled people, is about ½-mile along the Selborne Road from its junction with the Petersfield Road and its turning into **Greatham**. From South Lodge, a long drive turns away up a gently rising ascent through beautiful chestnut trees, towards a splendid position on the hillside, with excellent views across the village, an ideal site for the original *'manor house'*!

An old icehouse exists at the edge of a wood, bordering the grounds of Le Court. It is of brick structure, with some external ornamental stonework. An entrance passage, with two large recesses, leads to a circular brick-lined pit some 40-foot deep. The building is covered by a wooden mound and is believed to have belonged to the original mansion house on the site. It is one of the buildings which has been taken under the wings of **Greatham's** Conservation Area.

A manor house (or *'capital messuage'*) was recorded as early as the year 1286, held by Robert de Aquilon. In 1577, the site farm and demesne of Le Court became separated from the manor of **Greatham** and sold off to a Mr Lewkner. Later still, there is evidence that it was conveyed by Sir John Webb to a James Percy. In 1613, James conveyed the property to William Chase and Thomas, his son and heir. In 1638 it was still being dealt with by Thomas but, in 1646, was settled by himself and his wife Christine upon their son, also named Thomas. Records show that in 1656, Le Court was in the possession of Thomas Chase esq, of Empshott.

(The term 'messuage' simply means a dwelling house. Ed.)

Around 1802, the estate was in the hands of Thomas Limbrey Solater Mathew of Tangier Park, also including at that time what is now Manor House. In 1805 it was sold on to Charles Butler, who appears to have died in 1832, as his will was published in that year. In 1854, the estate is shown as being shared by two of his heirs, William Eldridge Butler (two thirds) and Walter Butler (one third), with the former holding the house at Le Court. W E was definitely at Le Court in 1851, being instrumental in acquiring the land for the new school to be built in **Greatham**. He went on to sell the house for £16,000 to Sampson Foster, who is shown as owner in the 1871 trade directory.

The property comprising the manor included arable land, pastures, woodland and farm buildings. There was probably a dwelling of some sort on the site, perhaps a timber-framed house, but none of this is apparent now. The ancient place name of Lee (or Le) Court was used when the manor house was re-built between 1865 and 1866. However, the English phonetic spelling of *'Lacourt'* (Lay Court) had been used on the tithe map of 1842, when it was listed as a farm, with a tithe assessment of 144 acres.

The re-build of Le Court was at the instigation of Sampson Foster and his wife Mary, who had moved down from Walsall, Staffordshire, when their son Joseph moved the few short miles from Alton to take up the appointment of Curate-in-charge at **Greatham's** 13th-century church. Sampson Foster had previously built up a company with his cousin, Sampson Lloyd, first acquiring coal and iron mines, then manufacturing engines and railway goods for the rapidly expanding railway system. By 1862, Lloyds Fosters and Company had become one of the largest employers in the West Midlands, with a work force of well over 3,000 men by 1866.

(The Foster family can claim a Royal lineage going right back to King Edward I (1239-1307), while a former Sampson Lloyd (1664-1724) was the founder of the world-famous Lloyds Bank. Ed.)

Having left behind them the newly constructed Old Park Hall in Walsall, the Fosters now had a fine stone mansion built at **Greatham,** containing nine principal bedrooms and constructed of local Selborne stone, with Bath stone dressings. Mary Foster's maiden name had been Fry and her nephews, H and A P Fry, were a firm of Liverpool architects who, in all probability. designed the new house for their aunt at Le Court. At a time of much poverty and hardship, it must have been a great boost to local people as a source of employment, both during its construction and then afterwards. The stable, courtyard and three lodges (which still remain) provided, along with the positions of maids and house-servants, employment for about 20 people.

Mary Foster died at Le Court in 1869, followed by her husband Sampson in 1870. They are buried in the family tomb in the old churchyard. Le Court passed into the hands of their eldest son, William Fry Foster, but all of their children received substantial cash legacies, including Joseph. It is William who is credited with providing both the land and the finance to build

Greatham's new church, just 200 yards from the old one, but no doubt there were contributions from other family members too. William died in 1884. Augusta Mary Sandford, widow of a Member of Parliament, bought the estate for £27,500, possibly as an investment on behalf of her son Francis.

Sadly, during her tenure, the estate then became rather run-down and neglected and was in fact left in a state of disrepair. Despite this, after nine years it was sold on by auction, for the sum of £25,000, in October of 1892, and the auction notice described the estate as follows:

"Situate in the very healthy, exceedingly picturesque and favourite district of Petersfield, and only about 2½ miles from Liss Station, on the Main London and South Western Railway, between London and Portsmouth, from whence the former is reached by an excellent Service to Trains in about an hour and thirty minutes.

It comprises a FIRST-CLASS FAMILY MANSION, of Gothic style and Architecture. Erected in the year 1865, in a very substantial and superior manner, quite regardless of cost, (it is) in an elevated position, commanding views of exceptional beauty and extent.

It is surrounded by beautiful pleasure grounds and finely timbered park; walled kitchen gardens, glass-houses, gardener's and bailiff's cottages; spacious stabling, two picturesque entrance lodges, conveniently placed farm buildings; rich meadow and arable lands in a high state of cultivation; a good proportion of woods of a very fine growth, the whole embraces an area of about 282 acres."

The new owners were to be Mr Heath Harrison and his wife Mary, who had arrived from a shipping business in the great port of Liverpool in 1893. The new Rector of **Greatham**, Francis Richard Bryans, arrived at the same time and wrote of the Harrisons:

"... they are a great acquisition to the place. They are young, very rich, kind and right-thinking people. I am glad to say they are also communicants. Le Court is wonderfully improved. That dull, gloomy hall has had daylight let into it and there are other improving alterations. They have put in the electric light and the whole house is suitably and beautifully furnished."

The by then Sir Heath Harrison died in 1934, having become a fixture of Hampshire life – Justice of the Peace, High Sheriff, Alderman, County Councillor and Magistrate. A fuller account of his life and achievements follows later in this history. His widow Mary died in 1938 and, as the couple had died childless,

the estate passed into the hands of Mary's sister, Madeline Knight, wife of General Harry Lewkenor Knight, CMG, DSO, who died in 1945. Their daughter married Major-General Arthur Barstow, who was killed in Malaya during 1942.

He had been uncle to Leonard Cheshire, and eventually Le Court was passed on to the Group Captain who founded the Cheshire Homes. Indeed, Le Court itself became the initial basis of these world-famous homes, with its first disabled resident arriving in 1948. Arthur Dykes was a patient in Petersfield Hospital, suffering incurable cancer, when Leonard Cheshire, who had known him previously, decided to move him to Le Court in order to look after him. At the time, Cheshire undoubtedly did not know where it was all going to lead!

The Victorian mansion was demolished in the 1950s, to be replaced by more practical accommodation for disabled people. The excellent purpose-built accommodation of today was completed with financial assistance from the Carnegie (UK) Trust. The recently deceased Lord Denning, former Master of the Rolls, was actively associated with the project right from the start, being present when the Queen Mother came to the official opening in 1954. He also went on to serve as the first Chairman of the Cheshire Foundation.

Leonard Cheshire died in 1992, himself the victim of the disabling Motor Neurone disease. A brief history of his life and work can be found later in this history. A stained-glass window has been installed in the Chapel of the Assumption at Le Court, consisting of six panels illustrating different aspects of 'GC's' life. He was always fondly called 'GC', this being based upon the fact that he became a Group Captain during his World War II exploits. One of the panels is a portrait of the man himself, by artist June Mendoza.

"A fine stone mansion", rebuilt in 1866; demolished a century later.

[SECOND EDITION.]

HAMPSHIRE.

PARTICULARS, WITH CONDITIONS OF SALE,

OF THE

VALUABLE FREEHOLD (AND SMALL PART VERY LONG LEASEHOLD)

Residential and Manorial Property,

KNOWN AS

THE GREATHAM MANOR ESTATE,

Situate in the Parishes of GREATHAM and HAWKLEY, adjoining Woolmer Forest, and about three miles from the pretty
and interesting Village of SELBORNE, in the midst of a beautiful district, commanding lovely views; comprising

AN ANCIENT MANOR HOUSE,

In excellent repair and condition, with GARDENS;

LARGE HOMESTEAD, A CAPITAL FARM HOUSE AND HOMESTEAD,

DETACHED FIELD HOMESTEADS,

And various COTTAGE DWELLINGS in and about the Village of Greatham,

Surrounded by rich Agricultural Land, containing an area of about

460 ACRES,

In Arable, Pasture, Water Meadow, Hop and Woodland,

Mainly in one fine occupation, and let at moderate Rents, which amount to about

£755 per Annum;

TOGETHER WITH

THE MANOR OR REPUTED MANOR OF GREATHAM,

WITH ITS RIGHTS, PRIVILEGES AND EMOLUMENTS;

ALSO A

LITTLE FREEHOLD DAIRY FARM OF RICH ARABLE & PASTURE LAND,

WITH

SMALL FARM HOUSE AND HOMESTEAD,

KNOWN AS

MILK VERE FARM,

Situate at Farringdon, about 3½ miles south of Alton, and containing about 6½ Acres,
let at £18 per Annum.

The whole presenting excellent opportunities for the Investment of Capital:

WHICH WILL BE OFFERED FOR SALE BY AUCTION, BY

Messrs. DANIEL SMITH, SON, & OAKLEY,

AT THE AUCTION MART, TOKENHOUSE YARD, CITY, E.C.,

On WEDNESDAY, the 27th day of JUNE, 1883,

AT ONE FOR TWO O'CLOCK PRECISELY,—IN NINE LOTS.

Particulars may be obtained of A. F. M. DOWNIE, Solicitor, Alton; of Messrs. RIVINGTON & SONS, Solicitors,
1, Fenchurch Buildings, E.C.; at the Mart, City, E.C.; and of Messrs. DANIEL SMITH, SON, & OAKLEY, Land Agents
and Surveyors, 10, Waterloo Place, Pall Mall, S.W.

Vacher & Sons, Printers, 25, Parliament Street, and 67, Millbank Street, Westminster.

1 D

Details of an Auction Notice of 1883
for the Greatham Manor Estate

For many years, Le Court used to run an Annual Fete, which attracted thousands of visitors, putting both the home and *Greatham* firmly on the map. Sadly, ever rising costs brought this splendid yearly function to a close. Last year, 1998, saw the Golden Jubilee of both Le Court and the Cheshire Foundation, as residents and staff celebrated 50 years of care and devotion.

Today, the Leonard Cheshire Homes offer both help and opportunities to more than 10,000 disabled people and their carers in the UK alone. Overseas, there are more than 250 projects in some 50 countries around the world. As for Le Court itself, it is a dual registered home, part nursing care and part residential. Apart from nursing, it also offers both occupational therapy and physiotherapy. There is a computer room, accessible for work, leisure or therapy purposes. An Activities Centre is the venue for many events, while shopping trips and leisure outings are also arranged.

In 1999, ambitious plans were then being prepared for another massive fund-raising effort, in order to expand and modernise the existing facilities. The key to its success was the chance it offered to sick and disabled people to make their own decisions about how they wished to live their lives. Sadly, as we enter the new Millennium, policy problems have arisen which put the very future of Le Court in doubt.

Government thinking is now aimed at making disabled people more reliant and independent, by placing them as *'care in the community'* patients. Many of those who have been selected to move, however, are appalled by the prospect of leaving their 'gently institutionalised' home. One possible solution may be to sell off the site altogether. No final decision will be made until late in 2000, but it is to be hoped that this splendid Cheshire Home can continue to flourish and maintain its long-held links with *Greatham*, where it all started over 50 years ago.

(The above account was adapted from a 'History of Le Court', an essay written by Angela Stone in 1987, later updated by reference to various documents and newspaper cuttings, plus a pleasant visit to meet Jenny Croucher, the Public Relations Officer in May 1999. Ed.)

PARTICULARS.

THE

GREATHAM MANOR ESTATE

IS A

VERY CHOICE AND VALUABLE

FREEHOLD PROPERTY

(A small part being very Long Leasehold for upwards of 1,000 years),

SITUATE

In the Parishes of Greatham and Hawkley (except a small piece, No. Part 1 on Plan, which is in the adjoining Parish of Liss), presenting a safe and good Investment, whilst its many enjoyable features, its natural advantages of a fine position in a Capital Sporting Part of the County of Hants on the borders of Sussex, within the Meets of the Hambledon and Lord Leconfield's Foxhounds, its proximity to the very picturesque Village of Liss (distant about a mile from the property), in the neighbourhood of which several good Mansions have been built, and to the Liss Station on the Portsmouth Direct Line of the London and South Western Railway (a journey of about 1½ hour from Waterloo), at which Station nearly all the passenger trains stop, affording excellent Railway communication to London and the South of England, would justify the erection of a suitable MANSION and thus render it a fine RESIDENTIAL ESTATE.

The Seats of several Noblemen and County Gentlemen are in the immediate neighbourhood or within driving distances, among which may be mentioned:—

Rotherfield Park (Arthur Jervoise Scott, Esq.), Pelham (Mrs. Lemprière), Chawton House (Montagu George Knight, Esq.), "The Wakes," Selborne (late the Residence of Professor Bell and previously of Rev. Gilbert White, the Naturalist), Blackmoor (Right Hon. Earl Selborne), Basing Park (Wm. Nicholson, Esq.), Thedden Grange (John Gathorne Wood, Esq.), Bentworth Hall (Hon. Mrs. Ives), The Grange, Alresford (Lord Ashburton), Hawkley Hurst (J. J. Maberley, Esq.), Binsted Wyck (Wm. Wickham, Esq.), Le Court (Wm. Foster, Esq.), Liss Place (G. E. Coryton, Esq.), The Grange, Empshott (Mrs. Scott).

THE PROPERTY

Occupies a lovely sheltered situation on the confines of Woolmer Forest, and commands a very distant prospect in all directions, being more immediately surrounded by the well known Selborne and other beautifully wooded Hills and Hangers, the surface of the Country being richly diversified by Hill and Dale; the lofty Promontory and the secluded Glen appearing in quick succession animating and giving special interest to the Landscape.

The District around the pretty Village of Selborne is fully described in the Rev. Gilbert White's well known and interesting work on the History and Antiquities of Selborne.

The Soil is a rich productive Loam resting on Marl and Chalk, and may be classed among the most valuable Corn growing, Hop and Grazing Lands of the County.

The Fields generally are large and well adapted for steam cultivation and the Estate is well Timbered.

The whole of the property is Freehold, except Lots 2 and 7, which are very Long Leasehold, and except such part (if any) of Lot 1, as is included in the site of a Barn and Half an Acre of Land (which cannot be identified), held for the Residue of a Lease of 1001 Years, granted in the 31st Year of Queen Elizabeth.

It is intersected by the Petersfield and Farnham Turnpike Road and surrounds the pretty Village of Greatham with its new ornamental Parish Church, some of the Cottages in the Village forming part of the property.

It is also bounded in part and intersected by 2 capital Trout Streams which afford good Sport to the Angler, and is situate about 4 miles from Liphook, 5 from Petersfield, 7 from Haslemere, 12 from Farnham, 7 from Alton, 14 from Godalming and 20 from Portsmouth, in a central situation with regard to some of the best Markets of Hampshire and Sussex.

Chapter Five
Manor House

A 'new' manor house (not surprisingly known as Manor House!) lies to the south of the Liss Forest Road junction. The house is large, with extensive grounds, and has been added to at various times over the years, but the oldest part is probably that which bears a stone plaque set into a wall, with the date '1680'. The earliest brickwork is identifiable by its 'galleting', the decorative mortar in-fill between the bricks, which is omitted on later work. It is probable that the house had humble beginnings, being first the 'farmhouse' of Manor Farm. Today however, with its myriad array of chimneys upon its steeply sloping roofs, it provides an impressive sight to its many visitors.

When the *'Greatham Manor Estate'* was put up for auction in London during June 1883, the *'capital old Manor House'* was described as a *'residential and manorial property'*, comprising the following:

'Built of stone, brick and tile and containing on the upper floor, 2 roomy attics. On the first storey, 5 good bed chambers, 1 dressing room and water closet. On the ground floor, large entrance hall 17 ft. 8 in. by 15 ft. 6 in., paved with Minton's tiles; dining room 19 ft. 6 in. by 15 ft. 9 in.; drawing room 16 ft. by 15 ft. 6 in.; pantry, fitted with cupboards; servants' hall; kitchen, with serving hatch to hall; back kitchen, with well of pure water and force pump; coal and knife house, lean-to, brick and tile; and good underground cellars.'

The earliest record of an owner is Thomas Limbrey

Solater Mathew, who bought the Manor House, along with other land and property, including Le Court, in 1802. Documents seem to show that a Thomas Smith was a previous owner, but is not made clear that this was the case. However, indications are that Manor House had already succeeded Le Court as *the* 'manor house', or seat of the manor, prior to this date. The original estate, which included *both* of these major properties, appears to have then been split up at a later date, probably sometime between 1810 and 1821.

(It is interesting that in 1792, in a dispute over parliamentary enclosure at Basing, a John Limbrey and a Mr Solater were the antagonists – see the names above! Ed.)

Charles Butler, who also bought Le Court, appears to have bought Manor House over a period of about 5 years, but then re-sold it to Richard Hearsey, a local farmer and landowner. Records also show that what remained of Charles Butler's lands were apportioned to his two sons, William and Walter, at the much later dates of 1858 and 1863.

As far as the Manor House is concerned, a deed of sale dated 1821 shows that Richard Hearsey sold it to Captain Henry Chawner of Newton Valence. As well as the Manor House itself, several other dwellings are believed to have been part of the same estate, namely *Manor Cottage, Tom's Acre Cottage, Case's, Swain's, Gold's Farm, Rook's Farm, Goleigh Farm, Ham Barn, Hatchmoor Farm, Berrygrove Farm, Scotland Farm, Lyss Place* and a milk farm at Farringdon.

A Mrs Elizabeth Ewen is shown as residing at the Manor House around 1875 – 1880, followed by a Mrs Unwin around 1895, but it is assumed that they were only renting the property during those periods.

It was Henry Chawner's son, Edward, who later sold the estate to George Edward Coryton in 1883, while a major five-year extension is commemorated by another plaque over the main entrance, dated '1898'. The Coryton sisters, Isolda and Georgiana, are thought to have been the first Manor House residents of that family, eventually swapping houses with their brother, Captain A F Coryton, who had previously lived at Gould's (or Gold's) House.

Between the Chawners (1821 - 1883) and the Corytons (1883 - 1971), Manor House became established as the main centre of village life for a century and a half, due mainly to the social standing

Manor House which dates back to the late 17th century.

of those two families who owned it. Certainly during the Coryton's residence, the grounds were often used for Church fetes and as a popular meeting place for the Hampshire Hunt.

(Captain E H Chawner was also 'lord of the manor' at Newton Valence. He died in 1916 at the age of 82 and his tombstone can be found in the churchyard at nearby Newton Valence. Ed.)

Since many of the outlying farms and lands belonged to the lord of the manor and were rented out to tenants, the Manor House obviously affected the direction of much local agricultural work, as well as of the people who carried it out. It must also have provided employment for housemaids, servants, cooks and gardeners, generally contributing to the fabric of village life.

As part of the Victorian refurbishment of Manor House, an intriguing water system was devised for the house. All the rainwater from the gutter system was drained into a filtering system, consisting of three tanks, each one containing gravel of finer grade than the previous one, with the last one draining into

a huge underground reservoir. This stored water was then pumped up into five water-tanks in the attic, from where the domestic water supply was then supplied. This system is believed to have been in use until around 1980.

L'Abri Fellowship

Manor House has been owned by an organisation known as the 'L'Abri Fellowship' since 1971, when it was bought by its Chairman at that time, Ranald Macaulay. It is a Christian study group, founded in Switzerland in 1955 by an American couple, Edith & Francis Shaeffer. The name 'L'Abri' is from the French word for shelter and, in this case, offers a resting-place for people to take time out from their busy lives and to ask themselves *what is life really about?'*

On a snowy day in January of 1971, Susan and Ranald Macaulay, along with their family, moved into the Manor House. They had been searching for a suitable place in which to start residential work and, when negotiations with the Corytons became finalised,

Augustus, Georgiana and Isolda in the Stable Yard

Frederick Coryton by the front door.

accommodation, the woodshed into a house, and the old bake-house into a lecture room. The orchard, planted over 20 years ago, continues to produce fruit for the residents, both permanent and temporary. It is a Christian study centre in a personal, family-style setting, but not a retreat, as the days are a healthy mixture of work, study and discussion. Students arrive from all corners of the earth, from as far away as Korea and from as nearby as Liss Forest. Each individual studies for half of each day and works for the community during the other half. Work is supervised by personal tutor, while there is access to a large library of books and video-cassettes.

Many former children of **Greatham** and its surrounding area will have fond memories of attending Manor House for its annual 'Children's Week' each summer, with outside activities such as horse riding and many indoor pursuits, which included pottery. Those who enjoyed swinging on the rope swing beneath the old cedar tree will be sad to hear that it was lost during the 'great storm' which swept across southern England in late 1987.

L'Abri offers its hospitality to both Christians and non-Christians, many of whom arrive in search of answers to their questions. Mature Christians come to learn more, while others are just trying to 'sort things out', perhaps spiritually, intellectually, morally

they were pleased to have access to this large house in the beautiful Hampshire countryside. Over the next few years, much had to be changed on the property. Manor House had become a quiet rural estate, but now it was 'all hands on deck' as drains were cleared, house repairs put into progress, gardens organised and the whole place converted into a self-contained international community within the village.

The stables were converted into living

Isolda, Augustis and Georgiana playing cricket on the lawn.

A view showing the porch way entrance to the Manor House

or emotionally. L'Abri does its best to encourage and offer guidance in all of these spheres. Thus Manor House's former effects on village or parochial life may now be diminished, but instead it now plays a much larger role in the affairs of the outside world.

(Thanks go to Gavin and Andrew for allowing me to visit Manor House on quite a few occasions and to Nick Houston for permission to use his excellent research notes. Finally thanks go to Jill Barrs, who brought me 'up to date' with the last 28 years. I was always impressed by the savoury smells of cooking during my visits – perhaps L'Abri should open a restaurant! Ed.)

Mrs Frederick Coryton at the back door overlooking the lawn.

Chapter Six
Greatham's old Church

The oldest building still standing in the area is the ruin of the old 13th-century St John's Church, whose *advowson* belonged to the Bardolf's in 1330 and descended along with the manor. The ruins are located at the junction of the main village road and the branch road that leads off to Liss Forest. Just across the branch road is an area of grass that was more popularly used in earlier years as the 'village green'.

Built from rubble (mixed sandstone and ironstone) with a sandstone *ashlar* dressing. Those good and honest men who built it would hardly recognise the village today. Ancient footpaths and foundations have long since vanished, now buried beneath the grass and undergrowth of the surrounding area. An earlier observer of **Greatham's** history mentioned that *'the romance of centuries hangs around the ivy-clad walls of its ancient church'*, while another describes the church as *'small and handsome, in the early English style'*.

('Ashlar' denotes a dressed, hewn block of stone, especially used to decorate the outer surfaces of buildings. Sandstone is sometimes also referred to as 'malmstone' in some descriptions of the building's construction. The term 'advowson' is the right of patronage to a church benefice or living. Ed.)

In his essay on Tudor Greatham, Doctor E M Yates produced a list of the Rectors that covered a century of those times. They were, in chronological order:

> *1486 Elias Hulme*
> *1496 Henry Bartelot*
> *1499 Robert Marshall*
> *1507 John Berne*
> *1520 Robert Singleton*
> *1532 William Mede*
> *1553 Evan Braunche*
> *1557 William Stoughton*
> *1562 John Gregory, with Richard Wise, Curate*
> *1571 John Abrall*
> *1572 Egidius Williams*
> *1580 Richard Colman*
> *1580 Jacob Williams*

A very sympathetic description of the old church appears in Arthur Mee's 'Hampshire with the Isle of Wight' travel book, first published in 1939:

" ... its old shrine is all but forgotten, the scene of its joys and sorrows for more than 600 years. The broken walls of the nave were richly clothed in nature's green when we called, as if to heal their wounds. Across the road, the village has a handsome modern church, but the 13th-century chancel of the ruined church, though seldom used, still has its 17th-century altar and its old

The remains of Greatham's 13th century church.

To the Church-Wardens and Overseers of the Poor of
the Parish of *Petersfield*
in the County of *Southampton*   and
to the Church-Wardens and Overseers of the Poor
of the Parish of *Greatham*
                    said
in the County of *Southampton*

Southampton
    to wit.   } WHEREAS Complaint hath been made unto us, whose Names are
            hereunto set, and Seals affixed, being two of His Majesty's
            Justices of the Peace in and for the County of *Southampton*
aforesaid (one whereof being of the Quorum) by the Church-wardens and
Overseers of the Poor of the said Parish of *Petersfield*
That *William White Sophia his Wife and their*
two Children Namely William of the Age of
three Years or thereabouts and Ann of the Age of one Year or
thereabouts have lately intruded and come into the Parish of *Petersfield*
                and *are* actually become chargeable to the
same : We the said Justices, upon due Proof made thereof, as well
upon the Examination of the said *William White the Father*

upon Oath, as other Circumstances, do adjudge the same to be true,
and do also adjudge the Place of the legal Settlement of the said
William White, Sophia his Wife and their two Children

to be in the Parish of *Greatham,*
in the County of *Southampton*

THESE are therefore in his Majesty's Name to require you the said
Church-wardens and Overseers of the Poor of the said Parish of *Petersfield*
            on Sight hereof, to remove and convey the said
William White, Sophia his Wife and their two
children
from and out of your said Parish of *Petersfield*
to the said Parish of *Greatham*   and *them*
deliver unto the Church-wardens and Overseers of the Poor there, or to
some or one of them, together with this our Order, or a true Copy
hereof, who are hereby required to receive and provide for *them*
according to Law.

GIVEN under our Hands and Seals, the *third* Day of *November*
in the Year of our Lord One Thousand Eight Hundred and *Seventeen.*

J Hookson

Chas Barton

*Notification of
responsibility for
'the poor' passing
from Petersfield to
Greatham, 1817.*

altar rails; and, lying in magnificent solitude in this deserted sanctuary is Dame Caryll, in alabaster on a splendid panelled tomb. The great hollow yew outside would have been a sturdy youngster when they laid her here in Charles Stuart's days."

Only the chancel survives, with a slate roof, pseudo-Gothic two-light east window, and two plain lancets (arched windows) in the north and south walls. At the eastern end of the south wall is a plain locker. The altar rails belong to a later age, being 17th-century, with balusters supporting the coping. The chancel arch, which is built up with a door giving access, is also 17th-century, three-centred with a projecting keystone and chamfered strings at the springing. These last appear to be 12th-century stones re-used.

(The wooden altar rails bear the date '1637', and are stamped with the initials 'M C', possibly those of the man who carved them or, more likely, as a dedication to the Lady whose story follows. Ed.)

The chancel contains a splendid panelled altar tomb, with an alabaster effigy of Dame Margery Caryll, who was born in 1592, only four years after the defeat of the Spanish Armada. Margery, who also appears on some documents to have been known as Elizabeth, was eldest daughter of Elizabeth (nee Uvedale) and John Freeland of **Greatham**, and was baptised at the old church on June 27th 1594. She was later married to Sir Richard Caryll of Lady Holt, Harting, West Sussex, at the tender age of 17. Sir Richard died when Margery was still only 24, while Margery herself died in 1632, aged only

40. These families were all local, having great power, wealth and influence.

(The Lady Holt estate was still owned by the Catholic Caryll family until sold in 1767. Sir Matthew Fetherstonhaugh had already bought Up Park in 1747, then started to expand his landholdings around Harting in 1755. Lady Holt was one of these added estates. Uppark today is a fine late 17th-Century country house, set high upon the South Downs, south-east of Petersfield. The house suffered from a disastrous fire in 1989, but has been lovingly restored to its former splendour. It belongs to the nation, being in the care of the National Trust. In 1874, the mother of H G Wells, the famous author, was housekeeper at Uppark.

On a trip to the south coast in October 2000, I witnessed a re-enactment of a Civil War battle by a company of English Heritage players within the walls of Portchester Castle. An accompanying leaflet gave details of the Tudor era, when the castle was 'sold to a local landowner, William Uvedale, as it was considered to be of no military use'. This was in 1628, so it is almost certain that William Uvedale was kin to Dame Margery, whose mother had been born a Uvedale. By an amazing coincidence, I visited Wimborne Minster, Dorset, within days of my stop at Portchester and found a stunning monument dedicated to Sir Edmund Uvedale, who died in 1606. Once again the date and name show evidence of a connection to Dame Margery's family, on her mother's side. The effigy of Sir Edmund is Italian, in the Renaissance style – though after a later restoration, he is mistakenly shown as having two left feet! Ed.)

Although Lady Caryll died in London, she was buried here at Greatham, with her will being dated June 23rd 1630. At a later period, the Carylls were greatly persecuted, due to their loyalty to the Stuart cause. Their property passed away from them, owing to heavy fines, and the last of their line died in poverty, and almost in exile, even though Richard had been created Baron Harting by King James II.

The covering slab of the tomb is of black marble, and the inscription is on an alabaster tablet under an arch pediment, carried by black marble columns with Corinthian capitals. It is surmounted by strap-work with a lozenge-shaped shield, bearing the arms of Caryll impaled with Freeland, as Dame Margery had been a Freeland by birth. The legend says that she died after pricking her finger with a needle while sewing, possibly causing blood poisoning.

(Could this be the origin of the story of 'Sleeping Beauty'? Ed.)

There are a number of inscriptions around the monument, and they all make interesting reading:

As indicated by the final inscription above, the monument to Dame Margery was erected by her

---

- "To the memorie of Dame Margery Caryll, who having sure confidence in the merits of our Saviour Jesus Christ, departed this life with great courage and comfort the 11th daie of May, Anno Domini 1632, in the 40th yeere of her age."

- "This vertuous ladie was the wife of Sir Richard Caryll of Harting, Knight, with whome she lived seven yeeres, and after his death continued his widowe all the time of her lyfe, beinge the space of 16 yeers."

- "And daughter and heyre of John Freelond, Gentleman, Lord of this Manor and Patron of this Church, by Elizabeth his wife, daughter and coheire of Thomas Uvedale of Colemeire, Esqr."

- "Thou marble tumbe though long ye mayst endure
  And dost within an honord corps immure,
  Yet raisd and freed thy prisonr God shall see
  When thou for ever shalt demolishd bee,
  A jewell then of price thou dost containe,
  Which thou consumed, for ever shalt remaine."

- "Johannes Love cognatus devotissimus"

kinsman (brother), John Love, who was known to be the Rector of **Greatham** at that time. The first Rector of whom there is any record is William Fidler, whose name appears in the register under the year 1574, during the first Elizabethan era. The name Nicholas Bailey appears from 1615 – 1640. Starting with John Love in 1657, by which time Oliver Cromwell and Parliament ruled England, the list can be followed right through to the present day.

The chancel walls bear witness to this, with tablets to the memory of some of the Rectors of the 19th-century: – the Rev Richard Newlin, who died in 1772 and must have been a contemporary of Gilbert White at Selborne; the Rev Richard Greene, who married Mr Newlin's daughter and died in 1786; the Rev G Berry Godbold, for 25 years the patron and Rector of the parish, who died in 1838; and his daughter, Harriet Jane, who died in 1824.

Richard Newlin and his wife Beata have the following inscription:

Near this Place
Are interred the Remains
Of the Rev'd RICHARD NEWLIN
Bachelor of Civil Law
And Vicar of the Parishes
Of Rogate and Empshot
As a Divine
He adorn'd his Station
With undeviating Integrity
And unaffected Piety:
In Social Life
With Purity of Manners
He happily Connected
A propriety of Expression
With pleasing affability:
His Actions
The Result of a considerate Mind
Exactly Corresponded with
The Justness of his Sentiments.
He died May 25th 1772
Aged 74.

In the adjoining Grave
Are deposited the Remains
Of BEATA the Wife of RICHARD
NEWLIN
who died the 24th Of July 1778
Aged 69.

Another marble tablet is dedicated to the memory of the Greene family:

Near this Place
lie interred the remains of
The Rev'd RICHARD GREENE M A
Rector of Radcliffe in Buckinghamshire
& Curate of this Parish
who died April 7th 1786
aged 48 Years

Also of
BEATA his wife
daughter of RICHARD &
BEATA NEWLIN who died
June 9th 1786, aged 47 Years
also of RICARDUS JOSEPHUS
GREENE
son of RICHARD & BEATA GREENE
who died Nov'r 25th 1793
aged 16 Years

The Reverend Godbold is remembered by the inscription:

Sacred to the Memory
of the Reverend
GEORGE BERRY GODBOLD
upwards of twenty-five years
Rector and Patron
of this Parish
Died April 26th 1838

His daughter died at a very early age, and has the loving epitaph:

Sacred to the Memory of
HARRIET JANE
Daughter of the Revd.
G B GODBOLD M A
Rector of this Parish
Died August 10th 1824
Aged 2 years and 9 months

"Lovely Harriet, fare thee well,
Far too good on Earth to dwell,
Almost Cherub here below,
Altogether Angel now."

A 'slateboard' now lies in the corner of the old chancel, and indicates that the old building, as was the custom in those days, was used for religious instruction of the local children, probably each Sunday afternoon.

Slateboard showing that the old buidling was used for religous instruction.

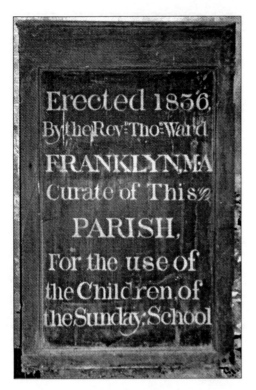

Erected 1836,
By the Rev: Tho: Ward
FRANKLYN.MA
Curate of This
PARISH,
For the use of
the Children of
the Sunday School

St. John's became a ruin in those years that followed the building of the new church, almost directly opposite, in 1875. Sadly, many parts of its structure were pulled down, to be used in the construction of its successor. The bells were transferred from the old belfry into the new church's wooden steeple. Fallen roof timbers were probably taken away by villagers for their own uses.

Similar in style to many other Hampshire churches, consisting of chancel, nave and north porch, St. John's became so thickly covered with plaster and whitewash that few of its original external features could be traced. By the end of the 19th-century, the still-standing remnants of the original church were deemed beyond repair. With no further funds available for its upkeep, the old church's future was seriously in doubt.

Despite the concerns of local people that the move would lead to demolition, and re-development of the site, and even after strenuous campaigning by such stalwarts as Gwen Brooker and Lt Col Michael Digby, the church was finally declared redundant in 1990. Thankfully, what remained stayed intact and, in February 1998, ownership of this historic building passed from the Church Commissioners into the hands of **Greatham** Parish Council. The church is now a Grade II listed building, as part of a conservation area.

It is gratifying that maintenance and restoration work on this splendid piece of local history is still being carried out, thanks to the tireless efforts of people like Hugette & Ray Jenkinson over a period of more than 30 years. Preservation work has continued under the auspices of the Society for the Preservation of Ancient Buildings (SPAB), who took over the site as a project in 1992. The Society is probably the oldest, largest and most technically expert group in its field, having been founded in 1877 by William Morris, the famous poet and artist, renowned for his splendid wallpaper designs. Over the past seven years, various people from all over

The old church photographed around 1954

the country, lodging temporarily with local people, have assisted in this worthwhile cause.

A final footnote as to the old church's future was given in the address by Gail Anderson, Chairperson of the Parish Council, at the Annual Parish Meeting in April 1999:

> " ... a meeting was held between interested parties to establish how a Trust could be set up to manage the old church. It was agreed that there should be eight Trustees, and of those eight, there would always be the County Councillor, the District Councillor, Chairman of the Parish Council, and a representative of the Parochial Church Council. A Trust Document is being drawn up for agreement and should shortly be in place. The Trust will be empowered to manage the practical side of maintenance to the old church, fund raising and application for grants, to maintain this ancient building as a monument for the village in perpetuity. The old church is already used for occasional services throughout the year, and it is hoped that the site will become a focal point of interest in Greatham."

The setting up of the **Greatham** Old Church Trust was completed early in the new Millennium, as a registered charity to manage the old church affairs on behalf of the Parish Council. The trust's stated objectives are (a) to preserve, repair and maintain the historic building and environment of St. John the Baptist old church for the benefit of the community and (b) to provide public access for the use of the said building as a place of Christian worship and prayer. All of **Greatham's** best wishes must be with them.

The ancient yew tree

Many churches in this part of Hampshire and neighbouring West Sussex have ancient yew trees. These were significant in pre-Christian times, often standing as monuments to longevity, as well as objects of beauty. When Christian churches were first built, yew trees would be planted as a symbol of immortality, respect for the tree having been taken from its pagan history.

Perhaps the most famous yew tree in the locality was the 'great yew of Selborne'. When it was unfortunately blown down during the turbulent gale of 1990, it measured 26 feet in circumference, and thus estimated to be 1,400 years old. In 1997, the yew tree in **Greatham's** old churchyard measured approximately 21 feet in girth. According to the Conservation Foundation, this would suggest an age of 1,020 years. Not as old as that at Selborne, but still living and therefore still growing. It is indeed an 'ancient' yew tree, certainly pre-dating the 13th-century church in whose grounds it stands. It is fascinating that this one tree has witnessed events that took place long before any of the present parish buildings were in existence.

(I am indebted to Anna Dale-Harris for the information regarding the 'Greatham Yew' – and to her three sons, Matthew, Edward and Hugo, who assisted in the measurement of its girth. Ed.)

Yew trees are monuments to longevity.

Thomas Pitter Widower of y Parish of Bentworth and
Margaret Hill Widow of Gretham were married Aug: 15th 1709.

William Rabyse a) Sarah White Widow both of y Parish of
Bramshott wee married by Licence Decem 15th 1709.

Zechariah Bridger was buried Decemr 22d 1709.

Thomas yr Son of John and Ann Bayly was Baptized
January 3d 1709. (1710)

James Knight and Mary Hill both of y Parish of Lysse
were married June 25th 1710.

James y Son of Wm and Mary Hearsey was baptd Novr 1st 1710.

Mary y Daughter of Robert and Elizabeth Taylour was baptized Novem 15th 1710.

Daniel White was buried December 7th 1710.

John Glabens of y Parish of Haslemere and Mary Purchas of Gretham
were married Feb: 7th 1710.

Mary y Wife of Thomas Hudson was buried Febr: 15 1710.

(1711)

Mary the daughter of Mr 8th Yalden and
Mary his wife was baptized July. 23: 1711.

Richard Bastin of Harting in y County of Sussex and Anne Condrey
of Gretham were married Oct: 7th 1711.

Bonard Burningham of Binsted and Anne Jeffery of Neatham
were married by Licence October 8th 1711.

Anne the Daughter of John and Anne Purchas was baptized
February 19th 1711.) Robert y SON of Robert and Mary
). Erle was baptized March, 1st 1711.

*Part of the
18th Century
Register showing
births, deaths and
marriages,
1709-1711..*

Edward an illegitimate Son of Mary Quersly was baptized
March 8th 1711.

(1712)

Sarah y Daughter of Richard and Elizabeth Web was baptized
Septem: 6th 1712.

William y Son of Mr William Yalden and Mary his Wife was baptized
Septemr 9th 1712.

Thomas White was buried Septem: 11 1712.

John Pink of Croxfeild and Rose Gahner of Greatham both of the
County of Southton were married by licence Octobr 4th 1712.

(1713)

Richard y Son of Robert and Elizabeth Taylour was baptized June 5th 1713.

Thomas Carwaker of Westmeon and Anne Chase of Gretham wer
married July 20th 1713.

Mary y Daughter of Robert and Mary Erle was baptized Aug: 16 1713.

Anne Quersley Widow was buried January 6th 1713.

(1714)

John y Son of John and Anne Putthas was baptized April 6 1714.

Ann y Daughter of Mr William Legg and Elizabeth his Wife was
buried Septem: 20th 1714.

William Newlin of Selbourn was buried at Gretham Oct: 30 1714.

Richard Callingham was buried Novem: 23 1714. (above written
in y small Pox as was his Broth:)

Oliver Callingham was buried Decem: 15th 1714.

Willm Goodale was buried Feb: 10. 1714.

Jean Lining was buried Feb: 19 1714.

(1715)

John Martin of Stedham in Sussex and Mary Gaylour of Gretham in the
County of Southton were married July 14th 1715.

Nicholas Chace was buried Septem: 2d 1715. ▶

Nicholas Clark of y Parish of Whitley in y County of Surrey and Mary
White of y Parish of Gretham in y County of Southton were married Septr 26th 1715.

Mary y Daughter of Thomas and Mary Grigg was baptized Sept: 27th 1715.

Anne y Daughter of William and Mary Mathews was baptized Octob: 13th 1715.

Mary y Wife of John Habens of Haslemere was buried Novem: 19th 1715.

Mary y Daughter of Thomas and Mary Grigg was buried Decem: 8 1715.

*Births, deaths
and marriages
1712-1715.*

MARRIAGES solemnized in the Parish of _Greatham_
in the County of _Southampton_ in the Year 18_30_

Henry Cobden _____ of _this_ Parish

and _Martha Small_ _____ of _this_ Parish
of Bramshott

were married in this _Church_ by _Banns_ _____ with Consent of
_____ this _twenty eighth_ Day of
June _____ in the Year One thousand eight hundred and _Thirty_
By me _____ _George Berry Godbold_

This Marriage was solemnized between us { _Henry Cobden his + Mark_
{ _Martha Small her + Mark_

In the Presence of { _Thomas Small his + Mark_
{ _William Trill_

No. 16.

_1831_

George Norton _____ of _this_ Parish
of Selborne _____ _Bachelor_

and _Sarah Hearsey_ _____ _Spinster_ of _this_ Parish

ere married in this _Church_ by _Licence_ ~~with Consent of~~
_____ this _seventh_ Day of
April _____ in the Year One thousand eight hundred and _thirty one_
By me _____ _George Berry Godbold_

This Marriage was solemnized between us { _George Norton_
{ _Sarah Hearsey_

In the Presence of { _Mary Anne Hearsey_
{ _John Foster_

No. 17.

Henry Gibbon _____ of _this_ Parish
Widower

and _Frances Chase_ _____ of _this_ Parish
of Selborne _____ _Spinster_

were married in this _Church_ by _Licence_ ~~with Consent of~~
_____ this _First_ Day of
December _____ in the Year One thousand eight hundred and _Thirty one_
By me _____ _George Berry Godbold Rector_

This Marriage was solemnized between us { _Henry Gibbon_
{ _Frances Chase_

In the Presence of { _Elizabeth Bennett_
{ _Thos Bennett_

No. 18.

_Part of the
19th Century
Marriage Register
1830._

Chapter Seven
The new Church

As previously mentioned, **Greatham** has its own 'fairly new' Church, St John the Baptist, standing just a few yards away from the old one, on the opposite side of the Petersfield Road. Framed by trees to the north and set in a distinct flat pasture of open glebe-land, the church, with its lofty spire, provides a splendid signpost to the village, especially when approached and viewed from the south.

The main edifice of the new church, designed to seat some 150 worshippers, was completed in 1875, during the Victorian age of religious fervour. It owes its existence to the gift of land, plus £5,000, attributed to William Fry Foster of Le Court, though it is probable that other family members also contributed. The architects were the Fosters' cousins, H and A P Fry, while the builders were J H and E Dyer of Alton. The church stands as a memorial to William's parents, who are buried in the old churchyard, while the stained glass window behind the altar, dated 1875, is dedicated to them.

William Foster's brother, Joseph, was curate in **Greatham** at the time, having taken up his post in 1866, aged 32 years. He later returned as the Rector in 1879, but alas died the following year, aged only 46 years. He and his wife, Letitia, were much loved by the local community and their memory lives on in another stained-glass window to the right of the church, dated 1883.

1891 proved a memorable year in the new church's early history. Eight stained-glass windows were installed, each one dedicated to a member of the Wright family. This was towards the end of Archdeacon Wright's term as Rector of **Greatham**. A magnificent lectern was also donated, along with a handsome pulpit, designed by an eminent architect of the day, James Fowler.

When the Harrisons arrived to take over Le Court in 1893, from the then great port of Liverpool, with its fine gothic-inspired Anglican Cathedral, the church at **Greatham** must have appeared rather stunted and uninspiring. It was probably a simple task for the Rector at that time, Rev Bryans, to persuade them that an improved church was a necessity. This was achieved with the addition of a fine spire and belfry in 1897, at a cost of some £900, to celebrate Queen Victoria's Diamond Jubilee of that year. That £900 included a donation of £100 from the Parish Churchwarden,

Timothy White.

The spire is constructed wholly of English oak and the original tower was itself heightened, to accommodate four two-light belfry windows. In all, an extra 70 feet were added to the tower and the bells were then re-hung. These two bells, originally in the old church, are dated with inscriptions. The first (1595/6) bears the words *"Henry Knight mad me"*, while the second (1630) has something similar in Latin – *"Briannus Eldridge me fecit"*. Henry Knight was from Reading, while Brian Eldridge was from Chertsey. A dedication service to the new spire and belfry was held in January 1898, with the Bishop of Winchester, Doctor Randall Davidson, officiating. Nine years later, it was the Harrisons who also provided the money to build the lych-gate at the church's entrance.

Two commemorative stone tablets in the church record the lives of the men who made the new spire possible. The first reads *"To the glory of God and in sacred memory of Francis Richard Bryans, born 7th February 1835, died 7th January 1909. Rector of this Parish 1893-1902. Into thy hands I commend my spirit"*. The second tablet is inscribed *"To the glory of God and in memory of the 60th Anniversary of the reign of Her Majesty Queen Victoria, the belfry and spire of this church were erected by Heath Harrison of Lecourt, in this Parish, 1897"*.

It is interesting to note that both Francis Bryans and Heath Harrison had been graduates from Brasenose

St John the Baptist with Swains in the foreground

*Looking across at
the new church
in Greatham
from the site
of the old one.*

College, Oxford. Although a generation apart, they had a great rapport and were obviously at ease with each other's company. Without this friendship, construction of the new spire may not have happened so easily.

Someone evidently started on some research back at the start of the 20th-century, as indicated by the following letter from the Diocesan Registry, Winchester, dated 11th September 1900:

"Dear Sir,

A list of Rectors could be supplied to you, but as we should have to employ an expert, and go back to 1282, the fee for same would be £4.14s.6d. The names, dates of institution and names of patrons would all be given.

Yours faithfully, Charles Wooldridge"

Whether or not this proved to be too expensive at the time is not known. The historical list of Rectors in Angela Stone's document dates back only to 1855. However, as has been seen in the chapter on the old church, Doctor E M Yates, named all the Rectors from 1486 to 1580. It was the last named of these, Jacob Williams, who copied out the previous records of **Greatham** onto parchment, as dictated by the parliamentary injunction of 1588. He was one of the few literate men of his time, and probably the only Rector of that century who actually resided in the Parish. This at a time when even the richest of farmers and landowners would attest their documents with only a cross.

At some time during 1901, The Church Times produced an article with the title 'A week's ramble in Hampshire', in which the following appeared:

*"... at **Greatham**, the next village, there is a modern church; but on the other side of the road is a roofed-in chancel and some remains of the small nave and north porch of the old one. Its condition is an eyesore to a pretty village in a pretty district. There are some small 13th-century lancet lights to the chancel, but is mostly debased work. This chancel has apparently been kept up after a cheap fashion, to serve as a shelter to the monument, with an efffigy in alabaster of Dame Margery Caryll, 1632."*

The Church has had many Rectors within its recent history, some of them serving for many years in succession. Prior to Francis Bryans, the most distinguished Rector of all was Archdeacon Henry Press Wright, who had spent a long career in service with both the Church and military forces. He served at **Greatham** from 1880 to 1892 and a fuller description of his career appears elsewhere in this narrative. Francis Bryans himself served some 9 years and was succeeded by Cecil Luttrell-West, who served for many years, from 1902 until dying at his desk, at the age of 58, in 1933. He was followed by Wilfrid Osborne Marks, from 1934 to 1943. More recently, Reginald Walter Tyler had an 18-year long Rectorship from 1948 to 1966, and was followed by John Russell, from 1967 until 1979.

The church has its own War Memorial close to the main road, *"erected by the inhabitants of **Greatham** in memory of their honoured dead, 1914–1919"*. Their names are as follows:

George Barker, Austin G H Bartlett, John

Berriman, Albert E Dean, Arthur R O Draper, Richard Ellis, Arthur W Foster DCM, William Hanson, Frederick C Hiscock, Bernard R J Jeans, Walter Madeley, Thomas E L Marsh, Ernest F Stokes, George E Wakeford, William P Wakeford, Oswald B Walker, Alexander F Wallis and Wellington K Webb.

A small inscription below honours those who died in the 1939-1945 war:

Arthur Edward Barstow CIE, MC, Albert W H Coombs, Frederick W Rumbold, Peter L Scolfield & Charles F Tull.

The 'CIE' above indicates 'Companion of the Indian Empire', while the 'MC' is of course the 'Military Cross'. Arthur Barstow was uncle to Leonard Cheshire, whose story appears elsewhere in this history. Ed.)

In 1957, **Greatham** was joined under one benefice by the Parish Church of Empshott, and this was further expanded in 1988 by the joining together with those of Hawkley and Priors Dean. This united benefice is illustrated by the four churches being shown together on the front of the Parish Magazine. Sadly, the Parish then lost the Rectory, sold on as a private residence. Canon Paul Duffet, before moving on to a new task in Cambridgeshire, believed that this reflected a change in the style of parochial management, with lay people now having more say in how parishes are run.

During 1986, local historian Angela Stone produced a history of **Greatham's** two churches, and Paul Duffet, Rector at that time, wrote the following foreword:

"At one time, it was only in the Cathedrals and larger town Churches that one would find some form of guide and history, to help the enquiring visitor. These days, easier access through travel has made the country Churches, in particular, popular to a public more informed and more interested in local history, than in the past. It is a fortunate Church congregation, which finds amongst its members someone interested and skilful enough to undertake the task of providing for these developments. Angela Stone has become the right person, in the right place, and has been able to draw together the folk memory of local people, alive to the importance of a community's roots, and the results of her own intelligent and lively research. We have therefore something to offer the pilgrims who come here, which we hope will make them feel that their efforts have been all the more worthwhile. We are also thankful to God that the past and present have been thus brought together, adding reality to the 'Communion of Saints' who make up the Church of Our Lord Jesus Christ."

Two more view of the new church, the spire and belfrey were added in 1897 on the ocasion of Queen Victoria's Diamond Jubilee.

Joseph Foster MA	*Curate in charge*	*1866-75*
Samuel George Dudley MA	*Curate in charge*	*1875-76*
Thomas Hooper MA	*Rector*	*1877-79*
Joseph Foster MA	*Rector*	*1879-80*
Archdeacon Henry Press Wright MA	*Rector*	*1880-92*
Francis Richard Bryans BA	*Rector*	*1893-02*
Cecil Francis Luttrell-West MA	*Rector*	*1902-33*
Wilfred Osborne Marks DSO, MA	*Rector*	*1934-43*
Paul Holman Biddlecombe	*Rector*	*1944-47*
Reginald Walter Tyler MA	*Rector*	*1948-57*
(and of Greatham and Empshott)	*Rector*	*1957-66*
John Arthur Russell A.K.C.	*Rector*	*1967-79*
Paul Stanton Duffett MA	*Rector*	*1980-88*
Gordon Woolveridge MA	*Priest in charge*	*1988-92*
(and of Hawkley and Priors Dean)		
William Charles Day B.Ed(Hons)	*Priest in charge*	*1993-95*
	Rector	*1995-*

In 1994, thanks mainly to the Diocese, but also with the assistance of donations and covenants from the congregation and other friends of **Greatham,** a Church Centre was added as an extension to the Church, dedicated and officially opened by the Lord Bishop of Portsmouth. The extension was very tastefully constructed to match the structure and decoration of the Church itself, and now finds itself being used for many Church and village functions.

(Hugette Jenkinson, lay-reader at the Church at the time of this account, produced a small booklet on the Church's history in 1996, based upon the previously mentioned research and pamphlet produced by Angela

St John the Baptist, Greatham
Patronal Festival & Millennium Flower Festival

The theme is
The Journey of Christianity

Friday 23rd - Saturday 24th - Sunday 25th
June 2000
11am - 7pm

Cover of the new Church Millenium Festival Programme

Stone in 1986. Ed.)

Hugette was able to update the list of Rectors from that produced by Angela Stone some ten years earlier. It starts from the opening of the new church in 1975:

Greatham Church has recently welcomed the appointment of a new Rector, the Rev David Heatley, at an evening service conducted by the Bishop of Portsmouth, the Right Reverend Dr Kenneth Stevenson. David introduced himself in a recent Parish Magazine by describing the induction service, which then followed on 18th May 1999:

"First of all, the Patron of the living presents the Incumbent-designate to the Bishop, and there are readings from the Bible and a sermon. Then follow, from the priest and the people, acts of commitment to Renewal and Growth, to the Word of God, to Prayer and to Unity, and the Bishop gives Charge to a Mission.
The actual Institution and Induction are medieval in origin and might almost be described as the last relics of the feudal system. The new Incumbent takes an oath of canonical obedience to the Bishop, so becoming 'his man', but in return, is given the freehold of the Living and the Bishop says 'Receive this cure of souls which is both mine and thine'.
This is the Institution, then follows the Induction by the Archdeacon who, putting the priest's hand on the church door handle, admits him to the 'real, actual and corporeal possession' of the Living, along with 'its rights, members and appurtenances'. The new Incumbent then rings the church bell. Then follows the Welcome, to which the Incumbent responds, followed by prayers and the Blessing."

As well as becoming Rector of **Greatham** and Empshott of course, David Heatley also became Vicar of Hawkley and Priors Dean. His 'Service of Institution and Induction' was well attended by members of all four local congregations, as well as by members of his former parish on the Isle of Wight, who turned up to wish him well.
(The terms 'living', 'benefice' and 'incumbency' are all of equal meaning, the grant of a property to an ecclesiastical officer for life. Ed.)
St John the Baptist Church celebrated its 125th Anniversary in the Millennium year of 2000. The holding of a Patronal & Flower Festival marked this significant occasion. This included events in the 'old church' as well as in the main church and church centre, thoughtfully linking the present-day back to Greatham's ecclesiastical past.

ECCLESIASTICAL DILAPIDATIONS ACT, 1871.

Benefice of *Greatham*

Diocese of *Winchester.*

IN pursuance of the 34th Section of the 'Ecclesiastical Dilapidations Act, 1871,' I, *Edward Harold* Bishop of *Winchester*, do by this Order state that the Repairs of the Buildings of the Benefice of *Greatham* in the County of *Hampshire*, for which the Executors or Administrators of the Reverend *Charles Bradford* the late Incumbent, are liable, are those stated in the Schedule to this Order, and that the Cost of such Repairs, for which the Executors or Administrators of the Reverend *Charles Bradford* the late Incumbent, are liable, amount to the sum of *£534. 0. 0.*

Given under my hand this *twenty second* day of *October* in the year of our Lord One thousand eight hundred and seventy *nine.*

E. H. Winton.

See SCHEDULE annexed.

N.B.—By The Ecclesiastical Dilapidations Act, 1871, § 36, "The sum stated in the order as the costs of the Repairs, shall be a debt due from the late Incumbent, his Executors, or Administrators, to the new Incumbent, and shall be recoverable as such at Law or in Equity."

§ 37. "The new Incumbent shall, as, and when he shall recover the said sum or any part thereof, forthwith pay the amount recovered to the Governors; (Queen Anne's Bounty) and if and whenever he shall recover any further part of the said sum, he shall in like manner forthwith pay to the Governors the further part so recovered."

Communications on the subject should be addressed to J. K. ASTON, Esq., Treasurer, Bounty Office, Dean's Yard, Westminster, S.W.

A request for money to cover repairs - £534 must have been a vast sum in 1879.

Chapter Eight
The Old Rectory

From the front this building looks most imposing, due to its height, and appears to have only two storeys, albeit very tall ones. However, appearances can be deceptive, because a false parapet on the front part of the house was especially designed to provide such an imposing facade.

Lying between the Gold's House collection of buildings and **Greatham's** Primary School, the house has been a private residence since around 1990, although it had ceased to be Church property for some time prior to that, evidence of tightened economic strictures on all of our churches. Built around 1819 at a cost of £1,000, it was improved, at a further cost of £804, in 1839. The frontage is plaster rendered, or 'stuccoed', with cornice and parapet, dating back to around that time.

There is an earlier three-storey ironstone structure directly behind this, with a tiled gabled roof and sash windows, while a later 19th-century addition lies on the eastern side. This means that the whole building is a combination of three different styles, built during three different eras. The final addition at the rear was built during the residency of Joseph Foster, first curate of the new church. The similarities of construction with both the earlier Le Court mansion and the new church can be clearly seen. It is more than likely that the same architects and builders were used for all of these buildings.

Back in 1696, a *'true and faithfoull terryer of ye parsonage of Gretham'* was carried out. This was basically a survey of the Rectory, the adjoining estate, and all lands deemed to pay tithes and glebe rent. The house was described thus: *"One parsonage house containing five rooms on ye ground floor, five rooms, one study, one little closet on ye middle floor, three little garrets, the house all tiled and in good repayr."* All the glebe lands are described, including land bounded by *'some grounds belonging to Goly'* – a reference to the present-day Goleigh Farm.

(A 'terryer' (or terrier) is a document or book, setting forth the extent, boundaries, rents and rights to land. Ed.)

Besides those glebe lands within the parish, two other parcels of land in Empshott, and one in Temple, in the parish of Selborne, also had to pay their tithes to **Greatham**. It certainly seems strange to our modern way of life that the Rector of three-hundred years ago was 'paid' in hay, corn, milk and cheese – and that cheese had to be made *'without fraud, every tenth day from ye 1st of May to Lammas Day'*!

An official letter from the Lord Bishop of Winchester in 1879 must have caused some alarm and despondency! It was related to the pursuance of the 'Ecclesiastical Dilapidations Act' of 1871 and was basically asking the 'estate' of the previous incumbent, the Rev Charles Bradford (deceased), to foot the bill of £534 for repairs to the Rectory. A list of the said repairs is still available, covering around six pages of foolscap paper. The cost doesn't seem so much these days, but must have been a vast sum at that time. It is not known how this affair was settled.

This view from the main road shows the three stages of construction.

(The term 'Rectory' obviously indicates the house in which the Rector abides, and a brief explanation of some Church titles is given below:
Rector: a parish priest, being the incumbent of a benefice (or living), having full authority over it and to whom the great tithes are paid – from the Latin 'regere', meaning to rule, guide or direct

Vicar: the incumbent of an English parish who is NOT a Rector, and thus does not receive the great tithes, but is paid a stipend from other sources (formerly called a perpetual Curate)

Curate: an assistant priest to the incumbent of a parish – from the Latin 'curatus', meaning one who is charged with the care of souls

I must say thank you here to Annaliese and Robert Nelson, the present occupants of The Old Rectory, for their kindness in allowing me to look around the place, and for furnishing me with some valuable details, including the 'terryer', a copy of which I include with this chapter.

*During the late 1960s and early 1970s, I was a regular visitor myself to the Rectory, during the time when my two daughters, Lorraine and Michelle, were members of either the Brownies or Girl Guides. Apart from my wife Joyce, who was 'Tawny Owl', other names which spring readily to mind are Winnie Knott (affectionately known to all as 'Knotty') and Rita Gerard, who was also a teacher at **Greatham** Primary School. Happy days!*

Certainly since I and my family arrived here in Greatham in 1967, and probably for many years before that, up until the time that the Rectory went into private ownership, the garden areas were used every summer for the Annual Church Fete. Ed.)

Old Rectory Repairs Order

Old Rectory Terryer's

Chapter Nine
Gold's (or Gould's) House

This house is located on the eastern side of the Farnham/Petersfield Road, opposite St John the Baptist Church. Both of the above names have been used in recent years, though during the latter half of the 19th-century, mention is made of 'Goles Farm', where William Goodeve farmed in 1859. The same farmer is also named in trade directories from 1847 to 1859, without an address, but it can be assumed that he was at Gole's for a number of years. William is buried in the old churchyard at Greatham, having been born in 1785 and died 1867. The 1875 to 1880 directories show a John Williamson, farm bailiff to a Mrs Chalcraft, again at Gole's Farm. It is assumed that Mrs Chalcraft was herself resident during this same period.

"The house, thought to be of 18th-century origin, has two storeys with attics. It is of ironstone construction with brick dressings, and has a tiled roof with two hipped tiled dormers. Casement windows are contained within cambered arches. There is a 19th-century porch and an additional rear wing. Alongside are two-storey stables, also of ironstone and brick dressing, with a single-storey extension which abuts the road."

The above brief description was given as part of a survey of **Greatham**, conducted it must be assumed, from the outside of the building only. This obviously tied in with the verification of its *'Conservation Area'* status in 1994. However, due to their enthusiasm and 'need to know' attitude, the present owners, Anna and Jonathan Dale-Harris, commissioned a survey of their own in 1995. The following is the surveyor's rather surprising report:

A report by P Smith, June 1995

Outwardly a late 17th-century ironstone-walled storeyed, sub-medieval house of the three-unit interval back-to-back fireplace and lobby entrance type, with Victorian porch at the front and Victorian kitchen additions to the rear. However, the roof contains a surprise, in the form of two clasped-purlin trusses (with collar and beam), incorporating long curved windbraces, unmistakably late-mediaeval (1450) and in parts heavily smoke-blackened.

(A 'purlin' is a main horizontal member in a roof,

Gold's House where the rear gardens provide a peaceful haven even in today's busy world.

supporting the common rafters. 'Windbraces' are curved braces, linking trusses to purlins. Originally intended to prevent distortion of the roof, they later became an ornamental feature of the design. A 'truss' is the framed structure, which supports the roof. Ed.)

A post still survives, extending from ground to eaves, embedded in the rear wall and framing what must have been the dais-partition of an open, or at least partly open, hall. The fact that the roof is so heavily blackened by smoke only towards the passage (present fireplace) end of the hall may indicate the existence of a smoke-bay. The purlins, chamfered and stopped, suggest that we have lost some sort of truss between the surviving passage and dais-end trusses. The surviving post has a cavetto (hollow) moulding, facing what must have been either the parlour, or solar, of a substantial late-medieval hall. It is arch-braced to the tie. Without this post, it would be difficult to prove that the present 6-foot wide ironstone walls replace an earlier half-timbered structure.

('Dais' indicates a raised platform, particularly at the upper end of a hall. A 'parlour' is a 'withdrawing' room leading off the hall, originally used for sleeping, but later becoming used as a private living room. A 'solar' is virtually the same as a parlour, at first-floor level – literally 'the room above the floor'. Ed.)

Because of the Victorian and subsequent alterations, it is difficult to be certain of the function of the secondary rooms after the 17th-century re-build, or the presumed reduction in the length of the house at the dais end. Before the destruction of the partitions at this

The gardens

end of the house, this probably served as a cold parlour and the heated room, at the entry end of the hall, as a kitchen. The building of the substantial rear kitchen probably resulted in the conversion of this 'outer room' into a parlour, but a modern fire-place fitting now obscures the old fire-place opening.

The 17th-century brick arched windows could easily be restored to their original size and appearance, by the reconstruction of the jambs, partly removed when the windows were widened. The projecting rear stair turret is indeed characteristic of late 17th-century domestic architecture, and contains somewhat mutilated stairs,

*Gold's House
with
St Johns
in the background*

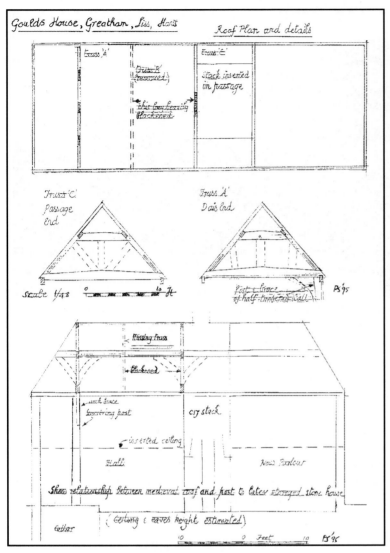

Goulds House, Greatham, Liss, Hants   Roof Plan and details

Truss 'A'

Truss 'B' (removed)   Truss 'E'

Stack inserted in passage

this lowly heavily blackened

Truss 'C' Passage End   Truss 'A' Dais End

Scale 1/48   0   10 ft

Post + brace of half-timbered wall   B '95

Missing truss

Blackened

wind brace surviving post   C17 stack

inserted ceiling

Hall   New Parlour

Shows relationship between medieval roof and post to later storeyed stone house

Cellar

(ceiling + eaves height estimated)

10   0 Feet   10   B '95

Details from the surveyors report on Gold's House.

nor easily strike fire with steel. Being often found in broad flat pieces, it makes good pavement for paths about houses, never becoming slippery in frost or rain; is excellent for dry walls, and is sometimes used in buildings. In many parts of that waste it lies scattered on the surface of the ground; but is dug on Weaver's-down, a vast hill on the eastern verge of that forest, where the pits are shallow, and the stratum thin. This stone is imperishable.

From a notion of rendering their work the more elegant, and giving it a finish, masons chip this stone into small fragments about the size of the head of a large nail; and then stick the pieces into the wet mortar along the joints of their freestone walls: this embellishment carries an odd appearance, and has occasioned strangers sometimes to ask us pleasantly, whether we fastened our walls together with ten-penny nails."

I have also heard the above method referred to as 'galleting', described as the insertion of small pieces of stone into freshly laid mortar joints, supposedly to strengthen the joints and add visual interest. Another story says that, in some areas at least, galleting was used to protect a house against invasion by witches – apparently witches are unable to cross anything made of iron. There appears to be a lot of the 'forest-stone' still lying about on some of the sandy banks within the Woolmer Forest area to this day, some 200 years after G W's reference to it above.

Another reference identifies the material as 'lower greensand – a hard, coarse stone, brownish in colour, according to its impregnation with Iron Oxide. Also known as 'carstone', it is usually found in pieces 1" to 2" thick. Used as nogging (in-fill) in framed buildings, its shows to good effect when set on edge for paving and is useful for galleting'. Ed.)

whose turned balustrade survives at the landing. The bolection-moulded panelling on the rear wall of the hall, if not a recent importation, should indicate that the re-building in stone is late 17th or early 18th-century.

('Bolection' merely indicates the portion of a moulding raised above the general surface. I am indebted to Anna and Josh for kindly showing me around their splendid old house during early 1999 and for providing the above survey and accompanying diagram. The 'ironstone' brickwork on this house, and in many others in the area, is mentioned in Gilbert White's 'Natural History of Selborne' and I quote his vivid description below:

"In Wolmer-forest I see but one sort of stone, called by the workmen sand, or forest-stone. This is generally of the colour of rusty iron, and might probably be worked as iron ore; is very hard and heavy, and of a firm, compact texture, and composed of a small roundish crystalline grit, cemented together by a brown, terrene, ferruginous matter; will not cut without difficulty,

An update on Gold's House, September 1999

(All the previous notes in reference to Gold's House had been put together and 'laid to rest' in early 1999, but having spoken to Anna Dale-Harris on subsequent occasions, she thought she may have a few thoughts of her own which would add colour to the history. I gratefully accepted this offer and Anna's addendum appears below. Ed.)

Dating back to 1450, Gold's House was originally a medieval hall house, with a two-bay central hall and floored bays at either end. It would probably have been owned by a wealthy yeoman farmer. In the late 17th-century, part of the original house was demolished, including the parlour, and the ironstone-walled storied house was built. At this stage, the house was given a lobby entrance, the service bay was rebuilt, and a central chimney-stack placed in the cross passage. During Victorian times, further additions included a gabled entrance porch, with stained glass windows, and a new wing on the garden side, featuring two first-floor oriel (recessed) windows.

Of particular historical interest to the current owners is the 'salt cupboard', uncovered in the entrance porch in the side of the chimney breast. This is believed to have been used for drying out the salt, by which meat would then be preserved. During exploration of the chimney itself, Josh found a small 4-foot square room on a level with the first floor, but only accessible from inside the chimney itself. This was probably a 'smoking chamber' for meat, and whole carcasses could have hung from the horizontal bar that still exists today. Just below this chamber, a bread-oven is also located.

The courtyard in front of the house was used over the centuries for animals and carts and, at one stage, the local hunt used to 'meet' at this point.

The 1920 notebooks of the Inland Revenue's rating surveyor reveal some interesting details. Described as 'Gold's Farm House', it was owned by a Mrs A F Coryton, but rented to Miss A H Jackson for £92 per annum. The house had no lighting or central heating, except for a gas supply in two rooms. It was described as 'very old' and 'awkwardly arranged', the rooms were 'low pitched' and it was remarked that there was 'some traffic on the road' – a familiar problem!

The layout of the house has hardly changed since then, except in the central area. Here, the site of the original hall, the wall dividing the dining room, study and butler's pantry has been removed, to create one large room. Upstairs, a small area above the lobby entrance, which formed a passage past the chimney breast between two bedrooms, was described in 1910 as a 'powdering closet', accessible from the second bedroom only.

Ownership

In 1804, during the reign of George III, a transfer document showed that Gold's had been once owned by John Purchase, then by William Sheet (the elder), and subsequently by William Sheet (the younger). It was now to be transferred to Thomas Goodeve of Blackmore (sic), yeoman, of the one part, and William Goodeve, yeoman, of the other part. The dwelling houses, barns, stable and out-houses of John Sholler, premises called Gold's, were transferred to William Goodeve, who was to pay a 'peppercorn' rent to Thomas Goodeve.

Found in the Winchester Records Office, an old deed dating back to 1813 describes the property as a 'messuage' called Gold's, with gardens, orchards, backsides and closes. Names and acreages were given, including *Craught* (1.5 acres), *Churchfield* (4.5 acres), *Jenkins* (1.5 acres) and *Readens* (8 acres).

Names that appeared on the house deeds are as follows:

*Elizabeth Street of **Greatham**, widow of William Street*
William Baker of Alton, mercer & draper, and wife Elizabeth (nee Street)
Thomas Goodeve of Blackmore, Selborne, yeoman
William Goodeve of Blackmore, Selborne, yeoman
Richard Knight of Norton, Selborne, yeoman, and wife Mary (nee Street)
Charles Henbest of Hawkley, blacksmith, and wife Ann (nee Street)
John Carpenter of Selborne, carpenter, and wife Sarah (nee Street)
Richard Paine of Farnham, Surrey, yeoman
Thomas Spencer of Selborne, yeoman
William Hall of Alton, brandy merchant
Robert Trimmer of Alton, attorney-at-law
Charles Trimmer of Alton, attorney-at-law
John Fullock of Empshott, gentlemen
William Smithers of Headley, gentleman

During this past century, the house is known to have been lived in by the following:

Alfred Maskell – Kelly's Directory for 1903
Colonel P H Greig – Kelly's Directory for 1907
Miss A H Jackson – Kelly's Directories from 1911 - 1923
Captain A F Coryton, his wife and three children, around 1935
Miss Isolda Coryton and Miss Georgiana Veal, around 1939 – they were Capt Coryton's sisters, who had previously lived at the Manor House. A swap was arranged, with Capt Coryton and family moving to Manor House and his unmarried sisters to Gold's House
Commander Arkwright, the Blameys and Sir Denny Ashburnham
*Norman and Evelyn Bryant, with their four children, 1959 – 94. Youngest son, John, was baptised at **Greatham Church** in August 1965. The Bryants were fruiterers and greengrocers, with premises in both Liss and Petersfield*
Jonathan (known as Josh) and Anna Dale-Harris, with three sons, have lived here since August 1994. Josh is a chartered surveyor

Chapter Ten
Gold's Barn

Just forward of Gold's House, towards the road and to the south, stands 'The Barn House', or Gold's Barn. As the barn is located just along the road from the ruined 13th-century church, it is quite possible that the barn was the one used for the collection of *'tithes'* back in medieval times. A tithe was a tax of one tenth of produce, collected on behalf of the church. As this would have taken the form of sheep, chickens, cattle or crops of all varieties, there was obviously the need of a barn in which to store it.

A few years ago the barn was in a sorry state, *'just about ready to be pulled down'* would have been the common view. Thankfully however, that wasn't the view of a certain passer-by! David Self, RIBA, who is a Chartered Architect, used to drive past the old barn almost daily and could see its potential, both as a challenging project and as a future home.

David and his family moved out of their comfortable house in Liss in late 1995, putting up with the conditions of a mobile home as a temporary residence, while they attempted to make the old barn habitable. David has designed the interior to retain all the original features, including sturdy oak beams, which date back to the 16th-century. With obvious skill and dedication of purpose, he and his son Kevin are doing a lot of the renovation work themselves.

Kevin has been studying at University, for a degree in Architectural Modelling, and as part of these studies has built scale models of the barn, as it would have appeared at three different stages of its history.

During the early months, over 140 tonnes of straw, mud and general rubbish had to be cleared from the barn's interior. Kevin remarked at the time that *"It feels like slave labour, but it's definitely great experience"*. It probably came as no surprise that, in the clearance work of both the barn and the overgrown garden, many pieces of old farm machinery were found.

Four years ago, the barn was covered with *'more holes than roof'*, as David cheerfully described it. As many of the original slate tiles as possible were salvaged, then mixed in with second-hand slates, selected to blend in with the existing range of shape and hue, in order to re-cover the roof. The rafters of the north aisle were rotten and had to be replaced. But those over the main part of the barn were remarkably sound, so the slating was carried out without the necessity of the undulating shape of the original roof having to be straightened.

The original timber boarding or cladding on the sides of the building had long been replaced, during earlier centuries, with thick walls of the local ironstone. Timber boarding now only survives on the eastern end wall and on the top section of the western end wall, where it faces the road.

The 'gun-ports', or arrow-slits, which provided ventilation for the crops stored in the barn, are now being fitted with 'direct' glazing. This means that there are no window frames used, as these would have reduced the already narrow apertures to silly proportions. Although small, they let in a useful amount of light and maintain the integrity of the original usage. The barn is generally far lighter than might be expected, as the central bay has full-height glazed screens on both the north and south sides, fitted inside the old cart-door openings.

David and his wife Wendy hope to move into their converted home later this year (1999) – let's hope they make it, because they were saying the same thing in 1996! There is still a tremendous task ahead as he continues the renovation of the building, with the intention of maintaining the internal timber frame as a monument to the past.

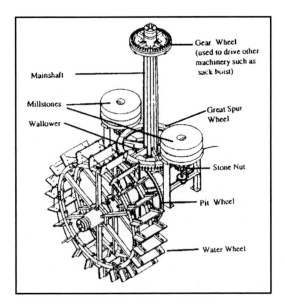

A typical arrange-ment of a water-driven mill wheel.

Chapter Eleven
Greatham Mill

Built around 1690, during the reign of William and Mary, the water-driven mill functioned as a flour mill for almost 250 years and, as far as can be made out, was last successfully tested around 1948. The advent of so-called industrialisation did not bring universal benefits to all. Traditionally, mills were run under the patronage of the local 'lord of the manor', and it must be assumed that this was the case in *Greatham*.

Prior to the building of these mills, individual houses would probably have owned and operated their own hand-milling wheels, to convert the inedible grain (wheat, corn, etc) into the flour which could then be used for the baking of bread. The water-driven mills gave the local lords the opportunity to ban such individualism. Instead, the farmers would have to bring their grain to 'the mill', where they would then have to pay for the *privilege* of having it ground by the miller, providing further income to the lord at the same time.

Greatham Mill is situated at the bottom of its own lane out on the Selborne Road, a 3-storey building of colour-washed brick with two gables, slate hung and slate roofed. The adjoining *Greatham Mill House,* originally two millers' cottages, is two storeys of brick, with a brick-dentilled cornice. There is a tiled roof with four gables to the rear, and the windows are of the casement type. A later extension connects the barn, which is of '*ironstone*' construction, with a tiled roof. In its 'days of glory', the house was a blaze of colour, thanks to its wisteria-clad walls.

The original surveyors negligently drew the river (Bull's Brook, a tributary of the Rother) as a direct flow through the mill. In fact, to raise the head of water sufficiently to drive the 14-foot diameter over-shot wheel required a dam, some 400 yards upstream, with a branching 'leat' to feed the millpond. The machinery is still largely intact, but the dam is broken and the leat downtrodden and overgrown.

(A 'dentilled cornice' has a series of small, square projecting blocks in the moulding. The term 'leat' indicates an open artificial trench for conducting water, while 'overshot' describes a wheel turned by water flowing into buckets on its far side from an overhead trough. 'Ironstone' describes the locally found stone, with its distinctive rusty appearance. Ed.)

In 1792, a policy was taken out with the Royal Exchange Insurance Company by one Thomas Goodeve, described as '*miller, of **Greatham,** Hants'.* The dwelling house, brick-built and tiled, was insured for £100, while his adjoining mill, brick and timber built, also tiled, was covered under the same amount. Utensils and 'trade' were separately insured, for a sum of £150.

(Kelly's Directory for 1855 listed one William Goodeve both as a farmer, and also as Collector of Taxes – a probable relative or descendant of Thomas Goodeve, as his (William's) gravestone shows that he lived from 1785 to 1867. Ed.)

An advertisement in the Hampshire Telegraph of April 1807, announced the auction of the property, to be held at the Dolphin Inn, Petersfield, later that year. Details of the land, including such old names as *Snailing's Knapp, Skinner's Mead, Snailing's Wood Field and Hart's Hill Field*, were given in acres, rods and perches – the latter two being almost forgotten units of measurement in these present days of 'metrication'.

Thanks to the records kept by the Hampshire Mills Group (HMG), based upon trade directory entries no doubt, the following residents at the Mill and its house are known to be:

Benjamin Blackmore Fielder (1852-59)
Mrs Mary Martin (1867-71)
Henry Wakeford (1875-1885)
John Ellis (1889-99)
Major Piggott (1907)
F W Lancaster (1911-15)
James Crass (1920)
Edwin Hull (1923-35)
Major Clifford Hugh Douglas (1939)

There are some obvious gaps in the dates given, but they present a continuous link, even though all of the above are not quoted as 'millers'. HMG state that the Mill ceased working in 1936.

Towards the end of the 19th-century, as indicated by the above list, the Ellis's, John and his son Frederick, owned the working mill on a lease for some 10 years, as they started up their family business. Kelly's Directory for 1895 listed John Ellis as '*Miller (water), **Greatham Mill'.*** Frederick, who died in 1940, left the business in the hands of two sons, John and Peter. John Ellis died in 1997, and it is his youngest son, Jason, who operates nowadays from Headley Mill (Bordon), with his Uncle Peter as a 'guiding light'. The firm, still called 'Ellis and Sons', celebrated their centenary in 1989.

Greatham Mill a cornerstone of village life for some 250 years.

In 1949, retired naval Captain Nigel Pumphrey (1910-1994) and his wife Frances (1915-1993) moved into the mill, and also farmed Hatchmoor Farm, mainly for the purpose of dairy and egg production. The buildings and cottages had previously been converted into a home, but the acre or so of land surrounding it was mostly field. With the able assistance of local gardener Jim Collins, they completely transformed the area into a magnificent garden and small arboretum.

Levels were altered, raised beds gave new perspectives, trees and shrubs were placed to provide shelter or lead on to another vista. Prominent amongst the many attractions were bog plants, a rose garden and some extraordinary fuschias. Frances Pumphrey had no formal training as a gardener, but put her enthusiasm down to her mother, who had been a keen amateur gardener. She always enthused about the job that Jim Collins had done – *"He is very, very good, I could never manage all this on my own"*.

Greatham Mill Gardens were first opened to the public in 1976, those who can will remember it as the 'year of the great drought'. The Pumphreys had to rig up an electric pump to draw water from the river. Such was their popularity over the next few years, that the gardens featured in the TV programme 'Gardener's World' in 1980. Each year, on Sundays between May and October, some 2,000 visitors would walk over the ironstone cobbles, which were once covered in flour dust from the millers' carts.

Lucinda Groves, granddaughter of the Pumphreys, along with her husband Edwin, inherited the Mill in 1994. With help and support from Elsie Collins and Barry Coffin, the couple attempted to keep things going up until 1996, even opening up the stables for 'cream teas'. An edition of 'Grass Roots' on local television publicised these efforts, while members of the HMG have also been busy on the site, offering their expertise.

But sadly, as the 20th century drew to a close, **Greatham Mill** had become infested with dry rot and woodworm and its gardens were no longer open for public pleasure. The verdict on the Mill at this time, from Tony Yoward of the HMG, was that *'It may be in need of TLC, but its condition is reasonably good'*. Fortunately, new owners have recently purchased the old place and have taken on the challenging, but ultimately rewarding, task of renovation.

*(I visited the Mill in early March of 2000 and was very pleased to meet up with Elaine Graves. She and husband John, along with children Jack and Lucy, had only recently moved into the place as their permanent home, but were already making tremendous strides forward in their attempt to bring the living accommodation up to pristine condition. Hopefully in future years they will bring **Greatham Mill** back to its former splendour.*
Towards the end of September 2000, I was happy to have the opportunity to once again visit the Mill. John Graves had called me a few weeks earlier to ask if I wished for an update or progress report on their efforts. Ed.)

He and Elaine had bought the old Mill at the end of 1998 and I let John's own words continue the story:

"Over a year of extensive restoration work then followed, which included completely re-roofing both the mill and house, converting the adjacent barn into a kitchen and re-plumbing, wiring and flooring the entire building. We (the Graves) moved in with the new century and work has continued since then, with the help of Martin Opie and Emily Newton on the garden. This is very different to how it was in the Frances Pumphrey's time because, although it maintains her layout, thirty-five years' growth has rather filled it up. For example, the central weeping willow planted by her has gone from being about 25 feet high to now being some 80 feet tall. Although the garden is no longer open to the public, it is hoped to open it for occasional charity days in the near future. It is also possible that, with help from the Hampshire Mills Group, work will soon start on restoration of the mill itself."

Chapter 12
Greatham School

The original 'National School' (boys and girls) was built just before the start of the 1850s, at an estimated cost of £257, alongside the old 13th-century church and what was then the village green. A document exists, dated 21st November 1851, pertaining to *'the matter of the* **Greatham** *Inclosure in the County of Southampton'*. William Blamire and George Darby, two Inclosure Commissioners for England & Wales, conveyed a parcel of common land to William Eldridge Butler of Le Court as a *'school allotment'* for the sum of £28. The same document names *'the Rector and Churchwardens ... of the said Parish of* **Greatham** *as Trustees for the National School'*.

In 1977, the school's oldest former pupil Mrs Rosa Lane celebrated her 94th birthday. She happily remembered her school days, when the children were allowed to use the village green as their playground. Rosa survived another five years until her death in 1982. Sadly, she just missed out on her telegram from the Queen.

Following the old school's closure, the building itself was converted in 1957, to be used for many years as the village community centre for all sorts of occasions, until construction of the new Village Hall was completed in 1973. It was then converted into a private dwelling, still bearing the name 'Old School House'.

From entries in the various Trade Directories over many years, the following information has been gleaned, which although not in itself the full story, does give a flavour for what has happened to the School during the last century and a half:

Miss Sarah Voller – *Headmistress, 1855, 1857 and 1859*

Mr William and Mrs Jane Bristowe – *Schoolmaster & mistress, 1875 and 1878*

Mrs Jane Bristowe – *Headmistress, 1880 and 1885, now termed a 'National School' (mixed) with an average attendance of 40*

Miss Goddard – *Headmistress, 1889, average attendance 50*

Miss Etheridge – *Headmistress, 1895, with a capacity of 60, average attendance 50*

Miss Harring – *Headmistress 1903, now termed an 'Elementary School' (mixed), with a capacity of 75, average attendance 68*

Mr Charles Hiscock – *Headmaster 1907, 1911, 1915 and 1920, with a capacity of 75, average attendance 60*

In December 1909, detailed plans were drawn up at the County Surveyor's Office, The Castle, Winchester, for the building of a new school for **Greatham**. These

There was no need for traffic calming in the school's early years!

*Early schooldays...
the happiest days
of their lives!*

plans are still in existence. The present school, still termed 'Elementary' (mixed), moved to its current site on October 30th 1911, to land given by Mr Frederick Coryton, father of the late Captain A F Coryton. A procession was organised from the old school to the new, with the children singing a hymn. It was constructed to allow a maximum of 120 pupils, and had an average attendance of 72 at that time.

> *Mr Charles Jeffery Wain* – *Headmaster, 1921 – 1944. In 1923, the title had changed once again, this time to 'Council School'*
>
> *Miss G M Hughes* – *Headmistress, 1944 – 1949*
>
> *Miss Gwen Brooker* – *Headmistress, 1951 – 1981*
>
> • *1950 – 130 children, aged 5 to 15, with 3 teachers*
>
> • *1958 – school changed from an all-age type to 'Primary', with 76 pupils and 3 teachers*
>
> • *1963 – lowest ever number of pupils, just 39, with 2 teachers, G B and Mrs Jean Crofts*
>
> • *1967 – Capt A F Coryton, of the Manor House, retired after 37 years as a School Manager since 1930*
>
> • *1970 – school modernised and extended, with*

*....and
in the early 1970's.*

(for the first time) inside sanitation and kitchen, with cooking on the premises

> *Mrs Daphne Caless* – *Headmistress, 1981 – 1984*
>
> *Mr R F 'Rick' Brewis* – *Headmaster, 1985 – 1989 (acting Headmaster 1984)*
>
> • *1984 – Mr Albert Baker, resident of Le Court, and a member of the MFPA (Mouth & Foot Painters Association), was appointed to the school management board. He later moved to a specially adapted house at the old shop in Longmoor Road, and became a great favourite with local children*
>
> *Mr Lawrie Wood* – *Headmaster, 1990*
>
> *Mrs Helen Patterson* – *Headmistress, 1991 – 1996*
>
> • *1991 – school roll totalled 136, in 5 classes*
>
> • *1995 – school roll totalled 173, with a 6th class added*
>
> *Mr Keith Brentnall* – *acting Headmaster, Sept – Dec 1996*
>
> • *1996 – October, 2 new class-rooms, toilets and reading area officially opened*
>
> *Miss Salma Badawi* – *Headmistress, since 1997*
>
> • *1998 – April, new hall, offices, staff-room and library extension officially opened. Upon his death at the age of 72 in 1994, Albert Baker had left a large amount of money to the school, which was used to supplement a county grant. A six-month project, which started in late 1997, extended and improved the premises to what they are today*
>
> • *1998 – school roll now 186, with a 7th class-room added*

In the new Millennium year of 2000, **Greatham Village Hall** was host to a memorable occasion, when 80 former pupils and teachers held a reunion. The event was organised by two ex-pupils, Molly McGinn and Graham Tarling. The eldest attendees included former teacher Mrs Phyllis Lee and Charlie Hanson, both now in their nineties. One facility now happily not required by the modern school was the air-raid shelter! *"The shelter is no longer there, but I can remember us all going into it with our barley-sugar and gas-masks"*, recalled Molly, who had been a pupil from 1940 to 1950.

*(I am grateful to Salma Badawi and her staff at the school for giving me permission to trawl through the school archives during the early months of 1999. As well as being able to compile this short history of the school itself, various other documents came to light, which assisted me on the overall project regarding **Greatham**. Early information with reference to the school only showed personnel as 'schoolmaster' or 'schoolmistress', but since they were the only ones named for the year, I have assumed that they were the 'head' teachers of their day. Ed.)*

Chapter Thirteen
𝔊reatham 𝔙illage 𝔥all

The present Village Hall is fairly centrally located in the village, almost opposite the Village School. Application plans for its erection were originally submitted in 1971, but work did not start until late in 1972, with its completion occurring sometime during 1973. The delay appears to have been caused by the drawn-out sale of the original village hall, as the money raised from that sale was to be instrumental in building the new hall. The hall is a timber-framed building of 'Colt' design, set on a concrete and brick foundation, and built at a cost of some £14,000.

Historical background

In the 19th-century, many quite different village hall trusts were created by benevolent local figures, for a variety of reasons. Some sought to encourage temperance, others to perpetuate their family name. Some believed they owed a debt to the local community, while the majority were genuine in their efforts to improve the local living conditions of their friends and neighbours.

It was traditional, in the main, that those individuals (and indeed their descendants) who created the trusts also became heavily engaged in the day-to-

Once the Village School, then the Village Hall and now a private residence.

day management of these institutions. Many trusts also went on to become registered as charities with the Charity Commissioners. Thus, management committees set up to administer the running of village halls generally included the trustees, with a sprinkling of representatives from previously established village institutions. These would include such as the Women's Institute, Royal British Legion, sports clubs and school governors.

Modern-day village halls tend to be multi-purpose, used for a wide variety of activities. **Greatham's** is no exception, providing a meeting place for local committees and public gatherings. Both local and national elections use the hall as a voting station, while on occasional weekends the hall is hired out to external bodies, such as caravan clubs, dog training sessions and caged-bird exhibitors.

Village Trusts

In 1949, a trust was set up to benefit the villagers of **Greatham**, by allowing them the use of some open land for sports facilities. The trustees were F W H Smith of Farm Cottage (the donor), who conveyed the land to A F Coryton of Manor House, Mrs A E Walters of Liphook Road (now Longmoor Road) and Bernard Hanson, MBE, of Moor House. For an annual charge of £15 for the life of the donor, and after his death to his sisters Constance Margaret Smith and Norah Maud Smith, and brother Eustace Smith, *"all that piece or parcel of land situate at Greatham ... and known as Dubbers"* was donated for the use of local inhabitants. This parcel of land is now the site of the new hall.

In 1959, another trust was set up by A F Coryton of Manor House, the Rev R W Tyler of the Rectory and F W H Smith of Farm Cottage, who conveyed *"a small piece of land in the Parish of Greatham, adjoining the Manor House, on which stands a building formerly used as a school. To be used as a village hall, to improve the conditions of life for the inhabitants of Greatham and the surrounding area, within two miles of the parish boundaries"*.

The old school house had long ceased its original use, when the new school had opened in 1911. The building, however, continued to be used for social functions and as a Sunday school. The setting up of a trust in 1959 appears to have been an attempt to formalise the situation.

Both the sports field and old school house were managed by separate charitable trusts, whose Chairman in both cases was Miss Wilcockson, of Cam Green Cottage, Church Lane. At a public meeting, held in May 1971, it was agreed that the old school house (village hall) was *'small, old-fashioned ... inadequate*

for modern recreational facilities'. It was decided that it should be sold off and the sale proceeds be used to finance a new village hall. After a prolonged battle between private bidders, the sale was finally completed in September 1972 and the 'Old School House' then became a private residence.

With the building of the new **Greatham** Village Hall, upon the same parcel of land ceded by the 1949 trust, the Charity Commissioners were persuaded that the two original trusts should be now amalgamated into one trust only, and this was accomplished around 1976.

A sports pavilion had been erected on the site in 1966 but, sadly, burned down in mysterious circumstances some thirty years later. 37 Engineer Regiment, stationed at nearby Longmoor Camp, had kindly lent their expert services to the construction of a car-park in 1973, and it is only fairly recently (June 1999) that this has now been re-furbished, after becoming quite worn during the many previous years.

In the late 1980s, when the Rectory closed down, this also meant that the Nursery School was without a home. Temporary accommodation was offered in the main Village Hall, but in 1990 an annex was added to the original Village Hall structure, and is now the permanent home to **Greatham** Nursery School, on lease from the Trustees. The Village Hall and its surrounding area continue to be run by a Committee of Trustees, presently under the Chairmanship of Tim Gould.

A 'Village Appraisal' was carried out in **Greatham** during 1998, and its results published during the latter half of 1999. One of the major outcomes of the Appraisal was the almost universal wish for the village to have some sort of leisure area and children's playground, with the most popular position for this being at the Village Hall site. To this end, a committee has now been set up, firstly to look into the possibilities and secondly to raise the required funds. It is to be hoped that progress can be made on this project during the coming years.

As another consequence of the appraisal, a village map entitled 'Greatham 2000' was produced, with copies available free to each house in the parish. The map shows a pictorial view of Greatham, made up from aerial photographs. One copy has been framed and now hangs in the committee room of the Village Hall. It is accompanied by two other framed mementoes of village life. The first is a very brief 'history', as produced and presented to the village by Alan Siney, cousin to Elsie Collins. The second is a facsimile of a plaque that used to hang in the original village hall. It reads:

"In memory of the interest and work of Isolda Louisa Coryton in this village & aided by the generous donations of her friends, this old National School, built in 1849, was in 1957 converted into the Village Hall".

Chapter Fourteen
𝔑𝔲𝔯𝔰𝔢𝔯𝔶 𝔖𝔠𝔥𝔬𝔬𝔩

The Nursery School is believed to have been established in the rear annexe of **Greatham** Rectory at some time during the late 1960s, and was run by Valerie Russell, wife of the Rector at that time, the Rev John Russell. When the Russells departed in 1979, the play equipment and goodwill were purchased by Sandra Allan, who has continued to run the facility for the past twenty years.

After the enforced closure of the Rectory in September 1988, the village's Nursery School became homeless, as they had become firmly established in the Rectory annex by this time. The nursery then moved temporarily into the main section of the Village Hall, but this proved an unsatisfactory arrangement, due to the inordinate amount of time spent both before and after each nursery school session, preparing and then clearing away.

Early in 1989, it was suggested that the nursery would be able to function more efficiently in its own accommodation. Plans were made to build an extension to the Village Hall, especially for this purpose. A band of willing helpers, including fathers, local residents and many friends from outside of **Greatham**, gave up their spare time, even their Christmas holiday, to ensure that the new nursery was completed on time.

Money needed to be raised for the extension, and this was helped by a grant from East Hants District Council, with loans from the same body and the village's own Parish Council. The annex was subsequently donated to the Village Hall trustees and leased back to the Nursery School at an agreed rent. Later, in 1990, further work had to be carried out and a gift of £4,000 from Mr Albert Baker, a local disabled artist, was presented to the nursery school at their Nativity play for the Christmas of that year. Albert later gave another £2,000 donation, money he had himself received as his reward as part of the 'Childline' scheme during 1993.

(An article devoted to the life of Albert Baker appears elsewhere in this history. Ed.)

Thanks to all this voluntary effort, local grants, fund-raising and donations, the Nursery School has been one of **Greatham's** success stories. This is illustrated by the fact that it was recently praised for its work by the government education watchdog, otherwise known as 'OFSTED' – Office for Standards in Education. The inspector said that the quality of teaching at the school, for children aged two to five, was very good. The nursery was 'well-equipped and strong in language and literacy, maths, and creative, social and personal development'.

*(Sandra Allan kindly supplied me with some of the above story. She informed me that a total of some £76,000 had been raised over the years, and that she would like to take this opportunity to thank the many people who have given such generous assistance. **Greatham** Nursery School looks forward to continuing its mission well into the third Millennium. The present lease is due to run out at the end of August 2003. Ed.)*

The Village Hall and Nursery School

Chapter Fifteen
Welldigger's Cottage

In February of 1967, Pat and Stan Stamp arrived in *Greatham* to take over the running of Blackmoor Post Office, and began living in the old cottage attached to the rear of the building. At some later time, a Mr Arthur Willis was carrying out some research into old buildings in Hampshire, with the intention to publish a book called 'History in Hampshire Houses'. This book no doubt eventually went into print, but the article referring to Welldigger's Cottage, 'A cottage at Blackmoor', was too late to be included. Having spoken with June Smith, who now lives in the cottage, and also to Pat Stamp, who now lives in Petersfield, between them they were able to provide a copy of the original article, which makes an interesting addition to this history. Since recent boundary changes, the cottage is now firmly situated within *Greatham*, lying just south of what is now the Game Centre.

'A cottage at Blackmoor'

It was a great pleasure, recently, to be invited by Mr S E Stamp, the sub-Postmaster at Blackmoor, to look over the ancient cottage at the rear of his Post Office premises — a building on which he was spending all his spare time, repairing and rehabilitating.

This was a most unusual and welcome opportunity; for if one goes to an old cottage which is being lived in, it is most difficult to get down to what may be called 'the architectural bones' of the building. Carpets mask the floors, curtains conceal the window-frames and seatings, and the walls are usually so thoroughly 'decorated', that their true nature is very effectively disguised.

In the Stamps' cottage, all this is revealed, and much else! How old is it? Well, it is clearly shown on a map of 1640, but the evidence of the building itself suggests a much earlier origin — perhaps as much as two centuries before that date, which makes it a very old cottage indeed.

The building is timber-framed, in a style not uncommon just over the border into West Sussex. Most of the timbering in the lower walls consists of uprights, horizontal timbers and rectangular patterning only appearing at the first-floor level. The whole framework is of oak, and there is evidence (in the form of mortice slots) that many of the timbers had been previously used

for some other purpose.

Although there is plenty of oak readily available around the Blackmoor area, it was probably a lot cheaper to buy timber, already shaped and seasoned from say Portsmouth Dockyard, and to haul it the 25 miles to the site, rather than hack a new tree-trunk into shape. Mortice slots are pretty conclusive of previous use; nail holes are *not*. When plaster is stripped off an old beam, a multitude of old nail holes are generally revealed, these having been deliberately made to provide a 'key' for the plaster.

Today we are invited to consider pre-fabricated buildings as one of the more modern achievements of our technological age. In fact, in the Middle Ages it was quite common practice for various sections of a timber-framed house to have been made up before construction started. This was usually done in a barn during the winter months, when outdoors work was impossible.

Cottages with timber framing, such as this one at Blackmoor, were built throughout the English countryside for at least three centuries, say from 1350 to 1650. It is only when we investigate the filling of the spaces *between* the timbers that we can get a close approximation as to the age of such a building.

Of course these fillings vary greatly, between outside walls which must face the ravages of the weather, and inside walls and partitions, which are protected in a dry environment. With the revival of brick making in Tudor times, bricks were preferred for use on exterior walls wherever possible — they did not shrink, and their regular rectangular shape made them easy to lay. There is a splendid example of a Tudor brick & timber building at Rook's Farm, just about half a mile along the road towards Petersfield.

But the panel filling of Welldigger's Cottage was done with a much more primitive material than brick. It consists mainly of small, roughly rectangular, blocks of a curious silver-grey local stone, known as 'Longmoor flint-stone'. It is extremely hardy and weatherproof, but its use indicates a pre-Tudor date for the building's construction, and it cannot have been nearly so easy to work with as bricks.

One of the interior walls, from which damaged plaster has been removed, reveals panels filled with that classic and ancient filling of 'wattle and daub'. It was of this wattle and daub that the Glastonbury lake-dwellers built their huts, the Saxons their churches, and the

English churls their walls, farms and cottages, through many early centuries.

(The term 'churl' indicates a man of low degree, a peasant, rustic or bumpkin being of similar meaning. This is not meant to be derogatory, but to contrast with an 'earl', or man of noble birth. Ed.)

One encyclopaedic definition of 'wattle' describes it as 'an interlacing of twigs and branches'. The craftsmen who built Welldigger's Cottage certainly rose above that meagre description! In each panel to be filled, they first fixed, between the main timbers, a row of uprights, stout clean hazel rods at intervals of eight inches or so. Then around these, horizontally, they wove in and out flexible spilt hazel bands. Thus the panel was filled by a firmly fixed wattle hurdle, and it remained only to give each side a generous application of 'daub' for the wall to be finished.

The daub used here at Blackmoor is interesting. It seems to have been compounded from a putty-coloured clay, well laced with straw to give it lateral strength. The materials may have been fetched from some distance, as the main ingredients of the local soil appear to be sand and peat. Wattle & daub made a highly durable wall, but as a space-filler it had the defect of shrinkage, as the material dried out over the years. So, to avoid draughts, it was the custom to plaster it over after a few years. As a rule, when this plaster is eventually removed, for whatever reason, it is done so roughly that most of the daub, and indeed some of the wattle, is destroyed with it. It is thus very fortunate that such a fine specimen of this traditional old walling remains in good condition here in Blackmoor – very rare indeed.

The original flooring in the cottage consisted of wide planks and slabs of timber, an inch or more in thickness. When these decayed and became unsafe, instead of them being removed, an equally solid one-inch floor was laid on top of them! Not unreasonably, Mr. Stamp has opted for a floor of concrete paving slabs in the largest of the ground-floor rooms. This living room, and the corresponding one directly above it, though very old indeed, are clearly an extension built onto one end of the original structure.

Access to the new upstairs room clearly presented a tricky problem. A straight but steep and narrow staircase was taken up to a passage-landing, which was so narrow that no bulky furniture could be moved along it. Therefore, the three windows in the upper room were actually built as doors – glass above and a solid wooden panel below – allowing very easy access to anyone who could manage to climb a ladder.

The most significant change to the cottage since it was first built has not yet been mentioned. The original roof would have been thatched, while it is now tiled.

Thatch, particularly when it becomes wet, is vastly heavier than tiles, so the roof timbers used to support it must be of considerably stouter construction – and also closer together. They are so here at the Blackmoor cottage. Mr Stamp cut a hole into the ceiling of the passage landing, with the intention of providing access to the roof space. He was met by such a forest of beams and rafters that all he could manage to do was push his head & shoulders through, take a brief look around, and beat a tactical retreat!

This heavy roof timbering extends over the latter-built extension, so that must also have been originally thatched. The present tiles are small in size and beautifully mellowed. A close inspection of them may help to establish their age. What does all this add up to, in the matter of overall history? There are many imponderables, but a safe bet would be that the original cottage dates back to somewhere between 1450 and 1500. The two-room extension appears to have been added between 1600 and 1650, while the thatching was replaced by tiling in the early 1700s.

It is most fortunate for this ancient cottage – and for all those who care for the welfare of such buildings – that in the years before he took to Post-mastering, Mr Stamp had considerable practical and professional experience in the highly technical and complex craft of renovation. Perhaps the finest point of the whole venture is that he has not embarked on this task in the hope of monetary gain, or to preserve it as a museum specimen, but rather to re-create a home wherein he and his growing family may live in comfort.

Welldigger's Cottage which could date back as far as the 15th century.

GREATHAM, HANTS.

About Two Miles from Liss Station, L. & S.W. Railway, and Four Miles from Liphook.

Particulars and Conditions of Sale

OF VALUABLE

Freehold Meadow Land

AND

COTTAGE PROPERTY

Situate close to GREATHAM VILLAGE, Hampshire,

COMPRISING

An Enclosure of Meadow Land

Known as THELE or BRIDGEFOOT MEADOW, in extent 10a. 2r. 24p.

A COTTAGE RESIDENCE

Containing 7 Rooms, with LARGE GARDEN.

TWO COTTAGES

Having a Frontage to Main Road leading from GREATHAM to LIPHOOK

A Plot of Meadow Land

With an Extensive Frontage to Main Road, in extent 1a. 0r., known as TADMORE.

TWO COTTAGES

Each containing 4 Rooms; together with LARGE GARDENS and a PLOT OF LAND, with Wheelwright's Shop.

A PLOT OF LAND, with Smith's Shop and Timber Stores, and

A Desirable Enclosure of Meadow Land

In extent 1a. 0r.

AN EXCELLENT MEADOW

In extent 1a. 2r., known as KINGSHOTT MEADOW.

A BLOCK OF SIX COTTAGES

Known as "KINGSHOTT COTTAGES," each containing 4 Rooms, with LARGE PRODUCTIVE GARDENS.

A Small Plot of Building Land.

A PAIR OF COTTAGES

Each containing 5 Rooms, with Good Gardens.

WHICH WILL BE SOLD BY AUCTION, BY

Messrs. MELLERSH

(Under instructions from the Trustee of Mr. George Wells) at

THE DOLPHIN HOTEL, PETERSFIELD.

On Wednesday, the 7th day of June, 1899,

At TWO o'clock to a Minute, in TEN Lots.

May be Viewed by permission of the Tenants, and Printed Particulars, with Conditions of Sale, may be obtained at the Dolphin Hotel, Petersfield; of Messrs. SMALLPEICE & Co., Solicitors, Guildford; and of Messrs. MELLERSH, Auctioneers, Land Agents and Surveyors, Godalming and Guildford.

Chapter Sixteen
Other dwellings

Goleigh Farm

17th-century Goleigh Farm is located on the southern side of the Liss Forest Road, about ½-mile distant from its junction with the main Petersfield Road. Formerly known as Goley Dean Farm, and Mill Farm before that, it is a two-storey building, with the eastern end of 'ironstone' construction with sandstone quoins being the oldest part, dating back to 1685. The ironstone western end has brick dressings, while the roof is tiled, with gable ends. The stone mullion windows are fitted with dripstones. There is a massive brick chimney and a broad two-storey gabled ironstone staircase projection, with brick dressing, on the northern side.

It is known that at one time, early in the 20th-century, Goleigh was split into two separate cottages, which allowed Captain Coryton to house the families of two of his stockmen, Benny Rumbold and Eddie Stokes. It is a shame that such a splendid old house now sits only yards away from the busy A3 dual-carriageway, but that's progress for you!

(A 'quoin' is a wedge-shaped stone or brick, used as an angle or corner stone. They are often larger than those in the rest of the wall, and sometimes ornamented or raised. A 'mullion' is an upright shaft, usually of stone, used to divide the sections, or 'lights', of a window. Ed.)

Deal Farm

Deal Farm, located on the opposite side of the Petersfield Road to Baker's Field, is of later vintage than Goleigh Farm, probably early 18th-century. Again of 'ironstone' structure, with brick quoins, it has two storeys, the upper storey being tile-hung. It is a timber-framed building, with ironstone in filling to the rear, and has a tiled roof with hipped gables, as well as a central chimney. It is furnished with wooden casement-style windows, and is surrounded with an ironstone garden wall. An 18th-century barn abuts the road. It is also of ironstone with brick dressings, and has a tiled roof.

(The term 'hipped' indicates a roof of which the slopes rise from the eaves on all sides, the 'hip' being the junction between two adjoining slopes. Ed.)

Deal Farm was to become the largest farm holding in **Greatham** parish, with an 1840 tithe assessment of 176 acres. Later, the land was split up between the Selborne and Coryton estates, with the farm and some of its land being bought by the Shotter family in the late 1930s. The family, consisting of three brothers and their sister, ran the farm under the trade name 'Shotter Brothers' until selling up in 1952.

Deal Cottages were originally a terrace of four cottages, listed at the time of the tithe survey as belonging to William Goodeve, of Deal Farm. Their 'rat-trap' type of brickwork at the gable ends was popular for only a few years towards the end of the 18th-century, which is when they would have been built. The roof was blown off during a storm in the late 19th-century, to be replaced with one of slate, which had come into wider use after the rapid expansion of the railway system.

(William Goodeve was referred to twice in the 1855 edition of Kelly's Directory – both as a farmer and 'collector of taxes'. He was also shown as farming from Gole's Farm in 1859. Ed.)

Both Goleigh and Deal Farms, as well as that belonging to Le Court, have survived well, possibly due to their having been built on sand, rather than on the local clay-beds. Whether or not this was down to structural problems, or an inability of those other long-defunct farms to support a family's tenure, is not known. **Greatham** has always been fundamentally a farming (or agricultural) community, with supplementary trades such as miller, cooper, blacksmith, wheelwright, cowkeeper and house-servant.

Deal Farm, Greatham 1948. A drawing by Alan Siney

In his will, dated 1910, James left the farm and land to his (second) wife Ann, and their children Emma Jane and Alfred, provided that there was to be a cash settlement of £200 paid by Emma Jane to Alfred. This eventually happened in 1929, according to records, some 18 years after Emma Jane had married William Albert Redman. The Redmans eventually moved into Forestside Farm, which was then located in Blackmoor.

Swain's Cottage

This handsome thatched building has been converted from an original three 17th-century cottages, situated on the north side of Church Lane, directly opposite the 'new' church. The structure is again of ironstone with brick dressings and is timber-framed to the rear. The thatched roof has eaved dormers, three in front and two at the back. There is a central chimney and wooden casement windows. At one time, one of the original cottages, on the end nearest the Church, served as the 'village sweetshop', attended by a well-known figure to older residents, one 'Nanny' Russell.
(I wont mention those who told me that they used to steal the occasional gob-stopper! Ed.)

Case's House

Located just south of the Selborne turning, the house is mainly 18th-century, but has the remains of an older cottage at its southern end. It is, in the manner of most of the old *Greatham* houses, of ironstone with brick dressings, and has a brick dentilled cornice. It has two storeys and sash windows with cambered arches. There is a wooden door-case, with pediment and plain fanlight. There is an additional 20th-century wing, with an ironstone garden wall with rounded brick coping. The name appears to have been derived from 'Chase's', as on the tithe assessment map of 1842, a field alongside the house was called 'Chase's paddock'.

Rook's Farm

Rook's Farm

This is another 17th-century building, located almost directly opposite the vehicular access to *Greatham* Primary School. It is a two-storey construction, timber-framed, with ironstone and brick in filling. There is a tiled roof, with three gabled dormers. The windows are of the casement type. The south-side wall is ironstone galleted, with brick dressings, while the upper storey is tile-hung. A later added porch has a tiled roof. There is a timber-framed and timber-clad barn, now being used as stables. These have a tiled roof, wooden stable doors, and non-opening small-paned windows.

Rook's Farm was sold by William John Hampden Chawner, for the sum of £450, on 12th December 1885. At the time, William was a Lieutenant in Her Majesty's Irish Regiment, serving and residing in Bengal, India. He was obviously one of the large family of Chawners from Newton Valence, to which their churchyard gravestones bear witness. The area of land was quoted as *'4 acres, 2 rods and 8 perches'*, and the purchaser was James Wells, who appears greatly in the history of the Redman family, described elsewhere.

Swain's Cottage

PARTICULARS.

LOT 1.

A BRICK AND TILED

FREEHOLD COTTAGE RESIDENCE

Known as "LISS COTTAGE."

Pleasantly situate in the Village of Greatham, about 2 miles from Liss.

Two Sitting Rooms, Kitchen, good Cellar, and 4 Bedrooms

There is a Capital Garden in extent about Half an Acre,

WITH WOODHOUSES AND OUTBUILDINGS.

It is in the occupation of Mr William Wells, and recently occupied by the late Mrs Wells

POSSESSION MAY BE OBTAINED ON THE COMPLETION OF THE PURCHASE

LOT 2.

A PLOT OF EXCELLENT, SOUND

Freehold Meadow Land

SITUATE IN THE PARISH OF GREATHAM, HANTS.

Known as THELE or BRIDGEFORD MEADOW,

IN EXTENT

10 a. 2 r. 24 p.,

ABOUT TWO MILES FROM LISS RAILWAY STATION.

It is let to Mr. Frank Kemp, with other Land, at £32 a year, Landlord paying the tithe-rent charge.

The rent is apportioned for the purposes of this Sale at £25 a year

Possession may be obtained at Michaelmas next.

The Timber will have to be paid for by the Purchaser at the sum of £24.

The adjoining Property belongs to G. F. Coryton, Esq.

LOT 3.

A PAIR OF BRICK, STONE AND TILED

FREEHOLD COTTAGES

Well situate with a frontage to the road leading from Greatham to Liphook, close to the Village of Greatham.

Each containing 4 Rooms, as let to Ben Cooper (monthly tenant) and John Pour (quarterly tenant), at 2s. a week each

There are Good Gardens in extent about Half an Acre.

Located just a short distance south of Case's, Manor Cottage is a two-storey 19th-century stone structure, with one end stucco and some repairs in brick. It has a thatched roof with dormers and two chimneys, with small-paned casement windows and a plain porch. The cottage was home to Mrs. Liliane Mansbridge, along with husband Frederick and step daughter Peggy, from 1947 until she died at Southampton in 1971, but her parents, Mr & Mrs Oliver George Skinner, had already been in residence there since 1923.

Before the 2nd World War, Mrs Mansbridge had taught as a dancing teacher in London and did in fact instruct the two young Royal princesses, Elizabeth and Margaret, first in Piccadilly, then later at both Buckingham Palace and Windsor Castle. She was a keen member of the local Women's Institute, with whom she used to produce a very successful drama group.

Pook's Cottage

Situated about halfway down Church Lane, this 17th-century cottage is of two-storeyed timber-framed construction, with ironstone and brick in filling. There is a tiled roof with three gabled dormers. The casement windows have glazing bars, while the upper storey is tile-hung. The ironstone south wall is 'galleted', with brick dressings. A later porch has been added, with a tiled roof. There is documentary evidence to show that, before the 'new' church was erected in 1875, Church Lane was originally called Pook's (or Pook) Lane.

King's Holt

This elegant house is probably around only 100 years old, occupying a commanding position on the hill to the east of the main road, with its entrance opposite what is now the 'EuroTec' building. Like so many other local houses at that time, it was built by the Kemp family of builders, then based in Alton. Originally part of the Whitehill (Blackmoor) parish, it is recorded as being the property of General & Mrs Chase-Parr in the trade directories for 1903-1911, followed by Sydney H Cotton around 1920.

In 1923, it became the residence of the Hope family, Herbert George and May Winifred. Their daughter, Isabel Susan, was only six months old at the time. She eventually married Peter Hiley in 1955 and, following

Manor Cottage

the death of her mother in 1960, the Hileys moved to King's Holt in 1962. Peter became a prominent member of the village, serving on the Parish Council and Village Hall Committee. When they moved to Steep in 1975, a parcel of land was sold, giving name to 'Hopeswood', a small council estate in Longmoor Road.

Greatham Moor

Situated nowadays alongside the busy A3 dual carriageway, this large house must have been a haven of peace in earlier days. Its most famous occupants would have been Sir Arundell Neave, Bart (1916 – 1992) and his wife Lady Richenda (1922 – 1994), both of whom were prominent in village life during their period living at **Greatham**. Older readers may remember that Sir Arundel was brother to the late Airey Neave, a Conservative Member of Parliament and shadow Northern Ireland Secretary, who was killed by an IRA car bomb outside the House of Commons, in 1979. The ghost of a lady dressed in grey and a white veil is purported to haunt the woods in the area, but nothing is known about who she may have been, so a mystery it shall remain.

Earlier occupants of the house can be gleaned from the various trade directories as follows:

Reverend William Smith (1875, 1878, 1880 & 1885)
Mrs Smith (1895)
William Rose Smith (1895, 1903 & 1907)

W R Smith was later to be knighted, becoming Sir William Rose Smith, and continuing to reside at Greatham Moor until around 1931. The 1935 and 1939 entries show that Mr H J Godwin was the owner during at least those years.

Tom's Acre Cottages

Originally one cottage, the present pair of cottages lies opposite the Selborne Road junction and used to face the 'Toll House'. An Inland Revenue rating surveyor's report from 1910 states that Tom's Acre was a 'service' cottage to the Manor House. It was owned by Captain A F Coryton and was at that time lived in by his coachman, a man named Rawlings, who paid a rent of 3 shillings (15 pence) per annum out of his wages.

Tom's Acre Cottages still sit across the road from the Selborne junction, but the Tollgate House has long since disappeared.

Cam Green Cottage

This old cottage lies just a short distance further down Church Lane than Pook's Cottage and is of a similar vintage. The name dates back to at least around 1842, when the tithe map of that year showed an area of about 60 acres, split up into Alder Common, Great Common and Cam Green Common. It is interesting to note that as late as the 1950s, a 'great tithe' rent was still being paid to the Church on this 'glebe' property.

Post Office

Although of little historical significance as a building, the Post Office tends to be the hub of village life and therefore well worth a mention. Apart from the Game Centre and the two village pubs, it is the main retail outlet and only remaining 'village shop' in **Greatham**. Situated at the northernmost end of the village and part of Woolmer Villas (dated 1903), it retains the name of Blackmoor Stores (as well as **Greatham** Post Office), reflecting the fact that it once stood in the parish of Whitehill (Blackmoor), until parish boundaries were amended in 1982.

It would appear that the postal facilities in

Greatham have moved around quite frequently in recent history. There is evidence to show that the Tollgate House, which once sat at the Selborne Road junction, was once the Post Office, run by Miss Amy Prince, who later became Mrs Amy Booth. There is a house along the Petersfield Road, south of the Game Centre, still named 'The Old Post Office'. Finally, the Game Centre was itself the Post Office for many years, until Sheila & Eric Sampson left in late 1991, having taken over the business from the Stamp family in 1976.

When the Sampsons left and the Game Centre became established, postal facilities moved to Blackmoor Stores, where Linda & Peter Stevens had been running the shop since 1982. The Stevens' themselves later moved away to Bishops Waltham and the combined shop and Post Office is now in the hands of 'Del & El' (Delma and Elwyn) Evans, who moved up from South Wales in 1997.

John Clarke, now living at 'Beeleigh', just a little further south down the Petersfield Road, ran the village shop for many years, prior to the Stevens, along with his wife Joyce, who provided a wonderful photograph showing how it used to be. Sadly, Joyce passed on in late 1999, but I am sure she wouldn't mind me using her own words here, as she described it in reference to her old photograph:

*"Our Village Shop! In its early years it was run and owned by Mr Grace, seen outside with his wife and the errand boy. They sold everything, including boots, shoes and dresses. They rented the front room of the house next door, where all the shoe boxes can be seen. The bus-stop outside used to be known as Grace's Corner. In those days, newspapers were sold by Mr Kirby in Pansy Cottage, the placards can be seen in the hedge. Eventually Mr Kirby bought the Graces' business, and the shop was than called Kirby's Stores for a number of years. Today in 1999, we have a bright modern shop. Although we can no longer buy boots or dresses, one can purchase a bottle of wine, the latest magazines and stamps for our letters – a credit and asset to **Greatham**."*

And now of course we all have to go to 'Grace's Stores' for our stamps, postal orders and gossip! Yes, there may be just a few older villagers left who remember when Mr Grace ran his business there in the early years of the 20th-century. Trade Directory entries for Blackmoor show that Herbert Grace was a shopkeeper from at least 1923, up until the outbreak of the Second World War in 1939.

Chapter Seventeen
Village Inns

It is not that long a time since **Greatham** boasted two public houses, 'The Queen' and the 'Silver Birch', which was formerly the 'Woolmer Hotel'. The Silver Birch was named as such sometime in the late 1960's, when the owners at the time were part of a family running another public house somewhere in the Salisbury area, also with a 'Silver' connotation, possibly the 'Silver Plough'. No doubt those owners thought the name more fitting, with all the silver birch-trees in this area, but the term Woolmer was far more historically significant, relating as it does to 'Wolfmere' — literally *'lake of the wolves'*. It is therefore surprising that the present name has lasted some thirty years. The inn was, for a short time in the late 1990s, home to 'Gianni's' Italian Restaurant, reflecting that today's customers often want rather more than just a drink during their evening out, especially with the stricter 'drink-and-drive' laws that now exist.

Inspection of an Ordnance Survey map printed around 1888 shows that there was a public house on the same site, called the 'Bricklayer's Arms', prior to the building of the Woolmer. This is borne out by the 1861 and 1871 censuses of Selborne, which then included part of what is now **Greatham**. In 1861, Thomas Kemp was shown as the publican of the Bricklayer's Arms, with three sons, but by 1871 he had been replaced by one

Hori (Horace or Henry?) Kemp senior, aged 77 years, as the innkeeper. The Hampshire Directory (Selborne) for that year showed both Kemp (snr) and Kemp (jnr) at this establishment. The White's Directory (Blackmoor) of 1878 indicated that the Bricklayer's Arms was now being run by one Henry Cooper.
(Hori Kemp appears elsewhere in the story – see the notes on Forestside Cottages. Ed.)

Various Kelly's Directory entries for Whitehill (Blackmoor) showed that the innkeepers for what was by now the *Woolmer Hotel* were:
Frederick William Pearson (1903)
Thomas Garner (1907 – 1911; also shown as 'jobmaster')
Sydney W Hawker (1915)
Mrs S Smith (1927)
Mrs Drusilla Hedley (1923)
Mrs Jean Roy was listed as 'proprietress' from 1931 – 1939.

The Queen is referred to in trade directories during the latter half of the 19th-century as the 'Queen's Head', though exactly when the name changed is not clear. At one time, it is believed that the public house was owned by the Blackmoor Estate and that apples from those famous orchards were used to make The Queen's own individual brand of cider.

'The Queen' in bygone days before traffic became a problem. The car parked opposite is probably filling up with petrol at Madgwick's Garage.

The Woolmer Hotel replaced an earlier hostelry, 'The Bricklayers Arms', on the same site.

as living in apartments at Kingshott Villas. Further trade entries show the business being run by John Goddard from 1915 to 1927 and then Harry Rixon between 1931 and 1939.

(The term 'jobmaster' describes a person who hires out horses & carriages, while 'victualler' indicates a publican or innkeeper, one licensed to sell alcoholic liquor. Ed.)

A visit to The Queen during early 1999 would have revealed three wonderful old photographs of the pub, taken at various times during the early part of the 20th-century. One was actually sent back to this country by a visitor from Tasmania, and evokes strong memories for older readers, showing a delivery to the pub by a cart drawn by the heavily built dray-horses of yesteryear. Sadly, after another change of ownership, these old photographs have now disappeared.

Even more sadly, The Queen was allowed more-or-less to 'run down', with a closure finally taking place sometime during 2001. It is now boarded up, with the site the subject of a planning application for the building of houses. Like many other villages in this modern age, the village pub appears to have become an anachronism, with people more than willing to stay at home for their evening's 'tipple' and entertainment.

The final curtain on Greatham's long hostelry tradition came in the summer of 2002, when the Silver Birch came to a similar fate. It too stands as a monument to the past, looking most forlorn behind a barrier of wire fencing. Battles are presently being fought against the awarding of planning applications on both sites, with the hope of eventually preserving at least one inn as a viable concern.

George Wells was described as 'blacksmith & wheelwright' in 1855, but by 1875 had become 'shopkeeper & farmer', and was believed to have taken over the running of the Queen's Head at this time. By 1878, he was also being described as a 'victualler', still at the same public house. This continued up until 1880, but by 1885 his name had disappeared and John Knight had taken over. In 1895, the pub had passed into the hands of one Samson Davis. He was described at one time as *'wine & spirit merchant, grocer and provision dealer'*, while the Queen Inn had *'good stabling and lock-up coach house'*. Samson was followed by Henry Herbert Hopkins in 1907, then Martin Kemp in 1911. In the 1911 - 1923 editions of the Kelly's Directory for Whitehill (Blackmoor), Samson Davis was then listed

The Wollmer Hotel proudly provided luncheons and teas. They particularly welcomed cyclists.

Chapter Eighteen
Village Businesses

EuroTec

The site that is used by EuroTec International PLC, to give the full business title, lies just to the north of the Game Centre. The present owners understand that the original buildings had previously been used for various purposes, such as a chapel, a cinema, an ice-cream factory and a printing works.

EuroTec was formed as a company in 1973, moving to its current premises in **Greatham** in 1978. The business has gradually expanded to include an additional warehouse and light industrial area, employing some 30 people. The company supplies automotive manufacturers with sound systems, such as loudspeakers and antennas. It is an international company with strong trading links to Europe, South Africa, the Far East and Australia.

Game Centre

The above named shop has been resident in the village since 1992, after the retirement of the Sampsons from what used to be the Post Office in late 1991. It is a retail and wholesale outlet for Hampshire Game Limited, which was established near Andover in 1977. The Company provides an extensive range, which includes feathered and furred game, venison, wild boar and even frozen legs of kangaroo. Almost all of the game supplied has been able to live and thrive in its natural environment.

Liss Forest Nursery

This wholesale-only plants & shrubs business is situated across the road from **Greatham** Village Hall. It is owned and run by Joyce and Peter Catt, along with sons Neill and Vincent, employing between 16 and 20 people, depending upon seasonable variation and demand. Joyce and Peter married in 1959 and live 'on site' alongside their nursery. Peter's father, Frederick Stanley Catt, had founded Bowyer's Nursery at Liss in 1952, and with Peter then at school-leaving age, he began working with his father. However, F S emigrated to New Zealand around 1962, leaving Peter to now start running the nursery for the people who had

EuroTec's in early days. Their premises ar now somewhat larger!

bought it.

At some later date, Peter decided to 'branch out', and along with a partner, founded Liss Forest Nursery, operating from The Wylds in Warren Road. He bought his present site, which had previously belonged to the Coryton family, in 1976. The first glass-house was erected in January 1977, with their bungalow home following later that same year. Peter has a justifiable 'claim to fame', in that he introduced the evergreen flowering shrub, *'Choisya ternarta'* — or 'Sundance' — to an admiring public. This shrub has gone on to become one of the most popular and famous in the world. He loves and prefers the 'hands-on' approach, but also gets involved in the day-to-day business of running his busy office.

'Grace's Store', now the only retail outlet still open, as the Village Post Office.

Chapter Nineteen
Village Organisations

Women's Institute

The *Greatham* branch of the 'WI', as it is affectionately called, was first set up in January of 1942. The first President at that time was Miss Isolda Coryton, sister of Captain 'Gussy' Coryton, last 'lord of the manor'. A few years after its inauguration, the *Greatham* branch amalgamated with Empshott, but became a singular branch once again, probably during the 1960s.

As detailed on a membership card issued to Winifred Lacy, one of the original members and mother to current member Elsie Collins, the main purpose of the WI is to *'improve and develop conditions of rural life, by providing a centre for educational and social intercourse and activities'*.

The WI is still going strong here in *Greatham*, with a current membership of around 24. There was great delight at a meeting in February 2001, when members congratulated Mrs Nancy Woodman on her having been awarded the MBE in the New Year's Honours List. Well-known ladies who have served the WI well over the years include Lady Neave, Frances Pumphrey, Olive Redman and Win Murphy, while the current Secretary of the branch is Pat Flack. At one time, the WI was able to boast a choir, which entered for the Petersfield Festival, while a drama group was once very popular, with Liliane Mansbridge of Manor Cottage as its producer.

A Remembrance Day parade at the new church.

Senior Citizens

It is a few years now since the term 'old age pensioner' was replaced by the more satisfactory 'senior citizen'. Certainly, here in *Greatham*, the Senior Citizens Club has been in existence since around 1963, drawing its membership at any one time from both the current and ex-residents of the village. Sometimes meetings are held at the Village Hall, but on many occasions individual member's houses are the venue. There are also many trips out in order to visit local showpieces and places of historical interest. It is believed that Mrs Holland of 'The Wylds' founded the local organisation and it was later run by Sir Guy and Lady Grantham of Hatch Lane, Liss, while Frances Pumphrey was an active member for many years.

Gardeners Club

The *Greatham* Flower and Produce Show started as an annual event in 1975 and has now completed a successful quarter-century. *Greatham* Gardeners Club became established in 1985, and in 1991 took on the responsibility of running the GFPS for the first time. Following the recent 'by-passing' of the village, Club members are now displaying their many and varied talents to add a touch of colour and beauty to the roadside verges and hedgerows, with the planting of trees and flowers at suitable sites.

Girl Guides, Brownies and Rainbows

Greatham Brownies was originally formed in 1920, but after flourishing for many years, it closed down in 1980. Thankfully, it has been re-formed and running again since 1996, with Debbie Hedicker as the current leader. The 2nd Liss Guides are stationed here in *Greatham*, under the guidance of Carol Rudd, while Jan Street is responsible for the running of the Rainbow group.

Chapter Twenty
Woolmer Forest

To the north and west of **Greatham** Parish lie the remnants of Woolmer Forest, one of eleven Royal forests dating back to the Middle Ages. The first known 'Keeper' of both Woolmer and Alice Holt forests, in 1068 at the time of Domesday, was Geoffrey de Marshall. This name related to the fact that he was 'Bearer of the Marshal's Rod' in the King's household. This title itself is the humble forerunner of 'Earl Marshal of England', created in 1315 and held ever since by the Earls and Dukes of Norfolk.

Located at the western end of the Weald, the forest straddles the borders of Hampshire and West Sussex, with the majority of its area lying on the coarse sands of Folkestone beds, although Bargate beds outcrop on the sides of the Hollywater valley. The whole of the Woolmer area had once formed an area within the great Saxon forest known as Andredsweald.

A typical description of the area, probably based upon that part now known as 'Weaver's Down', comes from lines of the poem written by the Restoration dramatist Thomas Otway, in 1860, entitled 'The Poet's complaint of his Muse':

'To a high hill where never yet stood tree,
Where only heath, coarse fern and furzes grow,
Where, nipt by piercing air
The flocks in tattered fleeces hardly graze.'

Driving along the A325 northwards to Bordon, it is hard to believe that you are crossing the probable site of a significant battle in ancient British history. Troops of the Roman Empire thought that their victory here was so important, that special commemorative medals were struck as a record. One of only two known examples of this medal was sold in 1992 for £87,000. The battle took place between two divisions of Roman forces.

The British had suffered badly under the reign of a leader named Allectus (AD 293-296), who had seized power for himself, after arranging an assassination. Soldiers loyal to Constantius I (AD 293-306), under the command of his ablest lieutenant, Asclepiodotus, crossed the Channel to put right these wrongdoings. The two armies met at Woolmer Forest, and the better-trained Imperial forces of Constantius were victorious. It is believed that Allectus' army chest, used to pay his mercenary troops, was lost. This is probably the origin of the 'Blackmoor hoard' of coins, found in 1873.

Constantius remained in Britain and married Helena, the daughter of King Coel of Colchester – the original *'Old King Cole'* of nursery rhyme fame. His son Constantine was proclaimed Emperor upon his father's death and went on to become Constantine I, or 'the Great', the first Roman Emperor to embrace Christianity, making it the religion of the Empire. He reigned from AD 307 to AD 337, reuniting the Eastern and Western Empires by the year 314. He made the city of Byzantium, on the Bosphorus, his capital, renaming it Constantinople in AD 324. Modelled on Rome, this new centre of Roman influence was more strategically placed at the crossroads of Europe and Asia.

The name Woolmer has changed many times. Amongst those that are recorded are Wolvermere (1226), Wolvesmer (1234), Wolmere (1372), Wulfmere and Wulmer. The term Wolmer was used after 1376, before settling at today's version. It is interesting that this is a 'forest' in the truest sense of the word, coming from either the Celtic 'furst', which means 'growth on wasteland', or the Latin 'foris', meaning 'outside' or 'beyond'.

Thus a forest was not necessarily a wooded area, in the sense in which it is used today, while 'foris' was a legal term, originally used to describe land not within the manorial system, which would be policed or managed by the King's forest wardens. As long ago as 1789, Gilbert White, the famous naturalist from Selborne, described it as follows:

*'The Royal Forest of Wolmer is a tract of land about seven miles in length by two and a half in breadth, running nearly from north to south; and is abutted on, to begin in the south and so to proceed eastward, by the parishes of **Greatham**, Lysse, Rogate and Trotton, in the County of Sussex; and by Bramshott, Hedleigh and Kingsley. This Royalty consists entirely of sand, covered with heath and fern, but is somewhat diversified with hills and dales, without having one standing tree in the whole extent. In the bottoms, where the waters stagnate, are many bogs, which formerly abounded with subterraneous trees'.*

This lack of trees may well have been due to the days of 'hearts of oak', when literally thousands of oaks were felled, for the construction of those great ships known as 'men o'war'.

Some 200 years on from that description, the area does now contain plantations of the ubiquitous Scots pine, and a sprinkling of silver birch, as well as the characteristic heather and bracken of heathland areas. The whole area was purchased by the Commissioner of Her Majesty's Woods, Forests and Lands in 1863. This was so that it could be used by the Army as a training ground, after its return from the Crimean War.

One of Woolmer Forest's more infamous characters was Adam de Gurdon, born around 1220. He was the third consecutive 'Adam' after his grandfather and father, inheriting the family estate at Selborne and East Tisted. By 1241, de Gurdon had succeeded his father as Bailiff of Alton, and was thus the farmer of royal lands in the district. However, he took sides with the rebel forces led by Simon de Montfort, Earl of Leicester, in the rebellion against Henry III. The rebel army was defeated at Evesham, Worcestershire, in August 1265 and de Gurdon's lands were seized and re-distributed amongst the King's supporters.

Adam and his followers set themselves up as a band of outlaws in woods and marshes, their wicked deeds spreading fear into the hearts of travellers in the Middle Ages. In May of 1266, they broke out of Essex and Hertfordshire, across the Chilterns and eventually into Hampshire, becoming established locally, close to de Gurdon's original homeland. From here, Adam and his men *raided the countryside, particularly the lands of those who adhered to the royal cause'*. Many writers attest that the legend of 'Robin Hood and his Merry Men' was based upon such adventures.

Prince Edward 'Longshanks' (later Edward I), on hearing of de Gurdon's deeds, challenged him to single combat. When Edward won the encounter, he spared him his life, at which point (perhaps understandably) de Gurdon changed his ways. His inheritance was restored to him and he became a faithful and trusty henchman, later being appointed Warden of both Woolmer and Alice Holt Forests. Having been restored to respectability, he settled in nearby Selborne and in 1271, granted a small area facing the church as a market place. It was known as 'La Playstowe' (play place) and today is recognised as 'the Plestor'.

An entry in the Rolls for Woolmer shows that de Gurdon was instructed to keep all trespassers in custody to await the King's pleasure. A further entry in 1285 shows that the Keeper of the King's hunting dogs was to be supplied with six oak stumps, in order to keep the dogs warm throughout the winter months. In 1286, de Gurdon was ordered to allow the Prior of Selborne to take *'six good oaks'* from the forest, as recompense for that heather & timber removed from the Priory by Edward I's household, when they had last been in the area.

A local building, on the minor road between Empshott and Hawkley, bears witness to de Gurdon's association with this area. Mounted on the side of the building is a plaque that has the inscription:

HOCHELEYE MILL
ANCIENT MILL OF THE BISHOPS OF
WINCHESTER
TAKEN FROM THEM BY SIR ADAM
GURDON
GIVEN BACK UNDER KING EDWARD AD
1280
BURNT DOWN AND REBUILT 1774
BECAME A COTTAGE 1880
I.I.M.

(For a more detailed description of Adam de Gurdon, I recommend a small book entitled 'Selborne', written by Rupert Willoughby. It also, of course, tells the story of Selborne and its association with Gilbert White. Ed.)

Successive English Kings continued the tradition of hunting within Woolmer Forest. Prince Henry himself, who later became the infamous Henry VIII of the 'six wives' saga, was said to have been the Forest Ranger at one time, while Thomas Chaucer, son of the famous poet (Canterbury Tales), also served in the same post around 1435.

During the 150 years or so that followed, many noble names graced the line of descent of the Keepers of the Forest. A great favourite was Ruperta Howe, born in 1673. Her mother, Margaret (Peg) Hughes had married Prince Rupert of the Rhine, cousin to King Charles II. When Rupert died, both Ruperta and her mother were still graciously accepted at Court, where Ruperta must have met Colonel Howe, Gentleman of the Bedchamber to William III. They married around 1690 and, on her husband's death in 1709, Ruperta assumed the post of Keeper, which she held with great authority for 31 years. She died at Somerset House in 1740, at the age of 67.

Many tales exist which are indicative of Woolmer Forest's colourful history. There is much written evidence of the hunting of fallow deer to the north, at Alice Holt, while red deer and wild boar were hunted to the south, near **Greatham**. Queen Anne is reputed to have stopped here in 1710, journeying from Southampton to London, and indeed there is a plaque which commemorates this event, mounted on a stone plinth on the aptly named 'Queen's Bank', from where there are fine views across the now open heath-land towards Liphook. The commemorative plaque once resided below a split oak tree, quite close to the A325, but was moved in the mid 1990s to its present site. 'Queen's Bank' once again lives up to its name.

Again, let the words of dedicated scribe Gilbert White describe the scene:

'Queen Anne, as she was journeying on the Portsmouth road, did not think the forest of Wolmer beneath her royal regard. For she came out of the great road at Lippock, which is just by, and reposing herself on a bank smoothed for that purpose, lying about half a mile to the east of Wolmer-pond, and still called Queen's-bank, saw with great complacency and satisfaction the whole herd of red deer brought by the keepers along the vale before her, consisting then of about five hundred head.'

There is evidence to indicate that some time after this event, around 1750, the herd had been decimated by a gang of poachers, known as the 'Waltham Blacks'. The so-called 'butcher' Duke of Cumberland, who had beaten the Jacobite armies of his cousin, 'Bonnie' Prince Charlie, at the Battle of Culloden in 1746, ordered his scarlet and gold uniformed huntsmen to round up what remained of the deer. They were then transported back to Windsor Castle, thus emptying the forest of its most ancient inhabitants.

A century and a half after Queen Anne's visit, Woolmer Forest was again graced by the Royal presence, on this occasion by Queen Victoria. However, this event was not commemorated until 1902, when Bramshott Parish Council announced that:

"In the year 1859, while Her Majesty's Troops were encamped at Woolmer, Queen Victoria and the Prince Consort, with the Princess Royal and the Prince of Wales, visited the Camp and, beneath the shade of an Oak Tree, partook of refreshments. To commemorate the event, a Tablet will be placed by the Bramshott Parish Council, with the consent of His Majesty's Commissioner of Woods, in the year of the Coronation of His Majesty King Edward VII, AD 1902."*

Woolmer today

In 1993, the publication 'Hampshire' recorded that Woolmer Forest was the only habitat in Great Britain to support all 12 indigenous species of reptile and amphibian, namely the common and sand lizard, grass and smooth snake, adder, common and natterjack toad, common and marsh frog, common newt, great crested newt and slow-worm. It is hardly surprising that the area has been graded a 'SSSI' (Site of Special Scientific Interest) since 1974, while Woolmer Pond had held the same status since 1971, as notified by English Nature. The latest revision of this status, along with the current boundaries, which include land at Blackmoor and Conford Moor, is dated 1993.

The 'natterjack' toad is a most endangered species. It burrows in the sand of Woolmer, its last native heathland site, and spawns in brackish water during April. The toadlets hatch out in June, and even fully grown, the natterjack is smaller than the common toad, being only eight to ten centimetres long. It has a yellow-green or olive-green skin, with a distinctive yellow stripe. Rather than walk or hop, it has a peculiar

Looking down on Woolmer Villas when steam trains ran on the Longmoor Military Railway.

run, while its croaks can be heard at a distance of about half a mile. Some naturalists postulate that the cement bunkers all over Woolmer Forest cause the soil to be alkaline in nature, thus aiding the toad to breed and flourish. The water in this area is certainly well known for its 'rusty' appearance, due to the high iron content of the soil, and the local river has often been referred to as the 'Red Rother'.

The Woolmer Forest SSSI also contains large and diverse heathland habitats which support vulnerable species of bird, as covered by a directive of the European Commission, and is therefore regarded as being of international wildlife value. These birds include nationally important breeding populations of nightjar, woodlark and Dartford Warbler, as well as breeding pairs of hobby (a small falcon). Also observed have been the stonechat, tree pipit, linnet, hen harrier and merlin (another small falcon). Any information regarding this area can be gleaned by contacting English Nature, which has a Hampshire & Isle of Wight team based at Lyndhurst, in the New Forest.

The SSSI includes the watersheds of two major drainage systems. The largest of these flows north to Holly Water, which forms a tributary of the River Wey. The smaller drainage system flows south from Longmoor Inclosure, to form a tributary of the River Rother. The drainage ditches and streams which criss-cross the site have cut broad valleys into the sandy soils, interspersed with rounded hills and ridges, whose tops are covered with extensive areas of dry heathland vegetation. Within these areas are found many nationally rare and uncommon plants such as tower mustard, mossy stonecrop, shepherd's cress and smooth cat's-ear. Also found are rare species of wasp and bee fly.

Teams of naturalists, including botanists,

ornithologists, entomologists, etc. make regular visits to the SSSI, observing and recording their findings as members of the Longmoor Conservation Group. Indeed, when the Ministry of Defence set up the conservation group in 1974, it became the forerunner of over two hundred such groups now organised wherever the Armed Services are stationed. Despite the fact that the Army still has authority over the area, and that access is often denied when the Ranges are in use, it is obvious from the facts above that once again, as with the AONB, *Greatham* is extremely fortunate to have the SSSI as a close neighbour. Once those red flags come down, Woolmer offers excellent opportunities for walkers and ramblers – but don't expect to keep on falling over rare species – these shy creatures like to keep themselves to themselves!

Mention of 'naturalists' brings us back to perhaps the most famous one of all, already mentioned in this account. Gilbert White was four times Curate-in-charge at neighbouring Selborne, and wrote a series of letters which eventually culminated in the publishing of 'The Natural History of Selborne' in 1788, just five years before his death in 1793.

In one letter, to Thomas Pennant, he was the first naturalist to ever write about both Woolmer Forest and Woolmer Pond. In fact he wrote that within the limits of Woolmer Forest were *"three considerable lakes, Hogmer, Cranmer and Wolmer; all of which are stocked with carp, tench, eels and perch"*. It is astonishing to read that in 1781, Lord Stawell was able to fish the pond *'with a net drawn by ten men'*. By 1927, one writer recorded that Woolmer Pond had *"now diminished to a miserable pool, no longer a lake but a marsh liable to flooding"*.

In recent years, the pond has once again been prone to drying up, during some exceptionally dry summers, with the drought year of 1976 being particularly harsh. However, it is unlikely that another treasure-hoard of Roman coins will be found, such as that of Gilbert White's era. Thankfully, during these past few months of the first half of 1999, a wet winter, followed by a wet spring, has seen water levels rise again to show the pond at its best, though it is difficult to see it ever again being permanently full of water once more.

Part of the original narrow guage railway line running through Woolmer Forest

Chapter Twenty One
Longmoor Camp

Longmoor Camp has long been a close neighbour of **Greatham**, situated above Apple Pie Hill, but there is little permanent military presence these days. One site is now used mainly as an equipment storage area, or Engineer Park, for the Royal Engineers, whilst the main barracks and surrounding heath-land acts as a training centre, for both Regular and Territorial Army units, as well as the Army Cadet Force. It is often asked where the name 'Apple Pie' came from, used as it is for both the hill and camp area just above it. Rumour had it that following a Royal inspection many years ago (probably in 1928) by King George V and Queen Mary, the King coined the term when he remarked that *'everything is in apple-pie order'*. But close inspection of an 1880s map shows that there was already an 'Applepie Corner' at the meeting of some tracks on the site, at the boundary between **Greatham** and Headley Parishes, so the mystery lives on.

Land for Army training was first bought at both Bordon and Longmoor in 1863, seven years after the end of the Crimean War. A Douglas Fir-tree, planted in 1849 from seed introduced from North America, still proudly stands in the grounds of what is now Ladysmith House. In 1900, when the British Empire still laid claim to a quarter of the habitable globe, the War Office planned some re-deployment of troops, using Longmoor as one of the locations. Work started by 23 Field Company, Royal Engineers, in August 1900 and was completed in May 1903.

The imminent arrival of troops in the area was not universally welcome at first. This is made clear by the following extract of a letter written the Rev Francis Bryans to his future successor, Cecil Luttrell-West, in August 1900:

"There is going to be a great change in the quiet parish, which I fear may upset everything in a little time. We are to have a second Aldershot. We have now about 100 soldiers putting up huts on the common for 3 or 4 Battalions, which I believe measures 3,000 soldiers or thereabouts, who are to take up their permanent abode here in about 3 months. In the course of a year or two there will be, as I have said, another Aldershot. The residents in the neighbourhood are very much annoyed, as Tommy Atkins in multitudes is not a very desirable neighbour, though it is the fashion now to back him up."

*(This does not appear to be a very Christian attitude, although more understandable in those days of stricter morals and conditions. A newspaper article of the day, in February 1901, sets the scene. Headed 'The Begging Nuisance', it reads: "At the Magistrates Clerks Office on Monday, before Mr W B Edgerton, Isaac Chase, tramp, pleaded guilty to begging at **Greatham** on the 2nd inst. and was sentenced to 7 days hard labour." Ed.)*

The first units to occupy the corrugated iron huts of the camp were 1st Battalion of the Argyll and Sutherland Highlanders and 2nd Battalion of the Wiltshire Regiment. It was these two units who complained so strenuously about the apparently unhealthy, damp marshy conditions, that the War Office decided to transfer the Infantry to Bordon, leaving Longmoor as the home for a Mounted Infantry School of Training.

In order to transport the necessary 68 huts over the 4½ miles between the sites, two 18-inch light railway *decauville* tracks, exactly parallel to each other at a distance of 22 feet apart, were laid down. The

Early pictures of Longmoor Camp

Layout of Longmoor Camp

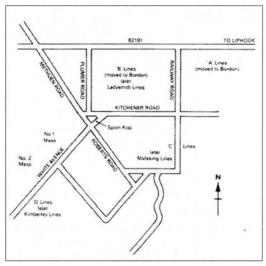

return journey to Aldershot.

John Thomas Hollidge was an interesting old character who lived in a corrugated iron shanty near the Camp entrance. He was a retired coachman, having served Queen Victoria. He would dress in a black frock coat with brass buttons, white breeches, coachman's leggings and a grey topper, daily exercising a pensioned-off dark-bay hunter, which had belonged to the Royal Family. The site of his 'residence' was required by the Sappers but, despite many attempts, they could not persuade him to leave. His story was that the old Queen had told him the hut was his for life and, as far as he was concerned, *"Here I stays."* He lived up to that statement until his death in 1931 at the age of 84.

An interesting addition to the story of Longmoor Camp is illustrated by a stone Royal Engineers Crest, mounted above the main entrance to No.1 Officer's Mess, built in the late 1930s. Incorporated within the crest is the cipher of Edward VIII, who reigned for only a few short months in 1936, before abdicating over his relationship with the American divorcee, Mrs Wallis Simpson. It is certainly a crest of some historical significance and rarity.

During World War II, the British Army Transportation Centre was set up at Longmoor and trained large numbers of Canadian troops for various trades, or for railway, port or water transport duties. Local residents who can recall those days remember most of them as cheerful soldiers, always ready for a laugh. Army lorries or regular service buses used to be crammed with soldiers, singing their way back to barracks after an evening out at Petersfield.

On the far side of Longmoor Inclosure, adjoining the Liss Forest Road where it is crossed by the old railway track, lies a poignant reminder of World War II. A memorial to the heroism of the pilot of a Royal Canadian Air Force pilot was erected in 1992, on the 50th anniversary of the crash of a Halifax bomber, as it returned from a bombing attack on Dortmund in Germany. With the plane on fire, Pilot Officer Richard Pryce-Hughes kept the stricken plane circling the area, allowing the rest of his crew to bail out

whole move took around two years (1903-05), but the foundation for a railway system had now come into existence, and its presence in the area remained for more than 60 years. A derailment of one of the 72-foot long huts proved irretrievable, and it was abandoned at Whitehill, where it was later refurbished, in 1904, to serve for many years as the local Police Station!

A photograph, believed to have been taken in 1906, shows the funeral cortege of a soldier, accidentally killed whilst serving at Longmoor. Members of the deceased's regiment formed a funeral party to accompany the coffin, as it was borne on a gun carriage all the way down the hill towards **Greatham** Church. After the funeral service, a firing party fired three volleys over the coffin, to the accompaniment of 'Reveille', and as the soldier was finally laid to rest, buglers played 'The Last Post' in his honour.

Longmoor Camp was privileged to host a Royal visit in 1907, by the Prince and Princess of Wales. 'The Times' of May 15th reported that this was to witness field operations. Arriving by motor car from Aldershot, headquarters of the British Army, the Prince switched to horseback to ride the final stage, escorted by Sir John French and staff from his HQ. After the military spectacle of an attack on Weaver's Down and lunch with Brigadier-General W P Campbell, commander of the troops, the Royal party was driven back on the

Horses at the mounted Infantry School of Training.

to safety, before it finally crashed on the moorland near to the **Greatham** road. Richard's two surviving sisters and nephew attended the unveiling ceremony. The memorial is soon to be refurbished, in tribute to the man who sacrificed his own life for the lives of his men.

As the war progressed, the lorries began to carry passengers of a very different background. The success of the 8th Army in the deserts of North Africa meant that thousands of prisoners-of-war were brought back to this country. The mainly Italian captives based at Longmoor must have made a strange sight to local people, dressed in their chocolate-brown battle-dress, covered in brightly coloured patches for identification purposes.

In 1965, upon the formation of the Royal Corps of Transport, Longmoor Camp became home to the Army School of Transport, and this lasted until 1977. Older members of **Greatham** may well remember being invited to the 'Farewell to Longmoor' function on May 31st of that year. The Band and Corps of Drums of the Royal Corps of Transport carried out the ancient ceremony of 'Beating the Retreat' for the last time at Longmoor, after an association of almost 60 years.

('Beating Retreat' is a ceremony belonging essentially to the Army and Royal Marines. Originally known as 'Beating Tatoo', the term was derived from an old Dutch word 'taptoe', adopted by the Army when it fought in the Lowland Wars. It was a signal to tavern keepers to close taps and serve no more liquor to the soldiers. The earliest known reference to 'Beating Retreat', under that specific name, appeared in a military order of the Army of King James II in 1690. Ed.)

When the School split up, one part moved up to Leconfield, North Humberside, and the other to Aldershot. Longmoor ceased to be used as a main military base for regular Army units and, in 1978, instead became HQ Longmoor Intermediate Training Area (LITA), controlling various activities, including Longmoor Training Camp and Longmoor Firing Ranges. The unit title was amended to Longmoor District Training Area, upon reorganisation of UKLF in 1991.

The Refreshment Room at the Soldiers Institute, Longmoor. In latter years Soldiers Institutes were replaced by the NAAFI.

Two churches were located within the Camp. St Martin's once stood at the northern end of Plumer Road (see map). Originally a forage-barn for the Mounted Infantry School, it was dedicated as a church in 1931. The building was demolished in 1978, although its many artefacts and windows had been moved to Leconfield in 1977. St Edward the Confessor Roman Catholic church was situated in White Avenue, next to the cricket pavilion. It had once been an abattoir and the rings for chaining cattle still remained in a few places. Conversion to a church took place in the early months of World War II, to serve the many soldiers of differing religions posted to Longmoor. It also ceased functioning as a church in 1977 and was pulled down in 1980.

There was an encouraging use of Longmoor Ranges during the first couple of weeks of April 2000. Schoolchildren from across Hampshire were taught how to 'Think Safe' at half-day sessions during this special event. A total of some 1,000 youngsters from surrounding areas, including those from nearby **Greatham**, took up the challenge of identifying dangers in eight different scenarios, set up by organisations including Hampshire Constabulary, Hampshire Fire & Rescue, Southern Electric, St John's Ambulance Brigade, local Councils and the Army unit at Bordon. It is gratifying to think that local facilities are being used in such a positive and constructive manner for the benefit of today's young people.

Chapter Twenty Two
𝕸𝖎𝖑𝖎𝖙𝖆𝖗𝖞 𝕽𝖆𝖎𝖑𝖜𝖆𝖞

Woolmer Forest is the main site of the now-defunct Longmoor Military Railway (LMR), which became its name once more in 1935, having been originally designated as such in 1905. This was when work on the track between Bordon and Longmoor was completed by various Rail Companies of the Royal Engineers, who were popularly termed 'The Sappers'. Started in 1903, some of the material used in its construction had been salvaged from the Suakin-Berber military railway, built during the Sudan campaign between 1882 and 1885!

Between 1908 & 1935, it had become known as the Woolmer Instructional Military Railway (WIMR), although it also had to live with the nickname *'Will It*

Move Railway', no doubt due to the difficult gradients encountered over the forest and heath. Although never part of the national rail system, it did provide a form of link between the main-line stations of Liss and Bentley. In December 1905, at the request of the War Office, a link-line had been completed from Bentley to Bordon, termed the Bentley & Bordon Light Railway. Bentley was on the London & South Western line, situated between Farnham and Alton.

During the years 1908-1910, along with the construction of a cutting at what is now Whitehill crossroads, a standard-gauge line was laid from Bordon down to Longmoor Camp. The final extension of the system, with a line down to Liss, started in 1924 but was not completed until 1933, while its connection to Southern Railway was not established until 1942. This was at a time when there was a need for Bailey bridges and other such equipment to be transported down to the embarkation ports along the south coast, in preparation for D-Day. It is no surprise to learn that, over its lifetime, the LMR had the largest number of different railway gauges in the world.

An interesting tale is that of the runaway engine. Those required for the day's work had been fired up and were building up steam-pressure. A loud bang reverberated around the shed and the next moment, one of the locomotives had crashed through the shed's shuttered doors and was dashing along the line with no sign of a driver. After demolishing a set of buffers, the engine toppled over an embankment into some boggy ground, with steam hissing and belching from every seam. Apparently, according to the Court of Inquiry, the hand brake had not been applied and, because the regulator was partially open, the build up of steam pressure was enough to set the pistons in motion.

Local resident Jack Dunn moved down to Longmoor Camp at a very early age in the 1920s, from Catterick, Yorkshire. Jack's father was one of the Royal Engineer drivers employed on the railway and the family were accommodated in Army quarters. As a boy, Jack would often take his father's breakfast down to the railway and then ride the footplate up to Bordon and back. In true traditional style, the food would be cooked on a shovel in the locomotive's firebox.

In May 1928, the LMR was honoured by a Royal visit. Their Majesties King George V and Queen Mary were shown the work being carried out on the

Longmoor Military Railway 1903 - 1924

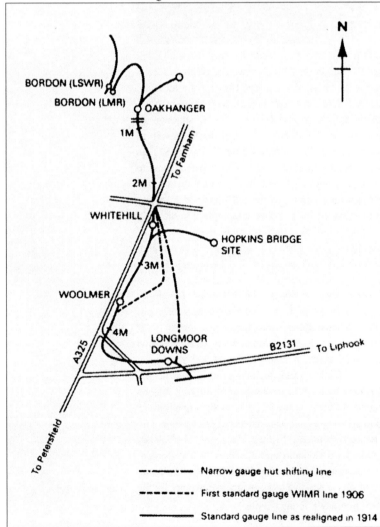

'Liss extension'. For their journey down the railway, the Kent & East Sussex Railway Saloon, numbered 'WIMR 7', was fitted out as an impromptu Royal coach, being furnished with various cushions and carpets from Officers' quarters around the camp.

Longmoor has an interesting connection with Waterloo Bridge in London! In June 1934, the old bridge was demolished and a temporary one erected. However, work on the new bridge did not start until 1938 and was then obviously disrupted by the outbreak of war. During the next few war years, the previously temporary construction was moved to Longmoor for storage purposes. It was then transported across the Channel during the D-Day operation, and used to bridge the Rhine at Remagen after the capture of Antwerp.

Throughout World War II, the LMR really came into its own, although its part in the Allied war effort has seldom been fully appreciated. By the end of hostilities in 1945, more than one-third of total RE manpower was employed on troops transportation and the greatest part of these, some 76,000 men, were trained at Longmoor. Apart from training, many thousands of passengers and tons of stores were carried through the Bordon - Longmoor area. At Longmoor itself, around 125 new military units formed up and went off to serve in all parts of the globe.

This involvement as a vital part of the War brought its own inherent dangers. During the summer of 1940, at around 6.30 one morning, the first of three bombing raids took place. Luckily, there were few casualties and only minor damage to some buildings and rolling stock. It is likely that the Luftwaffe, having been unable to penetrate London's defences that night, spotted the well-laid out pattern of Apple Pie Camp and decided that here was an inviting target. The BBC announced only that *'bombs had been dropped on waste land in Hampshire'*, an obvious attempt to try to maintain morale. Few permanent records of Longmoor's War years survive, probably due to the rapid and hectic turnover of both men and equipment.
(Charlie Hanson's memories of bombs falling on **Greatham** *are borne out by the above information. Ed.)*

Army cooking is not remembered with too much fondness by those who served and trained at Longmoor. Facilities were quite clean, fairly modern and spacious, but the large number of personnel to be catered for meant that, for the most part, the food could only be regarded as 'mediocre'. Sunday roasts were usually the favourite meal, being the highlight of the week. There was of course a 'NAAFI' and also a Church of England Institute, at which the soldiers could supplement their modest fare during evening visits. One old soldier recalls that the C of E was the best, as *'you could always*

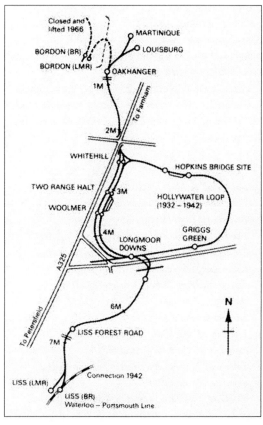

Final layout of the Longmoor Military Railway from 1924 to when it closed on the 31st October 1969.

get Horlicks, which was nectar after NAAFI tea'!

During its colourful history, the railway must have seen many events take place, but it could hardly have been expected to play the role of film star! But it did indeed form the backdrop for many films, from the late 1930s right through until the 1970s, after the system had officially closed. The first film to be made here was 'The Lady Vanishes' in 1938, which starred Margaret Lockwood and Michael Redgrave. The last, 'Young Winston' in 1972, starring Simon Ward in the title role, used the Weaver's Down to Liss line as a make-believe South Africa, set during the Boer War.

In 1955, during the making of 'Bhowani Junction', men of the 10th Railway Squadron, having recently returned from overseas service in the Canal Zone, required no top-up for their tans from the make-up ladies, as they played extras on the set. The Hollywater

The link from Liss across the road to Longmoor.

loop was transformed into an Indian landscape for the duration of filming. One of the stars of the film was Hollywood legend Ava Gardner and, while staying in the area, she was wined and dined by members of the Bordon Officer's Mess

The following list of films is probably not complete, but it illustrates the variety of railway sequences that were filmed at Longmoor over a period spanning five different decades:

> *The Lady Vanishes, starring Margaret Lockwood & Michael Redgrave (1938)*
> *The Interrupted Journey, with Valerie Hobson & Richard Todd (1949)*
> *The Happiest Days of your Life, with Margaret Rutherford & Alistair Sims (1950) Top Secret, with George Cole (1952)*
> *Melba, starring Robert Morley (1953)*
> *Bhowani Junction, with Ava Gardner & Stewart Granger (1955)*
> *The Inn of the Sixth Happiness, with Ingrid Bergman & Curt Jurgens (1958)*
> *Sons and Lovers, starring Trevor Howard & Dean Stockwell (1960)*
> *Weekend with Lulu, starring Bob Monkhouse & Leslie Phillips (1960)*
> *The Runaway Railway, with Ronnie Barker & Graham Stark (1964)*
> *Invasion Quartet, with Bill Travers & Spike Milligan (1964)*
> *The Great St Trinian's train robbery, with Dora Bryan & Frankie Howerd (1965) The Magnificent Two, starring Eric Morcambe & Ernie Wise (1967)*
> *Young Winston, with Anne Bancroft, Robert Shaw & Simon Ward (1972)*

The railway has no doubt seen many well-known railway

Troops in service dress (SD) waiting to board the train at Longmoor Station watched excitedly by three young children

engines in its chequered history, perhaps the most famous of all being 'Gordon the Blue Engine', friend of 'Thomas the Tank Engine'. Both were amongst the heroes of the children's book series, written by the Rev W V Awdry. The Army's blue engines were designed to pull heavy loads, and Gordon was built in 1897 at the Taff works in Cardiff. His name was given in honour of General C G Gordon, well known as 'Gordon of Khartoum'. Gordon was a 2-10-0 locomotive, Number 600, purchased in 1943 and probably used at Longmoor from that date, although only recorded as being there from 1957 onwards.

With the Bentley-Bordon line closing in 1957 and a gradual decline into disuse, official closure of all elements finally had to come. The last 'Public Day', held on July 5th of that year, was attended by over 12,000 spectators. To mark the occasion of the closure of the LMR, a ceremony was arranged by the Army School of Transport. Brigadier R A Nightingale MBE was then Commandant of the School, as well as Garrison Commander for Bordon & Longmoor. Senior officers of the Royal Engineers and Royal Corps of Transport (RCT), including former Commandants and Commanding Officers, attended a luncheon at the Brigadier's invitation.

Two well-loved engines, 'Gordon' and 'Errol Lonsdale', pulling their respective coaches, carried the invited guests out of Longmoor Downs station in opposite directions, 'Gordon' to Oakhanger and 'Errol Lonsdale' to Liss. This was to the strains of 'Auld Lang Syne', played by the Band of the RCT. When the trains returned, 'Gordon' was officially the last passenger train into Longmoor Downs, arriving at 1522 hours on Friday 31st October 1969.

Parts of the track-bed are still accessible to the public, and indeed it is possible to walk the whole loop which skirts what is now the Longmoor Military Ranges. Part of the 'Liss extension' has now been adopted as the very pleasant Riverside Walk, stretching from the Liss Forest Road right down to Liss Railway Station, and kept in good condition by the regular efforts of the Liss Conservation Volunteers. The three wooden bridges that now form part of this linear walk, reflect the history of Longmoor, being named after three of its former senior officers – namely *Rose*, *Nightingale* and *Briggs*.

It is now almost impossible to believe in the presence of such a railway system. For those hardy souls able to ramble and explore across the range area between **Greatham** and Whitehill however, it is still possible to come across the remnants of an old siding or railway track. Sometimes with the wind blowing through the trees, one may hear in the imagination the blast of a whistle or the hiss of a mighty steam engine.

Chapter Twenty Three
Albert Baker

Albert was born in London with deformed feet and without the use of either his arms or legs. To add to this tremendous burden, his home life was none too happy, his father being a cruel man, both to Albert and his mother. Beatings by cane were not uncommon. At only three years of age, Albert was sent for an assessment of his disabilities to St. Thomas's Hospital, thus beginning an institutionalised life until the age of fourteen.

Any education that Albert received at a number of different hospitals was constantly interrupted by surgical operations. It wasn't until just prior to his mother's death that Albert learned that many of the operations had been of an exploratory nature. His mother had signed a form, which allowed the surgeons to do whatever they wanted, even to the point of experimentation. Many of these surgical procedures left Albert in a worse condition and his life was one of constant pain.

He was eventually fitted with leg-irons and surgical boots, learning to walk a little by leaning against a wall and, to use his own phrase, *"pushing off"*. His only ray of light during those dark days was the drawing and painting that he had taught himself to do by mouth. At the age of seventeen, the authorities wished him to return to his mother's keep, but with an income of only ten shillings (50p) per week from public assistance, this was impractical – there were no disability allowances prior to the Second World War.

Instead, Albert spent the next three years in the hospital wing of a workhouse, a depressing time for this young man, where he was almost daily teased for being a cripple. Then in 1939, he was sent to Yorkshire, to a home for 'incurables and cripples', run by some monks who believed in a strict regime for their charges. Albert could still walk a little at that time and his greatest delight was to escape into the surrounding countryside. He was told, however, that any communication with women would lead to him being banned from the home!

Inspired by the beautiful scenery, Albert began to use his self-taught skill to paint postcards, then to sell them at a shilling (5p) each. However, Albert's artistic temperament did not fit in well with the other inmates, who constantly discouraged him, even pouring water over his postcards on occasion. In desperation, he wrote to his mother, who eventually agreed to his return to London, in order to live with her again.

Albert became an outpatient at King's College Hospital, where he received proper occupational therapy for the first time in his life and continued with his mouth painting of postcards. This continued for about three years, until his now-elderly mother could no longer cope. It was decided that he should apply for residence at the Cheshire Home of Le Court, here in **Greatham**. After all the trials and tribulations of his life so far, Le Court must have seemed like some sort of haven to Albert.

Meanwhile, Erich Stegmann, a member of the Mouth and Foot Paintings Artists Association (MFPA), with a gallery situated at nearby Selborne, had heard about this mouth-painter that painted postcards. Albert was enrolled as a student, with a tutor to provide proper art lessons. Albert's career was finally about to take off. However, in those early 1960's, standing at an improvised easel all day caused him a lot of pain and inconvenience and consequently his work suffered.

Fortunately, a local resident and friend of Le Court, Mr Charles Darby, was a skilled engineer and, after careful consideration and lots of measuring, a simple trestle-type support was devised for Albert – literally 'made to measure'. At the same time, the frame was also designed, by the use of cords and pulleys, to allow the adjustment of both large and small canvases to be within easy reach of Albert's mouth-held paintbrush.

Albert Baker at work at his 'made to measure' paint easel.

All this allowed Albert to pursue his chosen career with great success.

Albert became a full member of the Association, giving him financial independence and introducing him to the magic world of travel. In 1963, along with his friend Sam Symons, he attended the MFPA annual Congress in Madrid, over the Whitsun weekend, flying by the most modern airliner of its time, the famous 'Comet', the first ever jet-engined passenger aircraft. On the Sunday, with some spare time on their hands, Albert & Sam could have gone along to see a bull-fight, but in the event, settled on a football match – probably just as exciting, but certainly less bloody!

By 1979, Albert's art was becoming very well known and respected. Three of his paintings were exhibited at the MFPA exhibition at Croydon, and in September of that year he featured in the BBC programme 'In the Picture', a documentary which showed Albert giving three local children a painting lesson. He also opened a three-day exhibition of children's paintings and poems at Petersfield, where he himself donated some of the prizes, including one of his own paintings as 1st-prize in the raffle.

In March of 1981, Albert met and talked to Prince Philip and later his name was drawn in the ballot to see the Royal Wedding procession, from a special position in the courtyard of Buckingham Palace. He always remembered 1981 as one of his 'special years'. In 1984, he was appointed to the board of governors at **Greatham** School, later moving into Longmoor House on Longmoor Road. This had once been one of the village shops, but had been specially adapted to suit Albert's disability and to give him a measure of independence.

Albert was a great favourite with local children and became a great benefactor to them. Towards the end of 1990, he donated £4,000 to **Greatham** Nursery School, in order that an extension to **Greatham** Village Hall could be built as their new home. He timed the presentation of a cheque to coincide with the school's Nativity play, saying *"I didn't want to see it (the Playgroup) closed down, and Christmas seemed a good*

time to give the money".

In 1993, local children put forward Albert's name in a competition run by 'BT Childline', which recognised people's services to children. Albert came second in that competition, and was handed a cheque for £2,000 by the Duchess of Kent. It was no surprise that, at a later date, the same amount of money found its way to **Greatham** Nursery School.

Albert died in 1994 and his life was commemorated at a tree-planting ceremony in June 1995, when a cherry tree was planted in his name, in the vicinity of the Nursery School. Jim Harris of Bordon planted the tree, a great friend of Albert's, while the Rev Bill Day, Rector at that time, blessed the tree at the dedication service. A school barbecue and balloon race was held on the same day, and a collection of £855 was raised to help pay for new toilets at the school. Albert would be pleased that an OFSTED report some years later gave the Village Hall based nursery school a glowing report – *"well equipped and strong in language, literacy, maths, creative and personal development"*.

Albert will long be remembered for his great courage and sense of humour, as well as for being a benefactor to his fellow men. In 1985, as a member of the MFPA, he expressed a wish that the annual £200 donation to Le Court should be used towards an outing for all residents. After Albert's death, it emerged that he had left a large sum of money in his will, to be used for the extension and improvement of **Greatham** School. He was certainly a true friend of local children, and it is to be hoped that they will be able to draw some inspiration from his life, a victory for determination over disability.

Erich Stegmann, who had sought out Albert and his talent on behalf of the MFPA, was never forgotten by Albert. Although the following words are Albert's own, in reference to Stegmann, they sum up Albert's life so well, that it is appropriate to quote them here:

"What more charitable act can you do than restore a man's faith and confidence in himself? In the past, I felt so useless that I thought of doing away with myself. But he gave me the gift of self-respect which I had never known before."

(Most of the Albert Baker story is based upon a biography printed in 'Canvases of Courage' by Marc Alexander, and published on behalf of the MFPA. I am also grateful to Jill Roberts, of the Leonard Cheshire Archive & Library, who supplied me with some 'potted reports' referring to Albert. With the help of others who knew him, and local press cuttings, I hope I have been able to build up a reasonable profile of a courageous and talented man. Ed.)

Albert was a one-time resident at the purpose built Cheshire Home at Le Court.

Chapter Twenty Four
Leonard Cheshire VC, OM, DSO, DFC.

Leonard Cheshire was born in Chester in 1917, but grew up in Oxford, where his father taught at Exeter College. Leonard entered Oxford himself in 1936, to study law and languages. He later joined the University Air Squadron and his instructors soon realised that here was a natural-born flyer. On the outbreak of the 2nd World War, he received his mobilisation papers to join the Royal Air Force (RAF).

In September 1940 he was already Captain of his own aircraft and, on a raid on Cologne in November of that year, his plane was badly damaged by 'flak' (anti-aircraft fire). Despite this, he continued his run and released his bombs. Then, after a 5-hour struggle to control the plane, he brought it and its crew safely back to base. For this valiant effort he was awarded the first of three Distinguished Service Orders (DSO), and he also went on to gain the Distinguished Flying Cross (DFC) on two other occasions.

By April 1943 he had already flown 60 operations and had a best-selling book, 'Bomber Pilot', published. At the tender age of 25 years, he became the youngest Group Captain in the service – a fact that lived on for many years, as he was always affectionately called 'GC' in later life. This led to a 'desk-job', but eventually he voluntarily took a drop of two ranks, in order to continue active service. In fact he went on to command the famous 617 'Dambusters' Squadron, leading every raid personally for 12 months.

In April 1944, his method of marking targets, using red flares, was used in a raid on Munich, acknowledged by Cheshire himself as probably his greatest achievement of the war. His own light 'Mosquito' aircraft led the raid, followed by waves of 'Avro Lancaster' bombers. Reconnaissance aircraft confirmed the next morning that Munich had been devastated, a complete vindication of Cheshire's marking technique.

He continued to lead every Dambuster raid and, on the day after his 27th birthday, it was announced that he was to be awarded the Victoria Cross, the supreme prize for bravery under fire. However, five years of unrelenting war had taken its toll. The former brash and confident Oxford undergraduate found a new inner feeling of deep humility.

His final operation of the war was as an official British observer of the second atomic bombing raid, on the Japanese city of Nagasaki, in August 1945.

The terrible spectacle left its imprint on Cheshire's mind, although he always denied that it was this event which transformed him into a pacifist. Indeed, he recommended that Britain should build a stockpile of these dreadful weapons, as a deterrent to any future war.

Five months after Nagasaki, with the war finally at an end, Leonard left the RAF and returned to the challenges of civilian life. This did not prove easy, but after several minor ventures, he forwarded the idea of co-operative settlements for ex-servicemen and women. These would allow them to support each other and build up their skills, until they could stand upon their own two feet. He founded one such community in Leicestershire in June 1946, but afterwards negotiated the purchase of a larger, more suitable, house in Hampshire. Le Court had already belonged to his uncle, Major-General Arthur Barstow, and was now to be the start of Leonard's final and most famous venture.

After financial problems at the Leicestershire community, he was forced to sell of most of the **Greatham** estate and the venture could have failed almost from the start. It was at this low point that Leonard discovered that a former old soldier, Arthur

Leonard Cheshire

Dykes, was suffering from inoperable cancer at a local hospital. He was shocked to learn that there was hardly any place in 1948 Britain that could provide the necessary accommodation and care that such a person deserved. So he decided to look after Arthur himself, back at Le Court, and set about learning the basic nursing skills that would be required.

Leonard realised he had just found his new mission in life. *"It was so simple and serene and sure,"* he said, *"it made a deep impression upon me."* By the end of that year he was received into the Roman Catholic faith and Le Court began to accept other patients, even those suffering from tuberculosis, still a killer disease in post-war Britain. The community at Le Court gradually grew in size, accepting patients of all ages and with a variety of complaints.

By the end of 1950, the Cheshire Home at Le Court had become a registered charity and, with financial backing from the Carnegie (UK) Trust, plans were put in place to build a completely new estate, specifically designed for both the chronically sick and severely disabled. In fact a lot of the design was based upon the advice of Le Court's own pioneer patients. By now the Ministry of Health had agreed funding and the concept of an all-embracing 'Cheshire Trust' became a reality in March 1952.

Following many years of illness himself and with a failed relationship behind him, in 1956 Leonard met Sue Ryder, who herself had won respect for her post-war work relieving the suffering of concentration camp survivors in Poland. They married in 1959 and embarked on a joint mission to aid sufferers around the world. Both the Cheshire and Sue Ryder Foundations have become beacons, lighting up the lives of many people too ill or disabled to cope by themselves.

Leonard Cheshire was author to another two books, 'The Face of Victory' in 1961 and 'The Light of Many Suns' in 1985. He was awarded the Order of Merit in 1981 and created Baron Cheshire in 1991. His wife Sue was Baroness of Warsaw. Together they had two children, a son and a daughter.

As a poignant epitaph to his story, Leonard Cheshire himself succumbed to a disabling disease and died from Motor Neurone disease on July 31st 1992. His vision of offering choice, opportunity and independence to disabled people is kept alive through the work of the charity that bears his name.

The final chapter in this story came to a close in the autumn of 2000, with the death of Lady Sue Ryder at the age of 77. Although she had lived in Suffolk, Sue Ryder had many local contacts. As well being a frequent visitor to Le Court while her husband was still alive, she had set up her eighth Sue Ryder Home at Bordean House in Langrish and opened a charity shop in Petersfield town centre in 1978. A requiem service was held in St Lawrence's Church, attended by many of those people who had assisted her in her good deeds.

(This short history is based upon 'The story of Leonard Cheshire', a small booklet given to me by Jenny Croucher, Public Relations Officer at Le Court. She kindly entertained me for an hour one warm May afternoon, and also produced many other notes and newspaper cuttings relating to the history of both Leonard Cheshire and the home at Le Court. Ed.)

Pencil drawing of Le Court.

Chapter Twenty Five
The Corytons

George Edward Coryton's parents were John (1773–1843) and Elizabeth (1784–1824) and it would appear that he was raised in Cornwall. His sister Charlotte was a spinster, who started the school at St Mellion, near Saltash, while his brother Granville was Rector of that parish from 1841 to 1875.

George is known to have bought **Greatham's** Manor House from Edward Chawner, son of the late Henry Chawner, in 1883. However, the Kelly's Directory of 1885 still listed G E Coryton esq., JP, as living at 'Lyss Place', out on the Hawkley road in West Liss, while even ten years later, the 1895 entry listed his son Frederick Coryton esq, JP, still resident at Lyss Place. It may well be that Frederick's unmarried daughters, Isolda and Georgiana (or Georgie, as she was more familiarly known) actually went to live at Manor House during this period, although this is pure conjecture on the author's part.

In 1898, major alterations and extensions to Manor House were started under the supervision of Frederick Coryton, with the final building work probably being completed in 1904. However, it is recorded in local newspapers that the 'Coryton family' finally moved to **Greatham**, i.e. the Manor House, in 1900.

Further entries in the Kelly's Directory of Hampshire recorded the details as shown in the centre of this page as 'Lords of the Manor' of **Greatham**:

During Frederick Coryton's time, Manor House was regularly used as the meeting place for the Hampshire Hunt and in fact Frederick was well known as 'Master of the Hampshire Hunt', with his son Augustus serving as secretary from 1920 - 1933 and then again from 1948 - 1959. It can be safely assumed that the letters MFH above indicate 'Master of Fox Hounds'. During long years of service to the community, Frederick also found time to become the founder of **Greatham** Cricket and Football Clubs (1911) and the Liss branch of the British Legion (1919).

Nicholas Houston of Liss, while studying during his educative years at Eggar's School in Alton, carried out a detailed research into the history of Manor House, but puzzled over the hereditary line of the Corytons. On record is the fact that the house was bought by G E Coryton in 1883, and finally sold by A F Coryton in 1971. Many people thus assumed that these two gentlemen were father and son. However, a plaque exists in the house, with the initials 'F C', and it is now apparent that the Victorian improvements and extension to Manor House can be attributed to Frederick Coryton. Thus it may now be concluded that there were *three* generations of Coryton associated with Manor House and not just *two*, as may have been previously thought.

Frederick's son Augustus (born 1892) inherited the manor upon the death of his father. An inscribed tablet in **Greatham Church** celebrates Frederick's life

> "In loving memory of Frederick Coryton. Born at Lyss Place, Hampshire, March 1ˢᵗ 1850, died at Manor House, Greatham, November 12ᵗʰ 1924."
>
> "Lord I have loved the habitation of Thy house: and the place where Thine honour dwelleth."
> (Psalm XXVI, 8)

In 1931, at the age of thirty-nine, Augustus married his wife Violet and the couple moved from the Manor House to Gold's House during the same year. His widowed mother, Augusta, and her two daughters remained at Manor House, but Augustus appears to have returned at some later date, possibly around 1937. By this time Augustus and Violet had three daughters of their own, so it was a simple necessity of swapping residences with his unmarried sisters, Isolda and Georgiana. Isolda remained at Gold's House, while 'Georgie' later moved to live near Oxford.

Augustus Frederick Coryton has always been referred to as the 'last squire' of **Greatham**. He was

1907 – Frederick Coryton esq JP, MFH, of the Manor House
1911 – Frederick Coryton esq JP, of the Manor House
1915 – Frederick Coryton esq JP, of the Manor House
1923 – Frederick Coryton esq JP, of the Manor House
1927 – Augustus Frederick Coryton esq JP, of the Manor House
1931 – Augustus Frederick Coryton esq JP, of the Manor House
1935 – Augustus Frederick Coryton esq JP, of Gold's House
1939 – Capt. Augustus Frederick Coryton JP, of the Manor House

appointed a Justice of the Peace as early as 1927 and served as High Sheriff of Hampshire in 1956. He was active on the Parish Council for many years and was also a churchwarden at **Greatham Church**. He also served as a manager of **Greatham School** from 1930 until 1967.

Captain Coryton, always referred to as Augustus by his family, was better known by his close friends and associates as 'Gus'. He apparently led rather a sad life. He became an alcoholic and drank away much of the family fortune, before finally selling up. He and his wife Violet moved to Goleigh Farm, on the Liss Forest road in early 1971, upon the sale of Manor House to the L'Abri Foundation. Gussy died in 1976 at the age of eighty-four, while Violet outlived him by only another year, passing away at the age of sixty-seven. It is fitting that they lie together in the churchyard at **Greatham**.

They left behind them three daughters, Caroline Julia, Sara Jane and Lavinia Augusta Maude. All three have their baptisms recorded in the Parish Register between the years 1932 - 37. Sara Jane's entry in February 1935 records the family home as Gould's House but by November 1937, as shown by the entry for Lavinia, the Corytons were back as residents of the Manor House. All three sisters were married from Manor House. Sara Jane (aged nineteen) married Christopher 'Hoppy' Twiston Davies in 1954; Julia

(aged twenty-three) married Richard Fisher in 1955; and, finally, Lavinia (also aged nineteen) married Edward Grant-Ives in 1956.

(There is a fascinating footnote to the story of 'Lyss Place', the Coryton's family home at the turn of the last century. In July of 1999, the skeleton of a woman was found at the bottom of an old well on the property. The only clues to her identity were a wedding ring, two hairgrips and the remains of a pair of fur-lined boots. Thanks to the latest DNA research, the body has now been identified as that of Jessica (Jessie) McMahon, who had moved from Portsmouth to Liss during wartime evacuations, and went missing in 1942.

Jessie disappeared one evening after telling her mother she was 'going out for a minute'. She was never seen again, and rumour had it that she may have run away with a Canadian soldier, one of many who were stationed in this area. Local village rumours also gave suspicion that a local farmer's son was somehow implicated in her disappearance. Lakes and ponds all over the locality were dragged in the search for Jessie, but no one thought of checking the well at Lyss Place. Following the recent discovery, a formal inquest recorded an 'open verdict'. Jessie's remains have now been formally buried, but the truth about her death will probably remain a mystery for evermore. Ed.)

Augustus Coryton stands alongside a portrait of his father.

The Coryton family name

A small village in the county of Devon, just to the west of Dartmoor, still bears the name of Coryton and it is from this place that the Greatham branch of the family originated. The name is taken from the Celtic Saint Curig, who lived in the county in the early 6th-century. The Saxon missal of Leofric names it as Curigtown and it is not difficult to see how this later became corrupted into 'Coryton'. After the Norman Conquest, in 1086, the manor of Coryton was given to a family from Normandy, who then took the name 'de Corytone'. The Corytons moved to Pentillie Castle in Cornwall around 1600 and are commemorated by several monuments in the nearby church at St Mellion.

Chapter Twenty Six
Colonel Michael Digby, MBE, 1921 - 1996

Michael and his wife Dorothy, known to all as 'Dot', moved to **Greatham** in 1958, having lived for nine years at Headley. Their bungalow in Snailing Lane lies in the *ecclesiastical* parish of **Greatham** but in the *civil* parish of Hawkley. The postal address has always been named as Liss and, before the new national dialling codes were introduced, the telephone exchange was Blackmoor!

Born near the Thames in Berkshire during 1921, Michael was educated at Bedford School and destined for an Army commission at Sandhurst, until it was forced to close down on the outbreak of war in 1939. Instead he enlisted in the Royal Fusiliers and was eventually commissioned into the Royal Berkshire Regiment. He served in Iraq, North Africa and the Allied landing campaign on Sicily, where he was wounded in a mortar attack in 1943 and had to have his left leg amputated above the knee. It was the mark of the man that Michael returned to active duty on crutches, training recruits at Colchester, ready for their service in the Far East. It was here that Michael met Dot, a fellow officer, who hailed from Hertfordshire, the couple marrying at Colchester in 1944. Having also served at Aldershot and Reading, he was finally invalided out of the Army and went on to form his own

sales company, supplying the catering industry. He was awarded the MBE (Member of the British Empire) for his services to the Home Guard around the early days of the eventual 'Suez crisis' in 1954. For the nine years when the Digbys lived in Headley, Michael was closely associated with the local Theatre Club, Horticultural Society and Royal British Legion. He continued his support of the RBL upon his move south, becoming

Michael Digby photographed by Alec Fry of Liss

a member of the Liss branch and club. He also took great interest in educational matters, serving as a school governor at both Churcher's College, Petersfield, and Liphook's Bohunt Community School.

He served a total of 43 years as Councillor in all tiers of local government. He was Chairman of both Headley and Hawkley Parish Councils, a Hampshire County Councillor and District Councillor for the Hangers Ward of East Hampshire. One of Michael's colleagues on the first ever EHDC was Petersfield councillor, Elsa Bulmer. She paid this warm tribute to him: *"He was a great campaigner and was warmly respected for his hard work and enthusiasm. He always regarded as a great privilege his appointment as the first Chairman of the newly formed district council in 1974."* Michael had never served on the former urban or rural councils, but was the driving force behind the forging together of a unified council from the former Alton and Petersfield districts.

Michael Digby was a tireless campaigner on local issues. Often working behind the scenes, he was a firm hand on the tiller of numerous campaigns and projects. Amongst his many achievements was the creation of the Woolmer Industrial Estate at Bordon and, as Chairman of the Petersfield By-pass action group, saw this come to fruition in 1992. He was also in the forefront of the opposition to plans for the building of a crematorium, either behind the Church in **Greatham,** or south of the Ham Barn roundabout near Liss.

The Woolmer link-road was another battle that Michael fought on behalf of local people, but unfortunately his sudden death at the age of 74 came before either of the above battles ended. It is gratifying to know that both battles were ones that were won in the end, a vivid reminder of Michael's efforts. Both proposed crematoria sites were rejected, and the road that would take through-traffic out of **Greatham** also went ahead. Some way of commemorating his efforts was thought to be appropriate.

The Woolmer link-road was officially opened on what would have been Michael's 76th birthday. That section of road that leads off the roundabout into the village has since been named 'Digby Way', a permanent memorial in his honour. Dot Digby thought this most apt, as the road links the Headley division of the county council with the Hangers ward, both of which Michael represented during his many years of service.

Ray Flack, Chairman of **Greatham** Parish Council at the time of Michael's sad death, wondered how he could ever be replaced, either as a friend or colleague. *"He sat in on every other meeting of the Council, to give members the benefit of his long experience. I believe that it is largely due to his persistence and hard work that the Woolmer link-road is finally going ahead.*

It is truly sad that he should have died just a few months before work is due to start." There can be no argument with that.

Other colleagues were also unstinting in their praise, with such comments as *"fearless campaigner"*, *"never frivolous, but often theatrical"*, and *"man of the people"* amongst many others. Michael is sadly missed by all who knew him, he and Dot had recently celebrated their Golden Wedding anniversary in 1994. He leaves behind him a family of three children and several grandchildren. Dot continues with a busy life, being a very keen gardener, and also studying for a degree with the Open University. For many years previously she was a free-lance reporter, a regular contributor of articles to local newspapers, covering **Greatham** for some 30 years, then later the parishes of Liss, Hawkley and Selborne, until her retirement in 1990.

Chapter Twenty Seven
Heath Harrison, Baronet, JP

Sir Heath Harrison was well known in the County of Hampshire and his home, Le Court at **Greatham,** was certainly one of the most picturesque estates of which this highly favoured county possessed so many. Here, in a perfect sylvan setting, at an altitude of four-hundred feet, with sloping lawns, perfectly kept, lay gardens of refreshing charm, in the care of which Lady Harrison took a deep personal interest. With undulating park-land, surrounded by a mixture of fine forest trees, we had a country picture which could not fail to satisfy the most fastidious lover of nature, whilst the far distant views on a clear day extended across to Hindhead and the South Downs.

Sir Heath was born on October 1st 1857, second son of James and Jane Harrison (nee Heath), and formerly part of a ship-owning business at Liverpool, before retiring in 1893. He was educated at Malvern College and Brasenose College, Oxford, where he subsequently founded some exhibitions, whilst his insight in the cause of education was also expressed by the chair for Organic Chemistry he founded at Liverpool University. He married Mary Adelaide Howard of Colchester on October 2nd 1882, but there were no children of the marriage.

Heath and his elder brother, Frederick James, had been allotted shares in the family business, but Heath never played an active part in running the Company, preferring instead to pursue the life of a country squire. He came into Hampshire in 1893, having purchased Le Court at auction, for the sum of £25,000. He and his wife had previously dwelt at Horton Mount, Eastham, near Chester. In 1897, the spire and belfry were added to the present church of St John the Baptist at **Greatham,** at a cost of £800, contributed by Sir Heath in commemoration of Her late Majesty Queen Victoria's Diamond Jubilee.

The Hants and Sussex News reported the event in the rather flowery manner of the day:

"... devising to perpetuate the remembrance of the glorious Diamond Jubilee of our beloved Queen, he added a spire to the church, and truly it can be said that few, if any, memorials of the great historic event could be more seemly or worthy."

The main edifice (of stone in the decorated style) had been built in 1875, at a cost of £5,000. It was in 1907 that the fine oak lych-gate was erected, also the gift of Sir Heath and Lady Harrison, visible evidence of what was to be over 40 years of financial support to the church. A stone tablet inside the church commemorates the addition of the spire and belfry in his name, while the lych-gate itself is inscribed in similar fashion at its entrance, with Heath's and Mary's initials carved on its exit side.

During many years, Sir Heath occupied a position in the public life of the County. He was a Justice of the Peace (JP) for Hants, a County Councillor from 1901-1912, High Sheriff in 1916 and also a County Alderman between 1913-1927, taking a keen interest in the details of local government. He was created 1st Baronet in 1917. Whilst far beyond the boundaries of his own shire, his name is still widely known and greatly respected for the work he accomplished for the permanent stability and extension of the Union Jack Club, London, an Institution of incalculable benefit for our sailors and soldiers.

Heath was a very wealthy man and, unbeknown to all but a privileged few, he shared his great wealth, remaining a generous philanthropist for all his life. Among his most notable gifts was £25,000 to Liverpool's Anglican Cathedral. As well as giving financially to Winchester and Portsmouth Cathedrals, an endless list of donations to churches, schools, universities, lifeboats and other charities was his custom. He stressed however, on being asked for a contribution, that his gift should remain anonymous. It was only after his death that the full extent of his generosity was revealed by the glowing obituaries published at the time.

In 1931, Sir Heath donated a new lifeboat to the RNLI station at Ramsey, in the Isle of Man, and it was named the 'Lady Harrison' in respect of his good wife. Following his death in 1934, his widow herself donated another lifeboat, this time to the station at Port St Mary, also on the Isle of Man. This boat was inevitably named, after the man himself, the 'Sir Heath Harrison'.

The acreage of Le Court was about 600, including a farm that received Sir Heath's personal supervision, he was especially interested in the breeding of Jersey cattle. He purchased Le Court from Mrs Sandford, who had lived there for about nine years, and who had bought it from Mr Foster, who rebuilt the nine-bedroomed house in 1865. The previous owner had been Mr William Eldridge Butler, the whole estate being comprised within the three parishes of **Greatham,** Empshott and Selborne.

Sir Heath's tastes as an art patron were well revealed within his home, where there were many choice examples from the brushes of well-known masters. On the staircase was a large oil, representing the 'Procession of Our Lady of Boulogne' by Frith, whilst in the dining-room were examples of the work of Peter Graham, J Farquharson, Vicat Cole, WL Wylie (an Academy exhibit) and F J Herring. This apartment was adorned with a decorated ceiling, one of various improvements to be effected after Sir Heath's acquisition of the property.

Of course, this is only making a passing reference to some of the many beautiful treasures with which Sir Heath and Lady Harrison surrounded themselves and a volume could be filled if one attempted to describe them in detail. A very pleasing and interesting feature of the interior of the house, for example, was the set of ten beautiful pillars in the Hall, which were placed there by Mr Foster.

It has been said that busy lives are happy lives and every day, indeed almost every hour, brought Sir Heath some sort of responsible public duty. Yet he still found occasional leisure time for all kinds of open-air exercise and recreation.

The famous water-front at Liverpool - home of the Harrison Line and birthplace of the author.

(The above is mainly based upon 'A recent history of Hampshire, Wiltshire and Dorset' by P Campion, and is undated. I am also grateful to Graeme Cubbin of Merseyside, who was able to supply some further details. Sir Heath died on May 16th 1934, followed by Lady Mary Harrison in 1938, and both are buried in **Greatham** *Churchyard. Ed.)*

Postscript

By an amazing coincidence, I was researching another history, this time of the Army Apprentices' College at Arborfield, when I came across an article in *The Craftsman* magazine of 1979, giving details about the Harrison Line! At that time, it was stated that *"the Harrison Line is one of the oldest, and one of the few remaining private ship-owning firms in the United Kingdom, having started with little brigs in the wine trade 150 or so years ago"*. This would give a starting date of around 1830 and the full title of the firm was *"Thos & Jas (Thomas and James) Harrison Ltd, Liverpool"*. The tie-in between the two histories lies in the fact that the Harrison Line, over a long period of time, had actually had built for them a total of five ships that went by the name *"Craftsman"*.

Chapter Twenty Eight
The Shotter Family

*(This chapter in the history came to me in quite a round about way! I was already retired from my civil service post at Bordon, but visiting the Camp on occasion to keep up with the news and in touch with old friends. The lady who used to clean my office, Sylvia Lucas, spotted me one day and remarked that a friend of hers had in her possession a 'small book about **Greatham**'. Her friend, Janet Robson, was a distant relative of the author. I was eventually to receive a copy of this booklet and there was quite a lot in it that referred to the village. It is essentially a potted history of the Shotter family, some of whom were resident in the village many years ago. Ronald George Shotter, nephew of Emily wrote it, and I have included his tale almost verbatim, only modifying where I thought necessary. Ronald, who was born in 1929, has lived for many years in Croydon, and gave his permission for me to add his tale to the many others in this history. I am sure that it will add further insight into the lives of people associated with **Greatham** during the first half of the 20th century. Ed.)*

Emily Shotter, her Sisters and Brothers

Emily Shotter was born in the Hampshire village of **Greatham**, adjoining the parish of Selborne, of the Reverend Gilbert White fame. She was the youngest of a family of ten children, whose names appear below:

James (or 'Jim'), 1878-1944; Priscilla ('Dilly), 1880-1968; Gowan, 1882-1946; William, 1887-1956; George (1888-1970); John Henry ('Jack'), 1890-1980; Kate, 1891-1969; Lucy Elizabeth, 1895-1948; Albert Edward ('Bert'), 1897-1978 and Emily, 1903-1984.

Emily herself never married, but enjoyed being 'Aunty' to the following nieces and nephews, listed along with their parents' names:

Jim, Arthur ('Jack'), Charles, Gowan, Lily and Harry (who died young), all born to Jim and Louie Shotter; William, only son of William Shotter and his first wife, Louisa (nee Richards); Olive, Jack and Gordon, born to Kate and Charles Sayers; Phyllis, only daughter of Lucy and Sydney Pearce; Ronald George (that's me)

and Margaret Rose, born to Albert Shotter and Rose Elizabeth (nee Scruton).

Priscilla married a man named Mark Money, but they had no children, while George, Gowan, Jack and Emily Shotter remained single all their lives.

Emily Shotter's forbears lie buried in the churchyards of both the old and new churches in **Greatham**, their graves dating back through the 18th and 19th centuries. Her grandfather, George John Shotter (1817-93), had been employed in the drying of hops, gathered from the fields along the road to Selborne. Her father, William, had married Sarah Rance of Kingsbury, London, in 1877, whilst working in the area as a farm labourer. Emily was to lead a rural existence all her life, centred mainly on farming – or at least the daily running of farming households. She was born, and lived her first few years, in a cottage opposite the new church, not far away from the old, now ruined church. Copies of a large sepia-tinted family group photograph, taken around 1906 and showing the cottage, were given to all her nieces and nephews. Several copies are known still to exist. Incidentally, all the brothers and sisters, excepting Jim and Dilly, are present and the very old lady sitting at the front is my great-grandmother.
(This would be Swain's, located at the top of Church Lane. Ed.)

In those days, children left school at 12 years old. I know for certain that John Henry did, as did Albert Edward, my father, but I'm not too sure about Emily. At any rate, the older boys took up at work. Gowan became a postman, having to walk the 3 miles to Liss before he could begin his daily round; George did building work and was also employed at Selborne quarry; John Henry became a proficient gardener at Lee Court (sic), now a Cheshire Home.

The whole family (except possibly Jim) moved to Manger's Farm, East Liss, sometime prior to World War I, then on to a larger farm after only a very short time. Manger's Farm could be seen from the train, over on the right hand side, as it left Liss Station in the direction of Liphook. The larger farm was called Coombeland's, near the West Sussex villages of Milland and Rogate, just across the border from Hampshire. Emily's father had died in 1912 and this appears to have been before the second move. A medical (death?) certificate, signed

by Dr Cory of Liss and dated January 1913, was issued to John Henry, showing his address as Manger's Farm.

Around the start of the war, Kate and Dilly had already moved from home, taking up residential domestic work in various large houses. Some of these were in London, as shown by a collection of picture postcards. Jim and William had both married and were living in their respective new homes when, in 1917, Lucy also got married. Prior to that, she had worked at the old Churcher's College in Petersfield. These events led to a much-reduced family to look after the farm.

During the war, it was inevitable that Jack, Gowan and William should 'join up' into the Army. Both Jack (Royal Engineers) and Gowan (Gloucester Regiment) were injured in France and, after hospital treatment, were sent back home. Fortunately, they recovered enough to be able to cope with the hard work still required on the farm. This freed my father to join the Royal Marines in 1918 and he continued serving with them for a full 21 years.

Jack's 'injury' is well worth a mention here, as basically it was also a miraculous escape from death. He was in a dugout near Bethune in France, when a German shell came right through the roof before exploding. Everyone except Jack was killed outright. He was saved by a heavy table that upturned and protected him from the blast. The same table trapped and broke his leg but at least he lived to tell the tale.

Gowan began a milk round, operating from a pony and trap, but gave this up when the Milk Marketing Board was set up in the 1930s. Emily's mother died in 1931, leaving only Emily, George, Gowan and Jack to run the farm. This they did up until 1937, during which time Margaret and I were taken there on several visits, but we can only vaguely remember a few things about the farm. I was christened at Milland Church; no doubt a lot of these relatives were present.

One family story, often retold, concerns a swarm of bees that decided to settle down in the dog kennel. The dog was on its chain, unable to get away, and died from the stings. Gowan, who tried to rescue it, received about 80 stings himself and ended up in hospital. Apparently everyone else got stung that day, including my mother Rose, who just happened to be an unfortunate visitor! That farm received its fair share of visitors, mainly family of course, amongst whom I might mention were my cousins Olive, Jack and Gordon Sayers and William 'Billy' Shotter.

In 1937, the 'famous four' took up temporary residence at Rook's Farm, in **Greatham**. As far as I can remember, it was fairly small, with only one meadow. Our family stayed there on a short holiday once. There was a shepherd's crook hanging on the bedroom wall that I, for some reason, found rather 'spooky'. As I was only about nine at the time, I guess my mind invented a few things of its own! A coloured photograph of this farmhouse, and of the one mentioned next, appeared in the local Petersfield newspaper, together with an article on **Greatham**, earlier this year (1999).

(This article was in the Petersfield Post and marked the beginnings of my research into this whole 'history of Greatham'. Ed.)

In 1938, the four began calling themselves 'Shotter Brothers', a term which included Emily, but was only to be used for trading purposes. They also moved to Deal Farm, just a short distance northwards along the main road. This farmhouse, an oak-beamed 17th-century building, had farmlands of about 56 acres. It was a mixed farm, run on completely old-fashioned lines. Nowadays, this would be termed 'organic' and be well back in fashion! They did not allow tractors in the fields, as this *'compacted the soil underneath the ploughed top nine inches'*. There was no electric, gas or mains-supplied water.

'Shotter Brothers' are mentioned as 'Farmers, Deal Farm' in the 1939 edition of Kelly's Directory. Ed.)

The livestock included eight or nine cows and heifers; three or four pigs, including a boar; around 150 free-range chickens, eight or nine ducks, complete with pond, and a couple of guinea fowl; two working horses; an English sheep-dog 'Doone', who lived outdoors in a barrel for a kennel; a terrier 'Peter', who lived indoors and was George's pet; about eight or nine outdoor cats, two ferrets, up to 14 hives of bees; plus the young of all these animals. The crops grown were hay, oats, wheat, mangolds, turnips, swedes and potatoes. Clover was used as an 'undercrop'; there was a permanent grass pasture and a 1-acre orchard with well-spaced trees, where chickens, calves and pigs were free to roam. The river Rother ran through the farm, separating one rather sandy field from all the others, which were prone to clay. These created some lush areas and some true marsh, with rushes, alders and much wildlife.

During August and early September 1939, my mother and father (Rose and Albert), sister Margaret and I, stayed at Deal Farm on holiday. In those days of late summer, we all helped to gather in the corn, with father on top of the rick. On one such occasion, from around the corner of a large shed appeared the village postman, who handed Albert a telegram with the message *'Report back to barracks'*. One must recall here that he had only just retired after 21 years in the Royal Marines. A day or two later, on September 3rd, war was declared and Aunt Emily announced that we had better stay on, in father's absence. That's how I came to live with my aunt and three uncles in **Greatham** for the whole five years of the war. After a few weeks, mother and Margaret moved out, taking accommodation in a large house which formed part of the Westminster Bank in Petersfield, where mother

helped out with housework and did voluntary work in a forces canteen.

One morning, soon after the beginning of the war, I was in bed when I was violently shaken and I heard Emily shout out *"They're bombing the village"*. A string of bombs fell just to one side of the main road, from the farm almost to the church. Strangely enough, not one of them exploded; the vibration I had felt was due solely to their impact. One bomb fell in a pond just opposite the school, tearing a branch off an overhanging oak tree. So that was my first memorable experience as an evacuee!

During the war, work continued on the farm much as before, in the 'old-fashioned' way, despite visits and advice from *'whippersnappers from the Ministry'*. Sacks of super-phosphate were left to rot in the barn, rather than *'ruin the soil'*. **Greatham** was (and remains) close to Longmoor Royal Engineers Army Camp, so the bombing must have been intended for that target. One day, Emily cycled to East Liss via the Liss Forest Road, which branches off the main road at **Greatham** church. She had to cross the military railway track and, at that instant, a German plane machine-gunned the track. Fortunately, the bullets missed Emily, who carried on calmly with her pedalling. Another war connection I remember was that a field on the far side of the river was cut in two by wooden stakes and rolls of barbed wire, intended to slow down an invasion, but which merely rendered half a field out of bounds.

I'd like to mention a little about the individual characters of my aunt and uncles. Bear in mind that I lived with them for over five years, so had an intimate knowledge of their ways and means, which were largely Edwardian, or even Victorian by nature.

George, the eldest of the four, was of slighter build than his brothers. He had a lightly coloured moustache and his features showed the ruddiness of his outdoor occupation, his face lined with numerous small red veins. He was slightly hunched and, although some would term him 'wiry', he was very strong in those muscles needed for heavy farm work. He always wore a wide black leather band on his wrist, presumably to correct some injury. He was definitely 'the boss', although rather quiet and softly spoken, occasionally joking and joining in the laughter at a funny story or incident.

I never heard him argue but, when it came to deciding what or what not to do on the farm, his word was final. Apart from engaging in the general farm work, he specialised in ploughing by horse, expertly thatching corn and hayricks and looking after the pigs. This could mean him happily rising from his warm bed in the middle of the night if a sow was giving birth. He also had many beehives, but hardly ever got stung, which wouldn't have worried him anyway. He had his own pet dog called Peter.

George was very religious; he attended church almost every Sunday, knelt down to offer his prayers every night, and never allowed any work to be done on a Sunday, other than seeing to the animals. Hay or other crops would be left ungathered, it made no difference to him. He made sure I attended Sunday-school at the beginning when I was ten, until I was taken on by the church choir, which meant attending twice on Sundays and once during the week for choir practice. We would also sing at weddings and funerals, for which we received a shilling piece (5p). When I was big enough, I was given the job of pumping air for the organ, played by Mr William 'Bill' Redman.

(See the Redman's story elsewhere in this history. Ed.)

George believed in the Bible literally. One day I had asked him about the fossils being dug up from Selborne quarry, noted for yielding 'ammonites' almost as big as cartwheels. *'Aren't they millions of years old?'*, I must have asked him. *'No'*, he replied, *'the Flood came up to there and wiped out all previous life'*. To substantiate this he quoted a hill near Selborne, which he called 'Noah Hill'. He also informed me that stones grew in the soil, since every time he cleared them away, they would only come back the following year.

Both George and his brother Jack were good shots, so every now and again a rabbit would be brought home *'for the pot'*. I'll also mention that these two, though not Gowan, almost always wore blue denim working jackets, long before this material became so fashionable in the sixties. The only time this rule was broken was for special occasions, when a dark suit became *de rigeur*. The denim jackets were referred to as *'slops'*.

Jack is the next uncle on my list. To start with he was heavily built, though not what you'd call fat, and immensely strong. His old war-injured leg, for which he received a pension of *'eight bob'* (40p) a week, still caused him pain, but it didn't prevent him from doing the heaviest of the farm work. He had a large round face, like his mother's, and had rough, seemingly permanent chapped hands. These always became worse in the winter months and appeared to be set into the hand-milking position. Although of a religious nature, I can't remember him ever going to church or saying his prayers.

Leaving school at twelve, he had built up an amazingly vast knowledge of countryside lore and matters. On most Sunday afternoons, he would take me on long walks along byways in all directions. His favourite walk was towards Selborne, where we would ascend the 'Zig-zag', visit the wishing-well and go to the churchyard, with its venerable yew-tree, described in ages past by Gilbert White. Another walk would take us along a track from Liss Forest, past a large house with a lake, emerging on the Longmoor Road.

During these walks, and also when on the farm, he could identify and talk about any of the flora and fauna encountered, as well as pointing out obscure animal tracks. He couldn't give you their Latin names, these meant nothing to him, but he knew where to find little treasures. For example, the white-flowered sweet violets that grew on a bank near **Greatham** church, cranberries and *'herts'*. On one occasion, he showed me some stag-beetle larvae infesting an old oak stump that he was using for firewood.

Two mornings a week he gardened at **Greatham** rectory, using skills acquired at Lee Court, which I have previously mentioned. For the first few years of the war (World War II), the vicar here was Reverend Marks. In front of his rectory was an extensive lawn, separated from the main road by a wall, with a ditch on the outside. The lawn was decorated by a remarkable tulip tree growing upon it. On some summer evenings, after choir practice, a few of us boys went along to play *'tenny quoits'* (a type of tennis) on the lawn, under the shade of the tree. Dear Mrs Marks would then bring out refreshments, which could consist of a bowl of raspberries and cream, washed down with home-made lemonade.

When Rev Marks died, Mrs Marks gave Jack a pile of books. Handed on to me was Webster's Dictionary which, as in the Bob Hope and Bing Crosby song, was *'morocco bound'*. This is still a favourite possession, which inside contains the signature of Heath Harrison, who lived at Lee Court. Another book became a turning point in my life. It was a slim volume, entitled 'Lecture notes in Chemistry', and published by Blackie in about 1906. It included alternating blank pages for one's own notes, which started me off on the chemistry pathway for the rest of my schooldays and working life. One other thing I'd like to add about Uncle Jack was that he had a deep suspicion of life outside of his immediate surroundings. He never kept up with a changing world, especially the ever-increasing cost of living.

Gowan, although also once a powerful man, suffered badly and permanently from his war wounds. He still had shrapnel inside him and would spend long periods, huddled in an old padded chair next to the kitchen fire. He had a drawn face and smoked an old clay pipe, progressively shortened by breakage over the years. He had the appearance of the archetypal 'rustic' about him, and although the kindest of persons, we children were always slightly scared of him.

Gowan had a 'lady friend' called Alice, who worked in one of the big houses up at Hillbrow, and who came to tea just about every Sunday. After their meal, they would walk to the bus stop to catch the

Alton to Petersfield service, which in those days went via Hillbrow. They would always be arm-in-arm, with Gowan dressed in his best suit. Alice was such a refined type, addressing him as 'dear boy', that with Gowan's rugged looks, they truly made an incongruous couple. I never did establish their precise relationship but I have always assumed that they would have married, had it not been for Gowan's illness and wounds. I should add that, between his bouts of illness, he worked on the farm just as industriously as his brothers did. He died in 1946 and is buried in **Greatham** churchyard.

Emily is the last of the quartet that constituted the 'Shotter Brothers'.

Bear in mind that I lived with her continuously while she aged from 35 to 41 years, while I myself grew up from 10 to age 16, having stayed at the farm from 1939 to the spring of 1945, during the whole of World War II. I thus got to know her extremely well and she acted virtually as a mother to me.

To begin with, she was fairly tall, of average build, neither too slim nor overweight. She had a fine figure, a kind face and noticeably strong arms, no doubt a requirement for all of the tasks she had to perform. I have no doubt that people of her age group would have considered her as 'attractive'. Whether or not she had offers of marriage in her younger days, I don't know; neither do I know whether she chose willingly to keep house for, and look after, her three brothers after their mother's death, until they too ended their days. The fact of the matter is that she **did** devote the bulk of her life to her brothers.

Her chief function was to look after the farmhouse – no mean feat in itself. Cooking was achieved on an old-fashioned black-leaded stove, heated mainly by wood with a little assistance from coal. There could be as many as 13 to the traditional Sunday lunch and, if one remembers that every drop of water had to be fetched from the deep well, food preparation was quite an exacting task. In addition, she looked after the dairy produce. Milk would be placed in large bowls and the cream, which then rose to the top, was collected and churned into butter by hand once very week. She did all the household work and cycled regularly to the few shops and post office nearby for provisions. She always enjoyed helping out with the haymaking and harvesting in the autumn.

Another of her regular tasks, traditionally the woman's role, was feeding the chickens and ducks, then collecting their eggs, some of which were preserved in waterglass. Pickling, preserving, jam and winemaking occupied any of her 'spare' time. Jack would tend to the kitchen garden, providing her with an abundance of fruit and vegetables in season. There seemed to be plenty of apples available most of the year and Emily

had the job of sorting and storing them as necessary. Occasionally, she would accompany Jack, the pair riding a couple of old upright bicycles, on visits to their two aunts, Ada and Annie. These were her mother's sisters, the latter was married and living a fair distance away at Medstead, near Alton.

Emily was very religious, one would say almost puritanical, believing that any wrongdoing should be written down in a book. This applied especially to me! However, she rarely attended church, probably because she was extremely busy on Sundays preparing the dinner. This was inevitably eaten at 12.30 p.m. both Sunday and during the week. I would say that she was a very strict type, again as far as I was concerned. For instance, I had to be in by nine, as bedtime came just after the 9 o'clock news. This was brought to us by the only concession to modern technology – a portable wireless (radio) that had to have its accumulator (battery) charged at the local garage from time to time.

Also, I was discouraged from bringing home any friends. These counted as strangers, generally distrusted on the farm at any rate, who could be finding out about the family's business. I must add that we all got on well together, I was fairly treated and well looked after. Emily herself was treated with deference by her brothers and any visiting relatives. This particularly applied to her cooking, which was highly praised; indeed, it did have that 'farmhouse quality' that has largely vanished nowadays.

If one looks at the house from the road, Emily's bedroom was the one with the upstairs window, just to the right of the front door. Beyond that was a smaller room, used as an apple store. Behind the upper window to the left of the front door was a huge bedroom, in which my uncles and myself all slept, in beds that were scattered round the walls. This caused many visitors

Emily Shotter was born in one of the three original Swain's cottages.

*Notice of Auction
of Deal Farm
in October 1950*

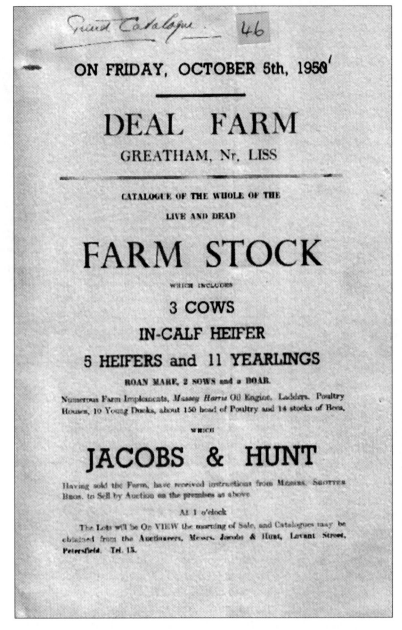

Print Catalogue 46

ON FRIDAY, OCTOBER 5th, 1950

DEAL FARM

GREATHAM, Nr, LISS

CATALOGUE OF THE WHOLE OF THE

LIVE AND DEAD

FARM STOCK

WHICH INCLUDES

3 COWS

IN-CALF HEIFER

5 HEIFERS and 11 YEARLINGS

ROAN MARE, 2 SOWS and a BOAR.

Numerous Farm Implements, Massey Harris Oil Engine, Ladders, Poultry Houses, 19 Young Ducks, about 150 head of Poultry and 14 stocks of Bees.

WHICH

JACOBS & HUNT

Having sold the Farm, have received instructions from Messrs. Shotter Bros. to Sell by Auction on the premises as above.

At 1 o'clock

The Lots will be On VIEW the morning of Sale, and Catalogues may be obtained from the Auctioneers, Messrs. Jacobs & Hunt, Levant Street, Petersfield. Tel. 15.

Notice of Auction of Deal Farm in October 1950

as a minor public school and only 17 scholarships were awarded each year; the other boys, some boarders, were paid for by their parents. At the start, I knew nothing about such schools and hadn't had a 'prep-school' tuition in such subjects as science and Latin. But I learned pretty quickly – I had to!

By the time I left this school, due to the war ending, I had come top in Chemistry exams every year and done quite well at Latin. I had started in August 1940 (the school stayed open during holidays) and, for the first term, used to walk into Petersfield to have mid-day dinner with my aunt and uncle, Lucy and Sid, along with my cousin Phyllis. They lived in a charming green square called 'The Spain'. Phyllis still lives in the town, but further along Borough Road. After that, Emily made sandwiches for me, except when I went to the British Restaurant, a wartime establishment where a good meal could be had for a shilling (5p). Several other pupils and myself had to travel to and from school on the hourly bus. Incidentally, my uncles used the appearance of the 12 o'clock bus, coming down the hill past 'The Queen' pub as a clock; it was a signal to stop work in the fields and get home for dinner.

to liken it to a hospital ward! It was freezing cold in winter, so ice would often form on the inside of the window. To the rear of this room was a small bedroom, reserved for visitors.

Just a few words now about the fifth inhabitant – myself! For the first year, I attended the village school, which had three classrooms and teachers. This meant that several age groups were taught in one class. I was in Miss Perry's class and was amazed to find that I came top in some exams, as I had been near the bottom in my home-town school in Joseph Street, Gosport. I was dully entered for the 'scholarship', the equivalent of the 11-plus. This I passed and found that I was to be taken on as a 'day boy' at Churcher's College in Petersfield, of which I had never heard. It is described

Scholarship boys had their season tickets paid for, and their books loaned, by Hampshire County Council at Winchester. By the start of summer term 1945, the war had virtually ended, so I moved back to my parents at Gosport, travelling by train every day, including Saturdays, to Petersfield. However, the Council now refused to pay my fares, which proved very expensive for my father. When I told the headmaster, Mr Bill Hoggarth, without hesitation he paid for the season ticket out of a special fund.

Amongst the many friends I made during the Greatham years were Derek Turner of The Mount, Blackmoor, and Clive Adlam of Blackmoor School

House, where his father was headmaster. Unfortunately, Derek died from 'polio' when he was only 21, a budding architect working for Crawley 'new town' and about to be married.

There now follows a list of wartime visitors to Deal Farm, to the best of my memory. Apologies for any omissions:

Alice Morling – aforementioned 'lady friend' of Gowan

Priscilla 'Dilly' Money of Rake, where she was school cook

Her boy evacuee, with whom we played cricket in the orchard

Kate & Charles Sayers and my cousins Olive, Jack & Gordon; Jack enlisted in the Army and was sent to Burma, while Gordon died during the war, aged 15; the family lived at Cowfold, Horsham, Sussex

Lucy & Sydney Pearce, a printer working for Childs, publishers of the local Petersfield newspaper

Their daughter, my cousin Phyllis, who enlisted as a munitions worker – once or twice she brought along her Army friend

William Shotter and his second wife, Nell, with cousin William; the elder William was a farm bailiff at Billingshurst, Sussex, while the younger went off to join the Navy

Jim Shotter (Emily's brother) and cousins Lily and Arthur (Jack); Lily joined up into the WRAF; Jack was married to Nora, while their children John & Janet were about my age; they lived at Cobham, Surrey; John, now married himself, to Wendy, still lives in Cobham

Albert & Rose Shotter, my father & mother, along with my sister Margaret; we came from Gosport, where Margaret still lives; Albert had re-joined the Royal Marines and was stationed with the Fleet Air Arm, HMS Daedalus at Lee-on-Solent, only a couple of biking miles away from home.

Among several non-relatives who came to see us from the village, I'll just mention two: One was Reverend Biddlecombe, who had succeeded Wilfred Marks; he painted a fine watercolour of Deal Farm, which Emily personally handed on to me and is still treasured; the other visitor was Captain Coryton (ret'd), who lived at the Manor House, and who held an annual cricket match in one of his fields; he made a point of walking every footpath in Greatham once a year at least, in order to keep them open.

When Emily fell ill with appendicitis, her sister Kate stayed with her for about a fortnight, as Emily refused to go into hospital. Without an operation, she almost died, but made a miraculous recovery, no doubt thanks to the efforts of Kate and Dr Cory of Liss. I remember the exact date when she started to recover – it was '4/4/44', April 4th 1944. Emily's brother Jim was another who came and stayed, probably for most of the summer of 1942. He had a long spell in hospital with severe thrombosis, so came to the farm to recuperate. Although still suffering some pain, he redecorated the outside of the farmhouse. The walls were cream and the woodwork green – the colours depicted in my watercolour.

I left the farm in 1945, paying only occasional day visits thereafter. Gowan died in 1946, so George and Jack found the work increasingly difficult. The farm was eventually sold in 1952, fetching £5,000 plus a small sum for the livestock and deadstock. After a spell with their sister Dilly at Rake, they finally moved to West Mark Bungalow, just inside the Hampshire border along the A272 Petersfield to Midhurst road. They had a meadow there and attempted a little farming with a few cows and other livestock. But, when George died in 1970, actual farming was then abandoned. Emily and Jack lived on there until 1978, when Emily had a stroke that caused her to become blind. By now, Jack had also become very decrepit and they both finished their days in a nursing home at Forestside, Sussex. I am happy to say that here they were frequently visited by many of their relatives.

(I was eventually able to make contact with Ronald Shotter and he kindly let me borrow both the family photograph c1906 and a copy of the auction notice issued for the sale of Deal Farm stock in the early 1950s. Ronald's early interest in chemistry, as mentioned in this story, evidently paid off, because he went on to become Dr R G Shotter, PhD. Referring to the photograph, those standing from left to right at the back are Kate, unknown, George, William, Gowan, Jack and Lucy. In the middle row, again left to right, are Sarah (Ronald's grandmother), Bert (Ronald's father), his great-grandmother Shotter, unknown boy, and William (Ronald's grandfather). The young girl at the front is Emily. Ed.)

Chapter Twenty Nine
Henry Press Wright, MA

Henry Wright was born in India in 1815. He entered Durham University in 1833, winning the Essay Prize in 1836. In that same year he moved to Peterhouse College, Cambridge, gaining a Gisborn Scholarship in 1838 as well as becoming a Classics Prizeman. He was ordained as a Deacon in 1841 and became Curate of Croscombe, Somerset. Awarded his BA in 1842, he was also ordained Priest and designated as the Curate of St Peters, Frome Selwood, the same year. In 1843, he married Miss Anne Nalder (it was the Nalder family who later purchased the incumbency of **Greatham** in 1882).

Moving to Yorkshire in 1843, he acted first as Curate at Guisley, in what was then the district of West Riding, and then became Curate of St Mary's, Quarry Hill, Leeds in 1845. Appointed Chaplain to the Forces of the Ionian Islands between 1846 and 1853, he then became a fully commissioned Chaplain. Going on to become Principal Chaplain to the Forces of the Crimea 1854-56, he was awarded Crimean medals and the Turkish medal.

He went on to serve as Chaplain to the British garrison at Canterbury in 1857 and remained Principal Chaplain to the Forces, with the rank of Colonel, until 1861, when he was released from duty but remained on the seconded list.

He gained his MA in 1861 and again served overseas, as Archdeacon of British Colombia, from 1861 until 1866. He returned to England, carrying out garrison work at Gosport and shortly afterwards at Portsmouth. Here he worked tirelessly for 10 years to restore the Garrison Church, before retiring from his Chaplain's duties in 1876.

Returning to Canada, he then took up duties as Archdeacon of Vancouver Island and Canon of Christ Church Cathedral, between 1876 and 1880. He returned to England for the last time in 1880 as Rector of **Greatham,** serving the parish with distinction until his death in 1892. His wife, Anne, with whom he had eight children, had died in 1880. Henry later re-married, but is buried in the old churchyard of **Greatham** alongside his first wife. He was a prolific writer, the author of some 14 books, as well as numerous articles, published letters and papers.

(I was able to speak with Elsie after being invited to join her at Helen and Tim Gould's house in early June 1999. Elsie not only furnished me with her personal memories, but put me right on a few other facts, for which I was most grateful. Elsie was also able to provide me with references to the Women's Institute and Senior Citizens organisations within **Greatham***. Ed.)*

I, _____ wishing to become a member of the _____Women's Institute, in the County of_____ promise to pay to the Treasurer of the Institute the sum of Two Shillings yearly while I continue a member. I also promise to keep the Rules and Bye-Laws of the Institute, and all Rules and Regulations made for Women's Institutes by the National Federation of Women's Institutes.

Member's Name *Mrs Lacy*
Date of joining *Jan: 27 1942*
Secretary of W.I. *Mrs Barchard*
Address of County Secretary_____
66A High St Winchester

Temporary Address of National Federation:
PUDDEPHAT'S FARM, MARKYATE, Herts.

National Federation of Women's Institutes.

MEMBERSHIP CARD

"For Home and Country."

Greatham

WOMEN'S INSTITUTE,

Hants

County Federation of Women's Institutes.

The main purpose of the Institute is to improve and develop conditions of rural life.

Chapter Thirty
Elsie Collins

Winifred Elsie Lacey was born on September 16th 1925, the eldest of three sisters, at 'Robin's', down towards the bottom of Church Lane, **Greatham.** The house is now called 'Pilgrim's Way'. All three girls were baptised at **Greatham Church** between the years 1925-1929.

Their mother was born Winifred Edith Osgood (1902–1976) at East Tisted, while her father, Leonard John 'Jack' Lacey (1899–1965), came from Hawkley. Upon leaving school, Jack worked for Augustus Coryton for some 39 years, before leaving to work in Hertfordshire in 1952. During that time, he had also served, and been wounded, in France during the 1st World War, seeing service with three different regiments – the Hampshire Yeomanry, the Royal Wiltshire and South Lancashire Regiment.

When Jack died, the couple had been living back in **Greatham**, at Baker's Field, for about a year and Elsie's mother remained there until her death 11 years later. The Laceys are buried together in the churchyard. Both had been much loved and well-respected members of the local community, being actively associated with many organisations.

Along with her two sisters, Phyllis Joan and Hazel Grace, Elsie and the family moved into Gold's Cottage, alongside Gold's Farm, around 1931. Jack Lacey's work for Captain Coryton was as a carter, while his wife worked as a 'domestic' at both the Manor House and Gold's Farm. Starting at **Greatham School**, Elsie would have stayed on, as was then the custom, until the age of 15, but the outbreak of War in 1939 meant that she left a year early. The headmaster during Elsie's school days was Mr. Charles Wain.

Upon leaving school, Elsie went to work at Highfield, in Hatch Lane, Liss, as a 'between maid' for Colonel & Mrs. Coates. She went on to become a cook for the household, meeting James 'Jim' Martin Collins, who also worked there, in his capacity as garden boy. For a few short months at the end of the War, Elsie went to work as a manager's maid at Ditcham Park, near Harting, which had become a British Society Sailor's Hostel. In August 1944, when the Hostel closed, she continued working then as a hospital ward maid at Wenham Holt, a nursing home up on the 'old' A3, near Rake.

Jim was called up into 'The Guards' in 1944 and went out to serve in Palestine during the 'troubles', which preceded the establishment of the Jewish State of Israel. Jim was 'demobbed' in 1947 and, on his return home, he first went to work as a forester for his grandfather, at Harting Coombe. Elsie left Wenham Holt in August 1949 and, on September 10th of that year, she and Jim Collins were married at **Greatham Church.**

The wedding service was conducted by Canon Barlow-Poole of Liphook, as Reverend Tyler was away on holiday at the time. Elsie can remember that she wore a very smart blue check suit that day, with navy blue accessories, and carried a sheaf of pink & white carnations. This was a time when 'the New Look', with its ankle-length skirts, became fashionable after the 'rationing' which had been applied to clothing during the war. Their wedding reception was a local affair, held in the old former schoolhouse, which seemed to accommodate all of **Greatham's** social functions in those days.

They both moved in to live with her parents at Gold's Cottage until 1953, when they made the short move to Ivy Bank South, located in Snailing Lane. Elsie had gone to start work at **Greatham Mill** in 1949 and Jim followed her there in October of 1952, having previously tended the gardens at Milland Vicarage and Highfield.

Jim looked after the gardens for Captain Nigel and Mrs Frances Pumphrey for the best part of 40 years, until February 1990, helping to turn **Greatham Mill** gardens into a wonderful display of trees, shrubs and flowers, and open to the public at certain times of the year. Elsie, also a keen gardener, would also be on hand, helping out with the 'potting up' and 'pricking out'.

In 1989, due to Jim's failing health, Elsie and Jim had to move out of **Greatham**, taking up residence in one of the Coryton Alms-houses, down at West Liss and, sadly, Jim Collins passed away a couple of years later. He is buried in the churchyard at **Greatham.** Elsie continues to live at West Liss, and relies upon her daughter Maureen for shopping trips to Bordon and Petersfield. She greatly misses being close to all her many friends in **Greatham**, but remains a stalwart supporter of the Gardening Club, Women's Institute and Senior Citizens and always on hand to help out at functions, wearing her usual cheery smile.

Chapter Thirty One
Brenda and Jack Dunn

John 'Jack' Edwin Dunn is a well-known character, not only in **Greatham**, but by many people in the neighbouring vicinity too. For many years, until he 'officially' retired in 1988, he was 'Jolly Jack the Butcher', always ready with a sunny smile and good advice at the butcher's counters in our local super-markets. Perhaps, however, his most famous claim to fame was that he was once the 'model' for the pub-sign that hung outside the 'Jolly Sailor',

Jolly Jack Dunn

situated on the old A3 heading south out of Petersfield.

Jack arrived in the **Greatham** area as a babe-in-arms in 1923, at the tender age of 10 months. His father Tommy hailed from Salford, near Manchester, while his mother Jane Ann originated in County Durham. Tommy Dunn had served with the Lancashire Fusiliers during the First World War but, after the campaign in the Dardanelles, had been transferred to the Royal Engineers and posted to Longmoor Camp. Here he worked on the Military Railway as a brakesman and shunter. With no Army quarter available, the family took lodgings, first at Grigg's Green, then Liss Forest and, finally, here in **Greatham** with the Madgwick family.

Jack started his education at the Army school at Longmoor Camp, also serving as a choirboy at St Martin's Church of England. He remembers that, as the church had originally been a forage barn, it was always a cold and draughty place. Because of this, the Chaplain had requested at one service that the congregation should remember the next week to put in 'a little something for the church heating'. When Jack collected the offertory that following week, imagine the look of surprise on his face when the weight of the collection was found to be mainly lumps of coal!

At the age of 10 Jack moved down to the school in **Greatham**, where his headmaster for the remaining 4 years was Charles Wain. An apprenticeship with a plumber at Liphook was short-lived and Jack changed his employment to a Heavy Goods Vehicle delivery firm, also at Liphook. With not even an ordinary licence to his name, and in the absence of the regular driver, Jack found himself delivering around six tons of timber and bricks all the way to Bournemouth one day. It was fortunate that he didn't fall foul of the law.

Jack remembers the first bombing raid on Longmoor Camp, not long after the outbreak of World War II. Having become disillusioned with a background of Army life, at the age of 17 Jack got himself down to 'Pompey' and joined the Royal Navy. He served throughout the conflict, surviving the Japanese 'kamikaze' attacks on his ship, the aircraft carrier 'Formidable', out on the Pacific Ocean. He recalls that he actually saw the plane heading for Nagasaki, carrying Leonard Cheshire on the second atomic-bomb attack on the Japanese mainland. He later spoke to the great man about this very incident.

('Pompey' has always been the affectionate nickname given to Portsmouth. The term 'kamikaze' is Japanese for 'divine wind' and describes those pilots who aimed their fully-loaded dive-bombers at Allied ships, committing the ultimate sacrifice as they attempted to destroy their enemy. Ed.)

Jack trained as a diver during his naval service and, on one memorable occasion, actually dived down to the wreckage of the 'Royal Oak' at Scapa Flow. This was a 'hush-hush' event at the time, as the authorities didn't want the general public to know that a German U-boat (submarine) had breached the British defences. Jack obviously survived all of his escapades and left the Navy as an 'acting' Petty Officer. During a training course at Whale Island in 1942, Jack had the good fortune to meet up with his future wife, Brenda, at a nearby fish and chip shop. Brenda Joy Gamblin was a local girl from Cosham. Their romance survived the War years and, in 1947, the couple married at Wymering Church, Cosham. As Jack later put it, 'There'll be no more gamblin' Brenda'! They moved into Pine Villas here in **Greatham** and have lived in the village ever since. A later move was to No 2 Forestside Cottages (now Bower Cottage), in Longmoor Road. It is here that the baptism register shows them living when their two children were baptised, Jennifer Ann in 1949 and John Richard in 1951.

After his wartime experiences, Jack returned to working 'on the lorries', while also carrying out some part-time work locally. For a while he worked in a bakery that was located behind a grocer's shop in Longmoor Road. The shop continued to function for many years until converted back to a private residence for the use of Albert Baker, whose story appears elsewhere. Jack recalls that where 'The Oaks' mobile-home site now resides was once a sandpit, while the chap who ran the grocer's shop also kept pigs on the site.

(The above-mentioned shop was still operating when I moved to the village in 1967. More information is contained in the chapter on the Lockleys. Ed.)

After about three years, Jack went to work at 'the NAAFI' up at Longmoor Camp for the next ten years or so. Stan Thomas, who used to deliver the meat to the NAAFI shop, told Jack that he 'would make a good butcher', so that is what Jack went on to do for the rest of his working life. After ten years with Mr Parsons in Chalet Hill, Bordon, he then spent around twenty years, firstly at the Gateway supermarket in Petersfield, then for the same company in their Liphook store. His 'official' retirement occurred in 1988, although he carried on in a part-time capacity until finally packing it in at the age of 68.

Brenda and Jack now live at number 9 Baker's Field, having previously occupied two other homes on the same site. Jack is still in demand at Christmas functions all over the place – he makes just about the best Santa Claus that you could imagine. He's a 'jolly sailor' indeed!

Chapter Thirty Two
𝕶ath & 𝕮harlie 𝕳anson

On a wet afternoon in early May of 1999, I was invited along to a chat with Kath & Charlie Hanson in their 'Kemptown' house. I was a bit stumped at first by this term, but Charlie explained that in years gone by, so many of the local houses had been built by the Kemps, that locals had christened the area 'Kemptown'. Entries in various trade directories and the head stones of many graves in the two churchyards are testament to the influence that the Kemp family must have had on the village of **Greatham**. This was over a period stretching back as far as 1850 at least, and certainly on until 1935, when Frank Kemp was still being shown as 'cowkeeper', as he had been since 1895, a period of 40 years.

*(Trade Director entries for **Greatham** do not tell the full story, as the northern part of the village was for many years located in the parish of Blackmoor. As far as the 'Kemps' are concerned, the Blackmoor entries from 1911 right through until 1939 record the following: 'George A. Kemp & Sons, builders, contractors, building material merchants, hoot water engineers & fitters, sanitary engineers, Elm Villa, TN 4, **Greatham**." Ed.)*

Charles Thomas Hanson has lived mainly in the same house, in which he was born, since 1910. His baptism is recorded in the Parish Register as having taken place at St John the Baptist Church on January 15th 1911. He is proud to have reached the ripe old age of 89 and is still very active, while Kathleen admits to being *'somewhat younger'* — but that's a lady's prerogative!

Charlie's parents were Ellen and William, who had arrived at nearby Longmoor Camp on an Army posting in 1903. They were both 'Brummies' by birth but William had served many years as a Royal Engineer, moving here to **Greatham** from Chatham in Kent. Kathleen came here in similar fashion, but not until 1928, along with her sister May, their father being another man (James Papps) from a military background — see the Lockley's story.

Greatham School provided Charlie's education, during the time when first Mr Hiscock was the Headmaster, followed by Mr Wain in 1921. Discipline was a different matter in those distant days and woe betide any boy who turned up at morning assembly without having first cleaned his shoes! However, Charlie survived the standard nine-year term of attendance, from the age of 5–14 years, and the discipline obviously rubbed off on him, as he decided to join the Navy.

Charlie's father William served as a Royal Engineer at Longmoor Camp in it's earliest days.

With his father having served his time in the Army, as well as his three elder brothers William, Jack and Bernard, Charlie must have decided it was time to break the family tradition. So, sometime in 1925, off he went down to Portsmouth to be interviewed by no less a man than Admiral Trumper! Charlie must have proved himself to be of 'the right stuff', being accepted for cadet training, and set off to join a Training Ship on the Thames, in the Port of London.

Charlie served on many different ships, borne out by his record of service, proudly displayed by Kath during my visit. Perhaps his most vivid memories are of being on a destroyer, HMS Sesame, accompanying one of the very first aircraft carriers, HMS Furious, as the pilots practised their skills at taking off and landing on a moving vessel. Charlie's ship and its crew had the task of picking up those who had literally 'missed the boat'! After between 5-6 years service, Charlie decided to try his luck in civvie-street. Looking for a job, a life abroad must have seemed a tempting idea at the time. As his brother Jack was out in Palestine, Charlie headed off in that direction. But after two years, with no prospects of permanent employment, he returned to *Greatham*, to where his parents were still living at Sundale Cottages, around 1933.

He found a job at a firm of plumbers over at Haslemere and settled down to learn a trade. Kathleen had been living in *Greatham* for 5 years by now and it was then that they began their future together. When Ellen Hanson died a couple of years later, Charlie was left living alone with his father. It seemed an opportune time for he and Kath to get married and this they did in March of 1937, down at Petersfield.

The following year, Charlie started working at Longmoor Camp. With a permanent job 'on the doorstep', the future must have then looked secure. But fate, in the shape of a certain Adolf Hitler, dealt the Hansons a blow in 1939, when Charlie was called up into the Army. He went to Aldershot to sign up for the Sappers (Royal Engineers) but another surprise awaited him. On hearing of his previous experience with 'the Andrew' (Royal Navy), Charlie was sent down to Marchwood, on Southampton Water, to join a ship!

It wasn't any old ship however, but a 'Port Repair Ship', which was essentially a floating workshop. Here Charlie served throughout the war, using his skills and engineering knowledge to assist in such projects as the 'Mulberry Harbour', vital in the planning for the invasion of Europe in 1944. Charlie was demobbed in 1945, having reached the rank of Warrant Officer class 1. He returned to Longmoor and carried on working there for another 30 years, until his retirement in 1975.

Kath and Charlie enjoy their later years, their lovely house and garden are a credit to them. They enjoy regular visits by their children and grandchildren, while Charlie still enjoys the occasional drive out in his car, to either Bordon or Petersfield. Daughter Elizabeth Ann and son David Charles were both baptised at *Greatham Church*, in February 1940 and December 1946 respectively. Our talk continued with a few other memories of events in the village over the years. Kath recalled her first 'work experience' at the age of 14, when she was asked to help the Gilburds, who owned Fern Farm, just at the bottom of their lane. The Gilburds sold dairy products to their neighbours, as well as operating the refreshment rooms at the top of the hill. It was Kath's task to turn the paddle on the churn, turning the milk whey into butter and cream.

(An entry in the Parish baptism register shows that, in December 1935, Harry Ralph and Jean Delma Gilburd presented their son, Pruett Ralph, for his baptism ceremony at the village church. Ed.)

The Gilburds owned quite a lot of land in *Greatham*, though that belonging to Fern Farm has decreased greatly in area since those days. The land now occupied by Wolfmere Lane was once Harry Gilburd's cornfield. Closer to home, as it were, Kath remembers the stick of bombs which fell on the village during the war, one landing in a field of carrots right alongside Fern Farm. Kath reckons that half of the local population probably dined on a diet of carrots for weeks afterwards! The Hansons both remember Joe Leggett as the man who worked at the piggery behind Forestside Farm, and also recall that 'another' Leggett ran an undertaker's business in Snailing Lane. They remember Billy Wells, operating from a barn on the site of where Ray Flack's garage used to stand (opposite The Queen public house), and also Nanny Russell at Swain's Cottage sweet-shop, serving out bags of gob-stoppers and sugar-mice! The corner where the toll-house used to stand, now known as the Selborne turning, was always known to them as 'Prince's corner', and indeed the toll-house itself was 'Prince's house', but they could not recall why. A certain Thomas Prince was shown as Parish Clerk in 1895. Then the 1907 and 1911 editions of Kelly's Directory named Mr George Prince (1846 – 1920) as shopkeeper at an address of 'Tollgate', and in 1915 a Miss Amy Prince as sub-postmistress at the same address, so all is explained!

As a footnote to this tale, the 1923 directory shows Mrs Amy Booth as 'shopkeeper', and this ties in nicely with the Lockley's story, where the inhabitants of the 'toll-house' were remembered as the Booth brothers – it would appear that Amy must have married one of them. Then from the Parish Register of Baptisms came further evidence – Herbert George Booth, son of Amy and Herbert Booth, was baptised on March 13th 1921, with the address being shown as 'Tollgate Cottage'.

Chapter Thirty Three
The Haywards, Forestside Cottages

Viv Hayward's grandmother outside the cottages many years ago.

These two adjoining cottages, No.1 and No.2, are situated at the northern end of **Greatham,** set a little way back from the western side of the Petersfield Road and now directly opposite the new roundabout exit at Digby Way. Before the parish boundary changes that took place in 1982, these cottages were part of Blackmoor, a fact still recalled by the adjacent 'Blackmoor Stores' & '**Greatham**

Post Office', part of Woolmer Villas. Forestside Farm is situated just a little further south and its having the same name would indicate that the two dwellings once belonged to the same estate, probably belonging to Lord Selborne at one time.

The two cottages are owned by the Hayward family but, at the time of writing (June 1999), the family is hoping that the 'Sold' notices outside really do mean that they can fulfil their dreams of moving to Kent. Margery Hayward, widow of Victor John Hayward, lives at No.1 and Sarah & Michael Hayward at No.2. Michael is the son of 'Marge & Vic', as they were locally and popularly known. Sadly, Vic Hayward died in 1997, at the age of 62, but will be fondly remembered for his cycling skills! Marge too was not averse to a spot of pedal pushing in her younger days.

Vic was born in Aldershot in 1934 but appears to have arrived in **Greatham** at an early age, living 'somewhere' down Church Lane. His father, John Alexander Hayward, was born at Harting and is buried in **Greatham** churchyard, while his mother Evaline (nee Fry) came from Beckenham, in Kent. Marge was born at Terwick Common, near Rogate, and met Vic at Petersfield Laundry, where they both worked for many years. Cycling was their means of transport in those days and romance seems to have blossomed 'over the handlebars'! After serving his two years of National Service with the Royal Engineers in the (Suez) Canal Zone, Vic returned home to marry Marge, at Terwick Church, in 1957.

For a number of years they lived a hectic life, literally swapping homes between their respective in-laws, before they were able to purchase the two cottages in 1963 and 'put down their roots'. Both the Haywards moved jobs, going to work at the Mint Laundry at Liss, until that business closed and they both became redundant.

With daughter Angela already married to a 'man of Kent', living in Maidstone, and Michael married to Sarah, a 'Kentish maid', it is no surprise that they intend Kent to be their family home from now on. If all goes well with the sale, Marge will move to be near Angela and her family, while Sarah and Michael are planning a move to Folkestone. **Greatham** wishes them a happy future.

(The following notes are based on a number of historical deeds relevant to the above-mentioned properties. The

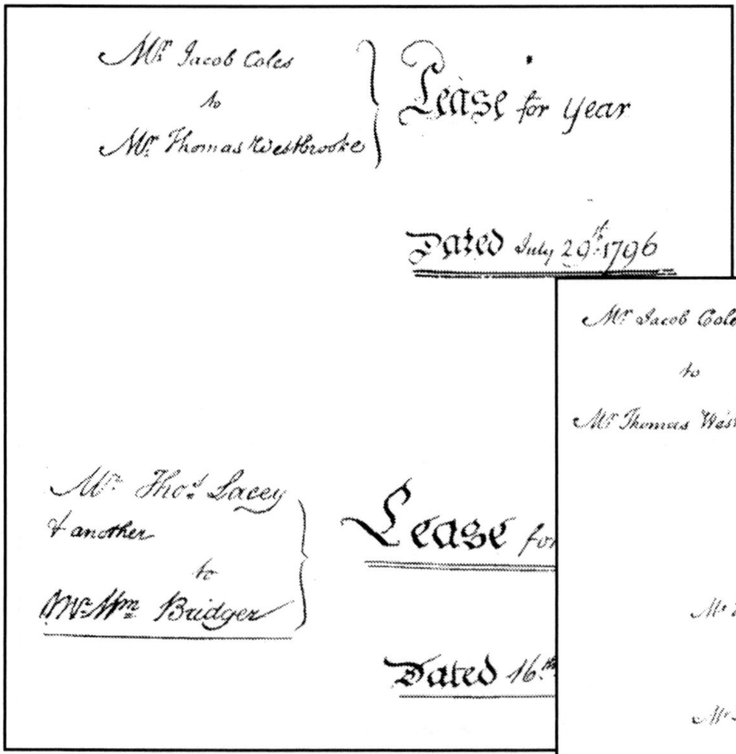

Mr Jacob Coles
to
Mr Thomas Westbrooke
} Lease for Year

Dated July 29th 1796

Mr Thos Lacey
& another
to
Mr Wm Bridger
} Lease for

Dated 16th

Forestside Cottages Lease for a year dated 29th July 1796

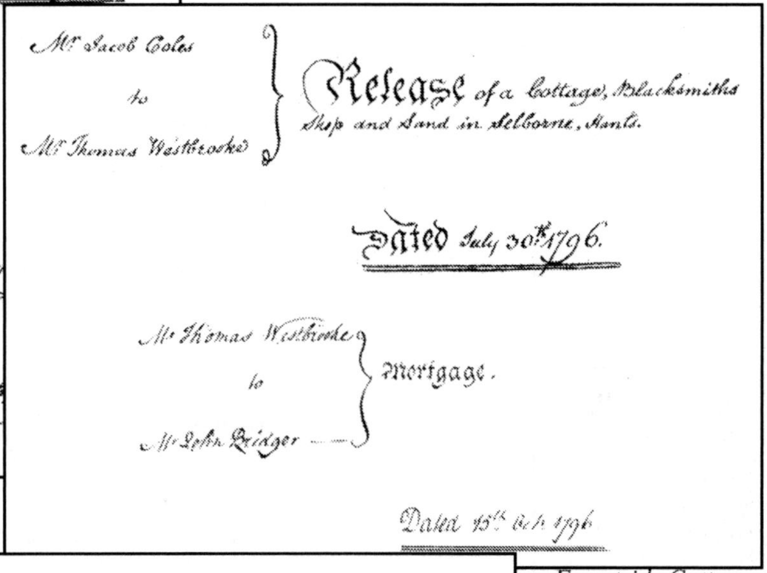

Mr Jacob Coles
to
Mr Thomas Westbrooke
} Release of a cottage, Blacksmiths Shop and Land in Selborne, Hants.

Dated July 30th 1796.

Mr Thomas Westbrooke
to
Mr John Bridger
} Mortgage.

Dated 15th Oct 1796

Forestside Cottages Release 30th July 1796

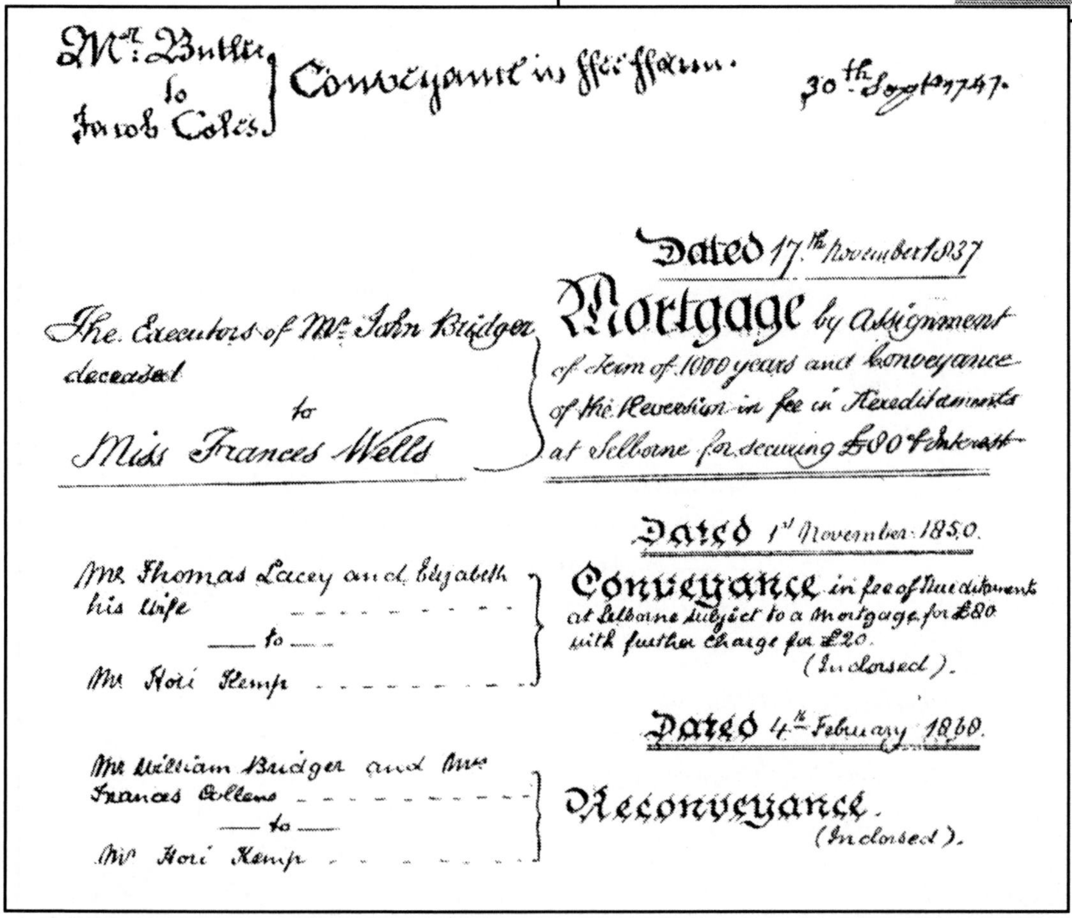

Mr Butler
to
Jacob Coles
} Conveyance in fee farm.   30th Sept 1747.

Dated 17th November 1837

Mortgage by Assignment of Term of 1000 years and Conveyance of the Reversion in fee in Hereditaments at Selborne for securing £80 & interest

The Executors of Mr John Bridger deceased
to
Miss Frances Wells

Dated 1st November 1850.

Conveyance in fee of Hereditament at Selborne subject to a Mortgage for £80 with further charge for £20.
(Indorsed).

Mr Thomas Lacey and Elizabeth his wife
to
Mr Hori Kemp

Dated 4th February 1860.

Reconveyance.
(Indorsed).

Mr William Bridger and Mrs Frances Collens
to
Mr Hori Kemp

Forestside Cottages conveyance agreement 4th February 1860

I Elizabeth Lacey, the wife of Thomas Lacey
of Selborne in the County of Southampton Husbandman
do hereby solemnly and sincerely declare that my
late Father Thomas Westbrook of Selborne aforesaid
Blacksmith married my late Mother Mary Westbrook
(then Mary Coles Spinster) and that of this his only
Marriage my late Brother Jacob Westbrook was the
eldest Son That my said late Brother Jacob Westbrook
married Lydia Hewlett and that of this his only
Marriage my Nephew John Westbrook now or late of
Battersea in the County of Surrey Shoemaker was and
is the eldest Son That my said Father died in or about
the month of April in the year One thousand eight
hundred and twenty two and my mother died in
or about the Month of March in the year one thousand
eight hundred and thirty one and my Brother Jacob
Westbrook and Lydia his Wife respectively died some
time before the year One thousand eight hundred and
thirty seven from which period the Cottages Gardens
Fuel House and Piece of Land situate at Selborne
aforesaid now occupied by my said husband and
Thomas Lacey Junior as tenants to How Kemp
continued in the uninterrupted possession and
enjoyment of my husband Thomas Lacey down to the
time of the Conveyance lately made thereof to the said
How Kemp And I make this Solemn Declaration
conscientiously believing the same to be true and by virtue
of the Provisions of an Act made and passed in the fifth
and sixth years of the Reign of his late Majesty
intituled "An Act to repeal an act of the present Session
of Parliament intituled an act for the more effectual
abolition of Oaths and Affirmations taken and made in
various departments of the state and to substitute
Declarations in lieu thereof and for the more entire
suppression of voluntary and extrajudicial Oaths and
Affidavits and to make other provisions for the abolition
of unnecessary Oaths".

Declared at Alton in the County
of Southampton this second day of   Elizabeth Lacey
November One thousand eight hundred
and fifty. Before me.

_____ a Master extra in Chancery. —

Forestside Cottages declaration by Elizabeth Lacey

I Hori Kemp of Selborne in the County of Hants Bricklayer Hereby declare that in consideration of the purchase by The Reverend Philip Haslewood of 55 Brompton Crescent Brompton in the County of Middlesex Clerk of certain hereditaments situate in Selborne aforesaid I do hereby acknowledge the right of the said Philip Haslewood to production and delivery of copies of the documents mentioned in the Schedule hereto (which are now in my possession and relate to the said hereditaments) and hereby undertake for the safe custody of the same As witness my hand this second day of February One thousand eight hundred and eighty six.

The Schedule
above referred to

Date.	Parties.	Deed
17th November 1837	Thomas Lacey of 1st part John Westbrook of the 2nd part Richard Knight & Ann his Wife & James Bridger of the 3rd part William Bridger of 5th part Frances Wells of the 4th part & said Thomas Lacey & Elizabeth his Wife of the 6th part	Mortgage
1st November, 1850	Thomas Lacey and Elizabeth his Wife of 1st part Hori Kemp of 2nd part and Frances Collens of 3rd part	Transfer indorsed on last Indenture
2nd November, 1850	Certificate of Acknowledgment of last Indenture by E. Lacey.	
4th February, 1868	William Bridger of the 1st part Frances Collens of the 2nd part and said Hori Kemp of the 3rd part	Reconveyance.

Witness:
(Signed) A. J. M. Downie
Solr. Alton, Hants.
(Signed) Hori Kemp

Forestside Cottages purchase declaration

Dated 2nd February, 1886

Mr Hori Kemp ———
——— to ———
Revd Philip Haslewood

copy
Acknowledgment
and Undertaking as to
Documents of Title ———

Gedge Kirby & Millett
1 Old Palace Yard
Westminster

Downie
Alton

Memorandum

By an Indenture dated the 2nd
February 1886, & made between Hori
Kemp of one part & The Revd Philip
Haslewood of other part, two pieces of
land situate in the Parish of Selborne
Hants to being nos 168 and 169 on the
Plan annexed to the Woolmer Forest
Inclosure Award & being an allotments
made as to 168 to the said Hori Kemp &
as to 169 to one John Upperton, were
conveyed unto & to the use of the said
Philip Haslewood in fee simple.

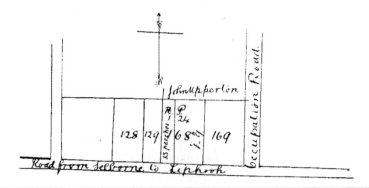

*Forestside Cottages
Transaction 1850*

These are to Certify that on the *Second* _____ day of *November* in the Year _____ One Thousand Eight Hundred and fifty _____ before us *Charles Trimmer and William Clement* _____ _____ Two of the perpetual Commissioners appointed _____ for the _____ County of *Southampton* _____ for taking the acknowledgments of Deeds by Married Women pursuant to an Act passed in the ~~Third and~~ Fourth Year of the Reign of His late Majesty King William the Fourth, intituled, " An Act for the Abolition of Fines and Recoveries, and for the substitution of more simple modes of Assurance," appeared personally *Elizabeth* _____ the wife of *Thomas Lacey and produced a certain Indenture marked 'A' bearing date the first day of November One thousand eight hundred and fifty and made between the said Thomas Lacey and Elizabeth his wife of the first part Flora Kemp of the second part and Frances Collens of the third part* _____

and _____ acknowledged the same _____ to be her _____ Act and Deed AND WE DO HEREBY _____ CERTIFY that the said *Elizabeth Lacey was* at the time of *her* _____ acknowledging the said *deed* _____ of full age and competent understanding, and that *she was* _____ examined by us apart from *her* _____ Husband touching *her* _____ knowledge of the contents of the said *deed* _____ and that *She* _____ freely and voluntarily consented to the same

EXAMIN'D COPY,

John S Bamley
Registrar of Certificates, &c.

Chas. Trimmer.
Wm Clement.

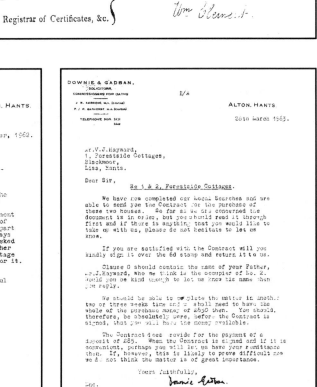

*Forestside Cottages
Transaction
1962 and 1963*

deeds, along with her own notes, were kindly presented to me by Sarah in March 1999, accompanied by an album of old postcard style pictures of **Greatham,** *lovingly collected by Michael's sister Angela. I am indebted to them both for their assistance. Ed.)*

1747 – 30ᵗʰ September (George III): Jacob Coles paid £35 for the land from John Butler (Gentleman), Lord of the manor of Temple

1796 – 30ᵗʰ July: Details of the land of ¾ acre adjoining farm (including a Blacksmiths shop and sand) being leased for 1 year to Thomas Westbrook by Jacob Coles for a 'peppercorn' rent, a nominal rent for land being held on a long lease

(It would appear that Thomas was married to Mary, probably the sister of Jacob, so they were in-laws. Ed.)

Jacob married Lydia Hewlett and they had a son, John Coles

1796 – 15ᵗʰ October: Indenture (an agreement, or contract) shows Thomas Westbrook (who died in 1822) and John Bridger paid £60 for ¾ acre in the manor of Temple, against a lane leading from Selborne into Woolmer Forest and including a Blacksmith's shop and outhouses

1837 – 16ᵗʰ November (Queen Victoria): William Bridger leased the land for 1 year, at a charge of 5 shillings, from Thomas Lacey and John Westbrook

1850 – 1ˢᵗ November: Thomas and Elizabeth Lacey mortgaged the land for £80, with a further charge of £20, to Hori Kemp
Elizabeth was the daughter of Thomas Westbrook, Blacksmith of Selborne, and Mary (nee Coles, who died in 1831)

1868 – 4ᵗʰ February: William Bridger and Frances Collens sell to Hori Kemp for the sum of £100, with a further payment of interest (£1.15s) to Frances Collens

1886 – 2ⁿᵈ February: Hori Kemp sold up to the Reverend Philip Haslewood

Hori Kemp was stated as being a brick-layer, and died in 1867, his will of that year leaving the property to his wife Elizabeth

(Kelly's Directory of Hampshire, dated 1895, identified one Hori Kemp as **Greatham's** *sub-Postmaster. This*

must have been the son of the first H K. The 1861 census of Blackmoor, as part of Selborne, showed Hori Kemp senior (real name Horace or Henry?) as being aged 77 years and innkeeper at the Bricklayer's Arms. If he had lived until 1895, he would have been 111 years old! Ed.)

Elizabeth Kemp passed the properties on to her daughter Elizabeth Emma, 3rd March 1892, with two tenants – James Lemon at No.1 and David Lord at No.2, before she herself died on 23rd October 1893

Elizabeth Emma then married Arthur Bellchambers on 26 December 1893

Eliza Bellchambers died on 24th Oct 1956, at the age of 89 years, leaving a daughter, Eva Blanche Bellchambers

1963 – 3ʳᵈ May (Elizabeth II): Victor John Hayward bought the premises, No's. 1 and 2 Forestside Cottages from Miss Eva Bellchambers for the sum of £850, his father John 'Jack' Hayward being already resident in No.2

(The entries above are only the 'bare bones' of a traceable history, and leave many fascinating questions unanswered. It cannot be seen whether the land was passed on with or without any dwellings, or indeed when the two cottages were built. If Hori Kemp sold the land to the Rev. Haslewood, how did the Kemps/Bellchambers obtain repossession – did the Rev. Haslewood only pay rent to Hori Kemp? Was Jacob Coles any relation to John Cole? Was John Westbrook the son of Thomas Westbrook? Was Mary Coles the daughter of Jacob Coles? I certainly cannot answer these questions, and invite readers to make up their own minds as to how the gaps in the story can be filled. Ed.)

Chapter Thirty Four
May and George Lockley
'The Welcome', Longmoor Rd

Georfe Henry Lockley was born in the village in 1921 and lived in No.1 Rose Cottages, at the bottom of the Liphook Road. Apparently, the road always used to be called Liphook Road, until the road-sign disappeared sometime during the war – possibly taken as a souvenir by one of the soldiers from Longmoor Camp. The old name was never re-instated, and since the war the road has been called Longmoor Road. George attended the village school, and remembers the headmaster as Mr Wain (*see notes on school history*).

George's parents were James George Lockley, who was **Greatham** 'born and bred', and his wife Florence, who hailed from Basingstoke. Next door to George and family in those far-off days lived one Billy Wells, whose parents ran 'The Queen', just a few yards along the main road. Billy sported a large bushy beard and was a well-known local character, not averse to a spot of poaching! He would carry a 12-bore shotgun under his arm and, when a target appeared, would not bother to shoulder the weapon, but aim from the hip. Apparently he didn't miss too often!

Billy was a wheelwright by trade, operating from a shed on the opposite side of the road to The Queen. George also remembers a small garage alongside the above shed, run by Frank Madgwick, which dispensed petrol via a hand-turned pump. A headstone in **Greatham** churchyard shows that Frank was born in 1897, and died in 1946.

(David Redman and Joe Leggett both refer to Billy Wells in their memoirs elsewhere in this narrative. Ed.)

George moved out of **Greatham** during the war, serving with the RAF from 1941-47. He married his wife May in 1947, and they lived for a couple of years at Forestside Farm, Longmoor Road, during which time their daughter Margery Ann was born. May had arrived in the village aged 11, with her father James Papps, originally from Westbury, Wiltshire, and his wife Kathleen, from Farnham. James Papps was a soldier in the Wiltshire Regiment for 56 years, and moved here on posting to Longmoor Camp. The family lived at Longmoor Lodge, at the top of Apple Pie Hill.

May and George moved to Baker's Field in 1949, but finally settled at 'The Welcome', returning again to Longmoor Road. It is now much enlarged from the original cottage, which was built by George Kemp, local builder, and one of the very large family of Kemps then resident in the **Greatham** area. May and George kindly offered to pass on some of their memories to me over a beer, at the end of March 1999. As well as confirming some of my previously heard tales, they were able to add a few of their own!

Both of the Lockleys can recall that a Joe Leggett ran a piggery in the field at the back of Forestside Farm,

The old Methodist chapel, knocked down in the early 1960's, constructed from corrugated iron and painted a cream colour, with green doors.

105

their previous house just a few yards down Longmoor Road from their present home. They knew Joe as a member of a large family from Grigg's Green, which corresponds with Joe's own story, printed elsewhere in this narrative. Joe is also remembered as running a 'Model-T Ford'. Both remember that the Wesleyan – or Methodist - chapel, knocked down in the early 1960's, was constructed from corrugated iron, and was painted a cream colour, with green doors.

(My own house, 'Chapel House', now stands on this site. Imagine my delight when, on the first Saturday in April 2000, while searching through a tray of old postcards at the Maltings Market in Farnham, I came across a wonderful picture of the old chapel. This was the first time since my arrival in **Greatham** *(1967) that I had seen such a picture – an enlarged and framed copy now adorns the wall of the hallway of Chapel House. When I visited Brenda & Jack Dunn some time later, they identified the smart looking chap standing outside the old chapel as 'Busty' Ansell, who lived at Glenthorne, just down the road. Ed.)*

About halfway between Chapel House and The Welcome is 'Broadleigh'. I can remember it myself as a village shop, run by the Pooleys, when I arrived in the village in 1967, but it closed as shop soon after that date. May and George remember that it had previously been run by a Mr Bertram Kirkby, operating as a general store and bike-repair premises.

Further down the road, just below what is now 'The Oaks' caravan site, was another village shop. I can recall that it was run by an elderly couple, the Pearces, back in 1967, followed next by the Angus family and then Lilian and David Booth, before it closed as a business. The Lockleys recall it being run by Mr Walters, when it had a bakery to its rear and a long wooden hut next to it served as a refreshment room.

The Lockleys also remembered that the old thatched cottage, now 'Swain's', just at the top of Church Lane, served as the village sweetshop. In fact there used to be three cottages and the sweetshop was the one nearest the church. From here, 'Nanny' Russell dispensed 'ha'pennorths' of pears from her orchard, as well as other such delights as toffee apples. Again this ties in with the story told by Joe Leggett.

The old Forge and Blacksmith's shop on the Selborne Road was run by Mr George Shepherd (*or Sheppard? Kelly's Directory uses both spellings, in its 1923 and 1935 issues*). A headstone in **Greatham** churchyard indicates that a Henry George Sheppard was born in 1891, and died in 1966. George was succeeded by Mr S G 'Fred' Ellis from 1959, until at least 1971. The old buildings were demolished in the early 1970s, when the road was widened, with the new 'Forge House' being built around 1977.

A Toll House used to stand on the corner at the Selborne turning; George Lockley remembers it being occupied by two brothers, Maurice and Herbert Booth. A Miss Amy Prince was postmistress there in 1915, but in 1923 a Mrs Amy Booth is referred to, so it would appear the Amy married one of the Booth brothers (see the Hansons' story for further confirmation).

What was once Blackmoor Post Office, and now the Game Centre, I can remember that back in 1967 it was run by the Stamps – now there's a coincidence! – and later by the Sampsons, a couple of cheerful Cockneys! The Lockleys remember that this had previously operated as a general store, run by Mr Alf Butcher, selling such as boots and shoes, haberdashery and old furniture, as well as groceries. Another gravestone in the churchyard shows that Alfred George Butcher, born in 1865, survived until the age of 86, dying in 1951, the year of the Festival of Britain.

At the top of the hill in Longmoor Road, Harry Gilburd ran some tearooms, from a lean-to at the side of the house, which was greatly used by the soldiers of Longmoor Camp. The small estate of 'Hopeswood' in Longmoor Road was literally that – a wood belonging to Hope! Mr and Mrs Hope were the owners of King's Holt, the large house on the hill just behind Hopeswood. Mr Peter Hiley, who sold the land for Hopeswood's development, had married the Hopes' daughter.

'The Oaks' caravan site stands on the site of a former sandpit, which used to be maintained by Punch Lee – could that have been his real name? The footpath across the common, between Longmoor Road and the new roundabout, has a largish pond of very brackish water, which always looks very menacing. Just to the rear of the 'pond' is the remnant of an anti-aircraft gun emplacement, a reminder that Longmoor Camp was a bombing target for the Luftwaffe (German Air Force) during World War II.

(I returned to see May and George towards the end of April 1999, to show them the above memoirs, and hoped that I hadn't got too much wrong! Their memories of other Greatham residents certainly cannot be faulted for accuracy, when checked against entries in various Kelly's Directories. Frank Madgwick was shown as a 'motor garage' owner from 1923-1939; Bertram Kirby as a 'cycle agent' right through from 1907 until 1939; Archibald Walters as a 'grocer, Longmoor Road' from 1920-1939; Harry Gilburd, changing from 'refreshment rooms, Longmoor Road' in 1920 to 'farmer' and then 'smallholder' by 1939; George Kemp, then later 'and Sons' were shown variously as builders, contractors and fitters for many years, from an entry in the Bennett's Directory for Liss in 1907 until finally in the Kelly's Directory at the outbreak of World War II in 1939. Ed.)

Chapter Thirty Five
Jackie & Bill Marie

On the evening of Saturday 13th July 2002, a party was held at 'The Devil's Punchbowl' hotel alongside the A3 trunk road at Hindhead to celebrate not only Jackie Marie's 60th birthday but also the forthcoming 40th anniversary of her marriage to Bill. A multitude of friends and relatives from far and wide assembled to wish this popular couple well on the next stage of their long and happy relationship, in particular their three children, Steve, Neil and Andrea.

Bill Marie was born at nearby Haslemere in 1938, son of William Roland Marie, who had originated from the Channel Island of Jersey. His mother Ann was one of the large Fry family, then living at Keeper's Cottage, down Church Lane in *Greatham*. Bill's grandfather, on his mother's side of the family, was employed for many years as the chief gamekeeper on the neighbouring Blackmoor Estate. Ann's sister Evaline was mother to the previously mentioned Vic Hayward, making Vic a cousin of Bill's. Evaline, or 'Aunty Evy' as she was known to all the family, is believed to have arrived in *Greatham* from Derbyshire and worked as a chambermaid at the Woolmer Hotel (later Silver Birch) for some twenty years.

Moving here to *Greatham* sometime around 1940, Bill was too young to recall the move, but it was to No.5 Kingshott Cottages on Petersfield Road. Bill started his education at *Greatham* School in 1943, and mainly recalls Miss Hughes as the headmistress, although Mr Wain would have still been there until 1944. He also recalls two other teachers as Miss Lee and Miss Jordan. Directly upon leaving school, Bill went to work for his Uncle Algy, at that time the head gamekeeper on Sir John Black's estate at Harting.

By 1946, the Marie family had moved south along the road by only a short distance, to No.4 Broadleigh Cottages, next door to the old Post Office. Here Bill stayed until he was called up for his compulsory two years' National Service in 1957. He was recruited into the Royal Wiltshire Regiment at their Headquarters in Devizes, from where he was sent to Cyprus during the troubles there at that time against the 'EOKA' terrorists fighting for amalgamation with mainland Greece. Bill returned safely to a barracks at Newport on the Isle of Wight, not far from the island's high

security prison, from where he was demobilised in 1959.

Bill then moved back to Broadleigh, still sharing the house with his Mum and Dad, as well as sister Pearl. Using his Army experience, he went to work as a waiter in the Officers' Mess at the Motor Transport School at Bordon. His father later purchased No.1 Pansy Lane, where he then lived until his marriage to Jackie Leece in 1962. Bill had met his future wife at a dance at what was known as 'The Rock and Roll Club', located behind The Welcome Inn at Petersfield. This well-known landmark was just across the main railway crossing near the station, but has long since been knocked down and replaced by the inevitable housing. Jackie and Bill married at St Mary's Church, Liss, in August of that year. Marriage – and Jackie's Mum! - obviously persuaded Bill to seek more remunerative

Granny and Grandad Fry, Bill Marie's maternal grandparents.

age of fifty.

After leaving Tews, Bill then worked for a number of different employers in the local area, including a time at Precision Printing here in **Greatham**, on the site that is now occupied by EuroTec. He was to be finally employed by Gould and Williams, an engineering firm over at Alton but, following a hip replacement, had to spend some time recovering at home. It was during this enforced quiet spell that he was able to provide most of the details of this story.

For a while, Jackie and Bill lived in No.2 Pine Villas in Longmoor Road but, with an expanding family, they had a house built in Pansy Lane, on land that belonged to Bill's father. They named the house 'Annest', which is where they still reside today. If you take the first two letters of each of their children's names, Andrea, Neil and Steve, you will work out where the name of the house came from! Bill has recently retired from work and Jackie is finding plenty of decorating to keep him as agile as possible, while she herself still works part-time.

William Marie Snr was a native of the Channel Islands before moving to Greatham.

Bill at the age of three, along with his mother and bay sister Pearl. The photograph was taken outside his cousin Viv's house at Forestside Cottages.

employment and he went into the engineering trade with Tews at Petersfield.

Jackie had been born at Liss in 1942; her Dad was Jack Leece, who worked for the old Southern Railway as an office manager at the depot in Havant. Her Mum Nellie worked for many years at the old Post Office in Liss, when it was the main distribution point for the surrounding area. Many people still use the term of '**Greatham**, Liss, Hants' as their postal address. Jackie went to the school in Liss, which then catered for all ages, from starting education at the age of five until the school-leaving age of fifteen.

No doubt influenced somewhat by her father's occupation, Jackie started her working life dealing with workers' accounts at the Southern Railway department at Woking, while still living with her parents at The Oval in Liss. Always keen on sports, she excelled at athletics and took up a long-standing interest in netball, carrying on playing for local teams right up until the

Chapter Thirty Six
Audrey and Bill Moseley

William 'Bill' Ernest Moseley was born and baptised in *Greatham* in 1933, being brought up at 'The Stores', which is now the site of the Game Centre and Welldigger's Cottage. Bill's father, Percy, had been a Warrant Officer Class 1, serving with the Royal Horse Artillery. Born at Gosport, Percy Ernest Moseley had been posted to Longmoor Camp at the end of World War I, then later, as a civil servant, found himself once again working at Longmoor. Here, he met and married Kathleen Isabel, who was the daughter of a long-established *Greatham* couple, Albert George Butcher and his wife 'Bessie', born Elizabeth Mells, of Liss. Albert owned and ran The Stores, under the title *'AG Butcher, Provision Merchant'*.

To the north of these premises, on the site of what is now the 'EuroTec' business, one large building was used as a cinema whilst a second building was operated as a garage, by Albert's son Bert. (This is not to be confused with the other garage further down the road, run by Frank Madgwick.) Bert Butcher later went on to become chief vehicle tester for Vauxhall, at their plant in Luton. Bill was able to show me a large photograph album, containing a marvellous historical record of his family. He was also kind enough to let me borrow some of the photos, which show the family house and business, as well as illustrating some of his relatives in the same setting.

(Kelly's Directory entries for Blackmoor, from 1911 right through until 1939, show Albert George Butcher as 'grocer', while those of 1935 and 1939 also now record Albert ('Bert') William Butcher as a 'motor engineer'. Ed.)

Bill attended *Greatham* School between 1938 and 1944, the headmaster at this time being Mr Charles Wain. Audrey Collins had been born at Cosham, but with World War II being imminent and the Portsmouth dockyard being a prime bombing target, she was one of the many thousands of children in this country who were 'evacuated' for their personal safety. Amongst many moves, Audrey was living at 'The Brown Teapot', West Liss, for some time, and attending *Greatham* School. It was here, at the tender ages of nine years, that Audrey and Bill first met. This must have been an auspicious meeting, because Bill himself moved to West Liss around 1950 and, in 1958 the happy couple married at St Mary's Church in Liss.

Audrey tells a story of her early childhood, which reflects upon the present-day scene quite well. She had only been at the school for about six weeks, when she and a younger boy were involved in what was probably one of *Greatham's* first traffic accidents. A chauffeur-driven car, thought to be travelling at some 70 miles per hour, knocked them both down, with the young lad, Michael Gallagher, suffering a broken leg. No doubt, back in those days, one would hardly expect a car at all, never mind one being driven at such speed.

Fortunately, both children lived to tell the tale, and Audrey remembers very well the great kindness

Bill's mother, Kathleen, sits proudly in her car outside the garage run by her brother Bert.

Bill shows his prowess at the controls of the road roller.

Bill joins the gang of workmen laying tarmac on the main parade square at Longmoor Camp.

in follow-on collisions. Unfortunately, a 13-year old local boy, out delivering newspapers on his bicycle, became trapped under the front axle of the lorry. Firemen had to use air bags to lift the heavy vehicle and the boy was lucky to escape with his life.

Thankfully, with the opening of the Woolmer Link road in 1997, the follow up of traffic-calming measures and the consequent reduction of the speed-limit to 30 miles per hour, such incidents will never occur again and **Greatham** should prove a much safer place in which to live in future years.

(Audrey and Bill now live down at Clanfield, and I am grateful to Shirley Redpath for having put me in touch with them. Their photograph album provides some nostalgic views of **Greatham.** *As a footnote, during a search through the Kelly's Directories, I noticed that an Alfred George Butcher was listed as an 'outfitter' at Longmoor Camp, from 1915 to 1939, he obviously made his living from the serving soldiers of those days. I mentioned this over the phone to Bill, considering the similarity in names and dates to his grandfather, Albert George Butcher, but he could not confirm any family link. It can only go down as an amazing coincidence. Ed.)*

shown by the school staff and children. They made every effort to visit her as often as possible, bringing her books to read, which enabled her to do homework and keep abreast of the school syllabus. On the other hand, the car's occupants made no enquiry at all as to the children's well being.

Probably the last serious traffic accident to occur in **Greatham** took place in January 1996. The driver of a 16-ton lorry lost control of his vehicle outside Theale Knapp Cottage, causing three cars to also be damaged

Transport was a much quieter affair many years ago, as Bill enjoys a ride with his Aunt and cousins.

Chapter Thirty Seven
The Redmans, Forestside Farm

Situated towards the northern end of *Greatham,* Forestside Farm lies between the 'Silver Birch' and the village Post Office, on the same side of the Petersfield Road. Not to be confused with another farm of the same name in Longmoor Road, Forestside Farm used to be situated within Blackmoor Parish, before boundary changes in the early 1980s. Since the whole top half of the village was once part of Lord Selborne's estate, the association between Forestside Farm and nearby Forestside Cottages may well not be just in the name.

Although the present farmhouse only dates back to the mid-Victorian era, a barn to the rear of the property is much older, probably 17th-century according to one expert who has studied its particular timber-framed construction. On the same site, an old thatched farmhouse was destroyed by fire many years ago. A sale notice of earlier years refers to the property as 'Temple Down', again giving an association with the Selborne estate, which has within it an area called Temple.

The farm is now the home of Mr Edgar Redman and his wife Olive (formerly Bridger), along with their only son, David. They moved into their farm in 1962, having previously lived at No 4 Leighwood, Benham's Lane, from 1959, where and when David was born. The farm was already a family possession, being the home of Edgar's father, William Albert Redman (born 1883), and his eldest son William James. Olive suddenly found she had four 'boys' to look after! W A died some two years afterwards, in 1964, at the age of 81.

W A Redman had married Emma Jane Wells, daughter of James Wells, in 1911 and, as the Wells family had already acquired Rook's Farm during 1885, W A and Emma took up residence there too. W A Redman was a dairy farmer, operating his business from Rook's Farm, and in the years around the 1st World War, he supplied milk to Longmoor Camp on a twice-daily basis. However, he is listed in the Kelly's Directories from 1915 to 1939 only as *'cowkeeper, Rook's Farm'.* It does seem a slightly understated term for someone running his own business!

William James was born in 1912 and died only recently in 1997, while Edgar was born in 1914. W J 'Bill' Redman was well known for his efforts on behalf of the church. A brass plaque alongside the church organ confirms that he was *'organist and choirmaster*

from 1932 – 1995, a faithful servant of his Lord'. This plaque was donated to the church by *'grateful parishioners'.*

The Redmans bought Forestside Farm in 1924, leasing it out at that time. An 1861 census of Selborne, which at that time included quite a large part of present-day *Greatham,* showed both George Wells and one of his sons, James, along with their respective families, living at Forestside, so the familial association was maintained. But when Rook's Farm became too small for their expanding business requirements, they moved into Forestside around 1930. By now their name had become 'W A Redman & Sons', the family business having always been dairy-farming in the main, and this continued for over 100 years all told.

(From those Kelly's Directories entries for Blackmoor, Forest Side farm (sic) was shown to be run by Frederick Etheridge (farmer) from 1907 until 1923, while the 1935 & 1939 editions show it to be the residence of William Albert Redman (farmer). Both of these gentlemen are mentioned in the memoirs of Joe Leggett, elsewhere in this history. Ed.)

David Redman loves to tell this tale about his grandfather. Being a regular visitor to the Sergeant's Mess at Longmoor, during his milk delivery round, he would often be invited to partake of the occasional tipple. He would leave the horse and float outside, tied to the railings. Fortunately the horse seemed to know his own way home, on those occasions when William had over-indulged. However, after one particular

Members of the Wells family carried out their trades of blacksmith and wheelwrights in premises opposite 'The Queen' public house.

session in the Mess, W A was perplexed to find that when he gave the order to 'gee up', the horse remained in position. It turned out that some joker had unhitched the horse from the float, pushed the float shafts through the fence rails – and then re-hitched the horse!

The Wells connection

1812	George Wells born	(headstone in old church-yard)
1816	Harriet, later wife of George, born	(headstone as above)
1834	George Wells baptised, son of George & Harriet	(register)
1836	James Wells, son of G & H born	(headstone in old church-yard)
1839	Harriet, later 1st wife of James, born	(headstone as above)
1841	Details from the census of that year:	
	George Wells, age 29, wheelwright	(b. 1812)
	Harriet Wells, age 25, wife	(b. 1816)
	George Wells, age 6, son	(b. 1834)
	James Wells, age 5, son	(b. 1836)
	John Wells, age 3, son	(b. 1838)
	Mary Jane, age 1, daughter	(b. 1840)

(The 1841 national census was the first to list the names of individuals. Occasionally it also named the house in which a family lived. Ed.)

1847	Daniel, son of G & H, born	(headstone in old churchyard)
1851	Details from the census of that year:	
	George Wells, age 39	}
	Harriet Wells, age 35	}
	George Wells, age 16	} All details relate to those of 1841
	James Wells, age 15	}
	John Wells, age 13	}
	Mary Jane, age 11	}
	Louisa Wells, age 8, daughter	(b. 1843)
	Ann Wells, age 7, daughter	(b. 1844)
	Daniel Wells, age 4, son	(b. 1847)
	Harriet Wells, age 3, daughter	(b. 1848)
1855	Anne Wells, age 11, died	(Register)
1855/1859 wheelwright		George Wells, blacksmith & (Kelly's)
1861	The census of Selborne included part of what is now **Greatham**:	
Forest-side	George Wells, wheelwright, wife, 1 son, 5 daughters	
	James Wells, blacksmith and wife	
1871	Details from the census of that year:	
	George Wells, age 59, licensed victualler	}
	Harriet Wells, age 55	} See 1851
	Louisa Wells, age 28	}
	Caroline Wells, age 19, daughter	(b. 1852)
	William Wells, age 16, son	(b. 1855)
	Ellen & Matilda, age 13, twins	(b. 1858)
	George Wells jnr., age 36, wheelwright	
	Jane Wells, age 35, wife	
	James Wells, age 35, blacksmith	
	Harriet Wells, age 32, wife, Selborne	(b. 1839)
	Alfred Wells, age 5, son	b. 1866)
	James Wells, age 2, son	(b. 1869)
	Martin Wells, age 4 months, son	(b. 1871)
	George Wells, Queen's Head, shopkeeper & farmer	(Kelly's)
	Daniel & James Wells, wheelwright & blacksmith	
1877	Emma Jane, daughter, born	(headstone in new churchyard)
1878	Post Office is at Mr Daniel Wells'	(Kelly's)
	Daniel Wells, postmaster	
	Daniel & James Wells, wheelwright & blacksmith	
	George Wells, farmer, shopkeeper & victualler, Queen's Head	
1879	Daniel Wells snr. died	(headstone in new churchyard)

1880	Post Office: Louisa Wells, receiver	(Kelly's)
	George Wells, shopkeeper & farmer, Queen's Head	
	James Wells, wheelwright & blacksmith	
1883	George Wells snr. died, age 71	(headstone in old churchyard)
	Harriet, 1st wife of James, died age 44	(headstone as above)
1885	Post Office: Mrs Louisa Wells, receiver	(Kelly's)
	Harriet Wells (Mrs), farmer (widow of George snr.)	
	James Wells, blacksmith	
	William Wells, wheelwright	
	James Wells bought Rook's Farm from William Chawner	(Abstract of Title)
	(John Knight now at Queen's Head)	
1889	Post Office: Mrs Louisa Wells, receiver	(Kelly's)
	(Samson Davis now at Queen's Head)	
1891	Details from the census of that year:	

Post	Louisa Wells, widow, age 57, Post Mistress	(b. 1834)
Office:	Daniel Wells, son, age 12, scholar	(b. 1879)
Yew	Harriet Wells, widow, age 74, own means	(b. 1817)
Cottage:	William Wells, son, age 36, carpenter/w-wright	(b. 1855)
	(John Knight, bricklayer, now at Church Lane)	
	(Samson Davis, publican – now called Queen's Inn)	
Rook's	James Wells, blacksmith/farmer, aged 55	(b. 1836)
Farm:	Ann Wells, wife, age 52, Newton Valence	b. 1839)
	Alfred Wells, son, aged 25, blacksmith	(b. 1866)
	Martin Wells, son, aged 20, cowman	(b. 1871)
	Emma Jane Wells, daughter, aged 14	(b. 1877)
1895	James Wells, blacksmith & farmer	(Kelly's)
	William Wells, wheelwright	
1897	Martin Wells, drowned at Foster's Quay, Emsworth, Aged 26 years (headstone in old churchyard)	
1899	Harriet Wells, died April 10, aged 82 (register) (confirmed by headstone in old churchyard)	
1907	As for 1895	(Kelly's)
1910	James Wells, died, age 7	(head stone in new churchyard)
		(confirmed by Abstract of Title)
1911	As for 1907, plus Jane Wells (Miss), cowkeeper, Rook's Farm	(Kelly's)
	Marriage of Emma Jane Wells to William Albert Redman	(Abstract of Title)
1912	William James Redman born, son of W A and E J	(register)
1914	Edgar Redman born, son of W A and E J	(register)
1923	William 'Billy' Wells, wheelwright	(Kelly's)
	W A Redman, cowkeeper	
1924	Ann Wells died at North End, Portsmouth	(Abstract of Title)
1935	William Albert Redman, cowkeeper, Rook's Farm	(Kelly's)
1937	Alfred Wells died at Grayshott	(Abstract of Title)
	William Wells died 7th February, aged 81 years	(graveside in new churchyard)
1959	Emma Jane Wells, died, age 82	(head stone in new churchyard)
		(confirmed by Abstract of Title)
1960	David William Redman born, son of Olive and Edgar	(register)

*(All the above details have been put together by trawling through old copies of census forms, registers of births & deaths, as well as the trade directories available. Some details did not quite add up and I have slightly modified things to correct any glaring errors. The 1841 census entries gave George's & Harriet's ages as 25 and 20, which did not fit the full story. I am pretty sure that the amended details are the right ones. Some of the dates of birth may be a year out, as I have only been able to estimate them. Taken overall, I hope that the details shown provide a fairly accurate record of the bloodline of one of **Greatham's** well-known families. Ed.)*

From the the above, it can be seen that George Wells was born in 1812, at a time when the country was ruled by a Prince Regent, later to become George IV. George Wells married Harriet and they had a son, also named George. Harriet was listed as a widow in 1891 and son George's name had disappeared from view after 1880. David Redman always knew that there was more than one Harriet in the family history, which does tend to confuse things!

The elder George Wells was shown as a wheelwright on his son's baptism certificate and sons did tend to follow in their father's footsteps in those days. So it is safe to assume that George junior is the one who went on to also become a wheelwright, before assuming

Abstract of the Title of Mrs E J Redman to Rook's Farmhouse, Greatham, in the county of Hants.

Dec 12th 1885: William John Hampden Chawner, then residing in Bengal, India, (a Lieutenant in Her Majesty's 18th Royal Irish Regiment) sold Rook's Farm, by conveyance, to James Wells, for the sum of £450. The purchase price included an area of land measuring 4 acres, 2 rods and 8 perches.

Feb 27th 1901: James Wells signed an indenture (agreement) with Edwin Albery of Midhurst, Sussex, entitling him and his heirs to hold the premises of Rook's Farm for the use of the Wells family for life. This included James and his (second) wife Ann, their daughter Emma Jane and son Alfred, and their heirs.

Oct 31st 1910: In his will, James Wells appointed Henry Trigg, of Pook Lane, *Greatham*, and his son Alfred Wells, to be the executors and trustees of the will. He also bequeathed Rook's Farm Cottage and 5 acres of land to his wife (Ann) and daughter Emma Jane during the life of his said wife, subject to a sum of £200 being paid by E J to her brother Alfred.

Nov 1st 1910: James Wells died.

Dec 28th 1910: Probate of the will granted to Henry Trigg and Alfred Wells.

Aug 23rd 1911: Emma Jane married William Albert Redman in *Greatham* Parish church.

Mar 17th 1924: Ann Wells died at North End, Portsmouth.

May 27th 1929: E J Redman (formerly Wells) paid Alfred Wells the sum of £200, in keeping with the will of her father James.

Dec 11th 1937: Alfred Wells died at Grayshott, Hampshire.

44, which would have been in 1883 or thereabouts. He re-married and this is borne out by the 1891 census, which shows his wife's name as Ann. The fact that both Harriet and Ann were of the same age led at first to the conclusion that they were one and the same person, but with the differing places of birth – Selborne & Newton Valence – being indicated, David's recollection is endorsed.

It was David Redman who was also able to confirm that the 'Jane Wells', listed by Kelly's Directory of 1911 as *'cowkeeper, Rook's Farm'*, was indeed Emma Jane, who was his grandmother, having married W A Redman in that year, when she was 39 years of age.

(Having spoken to David prior to a Parish Council meeting in early 1999 and discussed this 'history project', he invited me to visit the farm to look at some old documents and photographs. On a subsequent visit to Petersfield library to check some Kelly's Directories, who should be there doing their own family research but David and his mother! Obviously the bug had bitten them too! Ed.)

the responsibilities of publican at the Queen's Head, sometime during the 1870s.

There is also a George Wells who appears on the Register of Licenses for the Division of Alton, between 1911 – 1915. He appears to have been the licensee of the New Inn at Sleaford, working for Farnham United Breweries Limited, which in 1928 became part of the Courage group. His relationship to the Wells family of *Greatham* is not known, but the name and employment seem to go well together!

Daniel Wells, another son of the elder George, went on to act as the Post Master of *Greatham*. Sadly, he died at the early age of 31 in 1878, leaving his widow, Louisa, to take over the reins as Post Mistress. She is shown on the 1891 census as being a widow, with a son, another Daniel, who was obviously named after his father.

I was told by David Redman that James Wells lost his first wife, Harriet, who had died at the age of about

On the site of the present-day 'Todmore' estate used to be a large barn, used as both a wheelwright's and blacksmith's shop, purchased by the Wells family around 1853, when the property was known as 'Tadmore'. James Wells and William, better known as Billy, used to carry out their activities there, up until the 1930s, probably ceasing when Billy died in 1937. Older local people recall that these two were brothers, the sons of the first George Wells.

Amongst their many talents, apparently the Wells brothers tried their hand at dentistry! Upon hearing that one of the locals was suffering from rampant toothache, they decided to help out. First plying him with drink, they waited until he was well under the influence, then got out a pair of blacksmith's tongs, better known by them as 'Pig Nippers'! These were then used to try and remove the offending tooth, but to no avail. A few days later the unfortunate fellow reckoned that the toothache had disappeared, but he couldn't understand why one tooth stood out further that the rest!

As another sideline, it appears that the Wells brothers were also able to turn their hands to coffin making! The story is told of a gypsy woman who, on passing by, asked Billy if he had one that would fit. Billy promptly asked her if she would like to try one for size, which she did, remarking that it was fine, if a little tight across the shoulders!

Alongside Rook's Farm is the bungalow 'Amedee', which belongs to Hugette and Ray Jenkinson and was at one time the site of the orchard belonging to Rook's. Next to this used to be two old wooden huts, remnants of the Army camp at Bramshott, and placed on Redman land. Back in the 1920s, and possibly for a few years afterwards, they acted as a 'social centre' for **Greatham,** being used for dances, whist drives etc. They were later converted into four chalet-style bungalows, identified as No's 1 – 4 'The Bungalows', before falling into disrepair.

Further down the road, alongside what is now the site of the Village Hall, the two adjoining No's 1 and 2 Oak Cottages passed into the ownership of William James and Edgar Redman, along with the four bungalows, in 1960. They are now separately owned as private residences, having once been part of the Rook's Farm estate.

Abstract of the Title of Messrs W J and E Redman to land adjoining 1 Oak Cottages, Greatham, Liss, Hants., formerly part of Rook's Farm.

Jun 16th 1948: Emma Jane Redman, of Forestside Farm, Blackmoor, Hants., appointed her husband William Albert Redman, and her sons William James and Edgar, her executors and trustees.

Mar 2nd 1959: Emma Jane Redman died.

Jan 27th 1960: Probate of will granted to aforesaid executors.

Apr 6th 1960: The executors, W A and W J Redman of Forestside Farm, and Edgar Redman of 4 Leighwood Cottages, Blackmoor, assent to being joint tenants of the piece of land previously described. By the same assent, W J Redman became owner of No.1 Oak Cottages and Nos. 1 and 2 The Bungalows, *Greatham*, while Edgar Redman became owner of No.2 Oak Cottages and Nos. 3 and 4 The Bungalows, *Greatham*.

Aug 8th 1961: W J and E Redman conveyed a small strip of land on the northeast side to Alfred William and Bertha Ellen Kemp.

Redmans

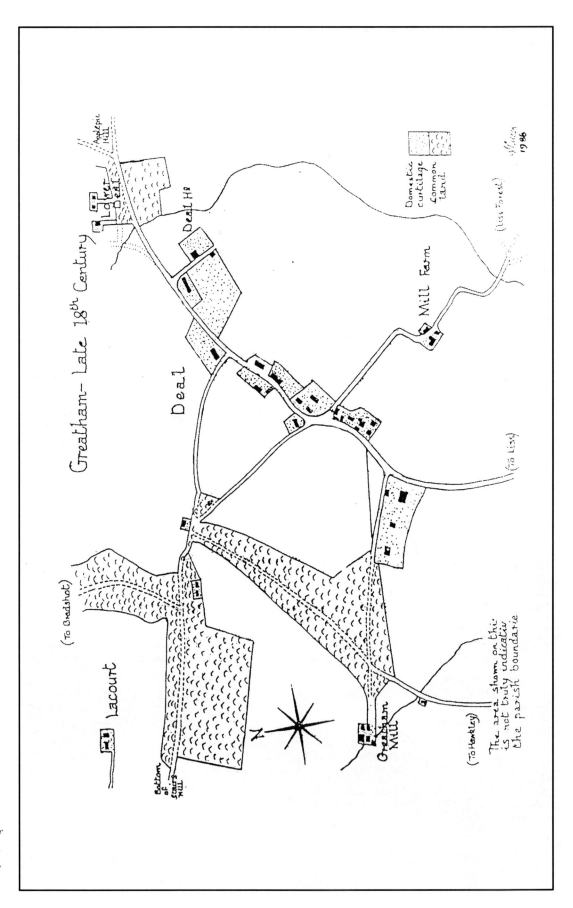

A simplified map of Greatham drawn by Alan Siney in 1986.

Chapter Thirty Eight
George Wakeford

George lives alone at No.4 Woolmer Terrace, off Benham's Lane at the northern perimeter of what is now the village of *Greatham*. Sadly, his wife Kathleen passed away only a few short weeks before I went to have a chat with him but, on an absolutely wet and miserable afternoon in April 2000, he cheered me up no end with his endless humour and story-telling.

George was born on December 7th 1911 in one of Lodge Cottages, which belonged to Blackmoor Estate. Considering that Benham's Lane was originally designated as part of Blackmoor Parish, one could definitely say that George is a local lad! Amazingly, he was the 12th of a family of 15 children – as he laughingly told me, *"They didn't have television in those days"*. George's father was one William Wakeford, who worked as a forester for Lord Selborne on the Blackmoor Estate. His mother, born Charlotte Knight, hailed from Worthing, down on the coast in 'dear old Sussex by the sea', as the old song goes.

George went to school in Blackmoor up until the age of 14. He recalls having to be at school for 9 o'clock and remembers that his mother used to keep him working at his household chores until about two minutes before 9! Such was life in those days. Upon leaving school, it is hardly surprising to find that he found his first employment upon the Estate, taken on as a 'dairy boy'.

This didn't last too long. Being a cheerful boy, George was always to be found whistling while he worked. For some reason, the dairyman took exception to this and one day threw a scrubbing-brush at young George, which bounced up off a duck-board and hit him on the back of the head. None too amused, George responded by throwing a whole stack of brushes back at the dairyman. The Bailiff quickly took George off his dairy duties and sent him off to work on the Estates fruit-trees, mainly on soft fruits such as loganberries.

He then found himself under the supervision of the large Mr Melbourne, who by coincidence came from Melbourne – yes, the one in Australia. By another

An old map of Selborne Parish, home to the Selborne Estate, where George Wakeford worked as a 'dairy boy'.

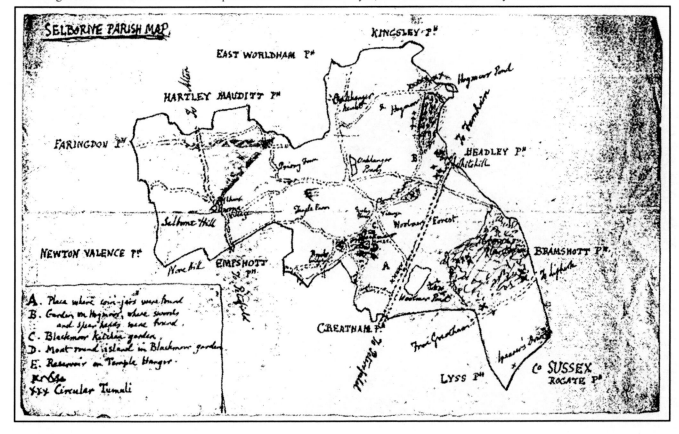

coincidence, two of George's brothers went off to make their living in Australia, in the famous Kalgoorlie goldfields of Western Australia. It was to be a whole 40 years or so before George saw them again, when he went off on a trip to track them down. Both of these brothers eventually died 'down under'.

George was working up a tree one day when, from an upstairs window of Blackmoor House, he was spotted by a young housemaid. When I had asked him 'how did you meet Kathleen?' his initial response was "Up a tree". Yes, a great sense of humour has George. Kathleen had been born in 1919, down at Ringwood in the New Forest. She was an adopted child, given the surname Edwards, and had moved up to Blackmoor to take up a position as a domestic servant, both at the Estate House and sometimes at Lord & Lady Selborne's London residence.

Early motor cars and motor cycles outside Madgwick's Garage

Kathleen's observance obviously paid off and eventually she and George were married at Minstead in 1940. Prior to this, George had served 6 years in the Merchant Navy – and on one occasion bumped into

Charlie Hanson, whose story appears elsewhere. On coming back to Blackmoor, George was offered the post of forestry foreman by Lord Selborne and, upon their marriage, the Wakefords were able to move into Keeper's Cottage on the Estate.

During World War II, George did attempt to re-join the Merchant Navy, but Lord Selborne was able to persuade him that his job at Blackmoor was too important to leave. However, George must have felt pretty much part of the war effort, as the cottage became surrounded by the temporary Army camp hutments which were all over the area in those war years.

After the war, the cottage was required to revert to its previous use, as a gamekeeper's home, and the Wakefords were offered the choice of several houses. Kathleen settled on 4 Woolmer Terrace, where they lived thereafter. George carried on his work on forestry, but would carry out all manner of odd-jobs in his own time, in an attempt to maintain a decent standard of living, while Kathleen was able to find periodic employment as a 'domestic'.

Eventually along came two boys, John and Michael, but tragically both their lives were cut short by cancer within a couple of years of each other in the mid-1980s. As a youngster, Mike used to accompany Lady Anne Brewis on her botanical surveys, particularly in the Noar Hill area, and a memorial seat was placed there by his many friends in **Greatham** during 1985.

As stated at the beginning of this little tale, George carries on living at his home of more than 50 years. Most people would say that he has led a hard life, but he puts this into context by telling of his father. William Wakeford lived at Froxfield and, when the Army Camp was being constructed at Bordon early in the 20th century, would walk all the way there to work during the week. He slept in a pigsty at nights, using clean straw as his bedding, and walked all the way back to Froxfield for his Sunday dinner as the treat for the week. Now those *were* the days!!

A George Wakeford is mentioned in 1567, being described as a 'husbandman' at the Quarter Sessions of that year. A Henry Wakeford operated **Greatham Mill** between 1875 and 1889, prior to its sale to the Ellis family. The names of George E Wakeford and William P Wakeford are inscribed on **Greatham's** War Memorial as having fallen in their country's service during the First World War. George cannot throw any light upon a family connection with the above-named, but says that the Wakefords were a huge family at one time, scattered all around this part of Hampshire. It would be no surprise to find that there is indeed a family connection, with a link going back over 400 years.

Chapter Thirty Nine
Joe Leggett's memoirs

*(As a result of an article published by the Petersfield Post in mid-February 1999, covering some of the historical buildings of **Greatham,** I had a phone call from an Elli Foster, of 5 Malthouse Meadows, Liphook. She told me that she had some written memoirs which referred to **Greatham,** as it had been in the years leading up to the first World War. The following document is an amended version of the original typed sheets, which she gave me, and forms the memoirs of Patrick J Leggett, best known as 'Joe', who was born in married quarters at Longmoor Camp, **Greatham,** in 1909. Ed.)*

Life in rural Hampshire, as seen through the eyes of a child, prior to the Great War of 1914-1918.

Longmoor, 1911.

It was at Longmoor Camp in 1911 that the reality of belonging to this world first began to register with me. I was then living in No.12 Married Quarters, within the camp. My father was Farrier Staff Sergeant Leggett of the Mounted Infantry Regiment, who had been stationed there since returning to the U.K. from South Africa, when the war (Boer War) out there ended.

My earliest memory is of mother being rushed off to Aldershot in a horse-drawn Army ambulance. She returned about two weeks later, by the same means of transport, with my sister Eileen, who completed our family to six, three boys and three girls, namely George (born 1900), Eva (1902), Charlotte (1906), Frederick (1907), myself (1909) and finally, of course, Eileen.

Longmoor at that time was a hutted camp, each hut clad with corrugated iron sheets, sides and ends painted green and the roofs tarred. There were many of them, dispersed around a large area from the western end of Weaver's Down to the moors overlooking **Greatham.** On the lower ground, by the road that led to **Greatham,** there were lines of stables fronted by two forage barns and an enclosed riding school. Also beside the road were an infant's school and a school for older children. My sister Charlotte attended the former, George and

Eva the latter.

The headmaster of both schools was a Sergeant William Redman of the Army Education Corps. He married a **Greatham** farming lady, a Miss Jane Wells, when he left the Army and, together with her, operated a dairy farm along the Petersfield Road at Rook's Farm. *(William Albert Redman did indeed manage a herd of dairy cattle from Rook's Farm in those far off days. He married Emma Jane Wells in 1911 and the couple eventually moved to Forestside Farm during the 1930's. The chapter referring to 'The Redmans' gives further details. Ed.)*

My brother George loved to give us younger members of the family a fascinating account of a great achievement by the Royal Engineers some years previously, when the camp at Bordon was about to be erected. The two lines of huts used to form the initial camp were on site at Longmoor, surplus to requirement there, and the Sappers were tasked with transferring them up to Bordon.

Each hut was reinforced by bracing and moved intact on rollers along the proposed military railway course. It was a Herculean task, cheerfully undertaken and successfully completed as per schedule. No doubt he (George) and the other boys at the school learned that from Sgt. Redman. When Longmoor Camp was better established, some of the huts were moved yet again to form married quarters, our No.12 being one of them.

For the children of the camp, life was just one long round of pleasure. The very atmosphere of military activity, with its parades and musical rides, displayed on the moors by personnel of the 15th Hussars, operation of trains on the track network, 'field days' on Weaver's Down, the aroma of saddle-soap, boot polish and metal polish forever wafting in the breeze – all these still set my nostalgia blazing, whenever I hear the name *Longmoor* mentioned.

It seemed the sun always shone over Longmoor, and its nearest places of habitation, in those far off days. So, when the band led the musical ride onto the local moors, there was a dazzling glitter from their instruments. It was a free show for all those who cared to come from the villages and hamlets, to witness the skills of superb horsemanship. They were frequent events and Father was always present in his capacity as Senior Farrier. He would be in full ceremonial regalia, the dreaded poleaxe being the main part of his accoutrements. George was quite good at giving Frederick and me a running commentary on what was happening, and when father passed by on his mount, would cry out in a voice for all to hear *"Look, there's Dad"*. He was very proud to be the Farrier's son.

Then there were the locomotives, which hauled the rolling stock all around the camp, with carriages on regular journeys to Oakhanger and Bordon. It was a free trip for the children of military families, provided they were accompanied by their parents. I can still recall the names of the engines, of which the Sappers who drove them were extremely proud. They were *'Sir John French'*, *'Woolmer'*, *'Bordon'* and *'Longmoor'*, while there was a smaller one, which was known as *'The London and Brighton'*. This had the letters 'L.B.S.C. Railway' painted on its sides, whereas the others all had their names in polished brass letters, on a red background, attached to their sides.

(Woolmer 0-6-0 replaced Bordon on the WIMR in 1910, and was used until 1919, when it was transferred to Hilsea, Portsmouth. It returned to Longmoor Yard in 1954 and, after restoration, was put on display on a short length of track outside the HQ building, until the railway's closure in 1969. Ed.)

One day the *'Sir John French'* was going to, or returning from, Bordon and came to grief as it negotiated a bend by a sandbank, opposite Woolmer Pond in New Road, or 'no road' as it was then called. Many long and most embarrassing days passed, before the Sappers managed to get it upright and back on track. There was a photograph of the event in the camp photographer's (Mr Harvey's) shop for many years afterwards. I understand that the picture is now on display in the Railway Museum at York. Each one of those engines had a character of its own and George could identify all of them, just by listening to the sound of their approach.

The lovely heather-covered Weaver's Down was a favourite for field-day exercises. That was always a good excuse for George to take Frederick and me to the summit, to get a good view of the exercise around the lower slopes. Not quite as exciting as the musical rides, but it attracted a lot of onlookers. Those lovely formations of pine-trees on the summit, moulded up with local stone were, as George said, the burial-grounds of Roman soldiers, who built the ancient Roman road on the southern side of the hill.

Our parents were the proud owners of a sturdy chestnut pony, which they used for pleasure with a 'governess' cart, much in the same way as a motor car is used in present times. Tommy the pony was stabled at Grigg's Green, so when he was finished after a drive, it was a labour of love for George to drive him to his stable, rack him up for the night, then return to Longmoor on a bicycle. He was never happier than when he was with Tommy.

My father was coasting along towards a full Army pension and, jointly with my mother, it was their ambition to find a suitable place, somewhere in the **Greatham** area, where they could start a small-holding. They hoped to work up a sound business to supplement the forthcoming modest pension. It was fun for me to go out in the governess cart, searching and enquiring about likely premises. Father was already in the habit of collecting large quantities of eggs from poultry farms at Four Marks and Ropley, for supply to the Officer's and Sergeant's Messes. It was proving to be a very profitable pastime.

Longmoor Camp was a hive of military activity. There was a fire station with a horse-drawn fire engine. Practice alarms were quite frequent and the engine would proceed to the scene, swinging perilously close to disaster as it was hauled by a team of galloping horses. An ambulance was kept at the same station, also drawn by a team of fast horses. Church parades were another big attraction to all ages. As usual, the sun shone on such occasions, reflecting a dazzling glitter from the brass instruments of the band that led the troops away to the service at **Greatham Church.**

Sometimes I was allowed to accompany my father as he did the rounds of the sick-lines for horses. I have often heard it said that a Farrier is *'one who shoes horses'*, but that is not all he does. The things I have seen my father practice, under the instruction of a Veterinary Officer, is a lot more than just shoeing horses!

I recall how terribly disappointed the three eldest members of the family were, when their beloved headmaster (Sgt Redman) retired from the Army to start up a dairy round. However, their despondency was short-lived, because they were able to see him every day as he delivered milk and other dairy produce to the

A sombre occasion as a military funeral cortage winds it's way thro' Longmoor Camp

married quarters at the Camp. Then later, when we had moved to **Greatham**, they had the pleasure of seeing more of him on his farm, almost opposite **Greatham** Village School. They felt there would never be another schoolmaster as kind and considerate as William Redman.

One day I was out for an evening ride with Mother and Father, when we turned into Benham's Lane. Father said that he was *"going to see a man about a dog"*, which was a favourite expression of his when he wanted to avoid a lot of explanation to my many enquiries. Benham's Lane was little better than a cart track through the fairly dense woodland of Lord Selborne's estate, on the perimeter of the extensive park-like grounds of Blackmoor House. After some distance, the woodland became less dense and we came upon a cottage on our right. A lady was in the garden, and my parents spoke to her. She said that she was Mrs Cousins, whose husband worked on the estate. They had a teenage son named Frederick and their cottage was situated within the grounds of Blackmoor House.

During the conversation, Mrs Cousins pointed to a house down on lower ground, across the grounds. My parents thanked her and we moved off down the boulder-strewn hill. At the bottom of the hill lay Benham's Farm, with a pond outside the entrance gate. Farm wagons sat in the pond, submerged to the tops of their wheels. Father pointed out that this was to keep the iron rims and spokes tight. A Mr Hall met us at the farm and accompanied us further down the lane to the house to which Mrs Cousins had pointed. To my young mind, Mr Hall was obviously '*the man*', but where was '*the dog*' Father had come to see him about?

Mr Hall showed my parents around a large rectangular plot of land, on which the house stood, and then produced the keys in order to look over the house itself. My brother Paddy (who was christened Frederick) suddenly arrived at the idea that we would soon be leaving Longmoor to live at Benham's Lane. Paddy was two years my elder and about to start school. He was becoming concerned about which school he would have to attend, disappointed that it no longer appeared to be the school at Longmoor. On our return journey it began to get dark, so before reaching the main road, Father stopped to light the two candle carriage-lamps. The village policeman was very keen to catch the drivers of unlit vehicles at that time. I seem to recall that the 'bobby' in **Greatham** was a PC Street at that time, later succeeded by PC Bowering.

Our quarters at Longmoor were good by comparison with the primitive conditions of the surrounding area. *'All mod cons'* of the time consisted of running water, for all purposes, while the fuel for heating and cooking was a free weekly issue. We had paraffin oil-lamps

These gateposts have long since gone, but Benham's Lane still runs besides Greatham's most northerly outpost of Rose Cottages.

hanging from the ceiling, but a power station was being erected to provide electric lighting for the future. Most important of all was a good sanitation system, with a sewage outfall that eventually seeped away from the filter bed under Weaver's Down into the denseness of Woolmer Forest.

When the news of a move to Benham's Lane became a certainty, there was much despondency once more amongst my elder brothers and sisters, who enjoyed having their school right on the door-step. They were destined for the village school at **Greatham**. This meant a long trudge by footpath, through woodland and across meadow, which would bring them out near the bridge over the stream, at the junction of Liphook Road and Petersfield Road. They would also miss all the privileges that they had enjoyed as '*barrack rats*'! (Not a very complimentary reference to the children of the Camp, but it was tolerated.) The day came when a GS (General Service) wagon, drawn by two shiny-coated Army horses, arrived to move all our worldly goods and chattels on that short journey to Benham's. Everything went smoothly, as you'd expect of a military operation.

Greatham, 1912.

Immediately we moved to Benham's House, it seemed to have a tonic effect on all of the family. To George, Eva, Charlotte and Paddy, the dreaded walk to **Greatham School** became a great daily adventure. They were all interested in the abundance of flora and fauna to be observed as they walked the footpath. After school, they just could not get home quickly enough to help in any way they could in the home, and on the rapidly expanding smallholding. George was in his element to be with Tommy the pony, who now had a proper stable of his own. Prior to our moving, he had been stabled at Grigg's Green, over a

Billy Wells

return again in early afternoon, free for the remainder of the day. In wet weather he would be taken into Camp in a two-wheeled Army cart with a tilt on it. The Colonel of the Regiment looked after his Farrier that way.

When we moved to Benham's, it was the winter of 1911-12, and I recall looking out of the window one morning to see a carpet of snow for the first time in my life. It was a lovely sight when the sun came out, to shine-up the distant hills surrounding Selborne. Tommy the pony seemed to be just as puzzled as I was, as he gazed at it through the top half of his stable door. There was a general freeze-up, with Woolmer Pond invaded by skaters from **Greatham,** Longmoor and Whitehill. Father made us a sledge and George rigged it up with a canvas sail, which was quite effective when a strong wind blew up.

The daily trek to and from school was a sure test of the stamina of those four children who attended, but to the amazement of our parents, they never complained. They loved the school, and soon discovered that the Headmaster, Mr Hiscock, was equally as kind and considerate as Sgt. Redman had been. Charlotte is the only one of those four still surviving. She has just entered her ninetieth year, and the hand-writing of a letter I have just received from her bears evidence of the excellent schooling she had been given in those far-off days, at both Longmoor and **Greatham**.

I loved going the rounds of the smallholding with my mother each day, to be told all about the animals and poultry. We had geese that started to lay eggs and I was told how the geese would sit on the eggs, so that the goslings would appear after days of incubation. There was a gander which recognised Mother as friendly, but he would eye me suspiciously and hiss at me as I passed by.

There was a young lad living at Benham's Farm by the name of Bert Hall. He was about the same age as myself, so our respective parents thought it would be a good idea for me to go up to the farm to play with Bert. All went well for a time, until the day we entered a barn just inside the entrance gate, containing hay and straw. Bert produced a box of matches and ignited one – we were lucky to get out of the blaze without injury. Farm-workers came on the scene and, with the duck-pond so close at hand, the blaze was soon extinguished. That was the last time we played together, but the scarred beams of the barn bore evidence of our having played there, remaining for all to see.

One afternoon, soon after our arrival at Benham's, I ventured to pass through the wicket-gate in the hedge, into a meadow adjoining our land. It led down to a stream that gently wended its way to **Greatham** and beyond. There was a bridge over the stream, where I could look down into the water, and I was fascinated to

mile away from the Camp.

Eva and Charlotte helped in the house, so that Mother could spend most of the day attending the welfare of the livestock. Pigs, chickens, ducks and geese occupied all the buildings at the bottom of a large orchard. They had previously been the kennels for a local pack of hounds. The house was the home of the Master of Hounds, while the stable was for his horse. The whole of the premises was a smallholder's delight – for my parents it was a *'dream come true'*.

Father was to remain a soldier for the next twelve months, but as the time for his 'de-mob' grew closer, so his duties at the Camp became less demanding. A Cavalryman would arrive at the house each morning on horseback, with a spare mount on a lead-rein for the Farrier to ride into work. It was interesting to see Father walk over to his mount, run his hands over its back and down each leg, then check the saddle for security, before mounting and riding away. He would see small fishes darting among the reeds. Sometimes there were small animals inhabiting the banks of the stream, which George said must be wild ferrets. *(I now know that they must have been otters.)* However I failed to notice a quick gathering of fog and, in trying to find my way home, got completely lost. Darkness fell and I was cold and hungry. It was lucky for me that a man named 'Billy' Wells heard my whimpering, located and identified me, and carried me back to my anxious family.

Billy Wells was a well-known character around **Greatham**. He lived in a house *(No 2 Rose Cottages)* on high ground at the corner of Liphook Road and Petersfield Road. As far as I know, he was a bachelor, who worked at his tradesman's barn opposite the public house *(The Queen)*. The local farmers knew him as a handy-man, who could always help them out with their problems and was nearly always on call.

*(Billy was indeed well known, coming from a long established family in **Greatham**, and a wheelwright by trade – see the Redman's story. Ed.)*

Billy knew every means there were for snaring rabbits, hares and foxes, as well as trapping pheasant and partridge. There was a ready demand for his catch among the villagers, as he went his daily rounds. His poaching activities were well known, with the farmers turning a blind eye to it – Billy was too valuable to offend! As he was a friend of my father, and had a brother, Jimmy, a blacksmith over at Grigg's Green, I have a feeling he himself may also have been a blacksmith at one time. He was also uncle to Mrs Jane Redman.

At this point, I would like to move my story forward to 1927, when I worked for my parents on a pig-farm beside the stream at **Greatham**, just behind Forestside Farm in Liphook *(now Longmoor)* Road. It was a Sunday morning, as Billy emerged from across the meadows with a sack over his shoulder. The sack was unusually bulged, so I asked him what was in it. To satisfy my curiosity he tipped the contents out for me to see. It was a large dog fox and he was quite proud of his catch. *"After I've been to 'The Queen', I'll skin him"* he said, as he went on his way. The next time I saw him, he was heavily bandaged and I asked him what had happened. He looked at me and *said "Haven't you heard?"* He then proceeded to tell me the tale.

He had gone home that Sunday, put the sack under the stairs, and headed for 'The Queen', turning out again at 2 o'clock, after his usual stay. Back home again, he had opened the cupboard under the stairs, with the intention of carrying out his plan to skin the fox. Now when I had seen that fox, it looked as if it had been dead for quite some time, but when Billy opened the door, the very much alive fox had confronted him

and viciously attacked him! His only course of action was to open the front door and let the fox escape. It had been a near thing for Billy, and a long time passed before he was seen again without his bandages.

That first winter at Benham's seemed to pass rather quickly, and although her mantle was still clearly visible on the distant hills around Selborne, the blue sky and warmer air in the lower grounds was pleasant. I was able to go up to the cottage on the brow of the hill to see Mrs Cousins, who would proudly show me the wonderful fretwork of her son, Frederick. I always had to ask her if I could get anything for her at Grace's Store, situated at the entrance to Benham's Lane. It was a long walk to the shop for a lad of not-yet four years of age, but I loved going there for Father's ounce of 'Royal Seal' tobacco, along with other sundries for Mother. When I arrived at the shop, I was nearly always in time to see one of the military trains on its way either to or from Bordon.

I often went with my father, collecting eggs from the poultry farms at Ropley and Four Marks. We now had a four-wheeled van for that purpose and, at each farm, Father would collect crates of eggs, each crate containing twenty dozen (240), with the van able to carry anything up to ten of these crates. There were two routes we could take to get to the collecting area, but the one I liked best was to turn right out of Benham's Lane, down through **Greatham**, then right again into the Selborne Road.

I liked that way, because we met people of the village, with who Father would stop to chat. Also, as we passed the school-house, there was the chance of seeing my brothers and sisters in the playground. On the corner of Church Lane there was a thatched cottage, where 'Nanny' Russell had a sweet-shop – Mother always made sure I had a copper to spend there. 'Nanny' Russell was such a kindly soul to all the

Mothers had no need to drive their children to school in Joe's day.

children, despite her whiskery appearance. No matter how small my purchase, there was always the bonus of a free pear from her own orchard. No pears have ever tasted so sweet since.

When we arrived at the bottom of Stair's Hill, there was a waiting place for trace-horses, which were there to assist heavily laden wagons as they negotiated the long, steep and winding hill. Also at that point was a notice-board, warning cartmen of the gradient, and demanding that bearing reins be slackened off, to become totally ineffective. I remember my father finding time to explain what the notice said – and why.

Tommy was quite capable of pulling our empty van up the hill without assistance from a trace-horse, but Father did not like to ride on the van. He would lead Tommy up the hill, stopping occasionally to reverse the van into the bank, so that Tommy could rest. When we reached the top of the hill, and Father got back onto the van, Tommy would put on a spurt, knowing that there was a drinking fountain at Selborne, where he could quench his thirst.

There was always a queue of wagons at the fountain, each cart-man had certain adjustments to make as he reached the drinking point, so that his horse or team of horses could drink freely. It would

This old coouple were able to stand by the main Farnham Road without having to dodge the traffic!

all require re-adjustment before the journey resumed. I had already been made aware of the fountain's history, it having been built as a memorial to Gilbert White, a former Vicar of Selborne, who did so much to preserve the beauty of that area. My brothers and sisters had filled me in on that subject.

After the fountain, we turned sharp left to ascend an even steeper hill than the previous Stair's Hill. This was Galley Hill, which went up through Gilbert White's much written about 'Hanger'. After Galley Hill, the lanes that led to our destination were very narrow, with grass growing on the surface, except for where the cart-wheels ran down the sides, and in the centre where the horses trod.

On those trips with my father, I hoped to get a first glimpse of a motor-car. I had seen trains, traction engines and even the occasional aircraft from Farnborough, as well as an airship that circled Longmoor and **Greatham**, but I was fated not to see a motor-car for some time yet. Our return journey from Ropley, with a precious load of eggs on the van, was quite perilous as we descended both Galley and Stair's Hill, and I can remember how the drag-shoe would be red hot when removed from under the wheel.

The winter of 1911-12 gradually faded away and I can remember looking out of my bedroom window one morning, to find every tree in our large orchard a blaze of various coloured blossoms. It was a marvellous sight, but prettier still when I was in the orchard later on, looking at it towards the sun. Spring was in the air, according to the family, and I wondered what they meant by that remark. They had seen spring on previous occasions, but this was the first time that it had come to my notice.

From that day onwards, the wildlife inhabiting our smallholding appeared to have received a message of urgency. Birds were working hard, gathering material to build their nests, the cuckoos were calling to each other, and the rooks that congregated in the tall trees down by the stream were setting up a tuneless chorus. Rabbits and hares were coming out into the meadow, while our geese were incubating the eggs that had been laid in February. Mother was reckoning up exactly when we could expect to see broods of goslings emerge. It was all explained to me in a most interesting way.

The chickens cackled with excitement as they left their nesting box and, each time that they did, our giant Rhode Island Red rooster would dash over to investigate what all the fuss was about. After feeding in the morning, our ducks would waddle off, with the drake in the lead, in single file to spend their day on the pond outside the gate of Benham's Farm. They would return again at feeding time; they too would soon be producing their offspring, but not all of them, as their eggs were in great demand at the Messes in the Camp. Yes, I was beginning to know the meaning of 'Spring is in the air' and, even now after a further eighty four years, the advent of Spring always turns my thoughts to **Greatham**.

About once a fortnight, a van belonging to the Surrey Trading Company came down the lane, loaded with all kinds of household requisites. The visit was so much appreciated by the residents of the four remote dwellings at Benham's and, as a reward for the effort, there would always be a large purchase of the goods carried. In addition to those wares carried inside the van, a vast array of pots and pans, baths and buckets, even scrubbing-boards, hung on the outside, rattling and clanging as the van negotiated the boulders down the lane.

This was always a loud signal that the van was on its way. At our house, being the last port of call, the driver was assured of some refreshment, whilst the horse had a well-deserved rest, a pail of water to drink from, and a munch of corn and chaff from its nosebag.

One day a tribe of gypsies from Grigg's Green came down the lane on a cart, followed by the head of the family, leading a sick horse. My parents knew them well and they had great faith in my father's ability to ease the agony of a sick animal. 'Old Tom', as the head of the family was known, led the horse into the orchard to where Father was waiting with his jacket removed, shirt sleeve rolled up and a 'colic ball' in his right hand. He opened the horse's mouth, grabbed its tongue with his left hand, and thrust the medicine down the horse's throat. The horse was then released and left in the orchard, where he was free to roll around if he wanted.

In the meantime, the rest of the tribe entered the copse adjoining our house to cut sticks of wood, then sat down on the bank of Blackmoor House grounds. There, they cut the sticks into uniform lengths, peeled them of their bark, and made clothes pegs of them with a few deft cuts of the knife. Their baskets were full of pegs in a very short time. Presently Old Tom came out of the orchard, now leading a far better looking horse, and the tribe departed, to sell their supply of newly-made pegs to villagers on their return trip.

As spring passed into summer, there was always something of interest to see in the fields. Grass in the meadows grew knee-high and, in the sweltering heat, teams of men with scythes could be seen cutting around the outer edge, one behind the other, each starting a new row. All day long they would swing their long-handled scythes, stopping occasionally to sharpen the blade on a whetstone. When they eventually reached the centre of a meadow, the newly mown grass would lie in neat rows, and the team would move off to carry out the same procedure elsewhere. The horse-drawn mowing machine was not in general use at that time on the smaller farms, nor was the threshing machine. Benham's Farm had many stacks of corn from previous harvests, waiting for an available machine to make a visit.

Although work continued on the farms in all kinds of weather, it is hard to believe how proud were the farm-workers of their endeavours. As though it wasn't hard enough for the ploughman and the carter, they still found time to polish the harness brasses and to decorate their horses manes and tails. At the end of each working day, the horses would receive attention to see them through the night, before the men went home to their cottages for their own well-deserved meal.

During that summer, I was surprised to note a very large gathering of local inhabitants outside the gate of our house. There was to be a game of Polo in the grounds of Blackmoor House, and some VIP's were about to arrive via Benham's Lane. Needless to say that the lane had itself received the 'VIP' treatment, for the carriage that would bring them. What a thrill! I expected to see the party arrive in a carriage, drawn by arch-necked horses with tight bearing reins, giving a high-stepping display.

Instead, as they descended the hill, I became aware of a strange noise. It was a motor-car, and I now know that the visiting party were Royalty. That was the very first motor-car I had the pleasure of feasting my eyes on. It stopped outside our gate and the party alighted, to be greeted and escorted to where the game was to be played. The car stood there all the time that the game was in progress, while its chauffeur went over to lean on the perimeter fence, from where he could see the play.

That was my chance to walk over unobserved, to get a close-up of that glittering piece of mechanism. To see one had become an obsession with me, but this was not just a passing glance, it was right there in front of me, to be examined at my leisure. At that tender age, I wasn't interested in Royalty, but I think I may now know who they were. My sister Charlotte, now in her ninetieth year, thought that it was the then Prince of Wales, later to become King Edward VIII, who abdicated to marry Mrs Wallis Simpson.

Also during that summer, there was a sports day at Blackmoor. Lord and Lady Selborne did a walkabout, encouraging all the children to take part in the various events. I raced against other children of my age, and won a prize – I think for that particular under-fives event, every entrant won a prize just for trying! However, Charlotte received a prize from Lady Selborne for needlework, a treasured, quilted needlework box, of which she is still very proud to this day.

George and Father worked hard together and, although the 'mod-cons' of Longmoor were missed,

the primitive conditions at Benham's were tackled and overcome. There was a sawing-horse near our back door, where they both spent some of their time each evening, sawing logs for domestic fuel, with a crosscut saw. The ringing tone of the saw, as it ripped through the branches fallen from trees, was music to our ears. Fallen branches were plentiful and ours for the gathering.

At dusk each evening, the toilet bucket needed emptying into a deep hole in the neighbouring copse. George and Father would carry the bucket, on a pole passed through its handle for that particular task. Father would light up his pipe, while George would smoke a Woodbine. His secret habit had been discovered before that, but his usefulness was too valuable for Mother to take much offence at his smoking. There was a deep well situated in the orchard. Water for all purposes had to be drawn from the well by bucket, chain and windlass. Quite a large amount was drawn each day and stored in vats, ready for daily use.
(One can only hope that separate buckets were used when carrying out these two tasks! Ed.)

George also took it upon himself, as a labour of love, to look after Tommy the pony. During the summer he had gathered, and made hay of, the grass that grew alongside the local lanes. As autumn approached, a large stack of hay ensured that Tommy had something to munch during those long winter nights, when he would be confined to the comfort of his stable. After the meadow next to our premises had been cut, and the grass made into hay and stacked, cows from Benham's Farm were allowed to graze there. Billy Wells had told me about their way of eating as much as they could, and

then lying down to ruminate.

I seem to have had no childhood fear of cows, and was so fascinated about what Billy had told me, that I entered the meadow when the herd was about to lie down, to watch their actions. If I watched the gullet, I could see the outline of the ball rise from the stomach to the throat, then the cow would start to chew. After chewing away contentedly for several minutes, I would see the chewed cud, as it was swallowed back into the secondary stomach. There would be a few seconds' pause, another cud would pass up the gullet to the mouth, and the rumination process would be repeated. As Billy Wells had pointed out to me, he felt that the real tranquillity of the countryside could be felt by watching the cows chewing the cud. His words, and the memories of those scenes, always come back to me.

Another thing that fascinated me was that when their rumination ended, one cow would always rise up and go down to the stream. As though it was a given signal, the remainder of the herd, with a few seconds interval between them, would follow suit. When they returned from quenching their thirst, they would wait patiently until Mr Hall called them in for milking.

In that same meadow, there was always a rich picking of button-type mushrooms during those misty mornings of early autumn. One morning when the mist suddenly lifted, it revealed a large gypsy tribe, with their large baskets filled to capacity with nature's rich crop.

As autumn turned to winter, I was getting more privileges than ever, it seemed that every day now I was getting out with my father. He was doing a lot of business with local farmers and smallholders. His duties at Longmoor became less & less as his time for retirement approached. His ability to render first-aid to all domestic animals, and his availability at all times, was well recognised by farmers and pet lovers over a wide area. It was on such calls, while treating animals, that I was able to accompany him, mainly to get out from under Mother's feet. One of the places I remember we visited is now a 'Cheshire' Home, although in those days we all knew it as Heath Harrison's. Although he could well afford a vet to attend to their many horses, Father was very much favoured when any of Harrison's animals were off-colour.

Another farmer in the village was a Mr Etheridge, I have a feeling that his farm was along the Petersfield road, just south of the bridge. On the other hand, it may have been near the pond, adjacent to the Woolmer Hotel, which is now called the 'Silver Birch'. Mr Etheridge was always so very kind to me and, when he died, all our family was extremely sad to think that we would never see him again. Not long after his death, there was a farm sale of all his livestock and equipment. My parents attended that sale, to purchase some very useful items, which became invaluable to us when we were farming in the years that followed.

Mr Frank Kemp farmed at **Greatham Hill**, behind the houses, and was also contractor to Longmoor Camp, for various types of transport jobs. He employed quite a number of carters. There were many little ailments among his horses, although I may add that they were very well looked after. Mr Kemp was so appreciative of Father's service, that in 1927 he let us have the piggery at the bottom of the hill.

Approaching **Greatham** from Whitehill, all the ground on the right was enclosed by the then familiar black, cast-iron fencing. Within this enclosure there was a dense growth of trees, shrubs and rhododendron bushes. On the other side of the road were the rifle-ranges, used by the soldiers of both Longmoor and Bordon Camps, with Woolmer Forest in the background. The first dwellings along that road were two cottages on the right, within the enclosure of Lord Selborne's Blackmoor Estate opposite Woolmer Pond, one of which was occupied by a family named Keen. The Keens were friends of my parents, I think there was a military connection from their days at Longmoor. They had a large family, all boys, which seemed to increase annually! I seem to recall that a daughter finally arrived, bringing the total to thirteen. A Mr and Mrs Jeaves lived in the other cottage, with daughter Mabel, a friend of my sisters.

There were no other dwellings until reaching Grace's store at the entrance to Benham's Lane. I do remember some of the names of the dwellers in the vicinity. Mr Fennel, who rode around on a bicycle with a basket on the front handlebars, peddled haberdashery

to the local ladies. He and his wife had a daughter named Joyce. A large family, the Wells, lived fairly close to the shop, their children being Jim, Arthur, Winifred, John, Veronica and Violet.

The James' were another family, with a son Jimmy, I believe that Mr James was a soldier serving with the Sappers. The Cooks lived in a house to the rear of those fronting the main road. They had two daughters, one of who was named Cissy. Harry and Mrs Scarlett also lived in that area. They had a daughter, Lita, and were guardians to a mentally retarded character, George Watson. Another family were the Gales, I think they had a son called Vic.

As time passed by, I realised that my days of accompanying Father to collect eggs and to visit farms where he would perform miracles on sick animals, would soon be coming to an end. I would soon be joining that happy band of scholars on their daily trek to **Greatham School**.

Greatham, 1913.

With these thoughts on my mind, I found myself wandering off along the footpaths that led to **Greatham School**, where I could meet my brothers and sisters as they came out. The bridge over the stream was where I would meet them, the stream held an attraction for me. I was gazing into it one day, when along came a traction engine, which pulled up at the bridge to replenish its tanks with water. It was hauling a complete threshing machine on about four long trailers, while in the rear was the crew's living accommodation.

The driver alighted and I saw that he had a wooden leg, but he was quite agile. He dropped a hose into the stream, moved a lever on the engine and, while water flowed into the tanks, filled his pipe with tobacco. Other men came out of their van and began discussing which way they should go.

After a lot of argument, the driver asked me if I knew where Benham's Farm was. I felt really grown-up to be able to reply in the affirmative, but my ability to give directions was another matter. So, when I said that I lived next door, he invited me to ride alongside him. This was just *like 'pennies from heaven'* to me, as it certainly made my day. There was a cast-iron seat for me to sit on and it was a joy to be able to point out the way home. It was quite a performance turning that great machine into Benham's Lane, some of the trailers had to be unhitched, then hauled along and re-coupled after the turn had been completed.

Eventually we were on our way again. One of the wheels sank at one point, causing further delay whilst a cable was run out and attached to a tree. A pin was pulled out of some contraption and the engine slowly pulled itself out of the soft clay into which it had sunk. There were further thrills as we negotiated the steep incline down to Benham's Farm.

The driver thanked me and I was lifted down from the seat to make my way home. I watched as the whole machine was driven skilfully through the gate, with little more than a few inches clearance. What a story I had to tell my brothers and sisters! There were lots more interesting things to see in the following days, when the machine would be operating in the rick-yard. All the men worked on stacks of corn, and after threshing, the ricks were rebuilt as straw for animal bedding.

When all the threshing was completed several days later, I just had to be at the gate to see the machine's departure. As the machine was negotiated through the gateway, the cheerful wooden-legged driver gave me such a friendly wave as he passed. I watched as it ascended the hill until it was out of sight. Whenever I saw a threshing outfit in later years, I always looked hard, hoping to see my friend with the wooden leg, but I never did see him again.

By 1913, Father had at last become a civilian. He had no difficulty in adapting to that status, having prepared for it during the year we had lived at Benham's. The economy of **Greatham** depended mainly on the number of troops at Longmoor, which was at that time full to capacity. Father had some valuable contracts for the collection of kitchen waste from the Messes, as well as for the regular supply of eggs, oven-ready poultry and fresh pork.

We kept our own pigs and had a butcher cum slaughter-man in Mr Lovell from Whitehill, who came about once a fortnight to kill a pig for the pork supply. With those contracts, plus the demand by local farmers for Father's knowledge and skill as a Farrier, the whole business was flourishing.

Unfortunately, Benham's was no longer large enough to meet growing demands. There was despondency once more in the family, at the mere thought of ever moving away from that place which had provided so much happiness. However, 'feelers' had been put out and results were coming in. My parents found themselves in a dilemma as to which premises to choose, and at last decided to look at the latest offer of Grove House, a gentleman's residence in Forest Lane, Grigg's Green.

This was an eight-roomed red brick house, built in 1907, standing in an acre and a half of ground, with a large paddock in the background. Next to the house was a long brick building, consisting of an outside toilet, fuel shed, coach-house, stables for four horses, as well as a harness room. All current 'mod cons' were installed. One look at the place and it was theirs – for an all inclusive rent of eight shillings and sixpence a week (42½ pence in present day currency).

Grigg's Green, 1914

We moved into our new home in easy stages. I am not sure whether we actually got there before or after Christmas 1913, but it was definitely winter, the house was very comfortable, and we quickly settled in. I remember how sad I had been, going along Benham's Lane, saying goodbye to all our neighbours and wondering if we would ever see them again. For me, eighty years would pass before I ever went down that lane once more.

Epilogue, 1993-1994

My son was over here from his home in Australia, and insisted on going to see the place he had heard me talk so much about, while he himself was growing up. Although I am now blind, except for the odd flicker of daylight, I sensed to my surprise that there was little change either to Benham's Lane or the dwellings. My wife and son were able to see the things I asked about, such as the wicker-gate that afforded entry into the adjoining meadow. It was a great day for me, just to realise I was actually back there, in a place I had so much loved.

In 1994, my son again visited from Australia, and we came to **Greatham** and stayed at what I remembered as the 'Woolmer', now the 'Silver Birch'. My mind went back to the times I often sat there in the governess cart, with Tommy secured to the hitching-rail, while Father called in there for his well-earned pint. During my stay, much to the dismay of my wife and son, I went

'The Woolmer Hotel' had long changed to 'The Silver Birch' by the time of Joe Leggett's return to Greatham.

off alone to trace the footpath to Benham's. Without assistance, I found the entrance and followed the rough track, making what I thought was good progress. Thinking that I would soon be at Benham's House, as I passed through some woodland, I heard the clear sound of almost continuous traffic. Realising that I was probably lost, I traced my way back to the hotel. Next time my son is over here, I intend to attempt that walk again, but this time with the benefit of my son's eyes!

Afterthoughts

I do apologise for the numerous times I have pressed the wrong key on this machine and for the terrible mess I have made in trying to correct my mistakes! I am not a touch-typist, but I do practice that technique, otherwise I would be unable to communicate other than verbally. Therefore, I trust that whoever cares to read what I have written will be able to interpret its true meaning.

I didn't intend to write further than my childhood at Longmoor and **Greatham**, but feel that I must add just a small amount more, to take it up to the outbreak of war. In August 1914, Father went back into the Army for the duration, while George became a trumpeter with the 19th Kings Own Hussars. Both survived that terrible war and, indeed, both served again in the 1939-45 fracas.

Upon leaving Benham's in those far off days, Father had owned a single-cylinder De Dion motor car which, upon his re-entry to the Army, went back to Brittnell & Crowther of Petersfield. Tommy the pony was commandeered to assist the war effort and Mother was left to run the smallholding as best she could. Charlotte, Frederick (Paddy), myself and later Eileen, all attended the school at Longmoor, staying there until the ages of fourteen. Our headmaster was Warrant Officer Haynes. My childhood ended when I started school. I too joined the Army, in 1928, and served until the end of the Second World War. I then became a civil servant for the Air Ministry and then with the MoD, Army Department at – of all places – **Longmoor Camp**!

(As Joe Leggett says himself, the type-written sheets which were handed over to me did indeed contain many typing and spelling errors, which is hardly surprising, when you learn that he has been blind for many years. I have tried to include as many of his own words as possible, and also of course to retain the original language and phrases of a man brought up before the First World War.

With the help of some local residents, I have changed a few names and places, where Joe's memory must have faded over the passing years. I do hope that I have not changed the original script too much, if so I apologise, all my motives were certainly well intentioned. Just about everyone who has read Joe's story has been able to either confirm one or two points, or to think of another story they had almost forgotten.

To follow this account, you will find the words of two letters, written by Lady Ann Brewis, now some 88 years of age, and the present resident of Benham's House. She kindly invited me to tea one day, and gave me permission to publish her letters. I trust you will find that they add a final footnote to Joe's fascinating memoirs. Ed.)

Lady Anne Brewis MA

Eldest daughter of the 3rd Earl of Selborne, Lady Anne has had a life-long interest in the flora and fauna of Hampshire. Soon after graduating in Zoology at Oxford, she married the Reverend John Brewis. But it was only after her husband's retirement, when they returned to live on her father's estate at Selborne (Blackmoor Estate), that she became a fully-active member of the Wild Flower Society and the Botanical Society of the British Isles. Following the death of her husband, she found solace and stimulation in the preparation of 'The Flora of Hampshire', on which she has worked tirelessly for over 20 years.
(From the dust cover of 'The Flora of Hampshire')

26 March 1993

Dear Mr Leggett,
Well I never! I do wish I had been in when you called. I am two years younger than you and I live here all by myself. My son lives at so-called Benham's Farm, which used to be two cottages, now knocked together, but he has a job abroad. I came here 25 years ago, with my husband the Rev J S Brewis, who had to retire early from St James's, Piccadilly, London, because he had Parkinson's. I can't tell you how delicious it was to come here from Piccadilly, and see the cows in the field, having their calves, etc.
I had never lived in the country all the year round before, as our jobs had

always been in some black town. When I was a child, my father was an MP, so we all lived in London, coming down to my grandparents (Lord & Lady Selborne) at Blackmoor House for holidays. The present Earl is my nephew, as his father, my brother, was killed in the last war.

So this was a smallholding in your time was it? At some point, it got into Blackmoor Estate and, as I first remember it, was used as a large cottage for someone who had about 8 children. The lane was unbelievably muddy, being on the Gault Clay. We children used to be taken round, bringing Christmas presents to all children on the estate; but Benham's Lane was too muddy for the car, so we had to go in the pony-cart, and even that stuck on occasion.

During the last war, there was a camp up at Ridges Green (the top of the hill), with a cement water tower. After the war the Army blew it up, and asked my father what he would like done with it. "Put it down Benham's Lane", he said. So that is why the lane is a bit better nowadays and passable for motor cars. Although I assure you that it is very much complained of even so. But I think that apart from it being bad for one's car, it is rather beautiful, like something from Beatrix Potter. I see rabbits, pheasants, foxes, deer and badgers running across it, and sometimes at night a woodcock flies up. Once I saw a kestrel fly up, with a young rabbit that it had pounced on from within the trees.

Isn't the view beautiful - and aren't I lucky? Well, as a matter of fact, there used to be three magnificent oak trees in the way of the view - you can't have seen it. My nephew cut them down, in order to put modern drainage into the field. I hated to see them cut down, but when that lovely view of the Hawkley hills was revealed, I couldn't complain!

So you used to go down to the stream - and to that little wooden bridge? It must have been a wonderful place for a child. The orchard had gone by the time we came. I think my father, who introduced apple growing to the farm, had a scheme for presenting his tenants with new trees, if they would cut down their old ones, which he said infected his orchards with 'woolly aphids'. When he arrived, alongside the house were a Bramley, a Belle de Boscoup, a somebody-or-other's Seedling and a Cox's Orange Pippin, all of which were destroyed to make way for a conservatory. That blew down in the gales of 1987-88!

The Bramley at the front still had one root in the ground, and I kept it there for the grandchildren to romp on, you probably saw it. I planted 8 new apple-trees on the other side of the house, but they have to be surrounded by a barricade, because of the deer. I remember them arriving in these parts at the end of the war, and they are now in swarms. The rest of the ground was a very mucky garden, which I grassed over, having an invalid husband, not wishing to pay a gardener, and wishing to have time for the wild flowers. Also, it was so nice to have the grass and trees after central London.

I used to have a car, and kept it in what had obviously been stables, I am sorry to say that some of it has now gone. It was a beautiful old building, though riddled with worm. About 15 years ago, the estate manager told me that it was beyond repair, and wanted me to buy an unspeakably hideous modern garage from a catalogue. I was hanged if I would, and said that I'd rather this one crumbled down on me first! However, my nephew says that he is going to mend it - only wish he'd hurry up. I've been waiting three years now, and as I expect you noticed, it's getting pretty bad.

If you have written some memoirs, please may I buy a copy? And if you come down here again, do come and see me by appointment. Do you still have any relatives here?

Yours sincerely
Anne Brewis

23 April 1993

Dear Mr Leggett,

What a wonderful and fascinating account of your early life here, my friends and I have been enthralled. To think that in this very kitchen where I am about to have my supper, you nearly cut your sister's leg off! And that you watched the Hunt (blue coats for the Hampshire Hunt and red coats for the Hambledon), I expect from the little room at the top landing, from which you also saw the fox creep into the outhouse.

There are still plenty of foxes, but also other animals which I don't think you had. Did you ever see a badger? They may have been here, but when in about 1923, I was cycling towards Brockbridge, and saw a badger cross the road from one wood to another, my grandfather wouldn't believe me. He was a keen naturalist, but had never seen a badger in all his life.

However, a year or two later, the hounds killed one, and now they are extremely common in all the hangers. They run along behind this house, coming from Bradshott and going towards Greatham Moor. Once there were some beautiful footprints in the hoar frost, but I have never seen them in my garden.

My daughter-in-law at Benham's Farm (they have knocked those two cottages together now) has been more fortunate. In that very hot summer of a couple of years ago, after one of the few showers, she looked out in the evening and saw three badgers on her lawn, shovelling up earth-worms for all they were worth. The only harm that they do is, that if you put a fence up along one of their regular paths, they will keep going the same way by burrowing underneath, letting in the rabbits! My nephew, the present Lord Selborne, has installed badger-gates in all his fields, across the badger runs. These are things that the intelligent badger learns to push open with his nose, but the rabbit doesn't have that sort of brain.

I expect you had red squirrels, we used to have lots at Blackmoor House. They were driven out in the twenties by the grey ones, of which we now have too many - beautiful, but little beasts. Along with the magpies, crows and jays, they destroy all of the baby birds and eggs, besides doing immense damage to young trees. They used to have a nest in one of our disused chimneys, jumping onto the roof from one of the nearby oak-trees, until I had that chimney stopped up.

I don't remember ever having seen a magpie until 1926, when we went to Switzerland, and I wondered at first what all the black & white birds were. They are very common now, supposedly because all the keeping went to pot in the two wars. There is always a nest in the wood behind the house. They watch the other birds build their nests, then when the babies are hatched, descend upon them. They feed their own babies on them for the whole of May. Did you ever see a magpie here in your time?

Then there are the roe deer. The first one I saw must have been around 1944, in the bog at Conford. A population explosion was just starting now they are in all the woods and all over Woolmer Forest. I have often seen them in what was your orchard, but which is now all grass. Beautiful they are, but most gardeners hate them, because they eat almost every garden flow, particularly the roses. I don't mind, as I have none of those things, and my grass is full of wild vetch, which they love. However, one can't grow any young tree without them de-barking it, one must erect a barricade.

I get harvest-mice nests in the long grass and once we had a stoat's lair nearby. The milk-bottle tops on the doorstep started having mysterious little holes in their caps, and one day my daughter opened the door to see a stoat running away. Later that year, there was a pair of young stoats playing together, rolling over and over just like any otter cubs, in the yard of Benham's Farm.

I loved your story of 'Sly' and the policeman getting into the swamp, and I have reflected that it must have been before they moved the Whitehill Pond a bit higher up. There are still the remains of an older road a lot nearer to Woolmer Pond, it is very boggy now, and it would not have taken much for a dog to decoy someone in.

If it is not asking too much, please may I have any similar tit-bits about Grigg's Green? I have botanised (sic) over there, as I have done everywhere else, working on 'The Flora of Hampshire' (see accompanying note), and wonder where your smallholding was. There is no small farm there now, but next to Queen's Road there used to be a nice damp meadow, grazed by a pony, where I found lots of nice flowers, but with a horrible cement-mixer right next to it! They have drained it now, and I imagine that they are going to build upon the site.

I have just passed on your letter to Lord Selborne because I knew that he would be interested. I know of three local magazines which would love to print extracts - the Alton & Petersfield division of the Hampshire Wildlife Trust, the Bordon & Longmoor Conservation Group, of which I am a member, and the Selborne Association would like your story of Galley Hill. Have I your permission?

Finally, I cannot think of how a limousine ever got down Benham's Lane in its condition of those days! I can just remember being taken to see that polo game, it was the Officers of Longmoor Camp who played it, but the war killed off all that.

Yours very sincerely
Anne Brewis

P.S. Yes, there is a ruin at the bottom of the garden, there is a sort of cement foundation. I was told it was where dogs had once been kept, I had no idea that they were 'hounds'.

The 'top end' of the Village shows the road to Farnham in the days of little or no traffic.

Chapter Forty
Alan Siney's story

*(The following historical collection is based upon articles written by Alan Siney and passed on to me by his cousin Elsie Collins, sometime during 2001, after I had already largely completed my own 'History of **Greatham'**. I was later given permission to edit the article, as Alan freely admitted that the original came about in random fashion. However, I hope that this editing has not detracted from Alan's purpose, I have only sought to put things into a more logical order, and into separate chapters, where thought to be necessary. I am happy to say that everything Alan remembered bore out many of the facts that I had already been able to gather together during my own research. I must also add that I had already been privy to some of Alan's work when I first started on this history, based upon the map and notes which can now be found on an illustrated manuscript mounted upon the committee room wall of **Greatham's** Village Hall. Ed.)*

Greatham - its history and my memories, by Alan Siney

Introduction

A little over a year ago my cousin, Elsie Collins, told me that a chap called Peter Gripton was compiling a complete history of **Greatham** and would welcome contributions from those who had memories of bygone days. At that time – and for some time since – I was busy on a series of projects relating to my own area and county of West Sussex and had to dismiss any plans to participate. Nevertheless, being blessed with clear memories of almost every detail of my boyhood spent in **Greatham**, it was never far from the back of my mind that it would become my duty to record those memories. When the opportunity came, it was on the spur of the moment that I decided to begin. Fortunately I found it easy, with no interruptions, no trips to the Records Office or scanning of reference books, the facts just flowed into my mind.

Elsie also showed me the account of **Greatham** life written by Dr Ronald Shotter, detailing his long stay at Deal Farm during the Second World War. I believe you will find it included elsewhere in this complete history. I remember the Shotters very well but only vaguely recall Ron, though I seem to remember his

sister Margaret, who only came to **Greatham School** for a short time.

An agricultural heritage

A griculture had seen great changes throughout the 19th-century; for the first half of it the Corn Laws operated, passed by the land-owning members of Parliament in order to protect their own interests. The Laws put an artificially high price on wheat and a high tariff on imports, which put the cost of good bread beyond the reach of the poor labouring classes. Along with land enclosures and the deep depression that followed the Napoleonic wars, the combined effects cumulated in the agricultural riots of the 1830s. Large gangs of hungry, displaced land workers roamed southern England, looting and burning.

Parliament wrote this off as a moral defect, rather than a socio-economic problem, and answered it by sending in armed troops. The 1834 Poor Law Amendment Act was passed, which ended the giving of outdoor relief by parishes and, in draconian fashion, the families of unemployed men were separated and thrust into Union workhouses. This made a mockery of their marriage vows; to the phrase *"let no man rend asunder"* should have been added *"except, of course, by parish officers in the course of their duty"*. Yet it was the Church that actually supported the Law's application at every level and was, indeed, the backbone of all civil administration.

Sir Robert Peel, as Prime Minister, was eventually forced into repealing the Corn Laws in 1847. By then, it became apparent that the lobby of Britain's expanding industrial might far outweighed the patronage offered by the land-owning gentry, who sold off the block vote of their tenants to whichever candidate proved to their mutual benefit. For the next two or three decades, British agriculture enjoyed relative prosperity, with an increasing demand for bread. But around 1870 imported wheat began to flow into the country. Steam-driven flourmills were built at the points of entry, from where railways could transport the ground flour to all parts of the land. This was followed by the import of wool from the Antipodes and, later, by meat being carried on large refrigerated ships from the far-flung corners of the globe.

British agriculture then fell into decline. Land values fell and most tenant and yeoman farmers lost their livelihoods; large country estates were now snapped up by men who had made their wealth from industry and commerce; the *nouveau riche* were no longer from the colonial background of tea, sugar and tobacco plantations as before. From a purely **Greatham** outlook, it may be significant that the row of Coryton alms-houses down at West Liss was dedicated to the memory of two ladies in Derbyshire, a county more closely associated with new estate owners from a background of iron and coal, as well as the Stock Exchange.

With wheat growing no longer a profitable concern, the face of the countryside changed from its predominantly arable look to a dairy farming appearance. Old tithe maps show that much of today's woodland was used for wheat during the era of the Corn Laws. A few small farming families, such as the Shotters of Deal Farm, clung on tenaciously, surviving only by thrift and a modest lifestyle.

New farm buildings show the changes that took place in the late 19th-century, as new owners used their capital to build large cattle sheds.

Those at Hatchmoor Farm, just along the Selborne road, had the capacity for about eighty milk cows. Old wheat mills, like the one at **Greatham**, which dates back a long time, were severely affected by the change to dairy farming. Those that did keep on working were restricted to grinding animal feed for local farmers. There may have been a brief reprieve during the First World War, but very few survived the 1920s.

Regarding maps, commons and roads

Deal Farm lay within the geographical locality known as Deal, which used to be distinctly marked on old maps as lying along the flood plain of the stream that forms one branch of the River Rother. This continued until more modern boundary changes marked it as the northern extent of **Greatham**. The organic matter that washed down onto this plain, over millions of years, left Deal with a fertile soil, so different to the heavy clay just above the ridge. How well I remember trying to break down the clay in the school gardens whereas, just down the road at Deal Cottages, the soil was black and friable. A drawing that I did in 1948 was loosely titled Deal Knapp Farm, but that was the name of the road that ran in front of the farm. Its gradient has been somewhat levelled from what I remembered when the hill was quite steep at the top. The term 'knap' comes from old English, and it can mean either 'to break flint' or 'crest of rising ground'.

The wide area in front of the farm was an old drover's road that followed across to join Church Lane by the cottage of Shepherd's Mead. *(I was rather perturbed to find, in later years, that a part of this ancient road, which ran between the hedgerows alongside the cottage, had been taken for private use, with the footpath widely diverted.)* The road then followed the existing green lane *en route* to **Greatham Mill** and Hawkley, along Snailing Lane. Church Lane itself continued on to Empshott, before turning northwards to Bradshott. All of these old roads had a dewpond at regular intervals, in order to sustain the herds of cattle being frequently driven to the larger towns. There was one just to the left of the foreground in my drawing, which also served as the main farm pond.

The tithe map and apportionment schedule of 1842 shows Deal Farm to have been the largest holding in the parish, with 176 acres, which extended along Church Lane on the western side of the main road and out to Forest Road to the east. The owner was William Goodeve, whose remains lie in the family tomb at the old church, while his memorial tablet enhances the north wall of the chancel. Deal Cottages belonged to Deal Farm and are shown on the first Board of Ordnance Survey map of around 1800. A little to the east of the cottages was Deal House, which was clearly of some importance, as it was also annotated on that survey map. Its position can best be described today as immediately to the rear of the bungalows that now form part of Baker's Field. It was owned by Thomas Trigg and occupied by the Blanchard family. It was possibly demolished soon after the middle of the 19th-century, as there was no mention of it when I was a boy, and such information handed down by those born in the village usually takes a couple of generations to become lost.

The sandy ridge, along the north side of the Liphook road at Lower Deal, is the edge of what was Woolmer Forest. This is a vast area of desolate heath on lower greensand, extending through Bordon to the north, reaching around almost to Liphook in the east, then on around to cover what is now Liss Forest. This was Crown Land and, when the military took it over in the late 19th-century, **Greatham** was reduced to a fraction of its former size. Over 10,000 acres (13 – 14 square miles) of the non-titheable wasteland of Woolmer was removed from the parish. When the War Department enclosed it, they placed boundary stones at intervals along the enclosure banking, between Longmoor Road at the top of Apple Pie Hill and right across to the Liss Forest road. A few years ago, I followed the boundary with my late brother Eric and discovered several of these stones still standing. I was also interested to find that, at the eastern side of the grounds of **Greatham Moor House**, a pair of gateposts still stood, where the house once had an entrance from the heath.

A sketch map that I produced is based upon those maps re-published by David and Charles, entitled the 1813 O.S. maps. With trigonometrical surveys beginning about 1790, they were carried out during the prolonged period that Britain endured under the threat of a French invasion. Such was their military value that the drawings and engravings were completed within the secure confines of the Tower of London. General publication was deferred until 1813, when it was (mistakenly) thought that Napoleon was now safely ensconced on the island of Elba. It is for this reason that I refer to them as 'circa 1800'. Another point to be explained is that the surveyors' drawings were cut and joined into county-size rectangles, for subsequent engraving onto copper plates, and it meant that the edging left a gap of about 100 yards between adjacent maps. Of all places, one of these gaps coincided with an important part of **Greatham** centred on the old church, with the line going to both the north and south of it. Thus, this locality has always remained a bit dubious.

What the map does show is that, before the turnpike road to Farnham was built in the early 19th-century, the old road from Liss (or now West Liss) curved towards the north-west at Deal. It crossed the stream some 100 – 200 yards downstream from the present road-bridge at the bottom of Longmoor Road. From the original crossing it roughly followed a course parallel to and south of Longmoor Road, along what is now Wolfmere Lane, to disappear as a sandy track leading into Woolmer Forest.

From that old crossing point, a track led along the northeast of the stream – I remember it well, with its bank capped by hawthorn trees. It later re-crossed the stream over a small brick bridge, giving access to a strip of wet, rough common grazing land, which stretched down the western side of the stream almost to the Liss Forest road. With the building of the turnpike and the Liphook road, one northerly spur of this track was maintained as a right-of-way. My eldest brother could just remember helping to drive a herd of cattle along that spur as a boy, but it is now built over and long since gone. The other spur linked the old road to Forest Farm, which once had a handsome barn. However this was in a ruinous state even when I was a boy and it was demolished some time later.

My map c.1800 therefore shows **Greatham** before the Farnham road was built and re-aligned to go up Queen's Hill. It was also before the Liphook road was built and before the Alton road even existed. It shows three pieces of common land with the roads through them shown in dotted lines, as was the custom. They were unconfined roads and the traveller was free to deviate from the track in whichever way he thought best. The track towards Snailing Lane crossed Alder Common. When this later became enclosed, there had to be maintained a right-of-way and so the present green lane from Church Lane across to the Alton road was laid along the western edge of the former common. Tracks over Great Common led westwards to the bottom of Stairs Hill and then to Empshott, while the locality where the road from Deal Farm joined with Church Lane, at Shepherd's Mead and Cam Cottage, was called Cam Green Common.

I collected these common names in the early Eighties, when I visited the Hampshire Records Office at Winchester. They are as given on the 1842 tithe schedule. I also found a reference to an Enclosure Act, which indicated that they became enclosed about a decade or so later. With over six million acres of common land having been enclosed in England during the previous hundred years, by the mid-19th-century Assistant Enclosure Commissioners were no doubt scratching around for work and bent on 'tidying up' any last remaining pieces. Established rights-of-way and old roads were usually retained, or at least suitably diverted, as public footpaths and bridle-ways. They remain so until well into this 21st-century, to be jealously guarded for recreational purposes. The Enclosure Act of 1870 was designed to prevent the further taking of common land for private occupation, but for most places it was already far too late.

My use of the term 'road' should not be taken in the modern context of a hard tarmac surface. Those old roads could be of deep mud for most of the time, impassable to wheeled traffic and unsuitable for even agricultural usage. In spite of advice from locals that he shouldn't attempt it, in 1822 William Cobbett took the route from Hawkley Green to **Greatham**, descending down from Hawkley Hanger on what we know as Tiddler's Hill. He spent some time admiring the views from the top before heading down and found it even worse than predicted. The surface was smooth, grey marl, so wet and slippery that his horse had to be freed to slide down much of the way on its hocks. Cobbett himself struggled to the bottom, hanging on to underbrush to slow his descent. Having passed through a farmyard (Scotland Farm), he found a lane that was at once both road and river and came to *"the indescribable dirt and mire of the road to* **Greatham***"* (Snailing Lane).

During his travels, William Cobbett wrote in great detail of the places through which he passed, making biting comments upon those injustices that he found.

He noted the parks and gardens; the quality of crops and the nature of the soil; in particular he stopped and talked to the labourers in the fields, questioning them about their wages and working conditions. The agricultural labourer of the day lived in abject poverty, his wages pegged by a Wages Board and based mainly upon the need for bread. So incensed was Cobbett by the miserable conditions of these poor workers that his fervent support for them was rewarded by a short spell in prison. It is thus disappointing that he made no mention of **Greatham**, beyond the state of its roads – *"I am thinking whether I ever did see worse"*. In itself, it is a noteworthy statement, coming from a man who spent years riding the rural byways of England, avoiding the turnpike roads.

It appears from Cobbett's writings that the direct roads to Farnham, Alton and Liphook had still not been built by 1822, but they had been completed by the time of the survey that followed the Tithes Commutation Act of 1836. Most turnpike trusteeships were disbanded about 1870 and the tollgates removed. I still vaguely remember the tollhouse at **Greatham Corner**, with its white lime-washed walls jutting out to where, today, they would be right in the centre of the Selborne junction. With the rise in motor traffic the tollhouse became an obstruction and, when it was demolished in 1937, we went down to the site with the old family pram to collect kindling wood. The last occupants were a family by the name of Booth, who then moved into Tom's Acre, a cottage on the opposite side of the road. It took many years for the name 'Tollhouse Corner' to disappear from local bus timetables.

Referring back to my map, it shows a building upon the site of the new school, which was only partially enclosed and open to the road. Thus it could

hardly have been privately owned and leads me to the conclusion that this may once have been the parish tithe barn, where farmers delivered one tenth of their crops to the church. This payment of tithes was introduced in biblical times by the Laws of Deuteronomy and became obligatory under ecclesiastical law over much of Christian Europe. It was made enforceable by secular law in England and much of the rest of Europe between the 8th and 10th centuries.

In England, tithe barns were made redundant by the Commutation Act of 1836, which commuted the payment of all tithes to an annual rental charge. The Tithes Act (1936), followed by further Tithe Redemption acts, paved the way to the eventual abolishment of tithes. They had been, to all intents and purposes, a legally enforceable property tax, promulgated by Parliament on behalf of the Anglican Church, whatever the payee's religious convictions or ability to pay. For over one thousand years, tithes had therefore been a bitter source of conflict between landowners and the clergy.

I have also included the 'pound' where it was shown on the 1842 tithe map, as one was normally erected just outside common land, for the impounding of stray animals. A cottager was normally allowed to tether his cow on the common, in accordance with the laws and customs of the local manor, but not allowed to turn it loose thereon. A straying beast could wander onto crops and farmers, trying to improve the quality of their stock, did not want them mixed with possibly diseased animals from the 'common herd'. These rules applied particularly before most land became enclosed. An impounded animal would be released to it owner, only upon payment of a fine, as levied by the manorial court. This type of feudal stranglehold by the 'Lords of the Manor' slowly released its grip throughout the 19th-century.

Captain Coryton and Manor House

Captain Augustus Coryton, of the Manor House, owned most of the parish. He was usually referred to, informally and out of earshot, as Gussy or just Gus. The house had been handed down to him, along with the estate, from his father (Frederick Coryton) earlier in the century. It was Gussy's firm belief that tilling the soil was man's only honourable profession, 'technology' being alien to his nature. At times he may have had the manner of the irascible old squire, but he firmly believed that country children should enjoy and learn about their surroundings, being able to wander about the countryside at their will. Thus, **Greatham** became our domain by right and we would wander wherever we chose, over field and meadow, the swampy land along the eastern edge of the parish, the

Manor House, for many years home to the Coryton family.

forest and moor and the sandy tracks that led beyond. We were inveterate tree climbers, stream dammers and fort builders, always expecting a new adventure to crop up at any moment.

We never went anywhere without a catapult, which could propel a pebble over a considerable distance. The 'proper' elastic would be bought from Allsworths in Petersfield and securely bound into the cleft ends of a forked hazel-stick. An old pair of leather boots, discarded in the hedgerow, would prove a great find, as the tongue would be used to make the projectile pouch. As for targets, well I should be ashamed to admit that this would be just about anything that moved! Not that we had anything to fear from the Captain, we would often meet him on his regular patrols of his estate, along with Bracken his faithful Golden Labrador. He would greet us in the friendliest of manners, often stopping to point out a visible feature or something unusual he had seen. Despite his bluff aristocratic manner he was quite a likeable character, but his mood could often depend upon his alcohol content!

The Manor House, as I recall, consisted of the original part, to which were added two later extensions. These were probably of the late-Victorian era, with a grand entrance hall and an impressive oak staircase. On the southern end, along the wall that enclosed the extensive gardens, was the farm entrance. A large duck pond on the right was half flanked with elm trees. There was an old paddock containing a very old and impressive oak barn, with a range of cart-sheds and other outbuildings of similar age and character. Around 1840 the house had been a humble farmhouse, with a holding of some 166 acres.

Captain Gussy worked his *Greatham* estate in true 19th-century manner, failing to come to terms with modern methods. With dwindling capital, it became inevitable that he would have to sell the Manor House and move to one of his smaller dwellings. The old house was split into separate parts and mostly sold to two owners. There was no interest shown in the large number of horse-drawn wagons and carts; nobody even bothered to take them for scrap so, eventually, they were pushed up together and burned, which must have been a sad sight. Fortunately I was not there as witness as, by that time, I was serving the Royal Air Force in the Middle East. My brother Eric went on to work for Sir Denny Ashburnham, who had bought Gould's House as his residence, along with nearby Goleigh Farm and several fields.

Gussy was one of the last of the old-style 'village squires', having had control of both administration and church, plus all within his domain. The landed gentry, who sat on District and County committees, couldn't boil an egg to save their lives and few would mourn

their passing. Yet it must be said that they formed the backbone and stability of rural communities, bringing in much-needed capital, which often went to good parish works. In a purely historic sense, it is difficult to envisage how a community would have evolved, both socially and economically, if the land had only been occupied by humble farmers, unable to offer much to their local parish. So perhaps these 'gentry' should be remembered as much for their charity as for their autocracy. With Captain Coryton's demise, the Manor House then ceased to be the venue for social activities and village functions, which had included the celebrations for the Jubilee of King George V and Queen Mary in 1935. I myself was present at the later function, heralding the Coronation of King George VI and Queen Elizabeth, in 1937.

The house now belongs to a religious community but I wish to relate one final story regarding its ownership by the Corytons. I had left Cowplain School after two years and, up until my military call-up time, I worked for Mees Limited, an electrical and radio business based at Liss. One day we were called out urgently to the Manor House, where smoke could be seen rising from below the large oak staircase. There had been an electrical fault and one of the house's gardeners-cum-handymen had seen fit to replace the fuse with a nail! No real damage ensued but it proves that, from such small and seemingly meanless deeds, the largest of houses can be lost forever.

The Siney family

My father was Reginald Alfred Siney, born at Longparish near Andover in 1895. His family moved to East Liss around 1907, where his father was head gardener at Easton House. This had a 'lodge house' at the driveway off the old A3 road near Hill Brow and was owned by a Miss Barton. Her family was quite wealthy, also owning an estate in Ireland. Father volunteered for the Hampshire Regiment soon after the outbreak of the First World War and was shipped out with his Battalion to north-west India in 1915. After Townsend had disastrously lost his army at Kut, the Hampshires were transported to the Persian Gulf to begin the slow advance up through Mesopotamia (Iraq), suffering many privations and dysentery and lacking the heavy stores and artillery of the Turkish defenders.

Father re-enlisted after the war and was in Ireland at the time of the rebellion. In 1921, his Company was marching back from the ranges outside Cork when an IRA mine exploded, killing seven soldiers and injuring many others. A battered bugle from that infamous incident now lies in the Regimental Museum

With Deal Cottages on the horizon, the prevailing traffic went directly up Longmoor Road in the 20th century.

school caretakers for many years throughout the war and she later became both a 'dinner lady' and a school manager, before her untimely death in 1974.

My parents had lost their first child Margery, who had died in infancy. Eric was born in 1927; Don then came along early in 1932, with myself the last of the clutch a year later. We were all born at Sandpit Cottages, just up Liphook (now Longmoor) Road, **Greatham**, on the left-hand side. A year or so after my birth the house was sold over our heads and we moved into an old wooden bungalow that used to stand opposite **Greatham School**. Originally built by William Redman, a local farmer and onetime schoolmaster at Longmoor Camp during World War I, one large hut had once served as recreation rooms for the local soldiers. This was later split into three separate 'bungalows', but we lived in a separate one at the northern end, which had once been the caretaker's house.

At the far end lived a Miss Bone and her brother, which brings me to an incident that happened when I was only two or three years old, but of which I have a vivid recollection. Early one dark morning, we were awakened by the sound of loud bangs, caused by house bricks being thrown onto our corrugated iron roof by Mr Bone! Father dressed hurriedly and went to fetch PC Dace, who lived in Wolfmere Lane, although by the time they got back, Mr Bone had left the scene. The outcome was that Mr Bone was later taken away by a couple of men who arrived in a van, and was never seen or heard of again. Why we had been targeted in such a manner I don't know, we were the best of neighbours and we boys were never allowed to upset anybody.

Deal Cottages

Sometime during 1937, Granny Arnold died at her home in Deal Cottages and we were allowed to move there. The rent at the bungalow had been ten shillings and sixpence a week, relatively high when my father only earned about £2 a week. Deal Cottages belonged to Captain Coryton and he only charged us six shillings and sixpence, so the move was certainly beneficial to us. Deal Cottages had been built as a row of four humble agricultural dwellings in the late 18th-century; each with two small rooms upstairs and the same downstairs. The end ones had the advantage of an attic built into the roof, with a small window high up at the gable end and reached by a steep narrow flight of stairs. There was no electricity or running water, but gas was laid on to a small gas stove and, later, a single gaslight was fitted in the living room. Prior to that I recall that, for many years, we played and read under an oil lamp on the table, while for around ten years I did my bedtime reading with the aid of a bedside

at Winchester. Leaving the Army in 1922, father found work at Longmoor Camp as one of the gang laying the military railway across Weaver's Down to Liss Station. When this was finished, he worked at the Longmoor Military Railway Stores right through until 1963. Retiring at the age of sixty-eight, he was later awarded the Imperial Service Medal. During World War II he served in the Liss Company of the Home Guard and, at an early age, my brother Don and I learned out how to handle the Lee-Enfield Mk4 rifle, often playing with the rifle upstairs. It was only after the war that father emerged with ten rounds of ammunition that he had kept hidden from us, in what must have been a very secure place. He eventually died in 1978 at a ripe old age.

My mother had been born Amy Lacey at Hawkley in 1901. Later she and the other five children moved to Woodbine Cottage, up the Hawkley road from West Liss. Her stepfather was employed as a carter for Mr Coryton of Lyss Place. At the age of twelve, mother passed a 'labour examination', by which she was allowed to leave school a year early. She went 'into service' as a parlour maid for Miss Barton, which is where she met my father. At Easton House she was allowed Sunday afternoons off and would walk home for tea with her family. This continued after her mother, Martha Arnold, and the younger children had moved to Robin's Cottage, down Church Lane in **Greatham**, entailing a round trip of some eight miles. Her mother finally moved to Deal Cottages, again within the village of **Greatham**.

Like all isolated parishes, Hawkley had to be self-sufficient. Thus my mother sometimes had to assist her own mother at the job of 'laying out' the parish dead, preparing them for burial. She was always cool, sensible and industrious, the type that neighbours run to in times of trouble. She and my father became the candle.

At each end of the cottages was a shared detached washhouse, with a pair of bucket privies built on and a couple of weather-boarded woodsheds for storage. There were two wells, one of which we shared with the next-door family, the Stokes'. They had two younger daughters, Ivy and Ena, of roughly the same ages as Don and myself. That well water was beautiful, being constantly drawn off and replenished with pure filtered ground water. It was as clear as crystal, always cool and sweet to the taste. The bucket did sometimes pick up a snail or two as it swung against the sides of the well, but it didn't bother us!

In the living room was a low black-leaded range of cast iron. This was the only form of heating and mother occasionally used it as an alternative method of baking and cooking, rather than the gas stove. Any number of saucepans and kettles would be placed on the range, to provide enough hot water for our ritual Saturday-night bath in front of the fire. For the 'weekly wash', father would draw off many buckets of water the previous evening, to fill the 'copper' ready for boiling and provide a bath-full of rinsing water alongside.

Father was a very good gardener, growing some heavy crops of tasty vegetables. Our neighbours did the same because, especially during the war years, self-sufficiency was a necessity. The soil was well enriched by the constant emptying of the lavatory buckets, keeping it as a nice black loam. We were always careful about keeping any sewage away from the well, so that it never became contaminated. In addition to his garden, father also grew a ton and a half or so of potatoes every year, on an allotment out on the Alton Road. This was rented from the Corytons at a nominal rent, I think it was only a couple of bob (10 pence) a year. The system of granting allotment by large local landowners, at a 'peppercorn' rent, had begun in the 19th-century, with the dawning of social conscience following the previous years of enclosure. Then, Parliamentary acts rode roughshod over ancient and common rights, denying the cottager the ability to either tether his cattle or to grow sufficient fodder to keep them alive.

Toilet facilities at home were very basic. Combined with the fact that all meat and groceries were collected once a week and that we had no means of refrigeration then, this would cause modern hygienists to throw up their hands in horror! Yet we must have built up a strong resistance to bacteria, never suffering from the tummy bugs and viruses that seem so prevalent today, while asthma was virtually unheard of. I was probably typical of most children in having to see the doctor only twice during my first sixteen years of life. One of these occasions was because of an injury and the other was when both Don and I had a dose of either mumps or measles. Even then the doctor was only called in because mother had noticed his car in the neighbourhood! There was no National Health Service in those days of course, and I think Dr Pope from Liss charged around half-a-crown per visit. However, we did have a free annual medical inspection at school by a visiting doctor, which mothers could attend if they so wished, plus free annual dental treatment.

If a man was off work through sickness, he was 'put on the panel'. This allowed him to receive modest National Insurance payments, towards which everyone had to pay a few pennies a week. Those on this 'panel' had to comply with a strict curfew – which I think was set at 8 p.m. – after which time they were not to be seen outside the house. I remember one fine summer's evening when a group of us had gathered at the garden gate, this included 'Nobby' Stokes from next door, who had broken his collarbone while playing football. 'Nobby' suddenly turned tail and ran inside, having seen a car coming over Deal Knapp. He had recognised it as the doctor's car – and it was past his curfew time!

From a very early age we were long-distance walkers, often taking the eight mile return trip to Rake, where we would have Sunday afternoon tea with our grandparents. They lived in a little cottage on a high bank alongside a sandy track that led to Harting Coombe, from just opposite the Flying Bull public house. Not far away lived father's youngest brother Vic, who would gallop up and down the track, giving us boys 'piggy back' rides. Sadly, Uncle Vic died of peritonitis in 1937. He was a mere twenty-nine years old and had been married for only about a year. Grandpa died the following year (1938) and Nan Siney followed him in 1941.

Our walk used to take us past the Liss Forest corner, there was a little shop there then, kept by an elderly couple named Mengham. Later we would use the lane that went past The Wylds to Ciddy Hall. This lane had been tarred and flinted for a hundred yards or so, but then it became a sandy track with lumps of protruding sandstone. Near The Wylds, where I remember a lake and a waterfall, large fir trees threw a lacy network of roots across our path. Sometimes we walked home in pitch darkness, which we thought a bit spooky, and we would then prefer to hold hands rather than our usual running about!

When he was six or seven Don was given a little bike and, as soon as he could ride it, announced one Sunday morning that he was going to ride up to Nan's. But on the rough track he came a cropper, when the steering stem broke at the front fork stanchion and he was thrown off his bike. He was lucky that a workmate of father's, Harry Hooper, had just built a cottage nearby. Harry heard the commotion and rode Don, now nursing a swollen lip, back home on his crossbar, with the two parts of the little bike slung over his shoulder.

During the warm summer months, we often took long Sunday evening walks of anything up to about five miles. There was a good choice of circular walks radiating out of **Greatham**, using both roads and footpaths. During one summer holiday, mother took Don and me for a picnic at Noar Hill, the steep hanger behind Empshott, and a new adventure for us at the time. The path climbed steadily upwards along the face of the hill, through magnificent beech trees. Some of them had fallen, their decaying corpses slowly being reduced by woodworm and fungus into the organic matter to feed the next generation. The higher we climbed, the more impressive became the view that appeared through tantalising gaps in the foliage. Eventually we could see over the escarpment of Stairs Hill, across **Greatham**, with the broad expanse of Weaver's Down and Woolmer Forest rising to the hills in the distance beyond. On one side of our scene were the South Downs and on the other the Surrey hills of the North Downs.

We came across a plateau of high ground where, on emerging from the beeches, we discovered what we called 'hills and dales'. These were the pits from where, over the centuries, chalk had been dug to burn into lime for sweetening the nearby fields. The lime would be used to neutralise the acids, produced by fermenting manure, the benefits of which have been with us since biblical times. The digging had resulted in a series of hillocks and shallow-sided pits, covered with fine turf, kept short by the constant nibbling of sheep and rabbits. It was a good place for a picnic and some boisterous running, up and down the slopes.

I have returned to Noar Hill a couple of times in the sixty or so years since that first visit. The last time was with my brother Eric, just before he died in 1994. It was a sad sight, because the 'Great Storm' of 1987 had left only the odd spindly beech standing, allowing the opportunist tress, such as ash and sycamore, to spring up and cover the hillside. It will take some intensive management over many years to allow the magnificent beeches to be restored. This will not be in my lifetime and, indeed, I fear it may never happen.

Attendance at church and youth activities

We Siney boys all sang in **Greatham's** church choir and later, when our voices broke, we all had a spell at pumping the church organ, for which we were paid threepence a service. This pumping took place in a dingy cubby-hole behind the organ itself, where a wooden handle protruded from the matchboard which lined the back of the organ chamber. This had to be pumped up and down like a blacksmith's bellows, the scene lit by a bare glowing electric bulb, hanging on its long flex from the belfry floor above.

Hanging down from the back of the organ was a lead weight, suspended on a cord, which moved up and down according to the air pressure in the system. Two thick pencil lines, drawn on the wood, indicated the low and high settings and it was our purpose to maintain the pressure between the two. When the organ was at rest there would be a gradual reduction in the residual pressure, which required a couple of occasional pumps to raise again. The thin, high notes required little air but the loud, throaty low notes that reverberated through the structure needed continuous pumping, with one eye kept on the weight to ensure that it didn't drop towards the low setting.

During the couple of years that I pumped the organ I only slipped up the once; the Rector was saying prayers during matins and my mind wandered off somewhere. I was returned to reality by the noise of Willie Redman thumping the pedals as he frantically tried to obtain a response. After the service I came out feeling rather sheepish. Willie glared at without saying anything – he didn't have to!

When the Reverend Marks died, **Greatham's** church services were officiated by visiting vicars for a year or so until around 1945, when the Reverend Paul Biddlecombe arrived for induction as the new Rector. He proved a very popular man, bringing fresh ideas to the parish, which included the introduction of girls to the choir. Paul raised his evensong congregation by the simple means of having a get-together in the village hall after the service. *(The 'Old School House' was the venue for 'socials', whist drives and plays, put on by the village's WI (Women's Institute).)* He was approachable to everyone and didn't perpetuate the 'parochial pecking order', as previous Rectors had traditionally done, by their setting aside of special arrangements for the local gentry at social functions. He enjoyed the company of youngsters and involved himself personally in a whole range of activities for their interest. He was a keen cricketer and played for the **Greatham** club team that flourished in the immediate post-war years.

It was quite a successful team, with a fixture list of games against other local parishes, the greatest rivals being neighbouring Liss. Lots of players, from both the home and away sides, knew each other personally, so there was a great deal of friendly banter both on the field and in the pavilion. I remember Wally Kean, who could hit the ball all around the boundary, once hit twenty-six runs off one over – it would have been more, but for one ball that was stopped just short of crossing the rope. Wally was just one son of the Longmoor Range-warden, who lived in an isolated cottage to the east of the railway sidings. After the war, Mr and Mrs Kean received a letter of congratulations from the King and Queen for having had ten sons and a daughter, all in uniform and serving simultaneously. They all returned home safely, including one son from a prison camp. Another good cricketer was Vic Wells, who returned from the war with all the fingers and part of one hand missing. Despite this, by using the thumb and what remained of its joint, he was still able to get a firm grip on his bat.

The cricket pitch was located behind the Manor House and had probably been there since the early days of the Coryton occupation. It certainly gave Gussy the ideal spot onto which he could spectate from the comfort of his own lush lawns. After a long period of non-use it certainly needed some renovation, especially the old pavilion, which was very dilapidated. The team worked hard on this, led by Vic Wells, who was a carpenter by profession. The entrance to the field was a gate down Forest Road, on the bend just before Goleigh Farm. Just inside the gate was the old estate creosote pit. Built of brick, with its own hearth and chimney, it was where timber could be dunked and allowed to steep in hot creosote. Cricket matches were then always played on a Saturday, long before the times when it became acceptable to play sports on Sundays.

Under the Rector's guidance, we also had a successful youth club, normally held in the old school and supervised by Mr Clive Gunner, a very conscientious man who owned the garage at West Liss. He was assisted by Mr Brian Matthews, when Brian returned from his war service. *(At a **Greatham School** reunion, held in 2000, it was great to meet up with Brian again, along with his wife Lily – nee Fiander.)* In the club we had a small snooker table and table-tennis, a couple of pairs of boxing gloves and a brand new BSA 'Major' air-rifle, used for indoor target shooting.

Amongst the visitors that came to see and address us was Professor Joad, who lived at Oakshott, and Group Captain Leonard Cheshire VC, who was at that time struggling to set up his nursing home in the dilapidated old mansion of Le Court. The old place had become a convalescent home for wounded servicemen during the war and, one afternoon, was machine-gunned by a German aircraft. We had heard it clearly but there had been no warning, it must have dropped from cloud cover to seek a suitable target. These were the so-called 'nuisance raids', but it was under one of these that a bomb was dropped on a school at nearby Petworth, killing twenty-eight boys and two schoolmasters.

For several months during one winter, a small group of us were taught woodworking and model making by a Mr Simonow, a Russian refugee who spoke very broken English and resided at Liss. He must have been a very clever engineer in his own right; one time he brought along a working model of a threshing drum that he had built. These lessons were held in a room above the Rectory coach-house. Paul Biddlecombe had cleared it out, providing a strong table as a workbench, along with some assorted tools that he had somehow acquired.

At some period during the war a family called Hawkins occupied the coach-house. Mr Hawkins was a stage comedian, although I can't recall his stage name. He may have been a serving soldier, or perhaps a member of ENSA, the forces own entertainment organisation. If that was the case, then perhaps the uniform he wore was only for honorary purposes. What I do remember, most vividly, was that he had a most glamorous only daughter named Jane. She was very mature for her age and wore her skirts even shorter than the wartime regulation length, thereby leaving the village youths goggle-eyed and breathless!

On some summer evenings, the Rector would take us along to **Greatham's** ancient church, along with the necessary materials to carry out urgent work to the masonry. It was my task to re-pack and re-point the loose and crumbling stonework above the entrance porch. Many years later, in the early Nineties, a group of students from the Society for the Preservation of Ancient Buildings (SPAB) spent their summer holidays in similar fashion. I went to see them several times, initially with Eric just before he died, and was at last able to properly identify some of the church's features. These included the marks of the fixings for the three steps to the pulpit in the south-eastern corner and

A typical area of heathland surrounding Greatham.

the sockets that housed the joists, which would have supported the raised minstrel's gallery at the western end. It was here that long-forgotten **Greatham** yokels must have stood, accompanying the congregation on flute and fiddle.

Some of those SPAB students had been to the Hampshire Archives office at Winchester, to see the plans and drawings that were made of the old church, before it was deliberately pulled down and made ruined. Interments still took place in the old churchyard after the new church was built around 1880. Possibly the first grave at the new church was marked by a stone memorial, erected by the comrades of a cavalry sergeant, killed in a riding accident at nearby Longmoor Camp.

It was a sad day when Reverend Biddlecombe left the parish after only two to three years. This followed the death of his father, who was the Rector over at Blendworth, where Paul was now offered 'the living'. I think this was a great loss to this parish, which always seemed somewhat divided. The northern parish boundary was at Deal Bridge, at the Longmoor Road junction. The largest proportion of village dwellings, up to the corner of Benham's Lane and along the road to Liphook, contained a greater population than all of **Greatham**, yet was placed within the Ecclesiastic parish of Blackmoor. I think this was in the civil parish of Whitehill, while both were within the rural district of Alton. Those who did join in parish functions felt more affiliated to **Greatham** than Blackmoor, which seemed a remote little hamlet, though they were small in number. The community spirit built up by Reverend Biddlecombe seemed to depart with him.

Wartime memories

With the threat of war in 1938 came the issue of gas masks to every man, woman and child. These had to be checked and fitted individually on every single person and I remember going down to the welfare hut at Liss for that very purpose. We walked down there; perhaps it was a weekend because, when we got there, it was full of people waiting their turn, families having to be fitted all at the same time. Later, once war had broken out, these masks had to be carried at all times. I can't remember how long it was before this ruling was relaxed, probably about four years. If you arrived at school without a mask, you would be quickly sent back home to fetch it, a dire warning ringing in your ears.

Once a week we had a gas mask drill where, having donned the masks, we all stood in line, whilst the lady teachers went along checking for condition and fit. This was done by putting two fingers in each side of the mask, to ensure that the tension was correct. Some of the younger children still had masks in the shape of 'Mickey Mouse'. There were a few children who were too frightened to even put on their masks, reflecting perhaps a lack of conviction in their parents. If coaxing failed, the teachers usually became stern and used a *"We'll have none of that nonsense"* approach, which seemed to work. Each mask was issued in a strong cardboard case, with a carrying cord. Some mothers used to 'decorate' the case for ease of recognition.

Upon the outbreak of war, my father and Mr Stokes built an underground shelter at the back of Deal Cottages, for both our families to share. They dug it out to a depth of five feet or so, then somehow managed to get enough boards and iron sheets to line the sides. Poles were then laid across the top to support corrugated iron sheets, heaped over with a lot of the dug out soil. Steps were constructed at one end, supported by boarded risers, while the doorway was shrouded with hessian potato sacks. A double-tiered bunk was made at the far end for us kids to lie on, while seats were arranged down the two sides for the adults.

Throughout 1940, many were the nights that we were woken by the sound of the siren at Longmoor and, usually, the one at Liss could also be clearly heard. This would cause us to slip on our socks, shoes and overcoats – no slippers and dressing gowns for us! – and run into the shelter alongside our neighbours. There was just enough room to accommodate the eleven of us and we would often have to stay there for several hours, until the 'all-clear' was sounded.

At No.3 lived Mrs Miller, an Irish woman who kept herself strictly to herself, along with her teenage son Mick. An elderly couple, Mr and Mrs Coombes, lived at No.4 with their younger son Gilbert. Sadly, their other son Albert was killed during that terrible war. The Coombes never stirred for an air raid, preferring to stay inside the shelter of what they obviously considered their 'safe' house.

The Battle of Britain was followed by the nightly 'blitz' during the autumn and winter of 1940 – 41. I recall in particular a couple of heavy raids on Portsmouth when, on the clearest nights, we could see the glow of the fires far away to the south and hear the rumble of bombs at a distance of some twenty miles. We could only imagine what it must have been like for those who suffered down there, it must have truly been *"hell on earth"*. The city had to continue to be 'up and running', with thousands of civilian workers employed in the Naval dockyards. Occasionally a brighter-than-normal flash would light up the sky, no doubt caused by a land-mine, one of those contraptions that floated down on its parachute and could flatten whole streets of houses. As we'd say, *"Poor old Pompey is taking a hammering tonight".*

The following year we had to have a local authority shelter, which was built by contractors, using Midhurst White bricks. For the four families the shelter was built as a pair, with pitched concrete roofs. Across the entrance was a 'blast wall'. Should that be knocked over, blocking the opening, a means of escape was provided at the rear by a two-foot square of bricks, set in sandy mortar and fitted with a steel plate. Should this emergency exit be required, the plate would have to be literally pulled from its setting, and the surrounding bricks loosened enough for them to be kicked out from the inside. Fortunately, we didn't often use this shelter; we found it stark and cold when compared to our snug homemade dugout.

I would like to describe what the 'blackout' was like, especially on an overcast moonless night; it was like being in a deep cave when the tour guide switches off the light. It was illegal to have even a chink of light showing from a window and householders had to fix up a complete cover, by all means possible. There were nights that I walked home from working at Mr Walters' bake-house when it was difficult to estimate the middle of the road. I couldn't even see the hedgerows, so it was usually safest to try and stay in the centre of the road – there was no traffic flying about then! Such blackness is hard to imagine nowadays as, however deep in the countryside you are, a town or village's streetlights will throw up sufficient light from miles away to indicate the largest silhouettes.

I can only recall two private-car owners in **Greatham** from pre-war days. Once restrictions came in, only those engaged on work of national importance were issued with petrol coupons. Of course there were 'fiddlers', there always will be, but they had be aware. Police could stop a vehicle at any time, which they often did, to question the driver as to the necessity of his journey and his entitlement to petrol. There was hardly a car on the roads at night; those that had to go out proceeded very slowly, as their shrouded headlights threw only a narrow beam of light into the darkness ahead. We walkers usually had plenty of time to step off the road for an approaching vehicle.

I think it may have been during 1940 when two former **Greatham** schoolboys, the Bowler brothers from Holt's Cottage, were struck by a car on the Whitehill flat, as they walked home from an evening at the cinema at Bordon. Albert, aged sixteen, was killed, while brother Frank was badly injured. This showed that, no matter how safe we thought we were, there was always the chance of an accident.

Two or three years after the outbreak of war, some rather strange figures began to appear in local fields, wearing dark brown uniforms. They were Italian POWs (prisoners of war), sent out by the County War Agricultural Committee. To begin with they were under a token guard, perhaps one armed soldier to a lorry load, but that was soon dispensed with and they were then left under the charge of just the driver of the lorry. They didn't have a particularly good reputation as hard workers, but most were pleased to be away from the war front, to which they had been reluctant conscripts. They had been poorly equipped, but now were issued with far better boots than those supplied by Mussolini.

One afternoon, I went over to a long swampy field along the western side of the river, behind Ten Acres, where a small party of 'Eye-ties' were helping an excavator driver to dig out a ditch. They were a friendly bunch and hadn't seen a catapult such as the one I carried. They were most impressed when I rattled a pebble through an oak tree at a fair distance. Then of course they all wanted a go. But being new to it, they were what we called 'cack-handed'. One of them was soon hopping about with a bruised thumb, much to the hilarity of his comrades.

Later some 'trusty' German prisoners were also sent to work, having been selected by a 'denazification' process, and they proved to be excellent workers. As the war came to an end, by which time the Italians had been repatriated, many of the Germans became 'live-in' workers at local farms. With their reputation for hard work, some actually stayed on after the war, perhaps marrying and settling down with one of the many land-girls they had worked alongside.

All clothing and fabrics were strictly rationed and priced with a number of coupons, which were issued in ration books. Imagine, if you will, that era before man-made fibres and hardly any imports of raw cotton. Those merchant ships running the deadly gauntlet of U-boats (submarines) were restricted to the transport of essential hardware. A lot of sheep could be produced at home, so there seemed no shortage of knitting wool. My mother, like most of her generation and status, regarded knitting, sewing and clothes making as normal routine, as they sat every evening hunched over their knitting needles and sewing baskets.

Wartime regulations stipulated that women's skirts, well those sold commercially anyway, should end one inch above the knee. Also, boys had to stay in short trousers up until the age of twelve. The latter was of no concern to us, as traditionally lads were always given their first pair of long trousers on their fourteenth birthday, when they would emerge from home to the cry of 'drainpipes'! And I think it is fair to say that most of the girls at **Greatham School** wore homemade frocks even before the war. Mr Wain was not necessarily referring to the rationing when he would announce that, if a boy came to school in new trousers, it showed he had an improvident mother. New trousers were for 'Sunday best', only to be worn at school when well worn and patched – and even then, to be passed down to the next biggest child.

In fact, it was often drummed into us that old Charlie would rather see us turn up at school wearing patched trousers than anything else. Curtains too would be mended and re-mended until they literally fell apart. Sheets had the worn middle parts cut out and were then sewn side to side, with the best parts of any remnants used to patch and mend other items. Mothers seemed to spend every evening making do and mending and, with four 'menfolk', as she referred to us, our mother was a typical example. She always seemed to have socks to darn, even when she wasn't knitting new ones. So even to many **Greatham** families, living on an income of around two pounds a week, the war didn't really seem so different to the days that had gone before.

It must have been around 1944 that I went over to Berry Grove Farm, West Liss, to see a 'Spitfire' that had made a forced landing in a nearby meadow. A crowd of fascinated onlookers watched as a party of RAF fitters removed the aircraft's wings, ready for loading the plane onto a sixty-foot 'Queen Mary'. The plane was undamaged, thanks to the skill of the pilot. There was only a long curving skid-mark where he had braked fiercely on one rudder, in order to slew the plane to one side and avoid a clump of trees. As I watched, I had no inkling that I would spend some forty years of my future working life on mostly military aircraft.

Daily life

Farm workers were issued with a supplementary cheese ration, delivered weekly to the foreman's house and doled out by his wife, Mrs Swyers. My eldest brother left school in 1941 to work on the farm, so he was entitled to this cheese. I'm sure that the lump given out to him was larger than the weekly ration for five people! There was also a weekly delivery of 'agricultural' pies, for farm-workers' families, which Don and I would collect during dinner time by cycling round to Mrs Swyers' place, just up the Alton Road opposite Hatchmoor.

The meat ration was apportioned to a particular shop; you could not normally get it from elsewhere. This ensured that every shop was supplied according to the numbers registered with it. Don and I in turn had periods when we cycled down to Liss on a Saturday morning to collect this weekly meat, from Lander's the butcher, which could be an education in itself! The queue normally stretched way outside the shop, the waiting seemed endless. But it could be entertaining, listening to the chatter and joking of the women, they

were all acquainted with one another. It was illegal to argue with your butcher, you had to take what was given, although you could state a preference. Some housewives would give Mr Culverson the manager a bit of a ribbing, trying to cajole him into adding a bit extra – a bit of this, or a bit of that. But he would have none of it, giving back as much as he got in the verbal exchange and usually adding *"Take it or leave it"*.

Presumably there was some prime beef about somewhere, but it must have been hidden away for 'special customers'. Most of what we got was tough and stringy, probably from an old dairy cow that would have provided dog meat in pre-war days! Some of it was so red in colour that there were many that argued that it was horsemeat. Later in the war, whale meat *(Was it called 'snoek'?)* was issued, but I don't think we were ever told of this fact before eating. Anyway, we were too eager to eat whatever was put on our plates. The meat tickets still displayed 'Scotch Beef' and 'Canterbury Lamb', but really this was a thing of the past and maybe a hope for the future! Whatever meat we got, the suet was always cut off and piled on the counter, with a piece being added fairly to each order.

Essential foods like butter, margarine, cheese and eggs were rationed separately and to one supplier, some of these dropping to just a few ounces a week. A wide range of tinned foods, preserves and dry goods was issued on a points system, for which each person had to save the required amount of coupons. Some tinned meat, like corned beef and 'Spam', were sometimes available but, as I remember, these could cost around thirty-two points per tin, so they were almost a luxury. Goods on this points system could be bought at any shop – but only when available.

The price of bread was pegged at a cost of fourpence farthing for the standard loaf, which was reduced from two pounds to a pound and three-quarters. It was coarser than the pre-war white loaf we had been used to, I heard one woman refer to its flour as sawdust! It took many years for the medical statisticians to resolve that the considerable drop in numbers of bowel cancer victims, both during the war and in its aftermath, was due to the fibrous diet of coarse bread and fresh vegetables. The farthing (one quarter of a penny) was retained as a unit of currency for a time after the war, at least until the price of bread was eventually freed.

No matter how stringent were the rations we never really went hungry, thanks to the providence of our mothers. Most of them had been brought up in a tough school of life, in poor families, and had long since learned to improvise. They had been taught to make anything out of anything, without it ever being boring or tasteless, and I am sure that we appreciated the fact that we were better fed than our parents had been in the first half of the twentieth century. My mother was one of six children of a farm carter who earned twelve shillings a week. At one time the family had been evicted from their cottage, with their belongings dumped in the lane outside, because father had hurt his back and so couldn't work.

Mother was very pleased when we brought home a rabbit – we **Greatham** boys were always focussed for a catch! When the corn was being cut, we would eagerly wait for the binders to reach the middle of the field and the rabbits would be forced to run out. Because the outer field was now stubble, we could easily outpace the rabbits over a short distance. Like the sparrows, rabbits were a major pest, nibbling off the new shoots of a wheat crop in spring. I have tried eating 'farmed' rabbit since, but find it tasteless when compared to the wild ones we caught ourselves – they were a special treat and always so tasty.

One afternoon during the summer holidays of 1944, I was in the harvest fields when I was asked if I would like to be the 'stan'ard boy', the previous lad having been sacked for absconding the previous day, without leave. This job involved leading the wagon between the rows of stooks, or 'shocks' as they were known locally, stopping every few yards for the wagon to be loaded. I would have to shout 'stan'ard' to the men on the wagon, so that they could prop themselves up on their pitchforks, before the wagon began to move off again. The term was obviously a shortened version of 'stand hard'. Later, I was told that Captain Coryton was applying for permission for me to carry on with the job after the start of the new term. I must have pleased Mr Swyers!

This bucked the trend all right. Only seventy years before, Education Acts had been framed to prevent children from working long hours in the fields, and here I was, thoroughly enjoying doing just that! Instead of being hunched over my desk, not daring to whisper to my chum at the next desk, nor allowing my gaze to wander around the room, both offences warranting a summary punishment, here I was, out in the sunshine and fresh air. It was lovely, working with those large, beautiful horses, getting paid a shilling and threepence an hour, at least half of a man's wage, all on the strength of a chit signed by the Hampshire Education Authority.

The sheaves were loaded in rick-building style, butts out and sides sloping outwards, to build up into a big wide load. Over the surface of the fields were shallow ruts, some eleven yards apart. These were drainage furrows, the fields being ploughed in strips of two rods. Each time the wagon was to pass over a rut, I would shout 'goblets', again to warn the men up top. For most of the time just one horse was used for loading but, usually, at the final stage and to pull the wagon to

the rick, a trace-horse was hitched up. I often took the full wagon to the rick and returned with it empty. I was surprised now at how easily the horse responded to even the gentlest tug of the reins.

I repeated this duty the following year. That summer of 1945 ended in very wet weather, with prolonged spells of rain, leaving much of the harvest still standing in the fields. I remember that the last of it wasn't gathered in until well into September, from two large fields called The Warren and Biddle's Piece, between Snailing Lane and West Liss. The stooks had been standing wet for so long that it took two men to tug the sheaves from the dense vegetation growing through their base. Tommy Swyers had to announce that he would not be attending the Harvest Festival that year. When all was safely gathered in, judging by the curses from the men trying to lift, the task had not been entirely without sin! Captain Coryton brought over a barrel of ale and I had my first taste of it, sat on a cart-tail, set up in a shed at Berry Grove Farm. At the age of twelve, I was now considered 'one of the gang' and I gladly returned for a refill.

The potato fields

Throughout the war, we worked in the potato fields and so had only a week for the Easter holiday, leaving another week to plant the new crop in May. The summer holiday was only three weeks, leaving another fortnight in October for harvesting the main crop. I was able to do this the first time in 1940 and, because I was not yet eight, was paid at only half the standard rate, which was then threepence an hour. By the end of the war, if I recall correctly, this had risen to tenpence an hour.

Planting the spuds was easy enough, one just walked a measured length of ploughed furrow, foot – spud – foot – spud, repeating this on the next furrow and so on. Harvesting was much harder work, which is why we set aside a whole fortnight. At first a double-shared horse plough was used, to go down the middle of a row, turning the soil in both directions. This did lead to a lot of sliced potatoes. We worked in pairs, dragging a basket for the 'eaters' and a pig bucket for the damaged ones, or ones below a certain size, which we called 'chatties'. Mr Swyers was a hard taskmaster, bellowing the length of the field if the plough stopped because a length wasn't completed. Then it was a quick dash across to the next strip, to finish it before the plough had time to turn around and return. There was no let up, most of the time we worked 'flat out', always trying to beat the plough.

The baskets and buckets were tipped into sacks, thrown down the length of the field, and we had to

Village life in the early 1950's.

make sure they didn't get mixed up. The sacks were constantly picked up by carters and taken to the nearest roadside. Here they would be weighed and adjusted into hundredweights. Many tons were sometimes loaded onto farm wagons and transported to Longmoor Camp, the remainder built up into clamps. The cleared ground was then levelled with a horse-rake and the withered haulms burned without delay, to kill any disease, on a row of bonfires. All the while Mr Swyers would patrol up and down, ready to vent his wrath if he found eaters mixed with the pig food, or vice versa.

We worked the same hours as normal school hours, with the usual mid-day break. Sandwiches were quickly devoured and, between bouts of horseplay, chasing the girls and throwing chatties at each other, we sat around the bonfires on upturned buckets, impaling potatoes on sharp sticks to bake them over glowing embers. They weren't particularly appetising, burned on the outside and still hard on the inside. It was a joy when the call came to 'knock off' for the day. We would empty what was left in our containers and trudge wearily to the top of the field to make our way home, some on foot, some on bicycles. Aching young backs are resilient however and quickly restored and, after a hot dinner, we would continue with our normal activities.

No one was forced to do this labour of course. The younger children, and those older ones who chose not to work, had to attend school as if it was 'in term'. But because they had given up holiday time, normal lessons were relaxed, with time spent on games and recreation. On the whole those who worked enjoyed the chance to earn some money and looked forward to the same opportunity the following year. I think we also realised the importance of such work to the war effort and, upon reflection, there was certainly no surplus of labour on the farms. I certainly can't see how those crops could have been lifted without our assistance.

Hard and demanding work it may have been, but most of us were well used to it and, with the imposed discipline of our upbringing, we had the moral stability to sustain us through it. In my family we were never 'given' pocket money, we earned every penny and thriftiness was encouraged. Mother bought us each a sixpenny National Saving stamp each week and, with our own earnings, Don and I had saved sufficient to buy new bikes by the time I was eleven. We had no qualms about having to 'work for our living'.

In time, the double-shared plough was replaced by a potato-spinner, which had rotating steel rods that churned along the rows, scattering earth and potatoes over a wide band. This resulted in less damage to the larger tubers and allowed two people to work side-by-side.

The war finally ends

In May 1945, Prime Minister Churchill broadcast to the nation that the war in Europe was won and that the following day was to be celebrated as 'VE Day', with two days devoted to a national holiday. A group of youths and some of the older boys in **Greatham** got together, deciding that the village was going to have the biggest bonfire it had ever seen, built out in the school field.

Our eldest brother, Eric, suggested that we borrow the large handcart from the yard behind Mr Walters' shop. The cart was very plush, more like a pony-trap, mounted upon a couple of automobile wheels. We took this down Smith's Lane to an area of swampy woodland, where there were many fallen fir trees of small and medium size lying on the ground, their roots having rotted away. With stout hearts and sturdy backs, we hauled out the biggest stuff we could manage and loaded the cart until its tyres were nearly flattened. Having hauled it up the steep gravel lane to Longmoor Road, the rest of the trip to the school was relatively easy. We repeated our efforts several times during the day and, as word quickly got around, other people soon began to turn up with all the flammable rubbish they could find.

It certainly did make the biggest bonfire in *Greatham's* history; built on a base of fir trunks, with a frame of piled-up poles to support its height. Just about everyone turned out to see the spectacle, joining in the singing and frivolities. But as with most celebrations, they were tinged with sadness for those boys from *Greatham* who hadn't made it through the war, bravely dying in their country's cause. There was Albert Coombes of Deal Cottages, killed whilst dispatch riding; Benny Rumbold's son Fred, from Goleigh, lost in Italy; David Shepherd, the postman's son from Ham Barn, who died in Japanese hands; Charlie Baker from just up the Blackmoor road, who joined the Navy at seventeen and went down on his first voyage; these are the ones I remember.

Four months later came VJ Day, following the atom bombs being dropped on Japan, and the celebrations were repeated. With millions of servicemen now returning to 'civvy street', our work on the land became no longer necessary by 1946. Then began a glorious period when village life was at its best. Everyone knew each other from shared experiences and no one had cars to insulate them from their neighbours. The spirit of togetherness, engendered by wartime trials and tribulations, was especially fostered by those young men returning from far-flung battles; they had spent years in the company of comrades, with their lives depending on each other. Despite the fact that they must have found it hard to settle back to a normal life, this they did, and *Greatham* became once again a united community.

Post-war days – and Bakersfield

The war had left hundreds of thousands of people homeless and the incoming Labour government embarked upon a major building programme. District Councils were awarded thirty-year government loans to build houses, so sites were sought on which to build. In *Greatham*, Bakersfield was chosen and the first two pairs of houses were built there during the summer and autumn of 1946. They were of Swedish design, with brick chimney-breasts and load-bearing walls of Midhurst Whites. They had clad partition interior walls and exteriors of large pre-fabricated timber panels. They were all allocated to *Greatham* people and we, the Sineys, moved into No.3 during the bitter winter of early 1947.

That was a never-to-be-forgotten winter. For those of more recent times, it was on par with that of 1962 – 63, but far more severe. The pre-war built power stations could not cope with the demand and, of these, a fair number had been destroyed during 'the blitz'. Coal stocks, upon which everyone relied, were frozen solid in their stockpiles and on stationary rail wagons. Some coal-yards encouraged people to get hand-carts and barrows and, armed with pickaxes, to go and collect their own coal. These dreadful conditions added to the drastic economic state of the nation. There was precious little sterling to be spent on imports, so restrictions and rationing continued in a long dreary period of post-war austerity.

It was during that winter's icy grip that we moved into our new home. With it being so close to Deal Cottages, father borrowed a four-wheeled rubber-tyred handcart from the Longmoor Military Railway stores, in order to move us. The new place was a revelation to us. For the first time we had a bathroom, with hot running water, heated by an efficient 'Glow-worm' range in the living room. Proper flushing lavatories fed into a sewage system that drained into a cesspool towards the back of the field. However, due to a lack of lead, and the spate of new buildings going up, there was a chronic shortage of underground supply cable. This meant that we continued using candles, oil lamps and flatirons for a further eighteen months before the main electricity was eventually laid on. At the same time, all cooking was managed on the range.

A small extension to the rear had a washing 'copper' and a separate deep sink for washing clothes so, even without electricity, things were far better for mother than they had been before. We also had quite a large garden, as the density of rural housing was then set at (I think) six to the acre, later changed to eight an acre. Because Bakersfield – or Baker's Field as others call it – had always been arable land, laid within a strip of the former flood plain, the soil was very workable, unlike the sedimentary clay up the hill.

All new dwellings then were semi-detached, with the exception of temporary 'pre-fabs'. If anyone had applied to build a privately owned detached house, I don't think they would have been granted a licence for the materials to indulge in such luxury. The next year two more pairs were built, of the same Midhurst

Alan and friend at the seaside!

Whites, followed by three pairs of 'Airey' houses, which were clad in wired-on concrete blocks. Finally the bungalows were added around 1963. It is interesting to note that Bakersfield was planned at a time when it was not foreseen that almost every working-class man would one day become a car owner, which would prove to be a severe problem in later years.

Weather-wise that year proved a contrasting one, as the atrocious winter was followed by a record-breaking summer. During the long heatwave, fierce forest fires ranged all across Woolmer Forest, so spectacular at times that they were shown on cinema newsreels. From the main road up to Whitehill, looking east, the flames could be seen leaping over the tops of mature pine trees. As the flames engulfed each tree, the resinous trunk would split with a crack like a pistol shot, sending a huge fireball hurtling into the sky. The exploding trees could be heard loud and clear from at least a mile away, seemingly in one continuous roar. Fires then started on the western side of the road, along the mile distance between the Blackmoor turning and Whitehill crossroads and across towards Blackmoor village. The fires went deep into the underground peat, where they kept on smouldering and breaking out anew. In the years that followed, it became apparent that this underground burning had caused sinkage, as patches of marsh grass broke through what had originally been heather and heath.

Latter days and leaving Greatham

I mentioned earlier that I once worked for Mees of Liss. They were happy days, with a wide variety of electrical work scattered over the rural area. One morning, on the way to Hawkley, we noticed a cat up a telegraph pole on the hairpin bend at the bottom of Hawkley hill. It was still up there when we returned, so we stopped the van and I shinned up the pole to bring it down. As I brought it halfway down, it jumped the rest and bolted across the field like, well, the proverbial scalded cat! Alf Woods the foreman saw this as an opportunity for some free publicity and phoned the Hants and Sussex News ('The Squeaker'), which subsequently printed the story. After that, I was often stopped and asked, *"Aren't you the one who ... ...?"*

I was later called up for my two years of National Service. It was something that I never regretted, as I 'signed on' in order to pursue an intensive course at the RAF Electrical School. This was to shape the rest of my working life, though I never envisaged spending the next two-and-a-half years living a primitive form of life under canvas in the desert! However, with the combined initiative of two good tent-mates, ours was the only one in the Squadron to have a wooden floor, carpet and (illicit) electrical supply. We had the benefit of a light and a small self-made heater in which to brew our tea. Mother had sent the element for this by Forces Air Mail — its surprising what you can find in a food parcel!

I finally left the village after my marriage in 1960 and moved to Surrey. Don returned to Baker's Field with his own family for a few years during the Sixties, before moving to West Sussex, while Eric remained in **Greatham** for the rest of his life. He is remembered as a village stalwart, being in turn secretary and chairman of **Greatham Football Club** for over twenty-five years. He was a founder of the Gardeners' Club and served as a parish councillor, later becoming the parish's tree and footpath warden. For several of his earlier years he was the local branch secretary of the National Union of Agricultural Workers, often having to cycle over the hills of Hawkley and Prior's Dean to collect dues and listen to grievances.

Eric worked at Longmoor for about twenty years and, when a new road was built in the barracks, it was named Siney Way in his honour. He retired in 1992 but still continued with some part-time gardening work. His sudden death in 1994 was a great loss to me, as I had only retired the previous year and we had just started to enjoy each other's company once again. We particularly liked long walks, setting off with our backpacks, containing the refreshments to have at some quiet spot along the way. These would often be trial runs for organised walks that he would sometimes take people on. The walks would take us far outside the parish boundaries, beyond those territories that we had learned intimately of on our childhood rambles. With a growing knowledge, I became aware of historic features and the many changes that had taken place – not all to my liking, I'm afraid!

Times of change

In 1990, on the 50th anniversary of the air raid, I went back over to the rear of Ten Acres to photograph the old oak-tree that had been stripped bare by the time-delayed bomb. To my dismay, it had long disappeared, along with long lengths of hedgerows and trees. It appeared that it had all been systematically razed to ground level by a market gardener, whilst burning his boxes. To the rear of Deal Farm I was confronted with a vast 'prairie', stretching over as far as Bradshott. Many fields had been joined into one, causing the destruction of miles of hedges and possibly thousands of oaks, and all to produce the lucrative but unwanted European wheat mountain during the Seventies. In my young days, agriculture had been our friend – essential to our survival. Could it now have turned this ugly? These methods had not even been resorted to during those days of a desperate need for more food, when County Agricultural Committees would step in to take over land they considered to be inefficiently used.

Other changes that have taken place in *Greatham* are too numerous for me to describe, but I will mention some for their historic interest. Imagine, if you will, the (then) A325 being the old standard two-and-a-half cars width. Even the relatively small pre-war lorries used to pass each other with extreme caution. The road was lined with a ditch on either one side or both, with the gullies that ran into them being kept constantly clear by council roadmen. There were far fewer puddles – or litter - on the road then. Our own roadman who worked *Greatham* was Paddy McGinn, who pushed his cart up and down from 'The Bluebell' at West Liss. His strip extended up to the old Alton R.D.C. boundary at the Liphook road. During the war, of course, there was little traffic, mostly it was of a military nature and even this tended to reduce towards evening. So the road actually became our playground, where we could kick a ball about and ride 'figures-of-eight' on our bikes, only occasionally having to step aside for an approaching vehicle.

Along the front of the Rectory wall was a wide verge and a brick-lined ditch, with a footpath between it and the road. I remember, when very small, my mother taking us along to see an Aldershot bus that

had run down into the ditch. On the other side of the road, on the corner of Church Lane, stands the old thatched Swain's Cottage, which was originally two tiny little cottages, before being extended to the rear. I vaguely remember old Nanny Russell, who lived in the southernmost cottage and kept a shop in her little front room. From here she sold sweets and oddments and apples from the orchard at the back, which stretched down to the field gate at Shepherd's Mead. I believe she died around 1936.

Because the roads were so narrow then, the village green was about twice the size it is now. A chain, which looped through oak posts, surrounded it, but eventually this disappeared when the salvage gangs came along during the war. The chestnut tree that was planted on the green was to commemorate the 1937 Coronation, but it was not a good choice, as the poor soil has since left it rather stunted. A little further on, between the old school *(now a dwelling)* facing the road, and the road itself, was a big beech tree with spreading roots. In front of this was a triangular area that had once been part of the village green. This was also fenced, around the Forest Road junction, across to the ancient churchyard wall and to the end of the graveyard. All this had once been the old school play area, accessible through a gate in the hedge, in front of the entrance lobby.

On the opposite side of the road to the old school, extending beyond the length of the Manor wall, was a line of elms, which I once saw on an old postcard. But I can only remember their stumps on top of the bank that formed this pronounced curve of the road. The trees, now sadly gone because of the deadly Dutch elm disease, provided a tough, durable timber, much used for carts and coffins. They were often seen planted equidistantly along hedgerows, unlike the oaks, which grew naturally. The planting of elms was sometimes stipulated to tenants in their land deals and inclosures.

Longmoor Camp, a great source of local employment for many years.

The field alongside the road southwards from the church lych-gate was always known as 'The Glebe', being owned by the church. It was used for pasture and never ploughed, as were all of the fields bordering Church Lane and reaching out to the Alton Road. This area, above the Deal flood plain, is predominantly heavy clay, so little or no attempt was made to cultivate it, even during the war. Nearly all the arable land in the parish lay to the east of the main road and south of the Alton road, extending down to West Liss.

Greatham appears as *Greteham* in the Domesday Book. It is thought that the name originated from the Anglo-Saxon term for 'an estate on gravely soil'. This hints that the first Saxon settlement was on the western side of the parish, on land rising towards the chalk escarpment. Certainly, flint nodules that have been found can only be associated with chalk, although some may have been deposited on clay eroded by chalk, or even worked their way to the surface. Around the north and east of the parish, any flint found on the lower greensand will have been deliberately moved there for a reason.

The Liss Forest road and Church Lane, being unclassified roads, were normally covered in flint chippings, rather than the granite pieces transported up from the West Country. Small flint slivers can be very sharp and the wise motorist would regularly check and de-flint his tyres to avoid punctures. Church Lane was badly pot-holed, showing where the stone had been rolled into the clay as 'hoggin', before it was tarmacadamed. This use of tarmac was a recent effort, my parents could remember the Alton road when the surface was still rough and stony.

Church Lane was an ancient right-of-way, which once carried on northwards to Bradshott *(now a public footpath)*. It was a charming locality, with the remaining characteristics of the common land it had been a century before. One could walk though an open grassy space, to the side of which nestled Keeper's Cottage in the edge of some oak woods. A wrought-iron kissing gate led into Le Court park, previously the seat of Sir Heath Harrison, High Sheriff of Hampshire. The last time I went through there, I felt lost! The area was covered in trees and shrubbery, as the cottages had turned into desirable residences. I confess that I didn't like the changes, as my love of trees is confined to the native hardwoods. The oak is a particular favourite, as its age and position can tell a story – a living monument of rural history. I like to see their place in the landscape, not to have the view smothered by alien foliage.

Greatham School

Mr Percy Gale, who had brought up several children in one part of Swain's Cottage(s) and was re-housed in Baker's Field in 1946, was (I think) the last surviving old *Greatham* boy to have attended the original old school, before it was replaced. Built to one side of the village green, in response to the Education Act of 1870, it was only a typical single-room Victorian schoolhouse but, considering the small population of the village at that time, proved to be just about adequate. A quite unbelievable number of children were crammed in, sitting on long benches with their slate-boards balanced on their knees.

When that 1870 Act led to compulsory education for all children in 1876, parishes received no central funding. Schoolhouses were provided from parish rates, collected from eligible ratepayers. These people were entitled to attend the parish vestry, which governed parishes in the days before elected parish councils were set up in 1894. Instead of land being purchased, schools were usually built at the edge of a green or on 'roadside waste', the term used for non-titheable verges held in common usage. *Greatham* probably had few ratepayers or benefactors to assist with expenses so, like other villages, the school had to be supported by the church, donations and subscriptions. National Schools had been built with aid from the National Society after 1830, but pupils also had to pay a few pence per week for their schooling.

An agricultural labourer, living in poverty, relied upon his children to work in the fields from an early age. They could not contribute towards education without great personal sacrifice. I once had the chance of scanning through the church book, which revealed that for most of the 19th-century, very few *Greatham* inhabitants could even sign their own names on birth and marriage certificates. The conclusion can be drawn

Swain's Cottage, once home to 'Nanny' Russell's sweet shop.

that, in an agrarian society such as was **Greatham's**, with very few tradesmen or artisans, the illiteracy rate was relatively high.

The 'new' school, as it stands today, was first used around 1911 – 12. The old school was subsequently used as the village hall, until the new hall was built on Dubbers Field in the 1970s. With the passing of another Education Act in 1902, control of elementary schools passed from local School Boards to County Education Committees. At the same time, the school-leaving age was raised to thirteen, where it stayed until after the First World War. Captain Coryton, as Chairman of the school managers, told one of his meetings that, when the officer came over from Winchester to inspect the new school premises, he was brought up from Liss Station by motorcycle and wickerwork sidecar.

I started my school life in the New Year of 1938, under the eagle eye of Miss Bowden. She was a rather stern Victorian old lady, with little sense of humour and a penchant for rapping one's knuckles with a ruler! The junior teacher was a Miss Perry, with a good sense of humour and a mischievous glint in her eye. For several years she travelled over from distant Fleet in her 'Baby Austin' car. The headmaster was Mr Wain — 'Old Charlie'. He had been a strict disciplinarian, but mellowed a bit with advancing middle age and, at times, could bring his class to fits of laughter. On the whole, we **Greatham** children were a happy bunch; we accepted life's limitations without whinging and, if any boy told his parents that he had been caned, it would take him ages to lose his reputation as a 'cissie'.

I certainly don't envy the children of today, with all their comforts and family cars. They spend far too much time indoors watching television and computer screens and eating what is now classed as 'junk food'. They have had to adapt to a changing world, where it is no longer safe for them to venture out alone. I am sure that we, of my generation, all wish our grandchildren could move back to the safe and stable society that we ourselves took for granted. Our lives were 'the great outdoors', both physical and active, of which I am still a great advocate.

In those days, the school had no telephone, and occasionally one of us boys would be dispatched by Mr Wain to the Manor House with a letter. Once, when my brother Don was sent on such an errand, Captain Coryton greeted him with the query, *"How about a spot of rook shooting, laddie?"* He quickly climbed into the Captain's 'Morris Eight' and they drove down to a field near Ham Barn, where Don was allowed to let fly with both barrels at a flock of rooks. Upon his return to school, when questioned about the length of time he'd been gone, Don replied *"Captain Coryton took me out rook shooting, sir"*. *"Oh, all right,"* said old Charlie,

trying hard to suppress the smile that was beginning to creep across his face.

As I've already mentioned, my parents were the school caretakers throughout the war years, for which they were paid a small joint monthly salary. And I do mean small, considering the hours that they put in! Each evening, mother would spread scouring sand over the wood-block floors and sweep the school right through, dragging the cast-iron desks to and fro as she went. This would be followed by a similar journey, this time with a duster. Father saw to the exterior work, such as cleaning out the lavatories, before raking out the boiler, banking up the fire, then closing it down so that it stayed hot until morning. Because of our parents' involvement, it became the custom that we Siney boys would be given the task, each day in turn, of managing the heating system. At least it gave us a good reason to occasionally excuse ourselves from the classroom!

The 'stokehole' was at the back of the school down some steps, where a large saddle boiler was encased in asbestos cement. It was gravity-fed from a water tank high up in the roof. There was no electricity, hot water circulated on the thermo-syphon effect through large bore pipes to the huge cast-iron radiators located around the school, which is why the boiler had to be below floor level. On its top was a big brass temperature gauge, with a line drawn at 180 degrees F. The objective was to keep the reading as close as possible to this line, without exceeding it.

We had to shovel in more coke as required, using a damper to control the temperature, which became simpler with the more experience one gained. A red line on the gauge indicated 200 degrees F and, should this temperature be exceeded, steam pressure would be forced up an expansion pipe to the water tank. This did happen once to my knowledge, just after Eric left the school, but also before either Don or myself were old enough for the job. Steam poured all along the school roof, classrooms had to be evacuated, and Mr Wain had to send one boy racing off on a bicycle to fetch a plumber from Mr Kemp's yard.

School sanitation was a fairly crude affair! At the rear of the tarmac playground were two brick-built lavatory blocks. These had rear doors leading to a chamber, in which a raised platform ran under the row of seats. Alongside was a gully, which ran out through a hole in the back wall. The platform had to be shovelled off every night, then covered with fresh peat. Every so often my father would go off with our uncle, Jack Lacey, down to **Greatham** Moor to dig up a fresh load of peat. The soiled heap would later be spread around the local fields. Our 'Uncle Jack' was employed as a carter by Captain Coryton.

In the boys' block the urinal was an iron trough

about six feet long, which my father had to 'bail out' into buckets, which were then emptied into a ditch in a thicket behind the school gardens. The wall behind the urinal was covered by an iron plate, about four feet high, and showed the evidence of the activities that went on! Competitions would be held to see who could pee the highest, with the sporty types trying to knock down flies, often accompanied by cries of *"Rat-at-at-tat, Rat-at-it-tit, I've shot down another Messerschmitt!"*

I can't remember if toilet paper was available then. If it was then we never saw it! Timber for wood pulp, and hence paper, was very scarce during the war. Our single-sheet national newspapers weren't discarded with the salvage collection; they were in much greater demand for other, more delicate reasons! Should the same need arise when at school, one would have to scrabble through the wastebaskets for some suitable remnant. As for washing our hands, well there was a sink and cold water tap available in both the boys' and girls' front lobby but, as far as we were concerned, if you couldn't see the dirt, there was no need to wash it off!

Once a year, a large green van would be towed into the school and parked on the back playground. On its side, in large gold or yellow letters, were the words Hampshire County Council – and it reeked of disinfectant! We kids called it the 'butcher's wagon', for it was not a popular sight, and it meant that the dreaded annual dental inspection was upon us! The same dentist accompanied the van for many years, a Mr Kench, who had – or was later to have – his own dental practice in Alton. He wasn't a suitable man to be treating children, his handling was as rough as his manner and we were always pleased to see the back of his surgery. A small generator ran at the back of the van to supply the lighting, but I think pedals were used to manually operate the drilling machine. Parents could decline their children's treatment, but I'm sure not many did. Otherwise it was relatively expensive to those on modest incomes. In fact, parents looked upon those visits as a great benefit, something they hadn't had in their own younger days.

Periodically we would also have a visit from the 'nit nurse', who combed and inspected our hair and heads for the dreaded lice. Anyone found to be infected was sent home, along with his/her brothers and sisters, for treatment with liquid paraffin. I recall one or two occasions when Miss Perry and Miss Coles, the infant teacher, had to undertake the inspection of each class in turn.

Greatham School possibly had eighty or so pupils before the war, which then rose to a little over one hundred with the closing of the school in Longmoor Camp and the arrival of some evacuees. These were city children and a school photograph taken in 1944 shows ninety-five children between the age of five and fourteen. At the beginning of the war evacuee reception centres were set up, with the school intended to be one of these, should a large-scale exodus from the cities become a necessity. A stout shelf was built, high up on the back wall of the boys' lobby, and then stacked with boxes of crockery. They never were used and were cheaply disposed of after the war. I recall that my mother had some of them, they remain in the family, all stamped 'Ministry of Supply' and dated either 1938 or 1939.

The school had a large playground, which was even less confined when most of the iron railings were cut down as salvage for the war effort. There was also a nice playing field of about four acres, with a football pitch, generally open in the summer months, so that we had plenty of space in which to run about. Throughout the war we had a concerted collection of salvage, with children often taking waste paper and metal to school. The paper would be placed into sacks and, once a week, the boys would carry it off to the collection point, located in a disused coach-house outside Gould's House. This was opposite the church and occupied by one of Captain Coryton's sisters. Another day it would be scrap metal that was collected. In a field close by there was an old hay-rake that had stood in a patch of nettles for years; it had become so old and rusty that we were able to tear it apart for salvage, finally rolling the large wheels, bigger even than ourselves, down to the road. All this at the tender age of seven or eight!

Because of the war, two air-raid shelters were built at the school, on the edge of the field beyond the playground. They must have been thirty feet long; each on a concrete base, covered by heavy gauge steel, with flat corrugations formed into a semi-circle. An entrance of steel plate was set at right angles at one end. Down each side ran slatted wooden benches and, at the far end, a metal ladder ran up to the escape hatch. One of the corners was partitioned off behind a canvas screen, in which sat an 'Elsan' lavatory container, which I don't remember ever being used. Nevertheless, there was one supplied for the infants and younger juniors, with the second for older children. When the siren went, we all got out quickly but in orderly fashion, using both of the lobby exits. Two older girls were delegated to assist the infant teacher with the smallest children. Once inside the shelter, now in almost total darkness, one of the boys would slide the hatch cover over an inch or so, to let in a shaft of welcome light.

Once we had settled down, we might have a 'spelling bee' or a session of 'I spy (with my little eye)', even if the object in question had to be imagined in the enveloping gloom! Then Miss Perry would say, *"Who's going to start a sing-song?"* and, hardly had the words left her lips, some children would begin on 'You are my sunshine' or perhaps 'I've got a sixpence, a jolly, jolly sixpence' or, another old favourite, 'Roll out the barrel'. These were all popular songs of a rousing nature that we knew off by heart. There were others of course, mostly of a derogative type towards Herr Hitler and his Nazis, and of a language that had to be kept strictly for 'out of school' hours! Sanitised versions were sometimes sung, much in the way that in a previous generation, the children had sung 'Boney (Napoleon) was a warrior, yea, yea, yea'.

On two or three occasions, Mr Wain entrusted me with the job of spraying out the shelters with disinfectant. He produced a bottle of 'Izal', which I then diluted with water from the stokehole. Using a standard ARP stirrup-pump, with the nozzle set to a fine spray, I thoroughly doused the insides, watching as all the creepy-crawlies ran for cover in the nooks and crannies. It probably kept the flies away from me for a few days too, as my clothes reeked of the stuff for ages afterwards!

During the Battle of Britain, I remember an urgent cry went up for any old aluminium to be collected. Along with some older boys, we went around with a handcart, calling out for pots and pans. Some of the local ladies donated serviceable items, which they obviously could ill afford and had little chance of replacing. That was the sort of attitude that prevailed during the war; the nation was fighting for survival and everyone played his or her part, without recourse to any sort of 'brain-washing'. **Greatham** children showed that they were able to do a hard day's work out in the fields, with the resilience that was required. This work, plus the physical games we had always played, gave us strength beyond our tender years. To illustrate this point, at the age of eleven and of only average size, I was able to lift up a hundredweight (50 Kg) sack of potatoes directly from the ground.

Sometimes, during a warm summer afternoon, we would be taken out for a lesson into the school field, under the spreading boughs of an oak tree. Again, depending upon the season, we would take further excursions out into the local countryside. Miss Perry would lead expeditions, of both junior and senior classes, on blackberry picking, with the berries being used for jam making. Or it could be picking rose hips to add to our vitamin 'C' intake, or even collecting acorns, which was then used for feeding the pigs.

During the winter, whenever the school playground was covered either in snow, ice or heavy hoarfrost, 'sliding' became a popular pastime. The standard boys' footwear in those days was a stout pair of studded boots and the first boys to arrive would start off the slide,

which then got longer and more slippery as time wore on. Eventually a continuous line of boys would be running round, trying to launch themselves at as high a speed as possible at the slide, in the hope that they could accomplish the fete of reaching the far end all in one go. Whatever else he did, old Charlie Wain was no spoilsport, he never attempted to stop this sort of activity. I never heard of anyone being seriously hurt, the headmaster obviously saw these activities the same as us – just part of the normal 'growing up' thing.

May 23rd was Empire Day, a day that we used to look forward to and on which I cannot recall it ever raining! We usually had a little parade around the playground, wearing coloured armbands. Then we would either march inside or squat outside on the tarmac, if it was warm enough. Captain Coryton would then introduce our 'visitor' for the day, usually either a retired military gentlemen or former Colonial civil servant. He would regale us with stories about the 'Empire' and the particular part in which he'd served. When he had finished speaking, he would turn to Mr Wain with a benign smile and the inevitable question, *"Now, headmaster, could you possibly allow the afternoon off?"* Old Charlie would stroke his chin and pretend to mull this over before responding, *"Well, erm, yes, I suppose that could be arranged"*. He would successfully hide the fact that it was all pre-arranged and that he had either booked an afternoon on the golf course or meant to spend it gardening – the two great loves of his life!

Mr Wain announced his retirement in the summer of 1944, with Miss Perry deciding to go at the same time. Neither of them had been able to get petrol coupons and in his case, Mr Wain had become weary of the daily bus journey to and from his home in Four Marks. It meant staying on late every evening to catch the available bus

Barrack Room accomodation at Longmoor camp

at 5.30 p.m., from the Selborne junction to Alton, with a further wait for another bus for the final stage home. Miss Perry had an even longer journey, all the way up to Fleet, but at least she was able to catch the Aldershot bus at 4 p.m. from right outside the school.

Old Charlie had been headmaster at **Greatham School** for over twenty years. *(I seem to remember having heard that his predecessor had been a Mr Hiscock.)* Charlie recalled that, on his very first day, there were boys climbing up on the school roof. He waited with his cane and 'greeted' them individually as they came down. Imagine the political implications today! I often used to climb up to the bell-tower, during those evenings when mother was cleaning the school – now made easier by the cycle shed at the rear – but the bell doesn't appear to have worked for many years. Perhaps it is still there, behind the slats, but the operating cord has long since vanished. *(Don reminded me that the school bell definitely rang out on VE night, when he and another boy climbed up on the roof and gave it a good old clanging!)*

The new head teacher was Miss Gwendoline Hughes, a large Welsh woman who seemed to hold a prejudice against the male gender in general. The new junior teacher was a Miss Simmons, who hailed from nearby Liss. In charge of the infants was Mrs Reeves, who by now had been there a couple of years. She had replaced Miss Coles, who in turn had taken over from the formidable Miss Bowden. Mrs Reeves was a grand looking woman, always smart in expensive-looking clothes, with an array of bracelets and lots of cosmetics. I don't think she got on too well with Miss Hughes, leaving after only a couple of terms. Her replacement was Mrs Jordan, a popular lady who rode down from Liphook on a new motorcycle. This was a 'Velocette', with its quiet twin-cylinder water-cooled engine, a neat little job. At the **Greatham School** reunion in 2000, she was warmly greeted by her former charges, a lot of them now grandparents.

The head teacher was keen to see some of her pupils go on to further education. Thus it was that in 1946, along with Ivy Stokes, Mary Arnold and 'Titch' Robinson, I sat the entrance exam for Portsmouth Municipal College. We all passed, but for me it was merely a rehearsal. Being under-age, I couldn't go to College until the following year. This left me virtually in a 'class of my own', so Miss Hughes got me into Cowplain Secondary Modern (Boys), which meant a long bus ride, via a connection at Petersfield. I had also sat for a free scholarship to Churcher's College – still there today in Petersfield – at the age of eleven, and was selected for an interview. But at that time, just before the 1944 Education Act was passed, scholarships were relatively few. Added to this was the fact that

Churcher's had a very large catchment area, which was boosted from evacuees from elsewhere. Thus there was a gap of several years when not a single child from **Greatham** was awarded a place at Grammar School.

Longmoor Camp

The Army Camp at Longmoor was a huge Royal Engineers railway depot and training centre during the war, with a station and sidings at Longmoor Down. Much of this site now lies under the A3(M) trunk road. A rail network linked Longmoor to the large military complex around Bordon and Oakhanger while, in the opposite direction, across Weaver's Down and over the Liss Forest road, it joined with the Southern Railway main line at Liss. There were also sidings at Woolmer, along the eastern side of the A325 between Whitehill crossroads and the junction of the Blackmoor turning. Here lay huge stockpiles of rails, sleepers and other heavy equipment.

At Longmoor itself were some very long railway sheds and workshops. In the eleven months between D-Day and VE-Day, almost 800 locomotives were overhauled and/or adapted for the re-occupied parts of Europe, as the retreating German armies withdrew. With them they took just about everything moveable, especially what remained of the locomotives and rolling stock.

Apart from locomotive engineering, every other aspect of railway maintenance and construction was put into practice for training purposes at Longmoor, including track laying and bridge building. Up on Weaver's Down, large pits were excavated for the purpose of demolition and sabotage training, entailing the cutting of rail lines and steel girders by explosive charge. The loud noises from such detonations echoed around **Greatham** on an almost daily basis.

The road from the camp down to the A325 was referred to as 'No Road', which derived from the signs that the War Department had to put up once a year, forbidding traffic to use the road on that day. Again, this old road is obliterated now, having been built over by the laying of the Woolmer link road.

The old road snaked through a vale beneath a sandy ridge and under a bridge constructed of creosoted timber, which carried the rail line from above the ridge and onto the down-gradient to Woolmer. On one occasion, a German bomber attacked this bridge, leaving at least two bomb craters nearby.

The Longmoor Military Railway ran continuous daily trains in both directions, and we children became accustomed to taking free rides whenever we could. Having been stopped to show our passes, which of course we didn't have, we had to resort to more devious methods of hitching a lift. We would hide amongst the chestnut trees behind the sidings, which were on the 'blind' side to the station. From here we could wait until the coast was clear, dash across and climb into an empty carriage, keeping our heads down until the train was merrily chuffing its way along the line, away from Longmoor.

One prime mover used on the railway was termed the 'Wickham Railcar', though we nicknamed it the 'whiz-bang', due to the fact that they seemed to go very fast. They were diesel engined, with only about a dozen seats, possibly used for ferrying officers around when traffic was light. One of these old cars has been recently restored, and can be seen at the Amberley Industrial Museum in West Sussex.

The Army always provided us with lots of entertainment. Convoys of various types often passed by and there were lots of military manouvres in the local countryside. Frequently there were route marches through the village, always in single-file by Platoon, the men staggered alternately to each side of the road, with rifles either slung or at port, to exercise the soldiers' arms. Every so often the call would go out for the men to whistle and, once one Platoon had started, everyone would join in, whole columns of men whistling and marching in unison to their marching tunes and the crunching beat of studded boots. The best sound of all was when they burst into song, with 'It's a long way to Tipperary' one of the favourites, putting an extra swing into the stride as they marched along.

Once, when an 'OP' (observation post) was set up in Baker's Field, mother made up a jug of steaming tea to take over to them. We always loved mingling with the soldiers, enjoying their company and the varied accents from all parts of the country. There were some that showed a degree of bitterness about 'civvies in cushy jobs' and once a remark was made about my father, being in his job at the stores in Longmoor Camp. When we told mother, she said that next time we heard remarks like those, to tell whomever that *"Father fought in the last war"*. Our pal Kevin's father was an RSM at the camp – a veteran of the First World War and now on the permanent staff, who had been permanently injured by a bullet through his foot. When this was mentioned to the soldiers, there would be a shout of *"Hey, his old man's the RSM"*, followed by a round of good-natured booing!

One evening a week, we would usually went to the cinema at Longmoor, in Seymour Hall, where the seats were initially threepence and sixpence, but later increased to sixpence and ninepence. Here, we could keep up with the latest glamour and glitter of Hollywood, when it was in its heyday. From the top of Apple Pie Hill, we would take a short cut through the

woods and over the moors, emerging in Seymour Road, directly opposite the cinema. On summer evenings, with double British summertime in operation, the return trip could be just as enjoyable. Inspired by some Western film epic, we boys would gallop through the woods, parties of marauding and whooping Red Indians being chased by gallant cowboys, with their white Stetsons and pistols blazing.

Methuen Road, the long straight road through the centre of the camp, was laid along the course of the ancient Roman road from Chichester to Silchester. To the north west, it skirted Woolmer Pond then passed through Blackmoor and Oakhanger. Woolmer Pond must have been quite a feature at one time. From the Blackmoor turning, looking east, one can see low hills consisting of tumuli and most of the area in between was once a large lake. It is on record that on one occasion, Queen Anne was *en route* to Portsmouth and her entourage took an excursion out from Liphook to picnic on its shore. When I was a boy, marsh plants were taking over, but there were still wide stretches of water and, during cold snaps – there seemed to be at least one every winter – we would go across the frozen lake, trying to control our bikes. This could be a great laugh if you ignored the bruised rumps!

It was also thanks to the military that we children had somewhere to swim, at a locality marked on the survey maps as Longmoor Inclosure. This lay in the pine-trees down at the bottom of the vale, south from the top of Apple Pie Hill. Here the convergence of

'The Bather' once used by soldiers from Longmoor Camp, now an angler's retreat, though alongside the busy A3 dual-carriageway.

natural streams had been diverted, in order to build a waterworks, complete with settling and storage tanks. A brick building contained a large oil engine, which could be heard thumping away continually as it supplied water to the high tower at Longmoor Camp. One natural stream took the surplus water into an area of swampland on the eastern side of the Rother, and it was across this stream that a concrete dam was built and a large pond excavated. It may have been primarily intended for training purposes, but became well used for recreation during the summer months. On warm evenings, groups of soldiers would stroll down the sandy tracks from camp to take to its waters.

The water was naturally soft but at times slightly brackish, due to the acidic area of its source. Modesty forbade women from approaching the area, it was an uninhibited 'man's world', but eventually some corrugated iron bathing huts were erected, possibly with ladies of the ATS in mind. On the concrete dam a springboard was installed and, at one time, an old whaler was floated out onto the water. There was a lot of horseplay as about twenty men tried to overturn it. Many **Greatham** boys learned to swim at 'the bather' without any tuition whatsoever, indeed some us would never have learned to swim without it. My first swim in a public baths was at a large open-air pool at Hilsea, on the northern outskirts of Portsmouth. We certainly wouldn't have bothered to cycle all the way down there and back if we hadn't already learned to swim much nearer home!

The 'Yanks' arrive

In the spring of 1944, Americans – the Yanks – came to Longmoor and lived in an encampment of large bell-tents on what had been the Army sportsfield above Apple Pie Hill. There were possibly about five or six hundred of them, all medical orderlies and their Commanding Officers, who were themselves doctors. The British soldiers, in their coarse khaki clothing, envied the Yanks' comfortable uniforms, their better pay and conditions and also, of course, their obvious attraction to the local girls. I never heard of any real enmity between their soldiers and ours, though of course there was always that famous quotation being bandied about – *"Overpaid, over-sexed and over here"*. To us children, they were very popular. We spent long hours sitting outside their tents, fascinated by their style of talk and mannerisms – just like the 'flicks'! Their lockers were adorned with photographs of their wives and sweethearts, as well as the occasional one of 'ma and pa'. They were always ready to talk about 'back home', with more openness and feeling than we had received from our own elders, and they were more than

generous when it came to their handouts of chewing gum and 'candy'.

American soldiers — or G.I's - were well fed in comparison to their British counterparts and it was clear to us that most of their food must have been brought across on the Atlantic convoys. They had chicken for Sunday dinner, whereas we looked upon that as a once-a-year Christmas luxury! They also had lots of tinned fruit and ice cream. One Sunday afternoon we were in the tent of two particular 'buddies' of ours, Rudd and Washer, when one of them walked over to the mess-tent and asked the cook could he give us something to eat. *"Sure, bud, fancy some peaches?"* he asked us, whereupon he opened a large tin of the same. They were delicious, something we had hardly ever seen, never mind eaten, in years.

There were several talented musicians amongst their numbers, enough to form a band and fine-sounding choir, who were often rehearsing. I went up there on my own one Sunday after evensong, listening to them until it was almost dusk. As I walked away down the sandy path down the hill, they were singing an anthem called *"Were you there when they crucified my Lord?"* It was only a few days later that I returned to the site, but they had all gone. All that was left of the cleared encampment were the circular marks of where the tents had once been pitched and the trodden paths of where the soldiers had walked; this was shortly after D-Day. The anthem that they sang that evening stayed with me but it was not until some forty years later that I heard it again, on the radio. It immediately made me stop what I was doing. I just sat down and listened – and did some thinking too.

The crashed bomber incident

I add this story as a tribute to that brave airman who, after ordering the crew of his crippled Halifax heavy bomber to bale out over **Greatham**, stayed at the plane's controls to crash it away from the village. I came over to **Greatham** in 2001 with Don, to check the precise details from his memorial, but was denied access due to the prevailing foot-and-mouth restrictions. So I can only relate this story as I remember it. I think the pilot's name was Pryce-Hughes, and he may have been a Canadian serving with the RAF.

Anyway, we were awoken in the early hours one morning by the sound of a large aircraft lumbering overhead, as it came around from north to south, followed by the loud 'crump' of an explosion. From our back bedroom window the flames could be seen leaping high into the sky, accompanied by the continuous cracking of exploding ammunition. We could tell that the crash had occurred on Weaver's Down towards the

Liss Forest road, not far beyond **Greatham Moor**.

Up at Oak Villas opposite the school, Malcolm Kemp, then a fifteen-year old Corporal in the Air Training Corps, was also awoken by the noise and thought that he may have seen a falling parachute. He shouted out, *"Is anybody there?"* and heard a reply from the far side of Dubber's Field. Guided by the calls, he went over and found an airman caught up in a tree by his parachute and suffering from a broken ankle. Malcolm helped him loose and down from the branches, then supported him back to the house. Soon they were joined by another airman and PC Dace, who had cycled around to locate the crew and had heard the shouting.

We went over to the crash site the following evening and, although the soldiers guarding it would not allow us to the main pile of wreckage, there were other pieces scattered around. I recall that the wreckage area was quite compact, as if the pilot was unable to level out, so that the aircraft had dropped straight down; the position of the engines showed that it had approached from the south. We re-visited on successive evenings until all the wreckage had been carried away, searching for and collecting the live ammunition that had been thrown clear of the fire by the impact. A few days later, David Potter, aged about thirteen and from Snailing Lane, found the pilot's severed hand lying in a clump of heather some distance away. It was carefully picked up by a Sergeant and taken away, wrapped in paper.

There had possibly been just enough moonlight for the pilot to see the broad empty expanse of Weaver's Down to the east, beyond the buildings of **Greatham**, particularly the church. He had circled the village, losing height, and ordered his crew to bale out close to habitation. He had then attempted a 'pancake' landing over on the moor. Fifty years later, a memorial was erected in his honour, overlooking Forest Road near the old railway crossing, probably some 300 – 400 yards south of where he had bravely crashed his plane. I believe some of his family attended the accompanying ceremony.

Bombs fall on Greatham and Longmoor

1940 had one of those long, hot summers that one would normally die for, except that in this case, that's exactly what many did, dying during the Battle of Britain. By August, the Luftwaffe (German Air Force) was concentrating its attacks on fighter airfields or sites of aircraft manufacture, so Longmoor wouldn't have been high on their list of priority targets. Nonetheless an attack did come along, on

a bright, sunny morning during the last week of our summer holiday. We understood later that the raiders had been intercepted over Longmoor and, turning westward, some aircraft then dumped their bomb-loads on **Greatham**, in an attempt to lose weight and escape more quickly.

We were still lying in bed, possibly planning the day's events when, suddenly, low-flying planes were roaring overhead, followed by a prolonged series of rapid shots in five-shell bursts, from the 40 mm Bofors light ack-ack (anti-aircraft) guns, located somewhere up Apple Pie Hill. Mother came dashing upstairs and we needed no invitation to run back downstairs in her wake. Although we had a dugout shelter at the back, she quickly bundled us into the space under the stairs, which had been cleared for an occasion such as this. In fact, it had been a good excuse to get rid of an old, unwanted possession, the family pushchair! Under the stairs we crouched to the sound of explosions; some of them were very loud and the house shook from the shock waves. Fortunately, no windows broke, possibly because the casement panes were so small.

I suppose it was less than a minute before all went deathly silent and, as we emerged from under the stairs, we could hardly see across the scullery, as layers of old lime-wash and distemper from previous decades had been shaken free, clouding the air with a white smoky mist. As it began to settle, mother made us calm down and get ourselves dressed, as she began to get our breakfast. As soon as we possibly could, we all walked across the stubble in Baker's Field, through the gap in the hedge and into Ten Acres, where we saw the first crater, to us it looked enormous.

Further over was another one, then a third and, as

The Halifax Memorial in Liss Forest. A memorial plaque to a brave wartime pilot.

Manor House was the home of Mrs Unwin in 1889.

were all woken by a further loud explosion, as one of the bombs, on a timer-fuse, went off on the far side of Ten Acres. It brought home to us the courage of the bomb disposal squads, who could be blown to bits at any moment as they attempted to de-fuse the bombs. We went over next morning to view the scene. A shattered tree had stark bare limbs, with a large crater exposing its roots and there were twigs and branches spread all around. It was only later that we found another crater near the driveway of **Greatham Moor House**. If there had been one more bomb in the stick (line), it would have fallen directly on Goleigh Farm.

A few days later, around 4 o'clock on a Friday afternoon, there was a deliberate air raid on Longmoor Camp. We were outside with the men, picking up the remaining corn in Ten Acres when it happened, so the carter had to quickly unhook their horses from the wagon and lead them away to keep them pacified. In the meantime, we were told to get under the wagon for cover. Although we could see across to Longmoor, it was all over too quickly for us to see the planes. It had been an incendiary raid, very likely from the fast ME110 fighter-bombers, which had quickly disappeared. As we continued to watch. Large plumes of black smoke filled the skies and we later found out that a number of wooden huts on the Weaver's Down side of camp had been destroyed by fire.

As father cycled home on his way from work, he passed Tommy Lee, who was on foot. Tommy, a deaf and dumb chap who lived with his family at Blackmoor, signalled to Dad that he had lost his bike in the air raid! No details of such raids were issued by the news media i.e. the BBC radio and newspapers. Only the 'official' line was given out by the Ministry of Information and a typical statement would be to the effect that *"A raid over the southern counties caused some slight damage, but no casualties"*. In such a climate of subterfuge, it was only to be expected that rumour and speculation became rife.

A few weeks afterwards came the final chapter in my air raid story. Don and I were always up and about long before the start of school, usually we were out gathering acorns, for which we could be paid a shilling a bushel. However, Don was out alone this particular morning, in the field opposite the Rectory. Returning to a piece of fence alongside Rook's Farm, he noticed a neat hole in the ground, almost under the hedge and only a few feet from the barn. His curiosity was aroused and, being very experienced for an eight-year old, he knew it wasn't a rabbit warren. Nor could it be a fox's hole, because there was no expelled earth. So he crossed the fence and picked up a large stone from a heap that was always left at the roadside for emergency repairs. This he dropped down the hole to sound out the bottom and

we approached the last one, Tommy Swyers – Captain Coryton's foreman – came towards us from the other direction. *"Don't go over there"*, he said, *"there's an unexploded one"*, pointing to an old oak tree, under which he had planted a hazel branch with a white handkerchief tied to it. He told us that he had been quite close to where the bombs fell, knowing immediately that one had failed to explode, so he had come over and marked it up. Shortly after the raid, my father called in. He explained that he had been pushing his bike nearly to the top of Apple Pie Hill when the aircraft swooped down overhead and the guns opened up. He had dropped his bike to dive into a ditch and had now come back to see if we were all safe.

After inspecting the craters, mother took us home and we all walked over to see Kevin Whatmough, our pal who lived in the bungalows. We met him and his mother walking down the road, carrying some bags. Kevin was really excited and told us *"We've got to get out, there's an unexploded bomb alongside our house, I saw it come down from my window"*. So we took him home with us, while his mother went off to report to one of her friends. Apparently, a number of bombs that had been dropped had not in fact detonated. One struck the large oak just behind Oak Villas, adjoining what is now the Village Hall. It had snapped off a large bough, before burying itself in a mud patch. Another had fallen in the corner of the garden of Rook's Farm, just a few feet away from Miss Bone's bungalow. Nothing short of dragging her out screaming would get her to leave, so she stayed put! Other bombs fell into the fields opposite the Rectory, quite close to the road. The road thus had to be closed while the bombs were made safe, meaning that all of us children got an extra week off school!

Two days after the raid, during another night, we

the metallic sound made him suspicious that it could have been made by one of the bombs from the raid.

Walking over to the school, he met up with a couple of older boys and they joined him at the mysterious site. After a closer inspection, they came to the unanimous conclusion that it was indeed a bomb hole! Rushing back to school, they waited for old Charlie to arrive and hurriedly burst out their story. One of the boys was dispatched to notify PC Dace, who immediately phoned the camp at Longmoor. It wasn't long before a bomb disposal squad returned and the deadly device was made safe, before being removed from its hiding place.

Rook's Farm was occupied at the time by a Captain Blakey, who was the military Padre up at the camp. He came over to the school later and gave his personal thanks to the three boys, and a pound note to be shared between them. They decided that, as Don had spotted the bomb first, he should have the lion's share of ten shillings. Captain Blakey had an only daughter, a pretty girl of similar age to us. Although she didn't normally associate with 'ruffians' like us, she was always nice and friendly when she chatted over the garden fence. I recall that my pal Kevin was quite taken up with her, but the rest of us always thought of girls merely as 'people who can't climb trees'!

Rook's Farm

While on the subject, I'll mention a little more about Rook's Farm. The next occupant after Captain Blakey was Major Clough-Taylor, whose wife was the sister of Mrs Coryton. He was a large, bald and humourless man, who showed a fair amount of hostility towards us and was, therefore, targeted for a prank! We had noticed that, when he went out each evening in his little Austin Seven motorcar, to share a bottle with his brother-in-law at the Manor House, he inevitably left the field gate unchained. This meant that he could push it open with the car bumper on his return, saving a few moments of his precious time.

One evening we put the chain back on its hook and took shelter behind a large holly bush by the school field entrance, to await results. As the car pushed against the gate, the gate bent visibly but it became evident that it wasn't going to open. Although we could hear him grumbling and muttering under his breath, he failed to hear the stifled giggles from across the road! One always had to be ready to run on these occasions, to avoid the inevitable clip around the ear if found out. And it was no good complaining afterwards to your parents, because you'd only be told *"It jolly well serves you right"* – and most likely get another clip into the bargain!

Behind Rook's Farm was an old orchard, which had long been the target for a bit of 'scrumping' whenever the apples were ripe and rosy. A later occupant of the farm was Mrs Wright. My lasting vision of her was as an angry figure, shaking her fist and yelling *"You thieving rogues"* at the three fleeing figures running off into the distance, their shirts bulging with their delicious, if illegal, haul. Mrs Wright was a long-time resident of **Greatham** – and of good standing. I'm sure she'd have been only too pleased to give us some apples if only we'd asked, but 'scrumping' was an old country tradition and all part of life's adventure.

Deal Farm and the Shotters

I certainly enjoyed reading Ronald Shotter's description of the three Shotter brothers and their sister, Emily, it was exactly how I remembered them. Soon after the outbreak of war, we started to keep our own chickens. For these, a ration of poultry meal was available, providing that you had registered the chickens and surrendered the egg coupons – you weren't allowed both! Before we had the hens, we would buy our eggs from Deal Farm, for which Miss Shotter always charged one shilling per baker's dozen (thirteen). When the hens were laying well, mother would preserve some in waterglass – a trade name for isinglass – and lie them in a large preserving pan. For breakfast we usually had porridge with treacle and some dried egg, which seemed to be in plentiful supply. I still can't understand why some people disliked the dried egg powder, we had it most mornings, made up into a flat omelette. We loved it, especially when it had been slightly browned, and served on bread, fried in dripping in the same pan. Because of the meagre ration of cooking-fat, every bit of dripping went back into the

Deal Farm

These commercial premises stand on the site of what is now 'EuroTec'.

ground. Here it exploded, shearing off a large circle of trees around it. Maurice Lacey didn't turn up for school on the next Monday and we learned that he had been badly shaken by the blast. The broken trees remained as a sight for many years afterwards, all overcrowded and spindly but few, if any, survive today.

Local farms, estates, tenants, people and businesses

At the outbreak of World War II, Captain Coryton's **Greatham** estate was still being farmed by methods that had been in use for half a century, with the exception perhaps of one Fordson tractor! Everything gathered from the land was lifted manually and transported by carts, their pairs of heavy shire-horses being led by carters. The two largest dairy farms were Hatchmoor, already mentioned, and Berry Grove down at West Liss, where Ted Austen stabled his horses. Ted was a 'bit of a wild one', a habitual mickey-taker, of whom I once heard Captain Gussy remark, *"That awful man Austen"*. Gussy was obviously aware of what went on, even though it was 'behind his back'! With Ted being of an excitable nature, this reflected upon the behaviour of his horses, as I was to find out as I began to know them all – and their temperaments!

Ham Barn was a much smaller farm which, after the war, was used for intensive chicken rearing. Here were stabled the horses belonging to Eddie Stokes. Eddie was a quiet man who showed little or no emotion, whatever the circumstances. His horses were a pair of Belgian Punches, which went by the names of 'Punch and Judy'. Although of a smaller breed than the traditional Shire horse, they were the most willing and manageable horses that one could wish for – and certainly of comparable strength to the Shires.

Down along the Liss Forest road stood Goleigh Farm, with its very old farmhouse. I well remember the old garden wall around its frontage, along with a gate, a reminder of those days when the road went through the farmyard, between the house and outbuildings. A tithe map annotated the road as 'road to Woolmer Forest' in 1840, when the farm was called Goley Dean. It then paid tithes on 85 acres, which stretched over to the main road – an area we knew as 'Stocklands' – and down towards West Liss. Goleigh reared calves and heifers until they were ready for breeding and joining the milking herds. The farm was worked by Benny Rumbold, an ex-World War I artillery sergeant, who sadly lost one of two sons on active service in Italy. He had a lovely deep rich voice, which he would put to good use at the Spread Eagle after a few pints. I recall that he sang something called 'The Old Screw Gun', to

pan, ready to be used over and over again!

I remember one particular incident at Deal Farm, I think I was about seven years old at the time. The threshing tackle had arrived and of course we went to see it, fascinated by its big chuffing traction engine and flywheel, driving the whirring threshing-drum. But it was also our purpose to kill rats and, as long as we arrived with that intention, our presence raised no objections. Sure enough, a large rat soon escaped over the mandatory wire-netting fence around the rick, dashing out into the frozen hard ploughed field. I gave chase and was almost within clubbing distance when I tripped and fell headlong into a rock-hard furrow, which knocked me unconscious. When I came to, it was to find myself slung over old Gowan Shotter's shoulder, as he carried me home. It was probably the only time Gowan had entered someone else's house, and he declined mother's offer of a cup of tea.

The Ministry had put a bounty of tuppence on every rat's tail and this was paid by the local Pest Control Officer. The rats bred like wildfire in the wheat-ricks and, one afternoon, I helped two men kill nearly 200 of these pests over at Spartham's Corner in West Liss. After the rats had been caught, out came the men's penknives and, with a quick swipe, off would come the tail. This would be followed by a quick wipe of the blade on their trousers – but at a later tea break, the same knives would then be used to carve off lumps of bread and cheese!

Ronald Shotter's story related how his Aunt Emily was cycling near the Liss Forest railway crossing, when a German aircraft machine-gunned the signal box. It was probably on a separate occasion when another plane aimed a bomb at the same target one Saturday afternoon. A group of Liss Forest boys were playing nearby and ran into a clump of fir trees that extended along the road from the signal box. The bomb fell into the trees, hitting one pine about twenty feet above the

the tune of the Eton Boat Song.

One of the local carters was Jack Lacey, who I've already mentioned as Uncle Jack, brother to my mother. He was an irrepressible extrovert, well known locally for his spontaneous wit. He could have a pub bar in an uproar before downing his first pint – which didn't take that long! I can still picture him and the way he walked with a rolling gait, one foot in front of the other, always the same stride, it never varied. *(Except, so I'm told, when he had to chase his daughters!)* He lived at Gould's Cottage with his wife, Edie, and his three daughters – my cousins of course - Elsie, Joan and Hazel.

Henry Fiander was another carter, whose stables and wagon sheds were at Gould's House. *(The stables have since been converted to a dwelling.)* Henry was an older man and small in stature but, despite being so short, a lifetime behind the plough had given him a naturally long stride. He loved his horses, treating them almost like his own children. Henry's working days ended tragically in 1944. He was driving his wagon along the road outside the Rectory, when a squadron of heavy tanks roared through the village. His horses panicked and poor Henry was thrown into the ditch and run over by one of his own wagon wheels. He never recovered from that unfortunate accident and died a year or so later.

Henry would sometimes go out shooting, one of his specialities being sparrows, which deserves an explanation! Many parishes used to have sparrow-shooting clubs throughout the 19th-century and then, during the First World War, the County sponsored both rat and sparrow shooting. There was a great increase in the rat population during both wars, due to the large amount of home-stored foodstuffs and a shortage of labour. The unfortunate sparrow was also looked upon as a pest, being a great threat against our essential food supplies. It is difficult to imagine today, but there used to be great flocks of these birds, probably thousands strong, which would descend upon the wheat crops and decimate them, leaving empty, broken stalks lying on the ground.

I met Henry outside with his gun one day and tagged along, crouching quietly alongside as he operated along the neatly trimmed hawthorn hedges, between the school field and the one behind it, known as Hop Garden. Every so often, a flock of sparrows would swoop down, almost as one, and settle in the nearby hedgerow, as if to rest from their boisterous activities amongst the wheat stalks. This was when Henry went into action; he sent a load of sparrow shot along the top of the hedge and, almost instantly, let fly with the second barrel, as the birds rose into the air, cutting them down in their hundreds. I helped gather

the corpses into heaps, which Henry then buried, using an old spade that he always carried.

There were many skilled countrymen working on the local farms around **Greatham**. One who particularly springs to mind was old Arthur Parfitt the shepherd, a simple type from a bygone era, with his bent back and bowed legs, always dressed in his old heavy corduroy trousers. I think he used to walk down from Hawkley but, when he had a large flock strip-grazing a field of kale, he would stay alongside in his shepherd's hut. This was built of corrugated iron on a wooden frame and mounted on wheels, which one of the carters would pull into the field for him. I can still see old Arthur now, bent almost double and moving slowly. He would have half-a-dozen hurdles over his back, hanging from the pitchfork over his shoulder, as he fenced off a new strip ready for the following day. Arthur used to say that, to be a good shepherd, you needed a *"hard heart and a sharp knife"*, a remark that was associated with the foot rot that needed to be cut away.

Freddie Aburrow was both a rick-builder and thatcher. The display of those handsome corn-ricks is seen no more, with the now general use of the combine harvester. They were usually built in pairs, with the gap between them set to just the right distance to draw in the threshing drum. The rick-builder took great pride in his work and aimed for the rick to be finished in a perfect symmetry of side and pitch. The sheaves were laid butt outwards to build straight sides and corners, but slightly sloping towards the eaves. Freddie would cast a critical eye over his finished work, in typical craftsman manner. From his vantagepoint, he could look out over the field and estimate just when to start the pitch of the roof, which had to be steep enough for the rain to run off the thatch, without penetrating the rick.

I started attending Sunday school at the age of

A pony and trap stand outside AG Butchers grocery store.

four, as did my brothers before me. I remember my first outing to the seaside in 1937. For the others, it was already an eagerly awaited annual event, usually to either Bognor or Southsea, but this was apparently the first time that it was done 'in style'. This was because Mr Fred Cartwright, proprietor of Cartwright's Coals of Liss, as well as a small-time farmer, had just bought a brand new Bedford coach, with streamlined duple coachwork.

Mr Cartwright had previously had a vintage charabanc, the type with a canvas hood and celluloid side panels that slid back on metal frames, to fold at the back. With this, he had founded the Liss and District Omnibus Company, which was kept busy all through the war, providing an hourly service between Longmoor Camp and Petersfield, via Liss Forest. He later added a Bedford Utility bus with wooden seat slats and, after the war, the business was bought out by the Hants and Sussex Company. They continued to run the same service for many years, using the same scarlet livery and always known to everyone as 'the red bus'. Another coal merchant in Liss, Charlie Hassell, delivered coal all through the war, using another old charabanc similar to Mr Cartwright's, but yellow in colour. I was told that, when this old bus was used for outings or weekend jobs, Charlie would first sweep out the coal-dust, re-fit the seats, then off they would go.

Just up the Liphook road on the left was a shop owned by Mr Archibald -- or Archie -- Walters. Archie was a baker by trade and he worked in the bake-house located behind the shop, leaving Mrs Walters to attend to the shop and its customers. Before the war, Archie delivered his bread and cakes throughout the locality, using a green box sidecar attached to a BSA motorcycle. Upon the outbreak of hostilities, he swapped over to a Ford Eight van, as he began to take his increasing trade into Longmoor Camp.

Archie built *(or had built?)* a wooden canteen, just past the shop and parallel to the road. Here, the rising population of soldiers would be able to buy a plate of chips and a tasty pie at reasonable cost. Just past the canteen, he then put up a large wooden hut, at right angles to the road, to be used as a recreation room for the same soldiers. Here, the off-duty men could play billiards or snooker, darts and cards, or just use the facilities for resting and reading. It was run by a Mr Willday from Liphook, who was a kind and gracious gentleman as well as a lay-preacher. He held church services on Sunday evenings and short prayer meetings during the week. These would be followed by hymn singing, to the accompaniment of Mr Willday's sister on the harmonium. With about 2,500 men posted to Longmoor Camp at any one time, the services were usually well attended.

The canteen met an early fate, being burned down soon after its erection, but was quickly replaced. Liss Fire Brigade still had a vintage Dennis fire engine at the time. If ever it passed the school field where we were playing, it seemed to have an impressive turn of speed, being driven flat out on its solid rubber tyres, with a fireman clanging its big brass bell. I once helped Mr Walters' partner build a deep-fat fryer for the canteen, made out of sheet steel. Admiring his skill, it was my job to hold the rivet-block against the closely spaced rivets, all along the sides on the inside, while he punched them home from the outside. With my arm being much slimmer than his, I was the one able to reach up the back from underneath and mark out the circular hole for the flue pipe.

I'll go onto the pig-farm story in due course but, before I do, let me continue with Archie and the bakery. As will be seen later, some evenings on the pig-farm gave very little to do and, with dung still on my boots, I would spend an hour helping in the bake-house. This was lovely on dark cold evenings, but a bit too hot if I went to help out during the summer months. Archie Walters was a busy man. Besides baking bread, he also came up with a wide variety of cakes for his delivery to Longmoor Camp. Two local women worked alongside him during the day and he himself used to work until the early hours most days. Everything was originally mixed by hand, but then a new machine appeared. His son was an engineer, working on Ministry of Supply contracts, and he gave his father this large electric mixer, which must have saved a lot of backbreaking work.

On one side of the bake-house was a large wooden flour bin, which was replenished from sacks stored upstairs in the loft, via a hopper and canvas chute. The brick oven was built across one end, with a gap to hold the wood and coal next to it. I loved to look inside the oven's fiery interior whenever it was opened. Then Archie would take this long-handled and fire-blackened paddle, shuffling the loaves around and rotating the trays of cakes. My primary task was to sort and pack the various orders onto their respective trays ready for delivery the following morning. A piece of paper would tell me the destinations -- NAAFI, C of E (Church of England canteen), YMCA, Salvation Army, etc. Under each heading would be the numbers of each item to be packed -- so many dozen buns, doughnuts, jam tarts, Banburys and so on. We would probably find them hard and a little tasteless, today, but he had to produce things with a limited quota of ingredients. Dried fruit, for instance, was like gold dust.

When Mr Walters came out after his tea, to start his stint for the night, he'd usually bring me a mug of tea. This was never sweet enough to my liking so, if the chance arose, I would dive under the bench to raid the sugar tub. I did this on one occasion, but the taste made me shudder – I'd grabbed some salt by mistake! With Archie close by, punching dough into shape, I had no choice but to carry on drinking! When it came round to Saturday evenings, that's when I'd pick up my pay, always accompanied by a bag of mixed cakes, to be eaten as part of our Sunday afternoon tea.

The pig-farm

At the rear of the Walters' premises, extending along the sand cliff and out into the sand-pit, a large number of pig sties were built, and it was at this pig-farm that I began to work most evenings, including Saturdays, for nearly two years. It had been built up by Mr Ernest Tarr, Archie's working partner, who lived at Sandpit Cottages just alongside. Ernie was a plumber by trade and worked for G A Kemp and Sons, a reputable family firm of builders. They had a workshop and builder's yard just up Queen's Hill, on the western side of the main road. Ernie could be a terse man with a quick temper, but we usually got on well and he would give praise when it was due. What I didn't know then was that he was still suffering the effects of a severe wound that he got during the First World War. He had then been in the Royal Marines, had lost a kidney and probably a lot more, and he eventually died at a fairly early age.

Each evening after tea, I would don my brace-and-bib overalls and be transformed into a ten-year old workman. My first job was to empty the copper, still warm from the previous night's boiling, then refilling it with about a hundredweight of potatoes, with 'swill' (kitchen waste) on top. I'd usually then get the fire lit by the time that Mr Tarr came out from having his tea meal. On dark winter evenings, there was little else we could do except go round with a hurricane oil-lamp, checking that all was well. If extra bedding was required for the pigs, we'd leave most of the cleaning-out until the Saturday, when we would also manage to get in three copper boilings.

A new type of pig food was manufactured during the war, known as 'Wembley Pudding'. Where it came from I don't know, except that it arrived by lorry in great big tubs. It must have been all sorts of vegetable matter, boiled, mashed and compressed almost to a solid, which had to be dug out of the tub and mixed with water. It must have been relatively expensive, but was most useful as a supplement, especially towards the end of summer, when normal supplies of 'pig potatoes' became scarce and began to rot. The storage of potatoes was of great concern and supplies of this staple food could not be taken for granted. With no imports, the main crop had to see the nation through the

Alan proudly shows off his prize pig Elsie

next twelve months, and it was not practical to store it all in sacks within buildings. If old 'Jack Frost' got to them, they'd turn black and become useless.

Thus, much of the crop was 'clamped' out in the fields. To build a 'clamp', the spuds were piled into long straight-sided piles, to a height of some five or six feet, lying on a thick bed of straw. The pile was then covered with another thick layer of straw, followed by several inches of earth. Along the apex of the pile, at intervals, a tuft of straw would be left protruding through the earth, to provide the clamp with ventilation. It could not be opened during the coldest weather but, if some potatoes were taken, this would be from the end of the clamp, and the exposed end had then to be well re-covered and protected. Another risk to the potato crop was from the Colorado beetle. Pictures of this black and yellow striped pest were widely displayed on public notice boards, with instructions to notify the authorities if such a beetle was seen.

The pig-farm swarmed with an old enemy - rats. The sandy cliff at the rear was full of their nests, but at least it provided another source of income with a bounty of tuppence a tail! The rat is a wily creature and a successful trapper had to learn his craft well, which I managed to do. *(If you don't get craftier as you get older, life's all been a waste of time!)* Instead of just laying the trap, whereby a large rat could tug itself free, I used to wire mine to a small log. This caused the rat to weaken and die in the trap. When there were lots of young 'uns about, Mrs Walters would give me lumps of rock-hard cheese rind, with the cheesecloth still embedded in it. This I would wire to the trap so that a small rat couldn't throw it about and, inevitably, others would join in. That way, I often caught two or three at a time and, using my 'Nipper' back-breakers, the haul used to mount quite quickly.

Periodically, a Mr Channings called in to pay me my bounty. As well as Pest Control Officer, he was also the Salvage Officer, presumably for Alton Rural District Council, as I seem to recall that those dwellings on the northern side of Liphook Road were then within the Parish of Blackmoor. Mr Channings was a smiling, round-faced man, to whom I took an instant liking. *"How many this time, son?"* he'd ask me, to which my response was to open the large dried-milk tin, full of mouldy rats' tails. *"Erm, I'll take your word for it"*, he'd say, *"how much do I owe you?"* Of course, I'd already worked it out and, once he'd paid me, he would say, *"Good, now you will throw those away, won't you?"* Which I always did, but never letting on that I'd had some assistance from 'Tom'!

Tom was a battle-scarred ginger cat with torn ears, which resided at the pig-farm. Mr Walters had taken him from a litter, born in the wild down Snailing Lane, correctly assuming that he would make a good 'ratter'. Tom disassociated himself from humans, but could be tempted to a saucer of milk. Otherwise he was self-sufficient and lived on his own kills. It was a simple matter to go to his lair and cut off the tails of any remains! Mr Tarr often kept his Four-ten gun and a box of cartridges in the copper-house so that, if a large rat got a bit too cheeky, showing itself once too often, it would soon be knocked over. Ernie was a sharp shot and always got a clean kill, whether or not the target was a moving one.

Our next-door neighbour, Mr Stokes, built a sty in his garden, keeping a pig for home consumption. I think one could get an allocation of pig-bran, providing that half of the pig was sold to the Ministry of Food. Certainly, if one kept two animals, they were shared equally between the home and the Ministry. However, no home was allowed more than one pig per year. Killing was done in the wintertime, but only by a licensed slaughterman. Mr Stokes' brother-in-law worked for Mark Mitchell, the Liss butcher. He would come up in his little Morris van to carry out the kill, whereas Mr Walters and Mr Tarr would get Bill Snell to come over from Blackmoor.

The pig would drop instantly as the humane killer pierced its brain, but its nervous system was so strong that two men had to kneel, or even lie on it, to cut its throat for bleeding. Naturally, as children, we had a certain amount of sympathy for the pig, but it was a job that had to be done. *(I was certainly pleased not to have witnessed the barbaric rituals related by mother, before the day of the humane killer!)* When the pig was still, it was carried to a large tub or bath and a copper full of boiling water would be used to scald the body, before it was scraped clean of hair. The scraper had a hook on the side, used to pull off the trotters and, with the pig all pink and rosy, it was then suspended from a beam via a double-headed hook through the back legs. The chitlings (intestines) were washed through and could be cooked just like sausages.

After hanging for two or three days, the carcass would be halved and cut into joints. These would be rubbed all over with hard salt, placed in large preserving pans between layers of salt, with a final layer of salt all over. No piece was left exposed to the air. Nothing was wasted; brains, head and feet would all be boiled down to make the most delicious jellied brawn. At home, this all took place in our shared wash-house, but never in such a way as to interfere with mother's traditional Tuesday – washday! Mr Stokes always boiled his pig food at the weekend, so that his wife could use the copper on her washday, which was Monday. With this co-operation between neighbours, there was never a cross word, and Mr Stokes often supplied us with a nice piece of pork.

'Old Shep'

One of the great **Greatham** characters was Mr Sheppard the blacksmith – or 'Old Shep', as he was affectionately known. Besides being the general farrier, like many rural exponents of his craft, he could make or mend just about anything. It could be a pair of matching wrought-iron gates, replacement parts for farm tools and equipment, repairs to carts of either wood or metal, even down to making the large wheel naves (or hubs) from baulks of elm, using only the most rudimentary hand tools. Each day, the ringing of hammer on anvil could be heard, as he fashioned horseshoes or whatever else he had been asked to do. His smithy was just along the road to Selborne by Hatchmoor Farm and, if ever we called in to watch him work, we would always receive a friendly greeting.

In fact, he was always pleased that we showed an interest in his work, only warning us against getting in his way, due to the fact that we may be burned or injured. We loved watching him shape the horseshoes, occasionally returning them to the forge, with its gentle roar boosted by his pumping of the bellows. The final heating would be followed by the hiss of steam as he water-quenched the shoe to harden it. Then he'd shoe the big farm horses, selecting the correct shoe, then heating it to burn into the hoof. Here, it would be bedded-in with a cloud of acrid browny-white smoke, sometimes with a growl of *"Stand still bugger 'ee"*, if the horse flinched and moved.

Extending beyond the length of the smithy was his yard, with its large-diameter iron plate and hollow centre, used for shrinking iron rims onto cartwheels. Besides the usual conglomeration of discarded bits and pieces, all of which *"may come in handy one day"*, the nettles surrounding the yard hid lumps of cast-iron Victorian machinery, long out of use. My father said that, before the first war, the local militia used to meet and parade in the blacksmith's yard. It was a most suitable place, with its firm surface established by decades of ash and cinder from the forge, probably the only open space in the parish that wasn't muddy or dung-strewn!

Old Shep was, like many tradesmen and artisans, a 'chapel man'. Every Sunday morning he was a man transformed, as he walked up the Liphook road to the Wesleyan/Methodist chapel, in a smart suit and trilby, swinging his walking stick in unison with his stride. Could this be the same man who, for six days of the week, was a blackened figure in a grease and soot-stained leather apron, and the inevitable brown fag end hanging from his lips? Indeed it was, as he entered what father often referred to as 'The Tin Tab' – 'tin', because the chapel was constructed of metal, and 'tab', short for tabernacle!

If one wanted to buy a piece of metal from Old Shep, he would weigh it carefully in his hand, with a slow up and down movement, before naming the price. I last saw him in 1958, when he did a job for me that must have taken several hours, yet his fee was so modest that I couldn't see how he could make a living. But he was content in his work and to live in a modest style. Soon afterwards, he suffered a protracted illness, which eventually led to his death. His old smithy was later demolished and built over by a modern house. A symbol of rural life from a bygone age, like in so many other villages, disappeared from **Greatham** forever.

Afterthoughts

In relating this account of my childhood, I don't think that I view things through rose-tinted spectacles, as life then was far removed from the attitudes and manners that prevail today. We made our own entertainment and pursued it mainly through outdoors physical activities. Naturally this did involve some mischief, but it was never done with a callous disregard for the feelings of others. Discipline, both at home and at school, was strictly enforced. We

The old Church

learned the rules and accepted the consequences of any misbehaviour. **Greatham** children became sound citizens and, as far as I was aware, there were no 'problem' children in the modern sense of the word. In our family, we received no pocket money, we had to earn all we got. But, with our savings and the weekly sixpenny National Savings stamp that mother bought, we saved up to buy our own bicycles and such things. We expected nothing besides the basic needs of food and clothing, sound helpful parents and the freedom to find our own enjoyment.

A fine example was set by our honest, hard working parents, living in harmony with their neighbours. Mothers worked miracles by their diligence, especially those whose husbands were away on active service, some for as long as four years. They dreaded the day that a telegram may arrive, yet still brought up their children to the same standards to which they themselves had achieved. Finally, my intention in writing down these thoughts is to give an account of the social and economic life of **Greatham** in the mid-20th-century, particularly during the Second World War, and its relationship to the past history of the parish. Having decided, almost on the spur of the moment, that this story should be recorded, I found that my memories hadn't been lost, but just filed away ready to be brought out and eventually presented.

Alan Siney, Rudgwick, West Sussex, 2001.

Epilogue

It seems a long time since I started putting together this history! Having retired in the summer of 2000, with the benefit and experience already gained on the story of **Greatham,** I was invited to start work on a project that had lain dormant for a number of years – that of writing the authorised history of my Army apprentices' school at Arborfield in Berkshire. It is an amazing coincidence that two other ex-apprentices from the same school reside here in **Greatham**, namely Ray Jenkinson and Mike Haben.

With the Army training centres at both Arborfield and, more locally, Bordon now likely to close down and move to Gosport in the near future, there was a pressing need to produce the Arborfield history within a definite timeframe – and that target was reached in July this year. So, although the **Greatham** history was my first major work, it will come a close second to the Arborfield history when it comes to printing and publishing.

On the Army book I was greatly assisted in the final layout and style by an old colleague, Ken Anderson from Worcester, without whose infinite knowledge of computing and publishing, I must confess I would have been struggling indeed to fulfil my mission. So it was with great pleasure that I took up his kind offer of further assistance with this particular history. He has taken my original text, documents and photographs, and put them together in his inimitable style. Any mistakes or errors are of my own making, I just hope that I haven't made too many of them.

Pete Gripton, 2003

This aerial view shows present-day Greatham, with Longmoor Road running off centrally from its junction with the Petersfield to Farnham Road. The photograph was part of a series used to produce a map of Greatham for the millennium year of 2000.

Appendix One
Parish Registers

Parish Registers

The oldest of *Greatham's* Parish Registers have long since been sent off to Winchester, where they now reside in the archives of the Hampshire Record Office in Sussex Street. The most recent registers of burials, baptisms and marriages are in the custody of the Rector and Parochial Church Council. For security reasons, they are kept locked in the safe at the Church.

Register of Burials

The first entry in the burials book dates back only to 1964, when William Albert Redman was buried on August 21st. It is fitting that his name should appear first, as the story of the Redmans, and before them the Wells family, is unbroken for the best part of 200 years. No doubt this family tree could be traced back much further if time permitted. Both families figure largely in the recent history of *Greatham*.

There follows a much-reduced list of entries from the burials book. Most names will be familiar to long-standing residents of the village. The names are chosen due to their appearance elsewhere in this short history, with no slur intended upon those names omitted.

Name in register	Burial date	Story reference
William Albert Redman	Aug 21 1964	Redmans
Leonard John Lacy	Feb 27 1965	Collins
Albert Frederick Mansbridge	Nov 17 1965	Manor Cottage
Kate Wilcockson	Dec 18 1965	Cam Green Cottage
Henry George Sheppard	Mar 14 1966	Blacksmith
Liliane Edith Emily Mansbridge	Apr 16 1971	Manor Cottage
Augustus Frederick Coryton	Mar 5 1976	Manor / Goleigh
Violet Alice Amy Coryton	Aug 10 1977	Manor / Goleigh
John Alexander Hayward	Dec 30 1980	Forestside Cottage
Michael Antony Wakeford	May 24 1985	Wakeford
Arundell Thomas Clifton Neave	Aug 12 1992	Greatham Moor
Frances Mary Pumphrey	Jun 1 1994	Baker / School
Richenda, Lady Neave	Jun 20 1994	Greatham Moor
Edward Nigel Pumphrey	Oct 10 1994	Greatham Mill
Richard Michael Digby	Sep 9 1996	Digby
William James Redman	Mar 3 1997	Redman
Victor John Hayward	Jul 14 1997	Forestside Cottage
Kathleen Wakeford	Apr 5 2000	Wakeford

During the period from which the above list was extracted, the main names of those Rectors signing the register were:

R W Tyler, J Russell, P S Duffett, G Woolveridge, W Day and D Heatley.

Register of Baptisms

The baptisms book goes back a lot further in time, with the first entry dated January 3rd 1903. The participating Rectors over this span of almost a century, with their first and last entry dates, are as follows:

C F Luttrell-West	No entry	July 1933
W O Marks	March 1934	November 1942
F S Smith	June 1943	March 1944
P H Biddlecombe	July 1944	November 1947
R W Tyler	May 1948	August 1966
J Russell	March 1967	September 1978
P S Duffett	June 1980	March 1988
G Woolveridge	November 1988	June 1992
W Day	June 1992	June 1998
D Heatley	June 1999	No entry

As with the excerpts from the burials, the number of entries chosen from the baptisms is also greatly reduced, with only those with a relationship to one or more of the stories covered in this history selected.

Name in register	Date	Parents	Reference
Mervyn Ventham	15/07/06	Sarah Ellen	Kelly's 1903-23
George Arthur Roke	09/05/09	Arthur Samuel and Bertha Kate	Kelly's 1927-31
Charles Thomas Hanson	15/01/11	William and Ellen	Hanson
William James Redman	22/12/12	William Albert and Emma Jane	Redman
Edgar Redman	24/09/14	William Albert and Emma Jane	Redman
Herbert George Booth	13/03/21	Herbert and Amy	Tollgate/Lockley
Winifred Elsie Lacey	18/10/25	Leonard John and Winifred Edith	Collins
Phyllis Joan Lacey	01/05/27	L J and Winifred E	Collins
Margaret Eva Madgwick	23/10/27	Frank and Eva	Motor garage/ Lockley
Hazel Grace Lacey	06/08/29	L J and Winifred E	Collins
Caroline Julia Coryton	17/09/32	Augustus Frederick and Violet Alice Amy	Coryton
William Ernest Moseley	06/05/33	Percy Ernest and Kathleen Isabel	Moseley
Sara Jane Coryton	03/02/35	A F and Violet	Coryton
Pruett Ralph Gilburd	01/12/35	Harry Ralph and Jean Delma	Hanson/Lockley
Lavinia Augusta Coryton	07/11/37	A F and Violet	Coryton
Brian George Roke	06/01/40	George Arthur and Cissy	Kelly's 1927-31
Elizabeth Ann Hanson	11/02/40	Charles Thomas and Kathleen Elizabeth	Hanson
David Charles Hanson	01/12/46	Charles and Kathleen	Hanson
Margaret Ann Lockley	27/06/48	George Henry and May Phyllis	Lockley
Jennifer Ann Dunn	30/06/49	John Edwin and Brenda Ivy	Dunn
John Richard Dunn	22/07/51	John and Brenda	Dunn
David William Redman	21/05/60	Edgar and Olive	Redman
John Leonard Bryant	08/08/65	Norman Leonard and Evelyn	Gold's House

(I am grateful to Hugette and Ray Jenkinson for allowing me to use their house, while trawling through these Parish Registers in the search for extra reference material. Although, as already stated, I have only utilised a fraction of the available data, all the details recorded do have a relationship to the stories told elsewhere in this history, thus closing off a few loose ends which may have occurred. Ed.)

Register of Electors – 2000/2001

As a final addition to the notes on 'registers', here is the extracted list of homes, numbers and house names from the most recent available Register of Electors, The Hangers Ward, Parish of **Greatham**. In the main, they are listed in alphabetical order by road name:

Bakersfield	*numbered from 1 to 26*
Benham's Lane	*Woolmer Terrace – numbered 1 to 7; Leighwood Cottages, 1 to 4; Fir Cottage, 1 and 2*
Blackmoor	*Snap House*
Church Lane	*Swain's Cottage; Pook's Cottage; Cam Green Cottage; Pilgrim's Way; Willow Lea; Winfield; Keeper's Cottage; Heath Harrison Cottages South; Copse House*
Farnham Road	*Manor Cottage; Tom's Acre Cottage – 1 and 2; The Manor House, plus The Stables; Old School House; Roseland House; Rook's Farm; Fairlawns – 1 to 4; Amedee; Oak Cottages – 1 and 2; Hill View; Deal Farm; Deal Cottage; The Queen Public House; Thele Knapp Cottage; Thele Knapp House; The Bungalow (Liss Forest Nursery); The Old Rectory; The Old Rectory Close; Gold's Cottage; Gold's House*
Farnham Road, West Liss	*Mistral; Ham Barn Cottages – 1 to 4; Bowyer House*
Forest Road	*Goleigh Farmhouse; Moor Park Farm;* **Greatham** *Green Cottages – 1 and 2; The Barn House*
Greatham, Liss	**Greatham** *Mill; Mill Cottage*
Greatham Moor	*Greatham Moor; Farm Cottage; The Coach House*
Hopeswood	*numbered 1 to 18*
Le Court	*Le Court Cheshire Home; Bothy Cottage; Colt Bungalow; Orchard Bungalow; South Lodge; Staff Cottage – 1 & 2; Study Centre; The Hill Station*
Longmoor Road	*Innisfallen; April Cottage; Acorn Cottage; Half Moon Cottage; Nutshell Cottage; Longmoor House; Darley, 1; River View, 1 and 2; Glenthorne, 1 and 2; Little Acorns; Lindisfarne; Mark Green; Coppins; Rivendale; Bower Cottage;* **Greatham** *Cottages, 1 & 2; Chapel House; New House; Laurel Cottages, 1 and 2; Forestside Farmhouse; Cloncarrig; Ashridge; Broadleigh; Wesley Villas, No 1 and The Haven, No 2; Lynden; Welcome Cottage; Gallinula; Byncleaves; Little Meadow; Hazeldene; King's Holt Cottage; Pine Villas – 1 to 4; Sundale Cottages – 1 to 4; The Bungalows, 1 and 2; Sharon; Manaccan; Treetops; Ascot House; Hillside Cottage; The Oaks, numbered 1 to 17*
Petersfield Road	*Brandon; Chalfont; Verona; Brambles; King's Holt; The Coach House; Holt End Cottage; Kingshott Cottages, 1 to 6; Broadleigh Cottages, 1 to 4; The Old Post Office; Rooklea; Welldigger's Cottage; Fulford; Witham House; The Silver Birch Inn; Forestside Farm; Beeleigh; Caryll's; Greenhaven; Woodside; Rose Cottage; Bracken Cottage; Woolmer Cottages, 2 and 3; The Old Coach House; Forestside Cottage, 1 and 2; The Mount; Pansy Cottages, 1 and 2; Pansy Lane, No 1; Annest; Woolmer Villas, 1 to 4 (includes The Stores); Rose Cottages, 1 and 2; The Game Centre*
Selborne Road	*Case's; Case's Cottage; Forge House; Haresclose Cottages, 1 and 2; Kemp's Place Cottage*
Todmore	*numbered 1 to 24*
Wolfmere Lane	*numbered 1 to 35 plus Moor Cottage*

Appendix Two
Trade Directories

The following are extracts from various trade directories of Hampshire

The most widely known trade directory is the 'Kelly's Directory', and most of the information below has been extracted from various editions over the years. In the 1907 edition, the following introduction appears:

"The Book still contains in some measure to be a gazetteer, as a topographical account of every Town, Parish, Village and Township, and descriptions of the principal buildings and objects of interest will be found in its pages.

Full information is given as to the County Councils; the Hundreds, Unions and County Court Districts; The Cathedral; the Churches, with the value of the Livings and the names of the Patrons and Incumbents; the chief Landowners, with details as to the Principal Seats in the County; the Hospitals and Charities, whether general or local; the Acreage, Soils and Crops, the Markets and Fairs; the means of Conveyance by Railway etc, etc."

1847 (Post Office)

GREATHAM is a parish 5 miles from Petersfield and 50 miles from London, in the Hundred of Finch Dean, containing 203 inhabitants, with 894 acres of land of various descriptions. Henry Chawner esq is 'lord of the manor'. The church is a small edifice, with a steeple and two bells, and is kept in constant repair. The living is a rectory, value £300 per annum, in the diocese of Winchester, in the gift of the Rev Thomas Agar Holland. The present incumbent is the Rev Charles Bradford.

FARMERS: William Butler, William Goodeve and Richard Hearsey.

Letters received through the Petersfield office.

(The 1847 edition also includes one recognisable name of a probable inhabitant of what is now the present-day **Greatham**, *shown as a resident of* **SELBORNE** *— which then included* **Blackmoor** *within its parish boundary.* **Blackmoor** *extended well into what is now the parish of* **Greatham**. *Ed.)*

Henry Wells, carpenter & wheelwright.

1855 (Kelly's)

GREATHAM is a parish 5 miles northeast from Petersfield, and 11 southwest from Farnham, in Finch Dean Hundred, Petersfield Union and division, North Hants. The population in 1851 was 212, with 2,123 acres of land of various descriptions. Captain E H Chawner is lord of the manor.

The church is a small edifice, with a nave, north porch and chancel, and 2 bells. The living is a rectory, value £275 per annum, in the diocese of Winchester, in the gift of the Rev Thomas Agar Holland; the incumbent is the Rev Charles Bradford. Here is a mixed National school. Mills Farm is a quarter of a mile south; Harford Pond, Parmenters, Ciddy Hall, Wild Green, 1½ miles south; Forest Field, 1 mile south; Brewis and Little Langley, 2 miles southwest.

GENTRY: William Butler, esq.

TRADERS: Benjamin Blackmore Fielder, miller; William Goodeve, farmer; Richard Hearsey, farmer; George Wells, blacksmith & wheelwright.

PUBLIC OFFICERS: Parish Clerk, Thomas Albery; Collector of Taxes, William Goodeve.

National School (boys and girls): Miss Sarah Voller, mistress.

Letters through Petersfield, which is also the nearest money order office.

Blackmoor: Henry Wells, blacksmith & wheelwright; William Wells, blacksmith.

1857 (Craven's)

The description for **GREATHAM** is scanty, with little information, but does provide a link between 1855 and 1859. The main residents are listed as:

GENTRY: William Butler esq.

TRADERS: Thomas Albery, Parish clerk; Benjamin Blackmore Fielder, corn miller; William Goodeve, farmer & tax collector; Richard Hearsey, farmer; Sarah Voller, mistress of National school; George Wells, blacksmith & wheelwright.

Blackmoor: Henry Wells, wheelwright; William Wells, blacksmith.

1859 (White's)

GREATHAM, 5½ miles NNE of Petersfield and 1½ mile N of Liss Station, is a village and parish containing 212 souls and 2,123 acres of land, on the borders of Woolmer Forest and bounded on the east by Sussex. The forest lands are now enclosed. Capt Chawner is lord of the manor, but a great part of the soil belongs to the Butler, Goodeve, Banister and other families. Le Court, a handsome mansion in the Gothic style, with pleasant grounds, is the seat of William E Butler, esq, and commands extensive prospects.

The Church (St John) is a small ancient structure and contains the tomb and effigy of Lady Margery Carlyll (sic), who died in 1632. The rectory, valued in KB at £6.5s.10d, and now at £275, is in the patronage of the Rev Thomas Agar Holland and incumbency of the Rev Charles Bradford MA, who has about 45 acres of glebe, and a good Rectory House, built in 1819 at the cost of £1,000 and improved in 1839, at the cost of £804. The school was built in 1849, at the cost of £257. Post from Petersfield.

Thomas Albery, parish clerk; Rev Charles Bradford, rector; William Eldridge Butler esq, Le Court; Benjamin B Fielder, corn miller; James Kemp, carpenter; Sarah Voller, schoolmistress; George Wells, blacksmith & wheelwright.

FARMERS: George Adams; Noah Adams; John Chalcraft (bailiff to Edward Chalcraft); John Figg; George Wells; William Goodeve, Gole's farm; J Payne, Mill farm.

1871 (Mercer & Crocker's)

The description given for **GREATHAM** is again very small, but fills a gap between 1859 and 1875. The principal villagers being listed thus:

Joseph Adams, farmer; George Anderson, farmer; Capt Edward Chawner; John Figgs, farmer; Rev Joseph Foster MA, Curate; Sampson Foster esq; Henry Gregson, gardener; Joshua Jellefs, farmer; Mrs Martin, corn miller; James Wells, wheelwright; George Wells, innkeeper; Joseph Young, carpenter.

Blackmoor: Henry Kemp jnr, bricklayer; Henry Kemp snr, Bricklayer's Arms; Thomas Kemp, farmer, Forest side; George Wells jnr, wheelwright; Henry Wells, farmer; William Wells, blacksmith.

1875 (Kelly's)

GREATHAM is a parish 5½ miles north-east from Petersfield, 1½ mile from Liss railway station on the Portsmouth line, and 11 miles south-west from Farnham on the road from Petersfield to Farnham, near the Sussex border, in the Northern division of the county (Hants), Finch Dean hundred, Petersfield union, petty sessional division and county court district, and in the diocese and archdeaconry of Winchester, and rural deanery of Petersfield.

The church of St John the Baptist is a small edifice, with a chancel, nave, north porch and 2 bells. The register dates from 1555. The living is a rectory, yearly value £275, with residence, in the gift of the Rev Joseph Foster MA, of Christ's College, Cambridge, who is the curate and resides at the rectory. The incumbent is the Rev Charles Bradford MA, who is a non-resident. A handsome church is now in course of erection by subscription. Here is a mixed National school. A part of Woolmer Forest is in this parish.

Captain E H Chawner of Newton Valence is lord of the manor. The principal landowners are Capt Chawner, William F Foster esq, and Mr William Goodeve. The soil is a good hazel mould and clay; sub-soil sand and clay; parish about equal pasturage and tillage. The chief crops are corn, roots and hops. The area is 2,031 acres of land of various descriptions; gross estimated rental £2,198; rateable value £1,912; the population in 1871 was 240.

Parish clerk: Thomas Albery. Post Office: Daniel Wells, receiver. Letters through Petersfield arrive at 6 a.m.; dispatched at 8.45 p.m. No delivery on Sundays. The nearest money order office is at Liss.

National School (boys & girls): William Bristowe, master; Mrs Jane Bristowe, mistress.

PRIVATE RESIDENTS: Mrs Ewen, Manor house; Rev Joseph Foster MA (curate), The Rectory; William Fry Foster, Le Court; Daniel Gunn; Rev William Smith, Greatham moor; Misses Williamson.

COMMERCIAL: James Kemp, farmer, carpenter, wheelwright and smith; Thomas Merritt, farmer, Mill ground; Henry Wakeford, miller, Greatham mill; Daniel & James Wells, wheelwrights & blacksmiths; George Wells, Queen's Head, shopkeeper & farmer; John Williamson, farm bailiff to Mrs Chalcraft, Gole's farm.

1878 (White's)

GREATHAM, 5½ miles NNE of Petersfield and 1½ miles N of Liss Station, is a village and parish on the borders of Woolmer Forest and bounded on the east by Sussex. It is in Petersfield union, county court district, petty sessional division and polling district (North Hants), Finchdean hundred and Petersfield deanery. It had 240 inhabitants in 1871 and comprises 2,031 acres of land. The forest lands are partly enclosed.

Captain Chawner is lord of the manor, but Lord Selborne and W F Foster esq are considerable landowners. Le Court, a handsome mansion with pleasant grounds, is the seat of W F Foster esq, and commands extensive prospects.

The Church (St John the Baptist), consisting of nave, chancel, south porch and a tower containing two bells, is in the early-English style, and was built in 1875 at a cost of £5,000. This was raised by subscription, to which William Fry Foster esq and his family were the principal contributors. It is intended to carry the tower up higher, to surmount it with a spire, and to hang a peal of bells. The chancel of the old church contains the tomb and effigy of Lady Margery Carlyll (sic), who died in 1632.

The Rectory, valued in KB at £6.5s.10d, and now at £275, is in the patronage of the Rev Joseph Foster MA and incumbency of the Rev Charles Bradford MA, who has about 59 acres of glebe and a good rectory house, built in 1819 at the cost of £1,000, and improved in 1839 at the cost of £804. The School was built in 1849, at the cost of £257.

POST OFFICE:– at Mr Daniel Wells's. Letters are received at 6 a.m. and dispatched at 8.45 p.m. to Petersfield. No deliveries on Sundays. Liss is the nearest Money Order Office

Thomas Albery, parish clerk; William & Mrs Jane Bristowe, National School teachers; Mrs Elizabeth Ewen, Manor house; Mr William F Foster, Le Court; Daniel Gunn; Rev Thomas Hooper MA, curate; James Kemp, farmer, carpenter, wheelwright & shoeing & jobbing smith; James Kemp jnr, shopkeeper; William Merritt, farmer, Mill ground; Rev William Smith, Greatham moor; Henry Wakeford, miller, Greatham mill; Daniel Wells, Postmaster; Daniel & James Wells, wheelwrights and blacksmiths; George Wells, farmer, shopkeeper and victualler, Queens Head; John Williamson, farm bailiff to Mrs Mary Chalcraft, Gole's farm; Misses Lucy, Harriet and Emily Williamson.

1880 (Kelly's)

GREATHAM is a parish 5½ miles north-east from Petersfield, 1½ from Liss railway station on the Portsmouth line, 11 south-west from Farnham and 47 from London, on the road from Petersfield to Farnham, near the Sussex border, in the northern division of the county (Hants), Finch Dean hundred, Petersfield union, petty sessional division and county court district, and in the diocese and archdeaconry of Winchester and rural deanery of Petersfield.

The church of St John the Baptist was built on a new site in 1875 at a cost of about £5,000, and consists of a chancel, nave, north porch and 2 bells. The old church is in ruins. The register dates from 1571. The living is a rectory, yearly value £275, with residence, in the gift of and held by the Rev Joseph Foster MA, of Christ's College, Cambridge. A part of Woolmer Forest is in this parish.

Captain E H Chawner of Newton Valence, who is lord of the manor, William F Foster esq and Lord Selborne are the principal landowners. The soil is a good hazel mould and clay; sub-soil, sand and clay; parish about equal pasturage and tillage. The chief crops are corn, roots and hops. The area is 2,031 acres of land of various descriptions; rateable value £2,010.6s.7d; the population in 1871 was 240.

Parish clerk: Thomas Ayling.

POST OFFICE: Mrs Louisa Wells, receiver. Letters through Petersfield arrive at 6 a.m., dispatched at 8.45 p.m. No delivery on Sundays. The nearest money order & telegraph office is at Liss.

National School (boys & girls): Mrs Bristowe, mistress.

William Bennett; Mrs Ewen, Manor house; Rev Joseph Foster MA (Rector), The Rectory; William F Foster, Le Court; Daniel Gunn; Rev Thomas Hooper MA (Curate); Rev William Smith, Greatham moor; the Misses Williamson; James Kemp, farmer, carpenter, wheelwright & smith; Thomas Merritt, farmer, Mill ground; Henry Wakeford, miller, Greatham mill; George Wells, Queen's Head, shopkeeper & farmer; James Wells, wheelwright & blacksmith; John Williamson, farm bailiff to Mrs Chalcraft, Gole's farm.

1885 (Kelly's)

GREATHAM is described in almost the same manner as in 1880.

The church of St John the Baptist is an edifice of stone, in the Decorated style, rebuilt on a new site in 1875, at a cost of about £5,000, consisting of chancel, nave, north porch and a low square tower, situated at the north-east angle, containing 2 bells. The old church is in ruins. The register dates from 1571. The living is a rectory, yearly value £275, with residence, in the gift of and held since 1880 by the Venerable Henry Press Wright MA, Peterhouse College, Cambridge, late Archdeacon of British Columbia. A part of Woolmer Forest is in this parish.

Le Court, the residence and property of Mrs Sandford, is a modern stone mansion, erected in 1866, situated upon an eminence, commanding extensive and picturesque views of the surrounding country; the grounds adjoining are about 280 acres in extent. George Edward Coryton esq JP, of Liss Place, who is lord of the manor, Lord Selborne and Mrs Sandford are the principal landowners.

The soil is a good hazel mould and clay; sub-soil, sand & clay; parish about equal pasturage and tillage. The chief crops are corn, roots and hops. The area is 2,031 acres of land of various descriptions; rateable value £1,920; 1881 population was 285.

Parish clerk: Henry Kirk.

POST OFFICE: Mrs Louisa Wells, receiver. Letters through Petersfield arrive at 5.35 a.m., dispatched at 8.30 p.m. On Sundays, letters delivered to callers only. The nearest money order & telegraph office is at Liss.

National School (mixed): built around 1850 with residence for mistress and 60 children; average attendance 40; Mrs Bristowe, mistress.

PRIVATE RESIDENTS: William Bennett; Mrs Sandford, Le Court; Rev William Smith, Greatham moor; the Misses Williamson; Ven Archdeacon Henry Press Wright MA, the Rectory.

COMMERCIAL: George Adams, dairyman; John Amey, farmer; William Gauntlett, cowkeeper; James Kemp, carpenter, wheelwright & smith; Henry Kirk, painter; John Knight, Queen's Head PH & shopkeeper; Charles Maybee, farmer; Thomas Merritt, farmer, Mill ground; Henry Trigg, farmer; Henry Wakeford, miller (water), Greatham mill; Harriet Wells (Mrs), farmer; James Wells, blacksmith; William Wells, wheelwright.

1889 (Kelly's)

GREATHAM is described almost exactly as in 1885. The yearly value of the Rectory living is quoted as £245. The rateable value of the whole area is also shown as being reduced, to £1,774.

Lord Selborne is a principal landowner. Parish clerk: Charles Tull.

George Edward Coryton JP, of Liss Place, is lord of the manor.

The living is in the gift of the Ven Archdeacon H P Wright MA (since 1880).

National School: now averages 50 children, with Miss Goddard mistress.

POST OFFICE: Mrs. Louisa Wells still receiver. Postal deliveries now increased. Letters through West Liss S O arrive at 2.25 & 5.35 a.m. and dispatched at 2.30 and 8.30 p.m.

PRIVATE RESIDENTS: Mrs Sandford, Le Court; Mrs Smith, Greatham moor; Mrs Unwin, Manor House; Misses Williamson; Ven Archdeacon Henry Press Wright, The Rectory.

COMMERCIAL: George Adams, dairyman; Mrs Amey, farmer & hop grower; Samson Davis, Queen's Head PH & shopkeeper; James Etheridge, farmer, Behham's farm; John Ellis, miller (water), Greatham mill; William Gauntlett, cowkeeper; Frank Kemp, carpenter & wheelwright, Walter Kemp, smith; John Knight, farmer; William Merritt, farmer, overseer & collector of taxes, Mill ground; Henry Trigg, farmer; Harriet Wells (Mrs), farmer; James Wells, blacksmith & farmer; William Wells, wheelwright.

1895 (Kelly's)

GREATHAM is again described much in the same manner as 1885.

The old parish church is now in ruins. The present church of St John the Baptist, rebuilt on a new site in 1875, at a cost of about £5,000. An edifice of stone in the Decorated style, consisting of a chancel, nave, south aisle, south porch and a low tower, at the north-east angle, containing 2 bells: there are 300 sittings.

The register dates from the year 1571. The living is a rectory, average tithe rent-charge £195; net yearly value £278, with 53 acres of glebe and residence, in the gift of Mrs Luttrell-West, and held since 1893 by the Rev Francis Richard Bryans, BA of Brasenose College, Oxford. A part of Woolmer Forest is in this parish.

Lecourt (sic), the residence and property of Heath Harrison esq, is a mansion of stone, erected in 1866, upon an eminence, commanding extensive and picturesque views of the surrounding country; the grounds adjoining are about 280 acres in extent.

Frederick Coryton esq JP, MFH, of Liss Place, who is lord of the manor, Lord Selborne and Heath Harrison esq are the principal landowners. The soil is a good hazel mould and clay; subsoil, sand and clay; parish about equal pasturage and tillage. The chief crops are corn, roots and hops. The area is 2,031 acres of land, of various descriptions; rateable value, £1,794; the population in 1891 was 288.

Parish clerk: Thomas Prince

POST OFFICE – Hori Kemp, sub-postmaster. Letters through West Liss S O arrive at 2.25 & 5.35 a.m.; dispatched at 2.40 & 8.30 p.m. On Sundays, letters delivered to callers only. The nearest money order & telegraph office is at West Liss. Postal orders are issued here, but not paid.

National School (mixed): built around 1850, with residence for mistress, for 60 children; average attendance, 50; Miss Etheridge, mistress.

PRIVATE RESIDENTS: Rev Francis R Bryans, BA, The Rectory; Mrs Cox; Heath Harrison, Le Court; Mrs Smith, Greatham Moor; William Rose Smith, Greatham Moor; Mrs Unwin, Manor house; the Misses Williamson.

COMMERCIAL: George Adams, dairyman; Sarah Clinch, (Mrs), apartments; Samson Davis, Queen's Head PH and shopkeeper; Frederick Etheridge, farmer, Benham's Farm; John Ellis, miller (water), Greatham Mill; Edward Kemp, farmer; Frank Kemp, cowkeeper; Frederick Kemp, carpenter & wheelwright; Jane Kemp, (Mrs), cowkeeper; Walter Kemp, smith; John Knight, farmer; Samuel Smith, farmer, Mill ground; William Rose Smith, farmer, Greatham Moor; Henry Trigg, farmer; James Wells, blacksmith and farmer; William Wells, wheelwright.

1903 (Kelly's)

GREATHAM is once again described as previously, with one main addition in that *'a permanent military camp is now in course of formation at* **Longmoor**'.

The living is in the gift of the Rev C F Luttrell-West MA.

Lord Selborne is a principal landowner.

Parish clerk: Thomas Prince. Elementary School (mixed): Miss Harring, mistress.

PRIVATE RESIDENTS: Frederick Coryton JP, MFH, Manor house; Mrs Cox; Heath Harrison, Lecourt; Rev Cecil Francis Luttrell-West MA, rector, The Rectory; Alfred Maskell, Goles; William Rose Smith, Greatham moor; Misses Williamson.

COMMERCIAL: Albert Butcher, grocer & post office; Samson Davis, The Queen's PH & shop-keeper, refreshment contractor to Longmoor Camp, ale & stout merchant; Frederick Etheridge, farmer, Benham's farm; Edward Kemp, farmer; Frank Kemp, cowkeeper; Frederick Kemp, carpenter & wheelwright; Mrs Jane Kemp, cowkeeper; Walter Kemp & Sons, smiths; John Knight, farmer; Alfred Lintott, farmer, Mill ground; Henry Trigg, farmer; Mrs Eliza Ventham, dairy; James Wells, blacksmith & farmer; William Wells, wheelwright.

Blackmoor: Mrs Chase-Parr, King's Holt; Frederick Etheridge, farmer, Forestside farm; Frederick William Pearson, Woolmer Hotel.

1907 (Kelly's)

GREATHAM is a parish on the road from Petersfield to Farnham, near the Sussex border, 2 miles north from Liss station on the London and South Western railway, 5½ north-east from Petersfield and 11 south-west from Farnham, in the Eastern division of the county (Hants), Finch Dean hundred, Petersfield union and county court district, and partly in the Petersfield and Alton (Whitehill sub-division) petty sessional divisions, and in the rural deanery of Petersfield, and archdeaconry and diocese of Winchester. The River Rother flows through the parish.

The old parish church is now in ruins. The present church of St John the Baptist, rebuilt on a new site in 1875, at a cost of about £5,000, is an edifice of stone in the Decorated style. It consists of a chancel, nave, south aisle, south porch and a low tower with spire at the northeast angle, containing 2 bells. The spire and belfry were erected in 1897 at a cost of £800, by Heath Harrison esq of Le Court, in commemoration of the Diamond Jubilee of Her late Majesty Queen Victoria: there are 300 sittings.

The register dates from the year 1571. The living is a rectory, net yearly value £250, with 53 acres of glebe and residence, in the gift of and held since 1902 by the Rev Cecil Francis Luttrell-West, MA, of Christ Church, Oxford.

Longmoor Camp, commenced in 1903, is a permanent military station used as a training school for mounted infantry, who are drawn from all regiments in the United Kingdom. The camp itself occupies about 40 acres of ground, and is available for about 1,000 troops. The rifle range attached to the camp is used conjointly by the soldiers from the camp at Bordon.

A military railway, running from Bordon Camp to Longmoor Camp, is used for instructional purposes by the detachment of the Royal Engineers permanently quartered here. Attached to the camp are Church of England and Catholic chapels, a military hospital and school. There is also a pack of drag hounds.

A part of Woolmer Forest is in this parish. Le Court, the residence and property of Heath Harrison esq JP, is a mansion of stone, erected in 1866, upon an eminence, surrounded by beautiful gardens, in a well-wooded park of 70 acres, commanding extensive and picturesque views of the surrounding country.

Frederick Coryton esq JP, MFH, of the Manor House, who is lord of the manor, Lord Selborne and Heath Harrison are the principal landowners. The soil is a good hazel mould and clay; sub-soil, sand and clay; parish about equal pasturage and tillage. The chief crops are corn, roots and hops. The area is 2,031 acres of land, of various descriptions; rateable value, £3,754; the population in 1901 was 533, including 166 military in Longmoor Barracks.

Sexton: James Lacey.

Wall letterbox at Manor House is cleared at 9.55 a.m., 2.45 & 8.10 p.m.; Sundays 8.10 p.m. Letters through East Liss S O. The nearest post & money order office is in the parish of Blackmoor, half a mile distant & the nearest telegraph office is at West Liss, 2 miles distant.

Elementary School (mixed): built about 1850, with residence for master & 75 children; average attendance 60; Charles Hiscock, master.

LONGMOOR CAMP: School of Instruction for Mounted Infantry. Commandant, Bt-Col F Hackett-Thompson CB; Asst Commandant, Major Sir H W McMahon bt, DSO, R W Fusiliers; Adjt & Quartermaster, Bt-Major A J McNeill, Seaforth Highlanders. Royal Engineers: 8th (Railway) Company, Capt E W S Mahon; 10th (Railway) Company, Capt H O Mance DSO; Military Hospital, Lt-Col R J Geddes DSO, MB, medical officer in charge & Lt P Sampson. Army Veterinary Corps, Capt O S Fisher; Army Chaplains Dept.: (Church of England) Rev C F Luttrell-West MA, officiating clergyman; (Catholic) Rev W Forrest CF; Army School, Miss Frances Scoular, mistress; Woolmer Drag Hounds, Major Sir H W McMahon bt, DSO master of the hunt.

PRIVATE RESIDENTS: Frederick Coryton JP, MFH, Manor house; Mrs Cox, Forest corner; Col P H Greig, Gold's house; Bt-Col F Hackett-Thompson, CB, Commandant, Longmoor; Heath Harrison esq, JP, Le Court; Rev Cecil Francis Luttrell-West MA, (rector), The Rectory; Major V R Pigott JP, the Mill house; William Rose Smith, Greatham moor; Miss Tassell, Kent Cottage; Miss Williamson.

COMMERCIAL: William Alexander, gardener to Heath Harrison; Henry Barnes, grocer; Thomas Barnes, fishmonger, Liss Forest; John Austin Bartlett, commercial traveller, Liphook road; Arthur Boys, farmer, Mill farm; Joseph Clarke, woodman for Crown lands, Brimstone lodge; Emma Downer (Mrs), refreshment rooms; Herbert Fidler, gardener to Mrs Chase-Parr; Hampshire County Council Stores Depot, Woolmer Forest division, Deal farm; Henry Herbert Hopkins, grocer and The Queen PH; Walter Kemp & Son, smiths; Frank Kemp, cowkeeper & cab & fly proprietor, Fern cottage; Frederick Kemp, carpenter & wheelwright; George Leonard Latham, insurance agent,

1 Bridge cottages; Thomas Luff, farm bailiff to W R Smith esq, Greatham Moor farm; James Marshall, builder, Liss Forest; John Patterson, clothier; George Prince, shopkeeper; Edward Russell, shopkeeper; Kathleen Sainty (Mrs), dress maker, 6 Bridge cottages; Edward Stead, storekeeper at Longmoor Camp, Longmoor Lodge; Henry Trigg, cartage, haulage & road contractor, farmer & traction engine owner (light), Deal farm; James Wells, blacksmith & farmer; William Wells, wheelwright.

Blackmoor: George Alfred Butcher, grocer; Samson Davis, apartments, Kingshott Villas; James Dickson, boot maker; Frederick Etheridge, farmer, Forestside farm; Thomas Garner, Woolmer hotel and jobmaster; Bertram Kirby, cycle agent; Charles McGuirk, barrack warden, Longmoor Camp; William Silco, refreshment rooms.

1907 (Bennett's Business Directory)

The following entries were found under the coverage of the 'Liss' area, and all annotated as '*Greatham*, West Liss':

Alfred George Butcher, grocer; George Kemp, builder; G A Kemp, builders & contractors; William Kemp & Son, farriers; Henry Trigg, carting contractor, Deal farm. Also was the entry: 'Queen Inn, *Greatham*. S Davis proprietor, wine & spirit merchant. Good stabling and lock-up coach house. Also grocer and provision dealer.' The Woolmer Hotel, *Greatham*, West Liss, is also entered.

1911 (Kelly's)

GREATHAM – the general description here remains as that of 1907, with the exception that the rateable value has increased to £3,815, and a first mention is made of a 'Wesleyan chapel'. *

The description of the churches is also unchanged, except that by now the lych-gate, erected in 1907 as the gift of Sir Heath & Lady Harrison, is added.

The living is in the gift of the Rev C F Luttrell-West MA. Lord Selborne is a principal landowner.

Sexton: James Lacey. School master: Charles Hiscock.

PRIVATE RESIDENTS: Frederick Coryton, JP, Manor House; Mrs Cox, Forest Corner (postal address, West Liss); Heath Harrison, JP, Le Court; Col Edward Charles Ingonville-Williams CB, DSO (Commandant of School of Instruction for Mounted Infantry), Longmoor; Capt Henry Cholmondeley Jackson, Longmoor Camp; Miss Jackson, Gold's Farmhouse; Rev Cecil Francis Luttrell-West, MA (rector), The Rectory; Bt-Col William Raine Marshall, Longmoor Camp; William Rose Smith, Greatham moor; Capt Augustus John Williams, AVC, Rotherdene.

COMMERCIAL: William Alexander, gardener to Heath Harrison esq JP; John Callen, farmer, Mill farm; Church of England Soldiers & Sailors Club (George Hall manager), Longmoor Camp; Frederick Drury, tailor, Liphook & Longmoor Camp; Herbert Fidler, gardener to Mrs Chase Parr; Frederick Wordsworth Hasleden, fishmonger, Forest Corner (postal address East Liss); Hampshire County Council Stores Depot, Woolmer Forest division, Deal Farm; William Herbert Harman, grocer, Longmoor road; Harvey & Co., photographers, Longmoor Camp; Walter Kemp & Son, smiths; Frank Kemp, cowkeeper; Frederick Kemp, carpenter; Martin Kemp, The Queen PH; Frederick William Lancaster, miller (water); Mrs Susan Lockley, refreshment rooms, Liphook road; London County & Westminster Bank Limited (sub-branch from Petersfield (Fridays 1 to 2.30 p.m.), Longmoor Camp – draw on LCWB, Lombard street, London EC; Thomas Luff, farm bailiff to W R Smith esq, Greatham Moor farm; John Moyser, chief rangewarden for Crown lands, Brimstone lodge; George Prince, shopkeeper, Tollgate; Frederick Robertson, hair dresser, Liphook road; Edward Russell, shopkeeper; Mrs Kathleen Sainty, dress maker, 6 Bridge cottages; Henry Trigg, farmer, Deal farm; James Wells, blacksmith & farmer; Miss Jane Wells, cowkeeper, Rooks farm; William Wells, wheelwright.

Blackmoor:

PRIVATE RESIDENTS: Mrs Chase Parr, King's Holt; Edgar James Tabor, The Laurels.

COMMERCIAL: Alfred George Butcher, grocer; Vernon Cuthbert Cains, boot repairer; Samson Davis, apartments, Kingshott Villas; John Henry Elston, boot repairer; Frederick Etheridge, farmer, Forest Side farm; George A Kemp and Sons, builders, contractors, building material merchants, hot water engineers & fitters, sanitary engineers, Elm Villa, TN 4 Greatham; Bartram Kirby, cycle agent, dealer, repairer & enameller, Broadleigh cycle works; William Smith, apartments, Woolmer Villas; George Wilson Wilburn, shopkeeper.

1915 (Kelly's)

GREATHAM is described in much the same manner as previously recorded in 1911. The rateable value has increased now to £4,775, and a population of 1,777 includes 1,128 military and 69 other occupants of Longmoor Barracks.

The living is in the gift of the Rev C F Luttrell-West MA. The Earl of Selborne KG, PC is a principal landowner. Sexton: James Lacey.

Post Office – Miss Amy Prince, sub-postmistress. Letters through East Liss, Hants, cleared at 9.55 a.m., 2.45 & 8.05 p.m.; Sundays 8.05 p.m. The nearest money order & telegraph office is in the parish of West Liss or Blackmoor, a mile distant. Pillar letter boxes – Le Court cleared at 8.35 a.m., 1.50 & 7.25 p.m.; Sundays 8.35 a.m. Liphook Road cleared at 9 a.m., 2.35 & 7.50 p.m.; Sundays 7.50 p.m.

Elementary School (mixed): built around 1850 and new school built on a new site in 1911, for 120 children; Charles Hiscock, master.

Woolmer Draghounds, Lt J F Montagu, master of the hunt

PRIVATE RESIDENTS: R F Bate, Cases; Frederick Coryton JP, Manor House; Mrs Cox, Forest Corner (postal address West Liss); Lt E H Crailsham, Rotherdene; Heath Harrison JP, Le Court; Miss Jackson, Gold's Farmhouse; Rev Cecil Francis Luttrell-West MA (rector), The Rectory; William Rose Smith CB, Greatham moor.

COMMERCIAL: Alfred George Butcher, outfitter, Longmoor Camp; John Callen, farmer, Mill farm; Church of England Soldiers' and Sailors' Club (George Hall, manager), Longmoor Camp; Charles Coles, gardener to William R Smith esq CB; John Goddard, The Queen PH; Hampshire County Council Stores Depot, Woolmer Forest division, Deal farm; William Herbert Harman, grocer, Longmoor road; Harvey & Co., photographers, Longmoor Camp; Arthur James, chief range warden for Crown Lands, Brimstone Lodge; Frank Kemp, cowkeeper; Frederick Kemp, carpenter; Sydney Kemp, smith; Bertram Kirkby, cycle agent, dealer, repairer, enameller & accessories, haberdasher, Liphook road; Frederick William Lancaster, miller (water); Mrs Susan Lockley, refreshment rooms, Liphook road; London County & Westminster Bank Ltd. (sub-branch from Petersfield; Thurs. 1 to 2.30 p.m.), Longmoor Camp; draw on head office, Lombard Street, London EC; Thomas Luff, farm bailiff to W R Smith esq CB, Greatham moor farm; Thomas Edward Paice, boot maker, Liphook road; John A Peskett, gardener to Heath Harrison esq JP; Miss Amy Prince, shopkeeper & post office, Tollgate; William Albert Redman, cowkeeper, Rooks farm; Edward Russell, shopkeeper; Mrs Kathleen Sainty, dress maker, 6 Bridge cottages; Albert Seagrove, hairdresser, Longmoor camp; Thomas Swyer, farm bailiff to F Coryton esq JP; Henry Trigg, farmer, Deal farm, TN 10 Blackmoor; Mrs Sarah Ventham, farmer; William Wells, wheelwright; George White, hairdresser, Liphook road. **Blackmoor:** George Alfred Butcher, grocer & PO; Samson Davis, apartments, Kingshott Villas; Frederick Etheridge, farmer, Forestside farm.

1920 (Kelly's)

GREATHAM is described virtually the same as for previous entries.

The living is in the gift of the Rev C F Luttrell-West MA (since 1903). The Earl of Selborne, KG, PC is a principal landowner.

Sexton: James Lacey. Schoolmaster (Council school): Charles Hiscock.

PRIVATE RESIDENTS: R F Bate, Cases; Frederick Coryton JP, Manor House; Sir Heath Harrison bart JP, Le Court; Miss Jackson, Gold's House; Rev C F Luttrell-West MA (rector), The Rectory; T W Rogers, Rotherdene; W R Smith, esq CB, Greatham moor.

COMMERCIAL: Ernest Atkins, C of E Club manager, Longmoor Camp; Mrs Herbert Booth, shopkeeper & PO, sub-postmistress; A G Butcher, outfitter, Longmoor Camp; John Callen, farmer, Mill farm; Edward E Carr, gardener to Sir Heath Harrison; Charles Coles, gardener to W R Smith; James W Crass, miller (water); Harry Gilburd, refreshment rooms, Longmoor road; John Goddard, the Queen PH; Harvey & Co., photographers, Longmoor Camp; Arthur James, range-warden for Crown Lands, Brimstone cottage; Frank Kemp, cowkeeper; Bertram Kirby, cycle agent etc., Longmoor road; Thomas Luff, farm bailiff to W R Smith, Greatham moor; Thomas Edward Paice, boot maker, Liphook road; W A Redman, cowkeeper, Rook's farm; Mrs Elizabeth Robinson, refreshment rooms, Longmoor road; Edward Russell, shopkeeper; Mrs Kathleen Sainty, dressmaker, 6 Bridge Cottages; Albert Seagrove, hairdresser, Longmoor Camp; George Shepherd, smith; Thomas Swyer, farm bailiff to F Coryton; Henry Trigg, farmer, Deal farm; Mrs Sarah Ventham, farmer; Archibald Walters, grocer, Longmoor road; William Wells, wheelwright.

Blackmoor: Sidney H Cotton, King's Holt; George Alfred Butcher, grocer; Samson Davis, apartments, Kingshott

Villas; Fred Etheridge, farmer, Forestside farm; Herbert Grace, shopkeeper; William Herring, motor garage; G A Kemp & Sons, builders, contractors etc.; Mrs Jean Roy, prop, Woolmer Hotel.

1923 (Kelly's)

GREATHAM is once again described in similar manner to 1907, except that it is now in the 'Petersfield', rather than the 'Eastern' division of the county. The river Rother flows through the parish.

The register dates from the year 1571. The living is a rectory, net yearly value £282, with 53 acres of glebe and residence, in the gift of and held since 1902 by the Rev Cecil Francis Luttrell-West MA of Christ Church, Oxford. There is a Wesleyan chapel. *

Longmoor Camp, commenced in 1903, is a permanent military station used as a training school for mounted infantry, who are drawn from all Regiments in the United Kingdom. The camp itself occupies about 40 acres of ground, and is available for about 1,000 troops. The rifle range is used conjointly by the soldiers at the camp at Bordon.

Attached to the camp are Church of England and Catholic chapels, a military hospital and school. A memorial of rough granite was erected by public subscription in 1919, in memory of 18 men of this parish who gave their lives in the Great War.

A part of Woolmer Forest is in this parish. Le Court, the property and residence of Sir Heath Harrison bart, JP, is a mansion of stone, erected in 1866 upon an eminence, surrounded by beautiful gardens, in a well-wooded park of 70 acres, commanding extensive and picturesque views of the surrounding country.

Frederick Coryton esq, JP, who is lord of the manor, Viscount Wolmer MP, Sir Heath Harrison and Sir William Rose Smith, KCVO, CB, are the principal landowners. The soil is a good hazel mould and clay; sub-soil, sand and clay; parish about equal pasturage and tillage. The chief crops are corn and roots. The area is 2,030 acres of land of various descriptions; rateable value £4,776; the population in 1911 (census year) was 1,770, including 1,128 military and 69 other occupants of Longmoor Barracks.

Sexton: James Lacey.

Letters through East Liss, Hants. The nearest money order & telegraph office is in the parish of West Liss or Blackmoor, a mile distant. Post MO & T Office, Longmoor Camp – William Campbell, sub-postmaster. Letters through East Liss, Hants.

Council School: built on a new site in 1911, for 120 children; C Jeffery Wain, master.

PRIVATE RESIDENTS: Surg-Capt R F Bate, RN, Cases; Frederick Coryton, JP, Manor House; Sir Heath Harrison bart JP, Le Court; Miss Jackson, Gold's Farm house; Thomas Lewes Rogers, Rotherdene; Sir William Rose Smith, KCVO, CB, Greatham moor; Rev C F Luttrell-West, MA, (rector), The Rectory.

COMMERCIAL: Mrs Amy Booth, shopkeeper; Albert George Butcher, outfitter, Longmoor Camp; John Callen, farmer; Church of England soldiers & Sailors Club (Ernest Atkins, manager), Longmoor Camp; Charles Coles, gardener to Sir William Rose Smith; Fred Cooper, chief range warden for Crown lands, Brimstone lodge; Harry Gilburd, refreshment rooms, Longmoor road; John Goddard, The Queen PH; Harvey & Co., photographers, Longmoor Camp; Edwin Hull, miller (water);

Frank Kemp, cowkeeper; Bertram Kirkby, cycle agent, dealer, repairer, enameller & accessories, haberdasher, Liphook road; Thomas Luff, farm bailiff to Sir Wm. Rose Smith; Frank Madgwick, motor garage; William Albert Redman, cowkeeper, Rooks farm; Mrs Elizabeth Robinson, refreshment rooms, Longmoor road; Edward Russell, shopkeeper; Albert Seagrove, hair dresser, Longmoor Camp; George Shepherd, smith; Thomas Swyer, farm bailiff to F Coryton; Henry Trigg, farmer, Deal farm; Mrs Sarah Ventham, farmer; Archibald Walters, grocer, Longmoor road; William Wells, wheelwright.

Blackmoor (addressed now as Blackmoor, East Hants.): Albert George Butcher, grocer; Samson Davis, apartments, Kingshott Villas; Frederick Etheridge, farmer, Forest Side farm; Herbert Grace, shopkeeper; Mrs Drusilla Hedley, Woolmer Hotel; George A Kemp & Sons (see 1911 entry).

1927 (Kelly's)

GREATHAM is once again described in the familiar manner. The population shown in 1921 (census year) was 1,921, of whom 1,038 were at Longmoor Camp.

The living is in the gift of the Rev C F Luttrell-West MA. Viscount Woolmer PC, MP, JP is a principal landowner. Council school for 120 children: C Jeffery Wain, master.

PRIVATE RESIDENTS: Surg-Capt R F Bate OBE, RN (ret'd), Cases; A F Coryton JP, Manor House; Sir Heath Harrison bart JP, Le Court; Miss Jackson, Gold's House; Rev C F Luttrell-West MA, rector, The Rectory; W R Smith, Greatham moor.

COMMERCIAL: Ernest Atkins, C of E Club manager, Longmoor Camp; A G Butcher, outfitter, Longmoor Camp; John Callen, farmer, Mill farm; Edward E Carr, gardener to Sir H Harrison; Charles Coles, gardener to W R Smith; Fred Cooper, chief range-warden for Crown Lands, Brimstone lodge; Stephen Fry, gamekeeper to Sir H H; Harvey & Co, photographers, Longmoor camp; Edwin Hull, miller (water); Frank Kemp, cowkeeper; James Kinally, draper, Longmoor Camp; Bertram Kirby, cycle agent etc, Liphook road; Thomas Luff, farm bailiff to W R Smith, Greatham moor farm; Frank Madgwick, motor garage; W A Redman, cowkeeper, Rook's farm; Harry Rixon, The Queen PH; A Roke, newsagent, Longmoor Camp; George Shepherd, smith; Thomas Swyer, farm bailiff to A F Coryton; Henry Trigg, farmer, Deal farm; Archibald Walters, grocer, Longmoor road; William Wells, wheelwright.

Blackmoor: Albert George Butcher, grocer; Herbert Grace, shopkeeper; G A Kemp & Sons, builders etc.; Mrs S Smith, Woolmer Hotel.

1931 (Kelly's)

The entries for 1931 are very much the same as for 1923. Regarding population, Longmoor Camp is not now included. The civilian population still quotes the 1921 census figure as 1,038, which seems rather high when the figures for 1923 are calculated as only 573.

The living is in the gift of the Rev C F Luttrell-West MA. Viscount Wolmer PC, MP, JP is a principal landowner. Sexton: James Lacey.

(The name of James Lacey was consistently spelled as 'Lacy' in many entries, but I have amended it to what must be the correct 'Lacey', having received a photograph of the gentleman from Ronald Shotter. The reverse of the photograph is annotated "With best wishes from James Lacey, Sexton at Greatham Church, May 1906 – December 31st 1940". Ed.)

PRIVATE RESIDENTS: Surg-Capt R F Bate OBE, RN (ret'd), Cases; Augustus Frederick Coryton JP, Manor house; Sir Heath Harrison bart JP, Le Court; Sir William Rose Smith KCVO, CB, Greatham moor; Rev Cecil Luttrell-West MA (rector), The Rectory.

COMMERCIAL: Albert George Butcher, outfitter, Longmoor Camp; John Callen, farmer, Mill farm; Edward E Carr, gardener to Sir Heath Harrison; C of E Soldiers & Sailors Club (Ernest Atkins, manager), Longmoor Camp; Charles Coles, gardener to Sir W R Smith; Frederick Cooper, chief range warden for Crown lands, Brimstone lodge; Stephen Fry, gamekeeper to Sir Heath Harrison; H Gilburd, refreshment rooms, Liphook road; Edwin Hull, miller (water); Frank Kemp, cowkeeper; James Kinally, draper, Longmoor Camp; Bertram Kirkby, cycle agent, dealer, repairer, enameller & accessories and haberdasher, Liphook road; Thomas Luff, farm bailiff to Sir W R Smith; Frank Madgwick, motor garage; William Albert Redman, cowkeeper, Rook's farm; Harry Rixon, The Queen PH, TN Blackmoor 12; George Robinson, hairdresser, Longmoor Camp; A Roke, newsagent, Longmoor Camp; George Shepherd, smith; Thomas Swyer, farm bailiff to A F Coryton; Henry Trigg, farm foreman to Viscount Wolmer PC, MP, Deal farm; Archibald Walters, grocer, Longmoor road.

Blackmoor, (addressed now as Blackmoor, Liss): Albert George Butcher, grocer; Herbert Grace, shopkeeper; George A Kemp & Sons (see 1911 entry); Woolmer Hotel (Jean Roy, proprietress).

*(There is also shown an Edward Hardy, motor petrol service station, which is likely to have been on what was then the main road through **Greatham**. Ed.)*

1935 (Kelly's)

GREATHAM is a parish on the road from Petersfield to Farnham, near the Sussex border, 2 miles north from Liss station on the Southern railway, 5½ north-east from Petersfield and 11 south-west from Farnham, in the Petersfield division of the county (Hants), Finch Dean hundred, rural district, county court district and petty sessional divisions of Petersfield, rural deanery of Petersfield, archdeaconry and diocese of Portsmouth. The river Rother flows through the parish.

The old parish church is now in ruins except the chancel, which contains a fine monument to Dame Margery

Caryll. The present church of St John the Baptist, built on a new site in 1875, at a cost of about £5,000, is an edifice of stone in the Decorated style, consisting of a chancel, nave, south porch and a low tower with spire at the north-east angle, containing 2 bells: the spire and belfry were erected in 1897, at a cost of £800, by the late Sir Heath Harrison bart, JP, of Le Court, in commemoration of the Diamond Jubilee of Queen Victoria: the lych-gate, erected in 1907, was the gift of the late Sir Heath and Lady Harrison: there are 300 sittings.

The register dates from the year 1571. The living is a rectory, net yearly value £261, with 53 acres of glebe and residence, in the gift of W S Luttrell-West esq, and held since 1934 by the Rev Wilfrid Osborne Marks DSO, MA, of Queen's College, Oxford. There is a Methodist chapel. *

Longmoor Camp, established in 1903, is a permanent military station. The camp itself occupies about 40 acres of ground, and is available for about 1,000 troops. The rifle range attached to the camp is used conjointly by the soldiers from the camp at Bordon. The garrison church of St Martin, built in 1930, seats 500. There is also a Roman Catholic chapel, a military hospital, school and welfare centre. A memorial of rough granite was erected in 1919, in memory of 18 men of this parish who fell in the Great War, 1914-18. A part of Woolmer Forest is in this parish.

The manor house is the residence of Miss Isolda Coryton. Le Court, the property and residence of Lady Harrison, is a mansion of stone, erected in 1866 upon an eminence, surrounded by beautiful gardens, in a well-wooded park of 70 acres, commanding extensive and picturesque views of the surrounding country.

Augustus Frederick Coryton esq JP, who is lord of the manor, Viscount Wolmer, PC, MP, JP and Lady Harrison are the principal landowners. The soil is a good hazel mould and clay; sub-soil, sand and clay; parish about equal pasturage and tillage. The chief crops are corn and roots. The area is 1,243 acres of land of various descriptions; the population in 1931 was 406.

Letters through Liss, Hants. The nearest M O& T office is in the parish of West Liss or Blackmoor. Post, M O, T & TED Office, Longmoor Camp. Letters through Liss, Hants.

PRIVATE RESIDENTS: Surg-Capt R F Bate, OBE, RN (ret'd.), Cases; Augustus Frederick Coryton, JP, Gold's house; Miss I Coryton, Manor house; H J Godwin, Greatham moor; Lady Harrison, Le Court; Rev Wilfrid Osborne Marks, DSO, MA, (rector), The Rectory; Oliver George Skinner, Manor cottage; William Francis Head Smith, Farm cottage.

COMMERCIAL: Albert George Butcher, outfitter, Longmoor Camp; John Callen, farmer, Mill farm; Church of England Soldiers' and Sailors' Club (Charles James Edwards, manager), Longmoor Camp; Charles Coles, gardener to H J Godwin esq;

Stephen Fry, gamekeeper to Lady Harrison; Harry Gilburd, farmer, Liphook road;

Edwin Hull, miller (water); Frank Kemp, cowkeeper; James Kinally, draper, Longmoor Camp; Bertram Kirby, cycle agent, Liphook Rd.; Longmoor Camp Cinema; Frank Madgwick, motor garage; William Albert Redman, cowkeeper, Rook's farm; Harry Rixon, The Queen PH, Tel Blackmoor 12; George Robinson, hairdresser, Longmoor Camp; George Sheppard, smith; Thomas Swyer, farm bailiff to A F Coryton esq; Miss Carr-Taylor, tea rooms, (postal address West Liss), Liss 120; Henry Trigg, farm foreman to Viscount Wolmer, Deal farm; Archibald Walters, grocer, Liphook Road.

Blackmoor (no further distinction shown between areas of Blackmoor): Albert George Butcher, grocer; Albert William Butcher, motor engineer; Herbert Grace, shopkeeper; George A Kemp & Sons (still as 1911); William Alfred Redman, farmer, Forest Side farm; Woolmer Hotel (Jean Roy, proprietress) TN 2.

1939 (Kelly's)

GREATHAM is described much the same as in 1935, with the following main amendments: Gas and electricity are available. Water is supplied by the Wey Valley Water Co. The manor house is now the residence of Capt Augustus Frederick Coryton JP Le Court is now the property of Brig-Gen. Henry L Knight CMG, DSO. The living is now in the gift of Mrs F E Luttrell-West.

PRIVATE RESIDENTS: Surg-Capt R F Bate, OBE, RN (ret'd.), Cases; Capt A F Coryton JP, Manor House; Miss I Coryton, Gold's House; Major Clifford Hugh Douglas, Greatham mill; H J Godwin, Greatham moor; Brig-Gen Henry L Knight CMG, DSO, Le Court; Rev W O Marks DSO, MA (rector), The Rectory; Oliver George Skinner, Manor cottage; F W H Smith, Farm cottage; William White MD, Rook Farm cottage.

COMMERCIAL: The Brown Tea Pot (Mrs N Renny), café (postal address West Liss), Liss 120; Albert George Butcher, outfitter, Longmoor Camp; John Callen, farmer, Mill farm; C of E Soldier's & Sailor's Club (James Edward Charles, manager), Longmoor Camp, Blackmoor 227; Charles Coles, gardener to H J Godwin esq, New cottage; Harry Gilburd, smallholder, Liphook road; Bertram Kirby, cycle agent, Liphook road; Longmoor Camp Cinema;

Frank Madgwick, motor garage, Blackmoor 225; Queen PH (Harry Rixon), Blackmoor 212; W A Redman. Farmer, Rook's farm; George Robinson, hairdresser, Longmoor Camp; Harry George Sheppard, smith, The Forge; Thomas Swyer, farm bailiff to Capt. Coryton; Shotter Bros., farmers, Deal farm; Archibald Walters, grocer, Liphook road, Blackmoor 257.

Blackmoor: A G Butcher, grocer; A W Butcher, motor engineer; Herbert Grace, shopkeeper; G A Kemp & Sons (as before) TN 264; W A Redman, farmer; Woolmer Hotel (Jean Roy, prop).

*(The preceding extracts give a fascinating snapshot of life in **Greatham**, for each of the years of which I was able to gain information. A lot of information will obviously tend to remain the same, but with time-spans of some 40 years (say 1855-1895 and 1895-1935), one can see how things developed, particularly with reference to the actual residents at each point of time.*

* The 'Methodist (or Wesleyan) chapel', first mentioned in 1911, refers to one on a site on the southern side of Longmoor Road (originally referred to as Liphook Road). It must have been of timber-framed construction, with a corrugated metal cladding. It was demolished sometime around 1965, making way for a pair of semi-detached houses. My own house, 'Chapel House' for obvious reasons, is the furthest up the road, while the other one retains the name 'New House'. I myself moved into Chapel House in late 1967, when the two house must have already been around two years old. Ed.)

Acknowledgements

Books and References

'Canvases of Courage', by Marc Alexander, courtesy of the Mouth & Foot Painting Artists Association;

'A picture of Hampshire' by John L Baker, 1986;

'A recent history of Hampshire, Wiltshire & Dorset' by P Campion;

'The Longmoor Military Railway' by Carter & Ronald, 1974;

'The story of Leonard Cheshire', courtesy of Cheshire Homes;

'Hampshire Place Names' by Richard Coates, c 1989;

'Rural Rides' by William Cobbett, 1830;

'The Melbourne Military Railway' by Cooper, Leggott & Springer, 1990;

'How old is your house?' by Pamela Cunnington, ARIBA, 1980;

Hampshire Record Office, Sussex Street, Winchester;

'The Bordon Light Railway' by Peter A Harding, 1987;

'History of the Manor House, *Greatham*' by Nicholas Houston of Liss;

'The Fosters of Le Court' by I L Jameson;

'History of *Greatham Church*' revised & updated by Hugette Jenkinson, 1996;

'Hampshire with the Isle of Wight', Arthur Mee, first published 1939;

'Branch lines to Longmoor' by Mitchell & Smith, 1987;

'The Oxford illustrated history of Britain', edited by Kenneth O Morgan, 1984;

'The Manor of Minley' by Brian A Myers, 1984;

'The Buildings of England – Hants & IoW', by N Pevsner & D Lloyd, c 1967;

'Discovering cottage architecture' by Christopher Powell, c 1984;

'Bordon Garrison through the ages' by Major R G Reed, TD, c 1982;

Notes and tithe map by Alan Siney, 1986;

'One Monday in November' by John Owen Smith, 1993;

'The Roman battle at Woolmer' by Giles Sparrow;

'History of *Greatham Church*' by Angela Stone, 1986;

'History of Le Court', an essay by Angela Stone, 1987;

'A chronicle of Woolmer Forest' by Dr Vivienne Tyrey;

'The Natural History of Selborne' by Gilbert White, first published 1788-89;

'A cottage at Blackmoor' by Arthur Willis;

'Selborne: Gilbert White's Village' by Rupert Willoughby;

'The new Hampshire Village Book', published by the Hampshire Federation of Women's Institutes 1990;

'Domesday – A search for the roots of England' by Michael Wood, 1986;

'Tudor *Greatham*' by E M Yates, MSc, PhD, AKC.

Personal Contributions

Sandra Allan, **Greatham Nursery School**;

Gail Anderson, Oak Cottages;

Salma Badawi, MA(Ed), Headmistress, **Greatham Primary School**;

Sue Bellamy, Hampshire Wildlife Trust;

Lt Col (ret'd) W J Briggs, Longmoor Camp;

Peter Catt, Liss Forest Nursery;

Catherine Chatters, English Nature;

Joyce & John Clarke, Beeleigh;

Elsie Collins, The Almshouses, West Liss;

Mary Collins, EuroTec;

Jenny Croucher, Le Court;

Anna & Josh Dale-Harris, Gold's House;

Jean Day, 1 Glenthorne;

Alan 'Dino' Dent, Sundale Cottages;

Dot Digby, Snailing Lane;

Brenda & Jack Dunn, Baker's Field;

Jason Ellis, Headley Mill;

Angela Gore (nee Hayward), West Malling, Kent;

Helen & Tim Gould, Snailing Lane;

Elaine & John Graves, **Greatham Mill**;

Kathleen & Charlie Hanson, Sundale Cottages;

Sarah & Michael Hayward, Forestside Cottages;

Isabel & Peter Hiley, Chichester;

Hugette Jenkinson, Amedee;

L'Abri Fellowship, Manor House;

May & George Lockley, The Welcome;

Sylvia Lucas, Bordon;

Jackie & Bill Marie, Annest;

Mrs W Murphy, Wesley Villa;

Annelise & Robert Nelson, The Old Rectory;

Amy Pickard, Baker's Field;

Olive and David Redman, Forestside Farm;

Jill Roberts, Leonard Cheshire Archive & Library;

Mr C P 'Titch' Robinson, 2 Rose Cottages;

Janet Robson, Camberley;

Brian Scard, The Game Centre;

David Self, Gold's Barn;

Alan Siney, Rudgwick, West Sussex;

June Smith, Welldigger's Cottage;

Basil Smith and Dr Christine Wain, Bordon & Whitehill;

Pat Stamp, Petersfield Book Shop;

George Wakeford, 4 Woolmer Terrace;

Doreen Williams, 19 Wolfmere Lane;

Tony Yoward, Hampshire Mills Group.

Index

Symbols

15th Hussars 119
1st Battalion of the Argyll and Sutherland High-
    landers 69
2nd Battalion of the Wiltshire Regiment 69
37 Engineer Regiment 50

A

Airey Neave 59
Alan Siney 50, 55, 116, 133, 135, 137, 139, 141,
    143, 145, 147, 149, 151, 153, 155, 157,
    159, 161, 163, 165, 182, 183
Albert Baker 48, 51, 95
Albert Shotter 85
Alder Common 60, 135
Alfred Maskell 43, 174
Alf Butcher 106
Alice Holt 2, 5, 65, 66
Alice Morling 91
Amedee 115, 169, 183
Amy Booth 60, 97, 106, 178
Amy Lacey 138
Amy Prince 60, 97, 106, 177
Angela Stone 18, 34, 35, 36, 182
Annaliese and Robert Nelson 39
Anna Dale-Harris 29, 42, 43
Ann Brewis 129
Apple Pie Hill 69, 105, 126, 134, 155, 156, 157,
    158
Arthur Bellchambers 104
Arthur Dykes 17, 77
Arthur Mee 24, 182
Arthur Willis 52, 182
ashlar 24
Audrey Collins 109
Avro Lancaster 77

B

Baker's Field 55, 93, 95, 105, 134, 147, 148,
    150, 155, 157, 183
Baron Harting 26
barrack rats 121
Barry Coffin 46
Beeleigh 60, 169, 183
Behham's Lane 2
Benham's Farm 121, 122, 124, 125, 126, 127,
    128, 129, 131, 174
Benham's Lane 111, 117, 121, 123, 125, 127,
    128, 130, 132, 142, 169
Benjamin Blackmore Fielder 45, 170, 171
Berry Godbold 27
Bertram Kirkby 106, 177, 178, 179
Bert Butcher 109
Bert Hall 122
Billy Wells 97, 105
Bill Hoggarth 90
Bill Marie 107, 183
Bill Moseley 109
Blackmoor Estate 61, 107, 117, 127, 129, 130
Blackmoor Post Office 52, 106
Blackmoor Stores 60, 98

Bordon 45, 65, 69, 71, 72, 73, 74, 76, 82, 85,
    93, 95, 97, 107, 118, 119, 120, 123, 127,
    132, 134, 143, 154, 166, 175, 178, 180,
    182, 183
Bowyer's Nursery 63
Bradshott 131, 134, 149, 150
Brenda Dunn 94
Brian Eldridge 33
Brian Matthews 141
Bricklayer's Arms 61, 104, 171
Broadleigh 106, 107, 169, 176
Broadleigh Cottages 107, 169
Buckingham Palace 58, 76
Bull's Brook 45

C

Cam Green Cottage 8, 50, 58, 167, 169
Canon Barlow-Poole 93
Carnegie (UK) Trust 17, 78
Caroline Julia Coryton 80
Case's House 11, 56
Cecil Luttrell-West 34, 69, 179
Chapel House 106, 181
Charles Bradford 38, 170, 171, 172
Charles Butler 16, 20
Charles Darby 75
Charles Henbest 43
Charles Hiscock 47, 175, 176, 177
Charles Jeffery Wain 48
Charles Sayers 85, 91
Charles Trimmer 43
Charles Wooldridge 34
Charlie Hanson 48, 73, 96, 97, 118, 183
Chawner 1, 15, 20, 21, 56, 113, 114, 170, 171,
    172
Cheshire Foundation 17, 18
Chichester 2, 3, 4, 155, 183
Choisya ternarta 63
Christopher 'Hoppy' Twiston Davies 80
Church Lane 6, 8, 50, 56, 58, 60, 85, 93, 98,
    106, 107, 113, 123, 134, 135, 138, 149,
    150, 169
Ciddy Hall 139, 170
Clive Adlam 90
Clive Gunner 141
Colonel P H Greig 43
Conford Moor 67
Constance Margaret Smith 50
Coryton 1, 15, 20, 43, 48, 50, 55, 59, 63, 64, 79,
    80, 91, 93, 134, 136, 138, 141, 145, 151,
    153, 159, 167, 168, 173, 174, 175, 176,
    177, 178, 179, 180, 181

D

Daphne Caless 48
David Heatley 36
David Redman 105, 111, 113, 114, 183
David Self 44, 183
Deal Cottages 13, 55, 134, 138, 142, 147
Deal Farm 8, 13, 55, 87, 90, 91, 133, 134, 135,
    149, 159, 160, 169, 176

Deal Knapp 134, 139
Debbie Hedicker 64
Denny Ashburnham 43, 137
Derek Turner 90
Devenish 1, 14
Digby Way 82, 98
Doctor E M Yates 24, 34
Domesday Book 1, 3, 6, 14, 150
Drusilla Hedley 61, 178

E

East Hants District Council 51
Edgar Redman 111, 113, 115, 168
Edith & Francis Shaeffer 21
Edwin Hull 45, 178, 179, 180
Egidius Williams 24
Elias Hulme 24
Elizabeth Ewen 20, 172
Elizabeth Kemp 104
Elizabeth Mells 109
Elizabeth Street 43
Elli Foster 119
Elsie Collins 46, 50, 64, 93, 133, 183
Emily Shotter 85, 89
Emma Jane Wells 111, 113, 119
Empshott 2, 6, 9, 16, 35, 36, 38, 43, 64, 66, 84,
    134, 135, 140
Erich Stegmann 75, 76
Eric Sampson 60
EuroTec 58, 63, 108, 109, 183
Eustace Smith 50
Evan Braunche 24

F

Farrier 119, 120, 122, 128
Flying Bull 139
Forestside Cottages 61, 95, 98, 99, 100, 101,
    102, 103, 104, 108, 111, 183
Forestside Farm 56, 97, 98, 105, 111, 113, 115,
    119, 123, 169, 183
Four Marks 120, 123, 153
Frances Pumphrey 46, 64, 93
Francis Bryans 33, 34, 69
Francis Richard Bryans 17, 33, 36, 174
Frank Kemp 96, 127, 173, 174, 175, 176, 177,
    178, 179, 180
Frederick Coryton 15, 22, 23, 48, 79, 136, 167,
    174, 175, 176, 177, 178, 179, 180
Frederick Stanley Cat 63
Frederick William Pearson 61, 174
Freeland 1, 14, 26
Froxfield 118
F W Lancaster 45

G

Gail Anderson 29, 183
Game Centre 52, 60, 63, 106, 109, 169, 183
Gardener's World 46
Gardeners Club 64
General Chase-Parr 58
George Darby 47

George Edward Coryton 20, 79, 173
George Henry Lockley 105
George II 6, 8, 15, 43, 104
George John Shotter 85
George Kemp 105, 106, 176
George Wakeford 117, 118, 183
George Wells 62, 111, 112, 113, 114, 170, 171,
    172, 173
Georgiana Coryton 79
Georgina Veal 43
Gilbert White 3, 27, 42, 65, 66, 68, 85, 88, 124,
    182
Gilburds 97
Girl Guides, Brownies and Rainbows 64
Godwin, Earl of Wessex 14
Gold's Barn 11, 44, 183
Gold's House 38, 40, 42, 43, 44, 79, 168, 169,
    177, 179, 180, 183
Goleigh Farm 20, 38, 55, 137, 141, 158, 160,
    169
Goley Dean Farm 55
Grace's Stores 60
Graham Tarling 48
Grass Roots 46
Greatham Mill 9, 45, 46, 93, 118, 134, 167, 169,
    174, 183
Greatham Moor 9, 59, 131, 135, 151, 157, 158,
    167, 169, 174, 176
Greatham School 47, 76, 93, 96, 107, 109, 121,
    127, 133, 138, 141, 143, 150, 152, 154
Greatham Yew 29
Great Storm 140
Grigg's Green 94, 106, 120, 121, 123, 125, 128,
    132
Grove House 128
Gwen Brooker 28, 48

H
Halifax bomber 70
Hampshire 1, 2, 5, 6, 7, 8, 9, 11, 13, 17, 21, 22,
    24, 28, 29, 34, 45, 46, 52, 61, 63, 65,
    66, 67, 68, 71, 73, 77, 79, 82, 83, 84, 85,
    90, 91, 93, 104, 114, 118, 119, 129, 131,
    132, 135, 137, 142, 145, 150, 152, 167,
    170, 175, 176, 177, 182, 183
Hampshire Mills Group 45, 46, 183
Hamptun 2
Harry Rixon 62, 179, 180, 181
Harting Coombe 93, 139
Hatchmoor Farm 20, 46, 134, 164
Hawkley 2, 8, 9, 15, 35, 36, 43, 66, 81, 82, 93,
    130, 134, 135, 138, 148, 161
Hawkley Green 135
Hawkley Hanger 135
Headmaster 47, 48, 96, 122
Headmistress 47, 48, 183
Heath Harrison 17, 33, 83, 88, 127, 150, 169,
    174, 175, 176, 177, 178, 179, 180
Helen Patterson 48
Henry Bartelot 24
Henry Cooper 61
Henry George Sheppard 106, 167
Henry Herbert Hopkins 62, 175
Henry Knight 33
Henry Press Wright 34, 36, 92, 173
Henry Wakeford 45, 118, 172, 173
Henry Wright 92
Herbert George Booth 97, 168

Herbert George Hope 58
Herbert Grace 60, 178, 179, 180, 181
HMS Furious 97
HMS Sesame 97
Hopeswood 59, 106, 169
Hori Kemp 61
Hugette Jenkinson 28, 115, 166, 168
Hugh Bardolf 14

I
Isle of Wight 4, 24, 36, 68, 107, 182
Isolda Coryton 79

J
Jack Dunn 72, 94, 95, 106, 183
Jacob Williams 8, 24, 34
James 'Jim' Martin Collins 93
James Crass 45
James Papps 96, 105
James Wells 56, 111, 112, 113, 114, 171, 172,
    173, 174, 176
Jane Bristowe 47
Jan Street 64
Jean Roy 61, 178, 179, 180, 181
Jenny Croucher 18, 78, 183
Jill Barrs 23
Jim Collins 46, 93
Jim Harris 76
jobmaster 61, 62, 176
Joe Leggett 9, 97, 105, 106, 111, 119, 121, 123,
    125, 127, 128, 129, 131
John Abrall 24
John Alexander Hayward 98, 167
John Bardolf 14
John Berne 24
John Carpenter 43
John Clarke 60, 183
John Ellis 45, 173, 174
John Fullock 43
John Goddard 62, 177, 178
John Gregory 24
John Purchase 43
John Russell 34, 51
John Skylling 14
John Thomas Hollidge 70
Jonathan Dale-Harris 40

K
Kath Hanson 48, 73, 96, 97, 118, 183
Keeper's Cottage 107, 118, 150, 169
Keith Brentnall 48
Kelly's Directory 15, 43, 45, 55, 61, 62, 87, 97,
    104, 106, 109, 114, 170
Kenneth Stevenson 36
King's Holt 58, 59, 106, 169, 174, 176, 177
Kingshott Cottages 7, 107, 169
Kingshott Villas 62, 176, 177, 178
Knapp Cottage 13, 110, 169

L
L.B.S.C. Railway 120
L'Abri Fellowship 10, 21, 183
Lady Harrison 83, 84, 176, 180
Lady Neave 64, 167
Lavinia Augusta Maude Coryton 80
Lawrie Wood 48
Leighwood Cottages 115, 169
Leonard Cheshire 17, 18, 35, 76, 77, 78, 94, 141,

182, 183
Liliane Mansbridge 58, 64
Linda & Peter Stevens 60
Liss Forest Nursery 63, 169, 183
Liss Guides 64
Liverpool 16, 17, 33, 83, 84
Lodge Cottages 117
Longmoor 4, 9, 13, 48, 50, 52, 59, 68, 69, 70,
    71, 72, 73, 74, 76, 87, 88, 94, 95, 96, 97,
    105, 106, 108, 109, 110, 111, 119, 120,
    121, 122, 123, 124, 125, 126, 127, 128,
    129, 132, 134, 135, 138, 141, 142, 146,
    147, 148, 152, 154, 155, 156, 157, 158,
    159, 162, 169, 174, 175, 176, 177, 178,
    179, 180, 181, 182, 183
Love 1, 14, 15, 26, 27
Lucinda Groves 46
Lydia Hewlett 104

M
Madgwick 94, 105, 106, 109, 168, 178, 179,
    180, 181
Major Clifford Hugh Douglas 45, 180
Major Piggott 45
Manger's Farm 85, 86
Manor Cottage 20, 58, 64, 167, 169
Manor House 10, 11, 15, 16, 20, 21, 22, 23, 43,
    48, 50, 59, 79, 91, 93, 136, 137, 141,
    151, 159, 169, 173, 175, 176, 177, 178,
    179, 180, 182, 183
Margery Caryll 26, 34, 179
Margery Hayward 98
Marshall 1, 24, 65, 176
Martha Arnold 138
Martin Kemp 62, 176
Mary Coles 104
Mary Foster 16
Mary Martin 45
Mary Sandford 17
Matthew Fetherstonhaugh 26
Methuen Road 2, 155
Michael Digby 28, 81, 82, 167, 81
Michael Hayward 98, 183
Miles Winsor 13
Milk Marketing Board 86
Milland Church 86
Millennium 9, 10, 18, 29, 36, 48, 51
Mint Laundry 98
Miss A H Jackson 43
Miss Etheridge 47, 174
Miss Goddard 47
Miss G M Hughes 48
Miss Harring 47, 174
Miss Wilcockson 50
Molly McGinn 48
Mosquito 77
Mrs Holland 64
Mrs S Smith 61, 179
Mr Stamp 53
Mulberry Harbour 97

N
NAAFI 71, 73, 95, 162
Nagasaki 77, 94
Nancy Woodman 64
Nanny' Russell 123
Nanny Russell 56, 123
Newton Valence 20, 21, 56, 113, 114, 171, 172

Nick Houston 23
Nigel Pumphrey 46, 93, 167
Noar Hill 140
Norah Maud Smith 50
Northern Ireland Secretary 59
Norton 1, 14, 43

O

Oliver George Skinner 58, 180
Olive Redman 64

P

Pansy Lane 107, 108, 169
Pat Flack 64
Paul Biddlecombe 140, 141
Paul Duffet 35
PC Bowering 121
PC Dace 138, 157, 159
Petersfield 1, 2, 5, 9, 10, 11, 13, 16, 17, 26, 33, 40, 43, 45, 52, 55, 60, 64, 70, 76, 78, 82, 86, 87, 89, 90, 91, 93, 94, 95, 97, 98, 107, 108, 111, 114, 119, 121, 123, 127, 129, 132, 137, 154, 162, 169, 170, 171, 172, 173, 175, 176, 177, 178, 179, 183
Peter Catt 63, 183
Peter Hiley 58, 106, 183
Phyllis Lee 48
Piccadilly 58, 129
Pilot Officer Richard Pryce-Hughes 70
Pine Villas 95, 108, 169
Pook's Cottage 58, 60, 169
Pook's Lane 58
Portsmouth Dockyard 52
Post Office 52, 60, 63, 98, 106, 107, 108, 111, 112, 113, 170, 172, 177
Primary School 38, 39, 56, 183
Priors Dean 35, 36
Priscilla 'Dilly' Money 91

Q

Queen's Head 61, 62, 112, 113, 114, 172, 173, 174
Queen Mother 17
Queen Victoria 6, 8, 15, 33, 67, 70, 83, 104, 175, 180

R

RAF Oakhanger 2
Randall Davidson 33
Ray Flack 82, 97
Ray Jenkinson 28, 115, 166, 168
Reginald Walter Tyler 34, 36
Reverend William Smith 59
Richard Caryl 14, 26
Richard Colman 24
Richard Cooke 14
Richard Greene 27
Richard Hearsey 15, 20, 170, 171
Richard Knight 43
Richard Newlin 27
Richard Paine 43
Richard Wise 24
Rick Brewis 48
Rita Gerard 39
River Rother 45
Roberts Road 2
Robert de Aquilon 14, 16
Robert Singleton 24

Robert Trimmer 43
Ronald Shotter 91, 133, 159, 160, 179
Rook's Farm 11, 20, 52, 56, 86, 111, 113, 114, 115, 119, 158, 159, 169
Rook's Farm, 20, 52, 86, 111, 114, 158
Ropley 120, 123, 124
Rosa Lane 47
Rose Cottages 105, 121, 123, 169, 183
Royal British Legion 50, 81
Royal Corps of Transport 71, 74
Royal Wiltshire Regiment 107
Ruperta Howe 66

S

Salma Badawi 48, 183
Sampson Foster 16, 171
Sampson Lloyd 16
Samson Davis 62, 113, 173, 174, 176, 177, 178
Sandra Allan 51
Sarah Voller 47, 170, 171
Sara Jane Coryton 80
Selborne 1, 3, 5, 6, 8, 9, 16, 27, 29, 38, 42, 43, 45, 55, 56, 59, 60, 61, 65, 66, 68, 75, 82, 84, 85, 88, 97, 98, 104, 106, 111, 112, 114, 117, 118, 122, 123, 124, 125, 129, 130, 131, 132, 134, 136, 154, 164, 169, 172, 173, 174, 175, 176, 177, 182
Senior Citizens Club 64
Sergeant's Mess 111, 120
Shepherd's Mead 134, 135, 149
Shotter Brothers 55, 87, 89
Silver Birch 61, 62, 107, 111, 127, 128, 169
Sir Arundell Neave 59
Sir Guy Grantham 64
Sir John French 70, 120
Snailing Lane 8, 81, 93, 97, 134, 135, 145, 157, 164, 183
Southern Railway 72, 108, 154
SPAB 28, 141, 142
Spencer Cowper 13
SSSI 67, 68
St. John the Baptist 11, 29
Stair's Hill 124
St Edward the Confessor 71
St John's Church 24
St John the Baptist 33, 36, 40, 83, 96, 171, 172, 173, 174, 175, 180
St Martin's 71, 94
St Mary's Church 107, 109
Sue Ryder 78
Sundance 63
Susannah Beckford 15
Susan and Ranald Macaulay 21
Swain's Cottage 8, 11, 56, 97, 149, 150, 169
Sydney H Cotton 58
Sydney W Hawker 61
S E Stamp 52

T

Tasmania 6, 62
Theale Farm 13
Thele Bridge 13
The Brown Teapot 109
The Queen 61, 62, 90, 97, 105, 111, 123, 169, 174, 175, 176, 177, 178, 179, 180
Thomas Cowper 15
Thomas Garner 61, 176
Thomas Goodeve 43, 45

Thomas Limbrey Solater Mathew 16, 20
Thomas Prince 97, 174
Thomas Spencer 43
Tiddler's Hill 135
Tim Gould 50, 92, 183
Tollgate Cottage 97
Tollhouse Corner 136
Tom's Acre Cottages 59
Tony Yoward 46, 183

V

Victor John Hayward 98, 104, 167
Village Hall 10, 47, 48, 49, 50, 51, 59, 63, 64, 76, 115, 133, 158
Viv Hayward 98

W

Wally Kean 140
War Memorial 34, 118
Weaver's Down 2, 65, 70, 73, 119, 120, 121, 138, 140, 154, 156, 157, 158
Welldigger's Cottage 52, 53, 109, 169, 183
Whitchill 6, 58, 60, 61, 62, 70, 72, 74, 122, 127, 128, 132, 142, 143, 148, 154, 175, 183
Wilfred Marks 91
Wilfrid Osborne Marks 34, 180
William 'Bill' Redman 88
William Albert Redman 56, 111, 113, 114, 115, 119, 167, 177, 178, 179, 180
William Baker 43
William Blamire 47
William Bridger 104
William Bristowe 47
William Cobbett 9, 135, 182
William Goodeve 13, 40, 43, 45, 55, 134, 170, 171
William Hall 43
William Mede 24
William Morris 28
William Rose Smith 59, 174, 175, 176, 177, 178, 179
William Sheet 43
William Smithers 43
William Stoughton 24
William Uvedale 26
Winchester 2, 6, 14, 33, 34, 38, 43, 47, 83, 90, 135, 138, 142, 151, 167, 170, 171, 172, 175, 182
Windsor Castle 58, 67
Winifred Edith Osgood 93
Win Murphy 64
Wolfmere Lane 97, 135, 138, 169, 183
Women's Institute 50, 58, 64, 92, 93, 140, 182
Woolmer Forest 4, 7, 9, 14, 42, 65, 66, 67, 68, 72, 104, 121, 127, 131, 134, 135, 140, 148, 160, 171, 172, 173, 174, 175, 176, 177, 178, 180, 182
Woolmer Hotel 61, 62, 107, 127, 174, 176, 178, 179, 180, 181
Woolmer Instructional Military Railway 72
Woolmer Pond 3, 67, 68, 120, 122, 127, 132, 155
Woolmer Road 2, 10
Woolmer Terrace 117, 118, 169, 183
Woolmer Villas 60, 67, 98, 169, 176
W A Redman & Sons 111